THE MAYFLOWER

THE MAYFLOWER

The Families, the Voyage,
and the Founding of America

REBECCA FRASER

ST. MARTIN'S PRESS
NEW YORK

THE MAYFLOWER. Copyright © 2017 by Rebecca Fraser. All rights reserved.
Printed in the United States of America. For information, address
St. Martin's Press, 175 Fifth Avenue, New York, N.Y. 10010.

www.stmartins.com

Maps © William Donohoe

Library of Congress Cataloging-in-Publication Data

Names: Fraser, Rebecca, author.
Title: The Mayflower : the families, the voyage, and the founding of
  America / Rebecca Fraser.
Description: New York : St. Martin's Press, 2017. | Includes bibliographical
  references and index.
Identifiers: LCCN 2017026873 | ISBN 9781250108562 (hardcover) | ISBN
  9781250108586 (ebook)
Subjects: LCSH: Pilgrims (New Plymouth Colony) | Massachusetts—
  History—New Plymouth, 1620–1691. | Winslow, Edward, 1595–1655. |
  Winslow, Josiah, 1629?–1680. | Winslow family. | Mayflower (Ship)
Classification: LCC F68 .F83 2017 | DDC 974.4/02—dc23
LC record available at https://lccn.loc.gov/2017026873

Our books may be purchased in bulk for promotional, educational,
or business use. Please contact your local bookseller or the Macmillan
Corporate and Premium Sales Department at 1-800-221-7945, extension
5442, or by email at MacmillanSpecialMarkets@macmillan.com.

First published in the United Kingdom under the title
The Mayflower Generation by Chatto & Windus,
an imprint of Vintage, a Penguin Random House company

First U.S. Edition: November 2017

10 9 8 7 6 5 4 3 2 1

Contents

CONTENTS

List of Illustrations

'Inhabitants of Virginia', from *Admiranda Narratio* by Thomas Hariot, published 1590, Theodore de Bry, coloured engraving after John White © Service Historique de la Marine, Vincennes, France / Bridgeman Images

Plimoth Plantation: the living museum at Plymouth, Massachusetts, which recreates the settlement as it would have looked in 1627 © David Persson / Shutterstock

Massasoit bronze statue in Plymouth, commissioned to commemorate the 300th anniversary of the peace treaty with the Pilgrims, Cyrus Dallin, 1921 © Courtesy of the Pilgrim Hall Museum, Massachusetts

William Bradford bronze statue in Plymouth, the companion piece to the Massasoit statue, though not cast until 1976, Cyrus Dallin © Courtesy of the Pilgrim Hall Museum, Massachusetts

Roger Williams Leaving Salem Under Obloquy, H. Brackner, 19th century © Courtesy the Heckscher Museum of Art, New York / August Heckscher Collection / Bridgeman Images

Beaver hat, worn in Plymouth by men and women, ownership attributed to Constance Hopkins © Courtesy of the Pilgrim Hall Museum, Massachusetts

Portrait of John Winthrop, artist unknown, bequest of William Winthrop, 1830 © Courtesy of the American Antiquarian Society, Massachusetts

The attack on the Pequot Indian Fort or 'palizado', illustration from *Newes from America*, John Underhill, 1638 © Courtesy of Paul Royster and the University of Nebraska-Lincoln, Nebraska

Anne Hutchinson bronze statue in Boston, Cyrus Dallin, 1915 © Courtesy of the Commonwealth of Massachusetts, State House Art Commission

John Cotton, illustration from the Boston Herald, 1930 © Courtesy of the American Antiquarian Society, Massachusetts

Site of the original 1636 Governor Winslow house, Careswell © The author

Miantonomo Monument, photograph from T. Bicknell Scrapbook © Courtesy of the Haffenreffer Museum of Anthropology, Brown University, Rhode Island

The Isaac Winslow House in winter © Courtesy of Cynthia Hagar Krusell

Portrait of Edward Winslow by an anonymous English artist, school of Robert Walker, 1651. The letter has these words at the bottom: 'from yr loving wife Susanna' © Courtesy of the Pilgrim Hall Museum, Massachusetts

SECOND PLATE SECTION

Portrait of Josiah Winslow by an anonymous artist, painted in London *c.* 1651 © Courtesy of the Pilgrim Hall Museum, Massachusetts

Portrait of Penelope Pelham Winslow by an anonymous artist, painted in London *c.* 1651 © Courtesy of the Pilgrim Hall Museum, Massachusetts

Penelope Pelham Winslow's embroidered silk shoe, made in England or France *c.* 1650. Material: pigskin, silk and galoon (silk-covered thread). Thought to have been worn by Penelope Pelham at her wedding to Josiah Winslow © Courtesy of the Pilgrim Hall Museum, Massachusetts

Monument to Sir William Waldegrave (died 1613), his wife Elizabeth and their ten children in St Mary's Church, Bures © Courtesy of Alan Beales, Bures

Smallbridge Hall, home of the Waldegrave family, which was visited twice by Queen Elizabeth I © Courtesy of Alan Beales, Bures

Penelope Winslow's deposition about her Waldegrave grandfather © Courtesy of the National Archives, Kew (Ref.: C8/338/282)

Ferriers © Courtesy of Alan Beales, Bures

Philip King of Mount Hope, engraved interior page for *The Entertaining History of King Philip's War*, Paul Revere, 1772 © Courtesy of the American Antiquarian Society, Massachusetts

Algonquian bowl of carved elm burl, known as King Philip's bowl, 1655–75 © By permission of the Massachusetts Historical Society

King Philip at Mount Hope: 'Western View of Mount Hope', illustration from *Other Indian Events of New England*, State Street Trust Co., Forbes, 1941 © Courtesy of the Haffenreffer Museum of Anthropology, Brown University, Rhode Island

The Bible in Algonquian, commissioned by John Eliot, showing the first page of Genesis, 1663 © By permission of the Master and Fellows of Jesus College, Cambridge

A *Map of New England*, printed by John Foster, 1677. Originally published in William Hubbard's *The Present State of New-England* © Collection of the Massachusetts Historical Society

And will the white man still pursue: lithographic print of Weetamoo engraved by J. Andrews & C.A. Jewett, 1889 © Courtesy of the Haffenreffer Museum of Anthropology, Brown University, Rhode Island

The Captivity of Mrs Rowlandson, illustration from *Harper's New Monthly Magazine*, Vol. XV, 1857 © Courtesy of the Haffenreffer Museum of Anthropology, Brown University, Rhode Island

List of Maps

A simplified map of the colonies of 17th century North America

A simplified map of southern New England in 1675, before King Philip's War, showing English settlements and American Indian tribes

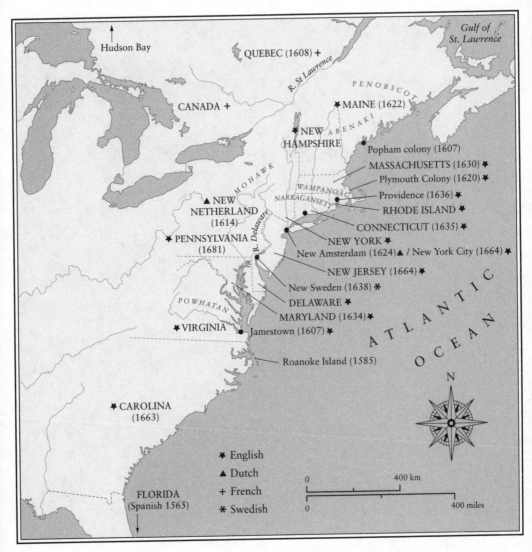

A simplified map of the colonies of 17th century North America

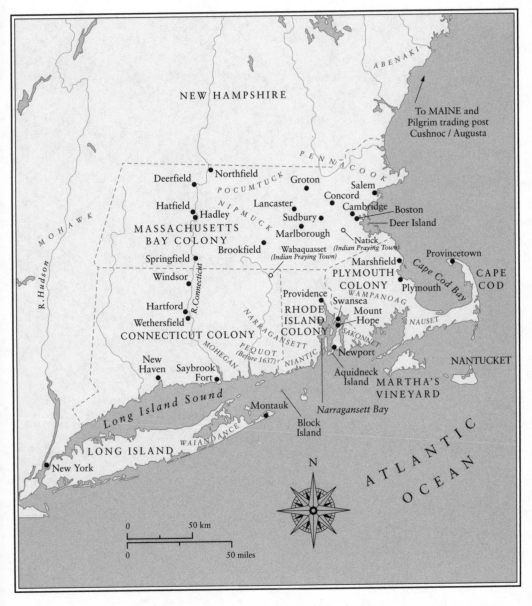

A simplified map of southern New England in 1675, before King Philip's War, showing English settlements and American Indian tribes

THE MAYFLOWER

1676

On 12 August 1676 as dawn revealed the dark pine trees and low shores of Rhode Island, the rising sun also lit up the dome-shaped rock called Mount Hope. From the ledge where his men had pitched camp for the night, the chief of the Wampanoag tribe, whom the English called King Philip, looked down and prepared to flee. He and his braves were completely surrounded by English soldiers.

Sixty years earlier, before the coming of the *Mayflower*, Philip's father's land stretched to Cape Cod. But by 1676 Mount Hope was his son's last remaining stronghold.

The Indians had been so successful at evading the English that Philip was convinced they were secure in this most secret home territory. He had not bargained for the tracking skills of Colonel Benjamin Church, the commander of the English, who was using Indian scouts to supplement the colonists' woodcraft. Philip had escaped too often, and Church was determined to trap him. In the duel of wits that had been going on for the past month, Church made careful mental notes of Philip's way of operating. One of Philip's men going out to relieve himself in the early morning had been shot at. Now gunfire was ricocheting wildly up the rock.

As the Indians returned fire, Philip threw off his meal satchel, cloak, jewellery and powder horn, which would weigh him down. Gun in hand, he started to leap through the wood into the swamp. The English were wary of swamps because they were so difficult to navigate. Philip had a good chance of escaping through its dark recesses as he had in the past.

Perhaps, though, he no longer cared very much what became of him. The fight had gone out of him after the English had caught his wife and treasured nine-year-old son. Clergymen in Boston were now debating bringing biblical precedent to bear on whether it was right to hang this boy – the child of a rebel – or sell him into slavery.

CHAPTER I

Droitwich

There was nothing in the annals of family history to suggest that Edward Winslow, and eventually his younger brothers, would migrate to live in a religious colony 3,000 miles away. Everything about his early life seemed comprehensively tied down by the entangling webs of tradition and desire for worldly position. His father, also called Edward, was an aspiring merchant, in the prosperous Midlands market town of Droitwich.

Edward senior dealt in grain and pease, had an interest in the salt business and travelled for work, mainly to Bristol, sometimes to London for a court case or to hand over clients' monies. He was in effect a paralegal, or legal executive – someone with a knowledge of the law but not sufficiently well educated to have been qualified – and seems to have been an unofficial notary or person of standing in the community who could be relied on for witnessing legal documents.

He mingled with the elite who ran the town. Though regarded as a decent and reliable chap, he was not quite one of them. He and his wife Magdalen were always scraping by, though she was of gentle birth and the Winslows themselves had seen better days. To her chagrin he never owned his own house. They moved home several times over twenty-five years. Sometimes they lived pleasantly in the sort of cosy sixteenth-century salt merchant's house which today is still seen in Droitwich High Street; at other times, as business waned they found themselves in smaller, damper lodgings.

Edward and Magdalen Winslow's eldest child was christened Edward on 20 October 1595 over the medieval font in the ancient church of St Peter in Droitwich. They went on to have four more sons – John, Gilbert, Josiah and Kenelm – and a daughter, Magdalen.

For several hundred years the Winslows had been recorded as living in Worcestershire as yeomen farmers. But at the end of the sixteenth century Edward senior's father, Kenelm Winslow, decided to stop being a yeoman farmer getting by on seventy-five acres, and became a cloth merchant.

There has been much debate about the Winslows' social status. In the more class-ridden age of the nineteenth century, rumours proliferated that they were of aristocratic descent. They themselves, however, were proud to use the term yeomen, which is what we would call middle class.

Yeomen could be wealthy enough to move amongst the gentry, and a reference in a seventeenth-century history of Worcestershire suggests that at some point Kenelm was a man of considerable estate, but then fell on hard times. However, it is generally agreed among historians that he owned a large house at Kerswell Green. Today it is a Grade II listed building, a thatch-roofed farmhouse from the late medieval period, with various alterations in the seventeenth, eighteenth and twentieth centuries – a fairly extensive half-timbered house with a large hall, gables and expensive brick elements.

Judging by the inventory attached to his will, Kenelm was a man who was accustomed to the elegances of the sixteenth century: he had table linen and napkins, and drank out of glasses. His meals were cooked in brass pans and served in brass pots and pewter dishes.

Kenelm was a daring and perhaps rather too entrepreneurial type, a trait his grandson Edward junior would inherit. Becoming a clothier or cloth merchant was one of the swiftest means to wealth during the sixteenth and seventeenth centuries. Worcester and Droitwich were boom towns because of the cloth industry. Ever since the Roman occupation, Droitwich's position on massive salt deposits made it prosperous. As well as being the best preservative for fish and meat before refrigerators, in the late Middle Ages salt's chemical properties became integral to the cloth trade, and Droitwich really took off. Salt was not only used for cleaning, dyeing and softening wool and leather but the trade also expanded into materials used in shipbuilding, such as flax and hemp, as well as medicines and ointments. A tradition of commerce and centuries of busy, crafty merchant activity and lucrative trade meant Droitwich was notably successful. And its propinquity to Worcester had a knock-on effect.

Worcester was famous for its rich red dye and was a centre for the international wool trade. Merchants in the late sixteenth century were the new success story. They were flexing their muscles, feeling their strength. Famously termed 'the middle sort of people', they were 'a composite body of people of intermediate wealth, comprising substantial commercial farmers, prosperous manufacturers, independent tradesmen and the increasing numbers who gained their livings in commerce, the law and the provision of other professional services'. Kenelm Winslow and his son Edward now had their feet fairly well set on the first rungs of this dynamic merchant community. It was the place to be.

Thanks to trade and exploration in the late sixteenth century, England was diversifying and spreading its influence internationally. As a result the landed gentry were being enticed into commerce. There were far fewer university places than now, and many gentry families made their sons apprentices. In an inheritance system of male primogeniture, apprenticeships for younger sons had social cachet, particularly in the London livery companies. Daniel Defoe summed up the change as 'this amphibious creature, this land-water thing called a gentleman tradesman'.

This process would have been particularly clear at Droitwich where the burgesses (the powerful merchants) 'be poor for the most part; because gentlemen have for the most part the great gain of it and the burgesses have all the labour'. Among those of 'the meaner rank' (which simply meant non-noble) who 'had and have salt-makings here' was Kenelm's son Edward. He rented salt vats from Robert Wintour.

Though Worcestershire was a centre for Catholic recusants, the Winslow family's leaning was straightforwardly Protestant. Edward was a client of the rising Puritan gentry of the county. Perhaps one of the traditions Kenelm passed on to his son was a taste for the fiercer, more fervent side of the new Protestant ideas through contact with Dutch merchants in the wool trade.

The Netherlands was where all English cloth was finished, and also the home of a legendary Protestantism. What a man believed – and why he believed it – was a constant subject of discussion which had a natural appeal for ruggedly individual merchants such as Kenelm whose success relied entirely on their own enterprise and brains.

Although Kenelm did not leave a huge amount of cash, his way of life was comfortable and elegant. He was a fairly successful figure in the merchant world. His son had expectations of various inheritances, and the fact that they did not materialise left Edward's wife Magdalen feeling hard done by, she having been brought up to better things.

Nevertheless, Edward Winslow became a well-placed member of the town's hierarchy. His signature can be seen on deeds of sale of salt vats belonging to various well-off families who had gentry status, such as the Wildes, the Wyeths, the Bucks and the Gowers. In various documents in what today would be called small claims courts he is described as 'gent'. This was a pleasing description, for not all yeomen were so honoured, and indeed the fact that Edward rented his vats and was taxed at the lowest rate of twenty shillings suggests he did not own his property but was living in rented accommodation. Given his slightly impecunious circumstances, and despite his energy and can-do abilities, he remained outside the magic circle of the burgesses and members of the corporation who in addition to owning the vats, ran the town and elected its two MPs. Although he was outside the inner circle, that did not mean that he was not longingly looking in. He just needed a bit of luck. In this socially mobile society, wealth and a grand house were all that lay between a yeoman and a fully paid-up member of the gentry.*

Edward senior was probably not formally schooled, but his eldest son Edward was prepared for a life amongst the county's prosperous elite by attending the King's School in Worcester. Only ten per cent of pupils were yeomen's sons; most of them were from the country gentry. Edward senior had a series of financial setbacks in this period but nevertheless, perhaps in accordance with his wife's upbringing, he decided his son must be educated at the leading school in Worcestershire (as it remains today).

Young Edward attended King's College from 2 April 1606 to April 1611, leaving aged fifteen and a half, having been clever enough to win one of the coveted scholarships. The requirements were that the candidate was already literate. Edward's mother was probably able to read and taught him. Thanks to her he displayed a 'native genius', with an 'inborn aptitude for learning'. Although Kenelm was probably illiterate – his inventory contained no books – his son must have been taught to read, as he handled legal documents. Now Edward junior was to be educated to high standards. There is no record of other boys in the family attending the school. His other brothers were of a more practical bent. One – Kenelm – was a joiner. Their father's hopes must have rested on the intelligent Edward.

The effect of an exceptional headmaster, Henry Bright, on Edward's

---

* Thomas Woodcock and Christopher Vane of the College of Arms believe that had Edward Winslow senior not suffered a financial setback which would make him flee to Ireland in 1620, he might well have crossed the threshold of gentility as so many did. But he did not have that sort of luck. A search of the records at the College of Arms has established that the Winslows did not feature in any Heralds' Visitations to Worcestershire in the period. Nevertheless the Winslows were a rising yeoman family who mingled with the educated of the county. Many years later Edward Winslow junior, who was now working for Cromwell, would take great pleasure in getting a coat of arms commissioned from the College of Arms.

receptive character was to give him an idealistic sense of what life might hold, and to expand his horizons far beyond Worcestershire. As the rector of several Worcester parishes, Bright may well have heard of the Winslows' clever son, especially as generations of the Winslows' friends and patrons, the Wilde family (sometimes spelled Wylde or Wyld), attended the school. In Bright's epitaph he is singled out as 'placed by Divine Providence in this city, in the Marches', to communicate a love of learning to the boys of England and Wales. The cataloguer of notables of the day, the antiquarian Anthony Wood, recorded Bright had 'a most excellent faculty in instructing youths in Latin, Greek and Hebrew, most of which were afterwards sent to the universities, where they proved eminent to emulation'.

Thanks to his reputation the school expanded to 150 boys. He encouraged intellectual tastes among the students and a curiosity that never left Edward, whose experience at King's honed his mind, and refined what became a vivid prose style as well as giving him a historical sense and humanistic enthusiasm so typical of the Renaissance world view.

Most important of all, Bright's scholarly interests meant King's pupils had the unusual privilege of being exposed to the work of leading Reformation scholars. The case for Reformation was eagerly absorbed by Edward's fervent personality. Not only did Bright have a profoundly held religious belief, he was also a powerful preacher. His teaching gave Edward his clear way of seeing things, and a recognition of the intense spiritual satisfaction to be found in Protestant theological ideas. Bright was an inspirational figure in a commercial landscape which might otherwise have been limited to the rapid-fire calculation of profit and loss.

Thanks to Bright, Edward was charged with new purpose, and his Protestantism became his driving religious impulse. He was a young man requiring only a match to set fire to the pressing desire within him to serve in some way. Bright was that match. The furnace started burning.

In 1605 when Edward was ten, Worcestershire was shaken by the national emergency of the Gunpowder Plot. It implicated the grand Catholic recusant families who lived within a few miles of Droitwich and Worcester, in huge, mysterious houses riddled with priests' holes. Anyone linked to them came under suspicion. Edward Winslow senior was connected to one of the conspirators, Robert Wintour, because he rented Wintour's salt vats. Wintour was savagely executed and Winslow suffered interrogation, but fortunately for him, it was agreed that his connections were strictly business arrangements.

There is a certain irony in this brush with danger, as Winslow was, in fact, a good Protestant. He became the trusted man to manage affairs for the Puritan-leaning Wildes, a family whose status in the world was rising at this period. John Wilde was one of Droitwich's MPs from 1621 to 1640, and Chief Baron of the Court of the Exchequer from 1646 to 1653. His father, Thomas Wilde, was the owner of a quarter of the advowson of St Peter's Droitwich and probably made Winslow a churchwarden in 1600. Other important patrons were the Puritan Coventry family. Edward senior was on affectionate terms with Thomas Coventry, a highly successful government minister who took it upon himself to be interested in his client's intelligent son.

The urbane Coventry was friendly with various open Puritans. He took a shine to the young Edward with his gleaming intelligence and evident commitment, discreetly assisting him at various times. It turned out that Edward's zeal for reformation would be far greater than Coventry ever dreamed.

Two and a half years after leaving the gentle milieu of King's, Edward was learning how to set type in the shadow of St Bride's Church in London. His employer, John Beale, published a whole range of books, including Puritan tracts at a time when it required commitment and nerve to do so.

We do not know how Edward got a job there, although it has long been believed that his family had a connection with the printing industry. His parents had married in St Bride's Church, traditionally associated with printers.

But the young man did not stay for long. In 1617, halfway through his eight-year apprenticeship, he broke his contract, and went to Leiden in Holland, thus ending any hopes of assured profitable employment as a Master of the Printers' Guild.

If his headmaster had lit a match, being in the company of Beale and other printers was the fuel. His faith was a matter of such urgency he was willing to throw away his professional career. Edward became the employee of Thomas Brewer, one of the most notorious Puritan activists of the age, responsible for all the illegal Puritan literature coming to England from Holland.

Leaving London for Leiden was an extraordinary decision. He

would now be an outlaw. The heroic Puritanism which held him in a grip of iron had begun to transform his life. He was deliberately seeking employment in a dangerous field.

Puritans were Protestants who believed the English Reformation had not gone far enough. The Elizabethan religious settlement returned the Church in England from Roman Catholicism to the Anglicanism established by Henry VIII. Anxious not to offend the population – many of whom had been disturbed by the Reformation in the first place – Elizabeth's government did not wish to make the new religious settlement too Protestant. But many of the English Protestant clergy who had been driven out by the Catholic queen Mary Tudor now returned from Geneva imbued with the ideas of important theologians of the sixteenth century, including Jean Calvin. Many of Elizabeth's chief ministers were Calvinists in points of doctrine such as predestination. However, they took the position that the state must dictate the form of the church. Bishops were an essential part of that. Calvin meanwhile promoted a system of church government run by Elders of the church or presbyters (from the Greek word *presbyteros*, meaning an elder).

How the church should be governed and how much it should be reformed became a running battle between the Elizabethan government and Puritan clergy. Bishops were not mentioned in the New Testament, nor were making the sign of the cross, saints' days or wearing vestments. In 1570 the Cambridge professor of theology Thomas Cartwright's dramatic conclusion that there were no bishops in the ancient church seemed definitive. But Elizabeth, her ministers and the church hierarchy held the line against a challenge to the Crown's authority. English clergymen had to subscribe to the Thirty-Nine Articles. Cartwright had no plans to create a separate church – he was a scholar, not a politician – but the genie was out of the bottle, and the issue became political. Clergymen found it hard to conform to an increasingly prescriptive Church of England under the hardline Archbishop Whitgift in the 1580s and 1590s. Puritan sympathisers were organised into secret groups. Extreme Puritans wanted a church which would not include the ungodly, as non-Puritans were increasingly believed to be.

Most Puritans, however, were ardent patriots at a time when Protestantism was threatened by an aggressive Catholicism, exemplified by plots to put Mary, Queen of Scots on the throne and an invasion of England by the Spanish Armada. They wanted reform, not expulsion from the Church of England. Separatism remained a term of abuse, and much disliked by the individual separatist churches themselves.

'Brownists' was the other term used for the breakaway Puritans, named after Robert Browne, a Cambridge intellectual, who was influenced by Cartwright's studies of the ancient church – though Cartwright himself deplored separation. Browne preached to small illegal churches in people's houses, and believed that bishops should be abolished and local congregations should choose their own ministers.

Persecution drove Browne to Middelburg in the Netherlands. Later he returned to the Church of England, but others of sterner beliefs went much further. The clergyman John Greenwood and lawyer Henry Barrow believed the Church of England was not only a false church but contained too many profane people. They were executed in 1593 after a trial for defaming the Queen's Majesty. The theologian Richard Hooker, meanwhile, defended episcopal government on the grounds that scriptural law must be interpreted by man's God-given reason, especially when it came to the government of the church. There was nothing wrong with using some ritual derived from Roman Catholicism.

On the death of Elizabeth in 1603, James I came to the throne. The Puritan factions expected the new king, a Scottish Presbyterian, to be sympathetic to their cause. James's progress to London had been met by the strange sight of 1,000 hopeful Puritan clergy standing by the wayside. They presented him with their 'Millenary Petition' asking for an end to conformity to the Elizabethan prayer book and far greater independence.

But James I was both clever and wily. He pithily declared Puritans 'agreeth with monarchy as well as God with the Devil'. The position changed. A whole new set of ecclesiastical laws forced the more committed Puritans out of the Church of England and made them separatists. James made it clear he would 'make them conform, or I shall harry them out of the land, or do worse'. He was determined, he said, to 'have one doctrine and one discipline'. It was to be one religion not only in substance, but 'in ceremony'. The democratic principles of the Presbyterian or congregational system were a threat to his rule. If he gave in to their demands he could envisage a future when 'Jack and Tom, Will and Dick, shall meet and at their pleasure censure both me and my council.' What it meant, he said, was 'No bishop, no king.'

Canons of 1604 enforced conformity. All those who rejected the faith and practices of the established church were automatically excommunicated. Puritan clergy must go before the Courts of High Commission to swear to these new canons or they would have to leave their parishes 'as being men unfit, for their obstinacy and contempt to occupy such places'.

And in the end, if you were a Puritan passionate about your religion, you left England. Otherwise you faced imprisonment or death.

John Beale, Edward's erstwhile employer in the City of London, doubtless had clandestine contacts with continental presses, given that he published various radical Puritan tracts. It is very probable that he was in touch with the Dutch secret presses that smuggled Puritan literature into England. His books were sold at the most radical publishers in England, Butter & Bourne. Nathaniel Butter was constantly being arrested for his seditious publications. One of Nicholas Bourne's apprentices, John Bellamy, was a young radical who became a celebrated printer and publisher specialising in Puritan texts about the New World.* He supplied books to Plymouth colonists. Edward must have got to know Bellamy because they remained good friends for the next thirty years.

Bellamy was a member of a separatist congregation in Southwark and the logic of his passionately held ideas may have added to Edward's zeal. Edward expressed an explosive hatred of the Spanish, 'that tyrannous, idolatrous, and bloody nation that hath inflicted so many cruelties upon the nations of the earth'. Such ideas were an abiding part of the English Protestant definition of itself in contradistinction to the power of Catholic propaganda like Foxe's *Book of Martyrs*, which influenced the mindset of a generation. First published in 1563, it included a polemical account of the sufferings of Protestants under the Catholic Church. Most serious-minded English Protestants believed the Pope was the Antichrist, but not all of them abandoned hearth and home for such ideas.

It has often been assumed that Edward Winslow's discovery of a passionate Puritanism began once he arrived in Holland in 1617. In fact his choosing to work for Beale in the first place suggests he was already a committed Puritan. He had been seized by a sort of valiant unquenchable fire – what the Puritans called a 'conversion' – and it

---

* Bellamy printed New World narratives and published the first report from the Plymouth Colony, *Mourt's Relation*. As politics took a radical turn in the 1640s Bellamy became a colonel in the Civil War, publishing Puritan tracts in the propaganda battle between Royalists and Parliamentarians. Edward turned to Bellamy to publish news about New England in the 1640s to show that much of the millenarian promise of the New World was being fulfilled.

became the mainspring of his existence. For the rest of his life it gave him a constant, restless need to serve, however dangerous the circumstances, whether in Holland, America or back in Cromwell's England.

Robust and energetic, Edward was longing to show his dedication. In Holland he would be joining people who were openly nonconformist. Printing the work of exiled Puritan divines, many of whom lived in the Netherlands, was strictly illegal. The material was smuggled in wine casks. It was the sort of work which could result in imprisonment or fines or worse.

By going to Leiden he was expressing his deepest nature. For above all things Edward Winslow was a man of action, made to be employed by Thomas Brewer. Brewer was an alumnus of Edward's school, King's in Worcester, and a merchant who had international businesses in both Holland and Worcester, so it is possible that local links had first got Edward interested. Brewer was a Worcestershire grandee, but the Wilde and Coventry families would not have associated with him. He was dangerous. English spies were watching his house in Leiden. To work directly for him required daring and commitment, both qualities Edward had in spades.

Brewer's footprints could be detected everywhere the Puritans made trouble. A heroic, reckless figure, he bankrolled many of the high-minded, impoverished English members of the various separatist Puritan churches sheltering in Leiden. The most numerous were the members of William Brewster's little church from Scrooby in Nottinghamshire. But there were also over thirty members of a separatist church from Sandwich in Kent, which had a fearsome reputation for sectarianism. They included the Chilton family. (Legend has it Mary Chilton was the first English person to set foot on Plymouth Rock in New England. In 1617 she was about eleven years old.)

At the same time that Edward left for Holland, his father's life began to unravel. A reputation for carelessness replaced trustworthiness. A series of misjudgements and questionable behaviour wreaked havoc with an already finely balanced ascent to prosperity.

All businesses can go through good and bad moments. There were stresses and strains, the result of overwork. Edward senior was handling money in large quantities at a period when he personally had need of it. By the time his eldest son left school he faced a Chancery suit for helping himself to gold sovereigns that he was delivering as part of a dowry settlement for a local landowner. (One of the reasons Edward left school suddenly may be because his father could not afford to send him to university.)

In his witness statement Winslow pleaded he had been let down over an inheritance and needed cash fast. He mentioned expectations of £170, the equivalent of around £17,000 today – a not negligible sum. He had to buy 'an extent of the moiety of certain houses and lands whereof he formerly had the inheritance'. He had borrowed money but of course intended to repay it as soon as he could. Perhaps he was never in a position to. Meanwhile, he was made undersheriff for Worcestershire by Sir Edward Wilde. Though it would have been more convenient to continue to live in Droitwich because of his new job, financial issues meant the family were forced to leave their own home for new premises in Clifton, a hamlet near Severn Stoke. Helping himself to loans without permission became a habit for the perennially broke Edward Winslow.

By 1620, unable to repay a debt, he had absconded to Ireland and went on the run there. He never returned to England. He left his wife and children to fend for themselves. The last we hear of him is in 1628, in Londonderry.

His ruined wife exited from her humiliation by retiring to Reading. She seems to have persuaded someone – perhaps Coventry or one of the Wildes – to pay for her son Kenelm's continued apprenticeship to the London Guild of Joiners and Sealers. In April 1627 she pulled off what her former circle in Worcestershire regarded as a distinct coup, especially considering her embarrassing family circumstances. Her daughter Magdalen married the gifted and artistic scion of the ancient Dorset gentry, a rising young clergyman named William Wake. The incumbent of Holy Trinity Wareham in Dorset, he was the former chaplain of the Earl of Westmorland and lifelong intimate friend of his heir, the Cavalier poet the Hon. Mildmay Fane. But this social triumph lay some time ahead.

Living with a seventeenth-century version of Mr Micawber was a lesson Edward junior never forgot. It may be that going abroad offered a convenient escape. He seems to have possessed almost superhuman energy. The early American historian Cotton Mather called him a Hercules used to 'crushing serpents'. Whatever the psychological reasons, this combination of character, energy and circumstance meant Edward was now looking forward to crushing the serpents of the Church of England.

He was a man of great jollity, of animal spirits. For all that his eyes were fixed on heaven, Edward was always full of a sort of barrelling common sense. Like most young men and women of spirit he straightforwardly liked fighting for a cause. Although going to Holland to work for Brewer was a matter whose seriousness engaged his whole being, it was also an adventure and an escape.

CHAPTER II

Leiden

Edward probably arrived in Holland in the late spring of 1617. The snows that encased the country in a thick white coat had finally departed and boats could navigate the canals again. This was the time of the Little Ice Age, the very cold winters that afflicted Europe for much of the seventeenth century. The sort of enchanted pale landscape just vanishing as Edward glided through a silent countryside can be seen in the work of contemporary Dutch artists. In England, frost fairs were held on the Thames. In the Netherlands the whole population went skating mad, strapped bones onto their boots and flew for miles along the canals that criss-crossed the flat countryside. The ice was a time for wild exuberance. Of all the European nations the Dutch seem to represent a sober way of life. But Edward came to think they were not as serious-minded as he might have expected – especially on Sundays when life did not take on the hushed feel it did in Puritan homes in England.

At the beginning of his adventure into the unknown, Edward was in a state of high excitement, neither impoverished nor wealthy but full of characteristic vitality. Travelling light, with the suit he stood up in, some sheets and a plate or two, he was a good-natured fellow, always interested in his surroundings and lit by an inner spiritual glow. He was looking forward to playing his part in the great battle between Protestants and Catholics – and dazzled by the thought of aiding Brewer.

Holland was the front line against the forces of darkness, the Roman Catholic Spanish Empire against which the seventeen Protestant provinces of the Netherlands had revolted in 1566. It held the sort of appeal Jerusalem once had for crusaders. The commitment to Protestant thought of all kinds was such that the Calvinist university at Leiden had become known for free expression and as a centre for publishing the work of exiled Puritan divines which James I forbade.

For the journey, first by horse to Gravesend, then ship, Edward was

wrapped in the sort of thick serge mantle that England and the Netherlands were celebrated for manufacturing. Though he was moving to
a foreign country, the huge English presence made him feel at home.
The English had begun to aid the Dutch in 1585. Over 100,00 Englishmen served in Holland, both in English and Dutch regiments as
mercenaries and as members of the peacetime garrisons. Towns such
as Flushing, Brill and Ostend were like English colonies. Many recruits
fought in Dutch regiments out of personal sympathy, to keep the new
Dutch Republic liberated from their former Spanish overlords.

In Leiden, all Edward's emotional needs were unexpectedly satis-
fied. He joined a separatist church headed by the inspirational minister
John Robinson, one of the most interesting theologians of his day.
The church – known as the Scrooby community, from its roots in
Nottinghamshire – was a mixture of independently minded people
like himself from all over England, and some Dutch followers.

And they changed Edward's life. It was one step to go to Holland,
only across the North Sea, quite another to travel 3,000 miles across
the stormy Atlantic to America. But three years after he arrived in
Leiden, Edward was ready to emigrate.

The Scrooby church initially had no thoughts of emigrating. The
core members under William Brewster and John Robinson had arrived
in Holland between 1608 and 1609. Escaping from the English authorities because they were an illegal body, their interest was in being able
to worship as they pleased. They had gone first to Amsterdam where
there were various other English separatist churches, of which some
of them had been members at different times. Subsequently they moved
to Leiden because of disagreements and because William Brewster had
contacts there from when he had been a young trainee diplomat. The
community was a modest gathering of exiles from an obscure part of
England but its members had extraordinary determination. The church
believed they had a covenant like the Jewish people of old. Their comparison was the working of God's will to save the chosen people in the
Old Testament. They constantly looked to the Bible for guiding
examples.

John Robinson was soon at the forefront of the vibrant intellectual
life of Leiden. From the beginning his church had been treated with
respect because Robinson was a major Protestant theologian, one of
the most brilliant minds of his generation. In England, the 1604 canons
had meant he had to resign his fellowship at Corpus Christi College,
Cambridge, where he had once been dean. In Leiden, he was invited by

the eminent intellectuals of the day to take part in debates about Calvinism. The notably tall and dark Robinson was not only a kindly man dedicated to his parishioners' welfare, he was an academic and thinker. Anywhere but in England, it was quite natural for him to enter the public dialogues which engaged the hearts and minds of the time.

The town government of Leiden gave financial support to all reformed foreign churches – English, French and German – that sought sanctuary within its fortress-like walls. The city's remarkable spirit made it a magnet for Protestant intellectuals. Leiden was the centre of the largest printing industry in Europe, as part of the United Provinces' proudly Protestant culture and dedication to religious freedom, and for thirty years it was a safe haven for exiled Protestant dissidents. For Edward, being with people who could understand his own religious yearnings was immensely exciting.

He lodged with his printing boss William Brewster. If Edward had been unconsciously looking for heroic patterns to live by, he found them in his landlord. Brewster had been a man of considerable position in his own neighbourhood in England. A pillar of the strongly hierarchical local community, a respected magistrate, the administrator of the estates of the Archbishop of York, he had lived in a manor house with a moat. Now he had a personal relationship with one of the most attractive figures in Leiden, the town secretary, Jan Van Hout. The connection had been forged thirty years previously when Brewster, then an eighteen-year-old trainee diplomat, had visited Leiden as part of an Elizabethan delegation in 1585–6.

The trusted protégé of the Elizabethan Secretary of State William Davison, William Brewster was at Peterhouse, Cambridge, in the 1580s at the time of maximum separatist interest. Davison's treatment at court – he became the scapegoat for the execution of Mary, Queen of Scots – may have made Brewster's intense nature more carelessly defiant. One way of bending the rules of the Church of England had been for gentry families to appoint Puritan vicars to livings, or to found Puritan lectureships for unbeneficed clergy. Their role was to preach in tandem with, and frequently in opposition to, the local vicar. But under James I's clampdown these vicars were no longer licensed. They were forced to go underground and make illegal churches. Leaders of these small gathered churches found so much they could not countenance in the new canons that in the end, reluctantly, a separate church was the only answer. They took their brave congregations with them.

It was Brewster who had taken it upon himself to hide John

Robinson, who had returned to his home town of Sturton in Notting-hamshire when he was expelled from his parish in Norwich. Robinson's church followed him. His parishioners were utterly bound up by the idea of coming as close as possible to the primitive church of the Apostles. Puritans considered reading the Bible the real way to salv-ation, but since adult illiteracy was so high, the Puritans also emphasised listening to sermons. In Brewster's church, a local congregation of the archbishop's tenant farmers and copyholders studied under benevolent guidance. At a time when the poorest people were not expected to be involved in church government, the circumstances of the Scrooby church's conception meant its membership was always unusually broadly based. But like all separatist churches, a feeling of personal spiritual conversion – which Edward himself had experienced – was paramount.

Once the fact that the Scrooby separatist church was gathering to pray in a room at Scrooby Manor had been betrayed to the church authorities, imprisonment, possibly death, were the future they looked at if they continued to practise separatism. The church members fled in the night, taking little more than the clothes they stood up in. They were more like a family than church acquaintances, their bonds inten-sified by neighbourliness and exile.

The exodus took place just as the war between the newly independ-ent northern Netherlands and Spain was reaching a twelve-year truce. The warm-hearted and generous-minded Van Hout, remembering Brewster from the noble past, welcomed the Scrooby church, and his patronage smoothed their path. Van Hout helped the church success-fully apply to the city authorities for permission to settle in Leiden, perhaps even wording their application. He found them lodgings and introduced them to wealthy merchants who employed them as weavers. Those who wished to elevate their sons to get them into Leiden Univer-sity used William Brewster's skills as a tutor. Van Hout's nephew, the historian Jan Jansz Orlers, who was one of the mayors of Leiden, helped with the distribution of books printed by the Brewster Press (also known today as the Pilgrim Press). He took them to the Frank-furt Book Fair, even then an important event for the publishing industry.

The Brewster family had included MPs in their ranks and had been in Nottinghamshire for at least 200 years. They were educated profes-sional people – clergymen, diplomats and magistrates. Now William Brewster's son Jonathan – who could once have reasonably expected to attend Cambridge – was in the cloth trade and his father was dependent on Brewer's charity.

One of the Scrooby community was an autodidact of great culture and vast reading named William Bradford. He was about Edward's age and came from a well-to-do South Yorkshire family of farmers. He told Edward that of all the 'godly' who had escaped to Leiden, William Brewster had suffered the greatest loss. Older than most of them, he had exchanged an important government position and status for a hard way of life. His health had been lost through imprisonment in Boston, England.

Most of the original church found work in the cloth industry. A good many had had some experience of piecework weaving in their cottages in England. Brewster's uncertain health meant he was grateful when the ebullient Brewer employed him as a sedentary publisher. Edward was proud of his new friends Brewster and Bradford. Because of his celebrated learning, Robinson had rather reluctantly become a star turn in the acrimonious debate at Leiden University between Calvinists and Arminians,* and Edward thrilled to see Robinson's keen brain and rhetorical skills defeat his opponent. Bradford reports Robinson as winning a 'famous victory for the truth'. For the rest of his life Edward Winslow would have a slightly grandiose hankering to be at the centre of things. In Leiden he was in the thick of a new battle for the soul of Protestantism.

Edward was billeted with the kindly Brewster in a small dark alley round the corner from the Pieterskerk. Today it is called William Brewster Steeg, but when Edward lived there it had no name, being generally known as the Stinck Steeg or Rubbish Alley. The damp lodging crumbled away long ago, but the remains of the wall of the house where Brewster lived and where Edward helped print books can just be made out. His host was a shabby yet indefatigable figure, impoverished, exiled and very close to the edge. Melancholy determination was the air most common to him, although in his presence Edward found the sort of affirmation he was searching for.

Brewster was paid by Brewer to be the publisher of all the Puritan literature now flooding towards England. Some dated back to the Puritan rebel texts of Elizabeth's time, including the writings of Thomas

---

* Arminians were followers of the Dutch theologian Jacobus Arminius who disputed Calvinist doctrines, especially predestination. Known as the Remonstrants in 1619 after the Synod of Dortrecht, they were expelled from Holland.

Cartwright. There were also contemporary offerings, the thoughts of other exiled theologians who had suffered for their beliefs.

The Brewster Press had a distinctive logo, a bear with heraldic plumes. The books were often practical. John Robinson wrote a defence of lay preaching, *The People's Plea for the Exercise of Prophesying*, one of Elizabeth I's particular dislikes, while Thomas Digton explained why people should not kneel in church, nor make the sign of the cross during Baptism. There was a Dutch translation of John Dod and Robert Cleaver's *Ten Commandments*. This Puritan bestseller of the day was a sort of compendium guide to Puritan ethics. Edward's education gave him the great advantage of being able to read both Latin and Greek. References in such languages formed a formidable part of the esoteric ecclesiastical arguments he and Brewster were setting, and he found plenty to get his teeth into.

Living with English Puritan heroes, Edward walked with amazement the cobbled streets where in recent memory the Dutch had fought their great war of liberation against their Spanish overlords. Every Dutch town had its history of death endured for the Protestant cause against the Catholic Spanish. Leiden's was seminal in the history of the republic because it had been victorious, the starving inhabitants withstanding siege by the Spanish armies. Eventually the Dutch cut the dikes so that ships could sail to Leiden's rescue, but farmland reclaimed over the centuries was destroyed as a result. The siege was the city's defining event whose memory formed part of the dominant culture, the subject of hundreds of paintings and tapestries.

William the Silent granted Leiden the honour of a brand-new and emphatically Calvinist university. The oldest university in the Netherlands, it was founded six months after the year-long siege ended. Beside it was planted its famous garden, the Hortus Botanicus, created by the adventurous Leiden professor of botany Carolus Clusius, who introduced the Turkish tulip to Holland – and thus to Europe.

With its motto *'Praesidium Libertatis'* – 'Bastion of Liberty' – the university became a refuge for free-thinking philosophers. The backer of the Brewster Press, Thomas Brewer, cunningly enrolled as a mature student, guaranteeing him safety from prosecution. The university prided itself on the privileges of its members, who were allowed a freedom of debate remarkable for the time. Once enrolled at the university their rights were an iron wall against any angry monarch such as James I demanding their extradition.

Holland's generosity to so many groups of religious exiles rewarded her materially. By the early 1600s she was the centre of industries brought there by merchants and artisans from Brabant and Flanders and Jews from Portugal and Spain. The result was an astonishing economic transformation. For the next century and a half Holland became the foremost commercial power in Europe. Like England, Holland saw an astonishing expansion in its wealth through new institutions such as a stock market and joint stock companies which increased its share of world trade. These were ways of pooling money or capital that became highly successful vehicles of exploration because the risk was spread.

At the time Edward was in Leiden, the contemporary painter Frans Hals was often commissioned by Dutch town worthies to paint group portraits. His images show the sort of people the English government crossed swords with. The strong faces of the burghers suggest a bourgeois confidence which was a novelty in Europe. Seriousness, optimism and vigour rightly belonged to a people who established the Dutch Republic against all the odds. It confirmed their sense of themselves as the Elect.

The Scrooby church met in a building that can still be seen today, a large house called the Groeneporte or Green Gate on the Kloksteeg. It had a deceptively narrow front, but the grounds extended back 300 feet into a broad garden. Robinson and his family lived in the house, and at least twelve other families – including those of his wife and three sisters-in-law – inhabited what were noted in town records as twenty wooden cottages in the garden.

This arrangement added to the community feeling of warmth and intimacy, but it was really because Leiden was so overcrowded due to the refugee crisis that throwing up shacks in any empty space had become the rule. Born to a wealthy yeoman family, Robinson married one of the White sisters. All four sisters and their brother were involved in the church at Leiden.

The extended Robinson/White family was well-to-do, but many of the rest of the original Brewster church who gathered for services at Green Gate were badly off. As former tenant farmers on the Archbishop of York's lands they had always struggled to get by, but in Holland they were at the harsher mercies of Dutch masters where spending twelve hours at their looms was normal. Safe in Robinson's house, they held services and discussed the Bible in a way which had been forbidden to them in England. That was reward enough. We may imagine them, their wan heads rising from simple white collars bowed in prayer for hours. All kinds of discussion took place. Robert Cushman, one of the community's agents in England devising strategies to get the church out of Holland, was a deacon of the church whose strong convictions made him fond of lay preaching. A keen student of the Bible, this wool merchant left Canterbury for Leiden probably because he had links with the group of forty separatists from nearby Sandwich on the south coast who also joined Robinson's church. They had close links with Thomas Brewer, who had an estate nearby.

Cushman was an especially intense personality, with many business connections which made him a natural choice to arrange to get the community out of Holland. For him, emigration was a solution if there was nowhere for people to exercise their talents, what he called 'that knowledge, wisdom, humanity, reason, strength, skill, faculty, &c. which God hath given them'. People living as outcasts, uselessly passing the days, were 'not slaves'. Therefore they should see whether there was another country where they could 'do good and have use towards others'.

Robinson was rigorous and daring, and he found evidence in the Bible that there should be an active role for women in church services. According to him, 'if immediately, and extraordinarily, and miraculously inspired', women 'might speak without restraint' during a church meeting. Perhaps affection for his many sisters-in-law and their powerful presence encouraged him to celebrate women's intellect and rationality. Women were allowed to make a profession of faith, even accuse a brother they believed to have sinned. Finally, if a man would not dare accuse the church of some wrongdoing, 'yea, in a case extraordinary, namely where no man will, I see not but a woman may reprove the Church, rather than suffer it to go on in apparent wickedness, and communicate with it therein.'

The Scrooby congregation contained another feisty female member, the surprising matriarch of the Chilton family from Sandwich. Most unusually for a woman the spirited Mrs Chilton had been amongst several members of her congregation named as being expelled from their local church. There was also a midwife in the church community, Mrs Sarah Willett, whose daughter sailed on the *Mayflower* as the ward of the Carvers. In his magnificently open-handed way, Thomas Brewer was supporting her, further suggesting a female-friendly atmosphere.

Despite their half-starved lives and grinding existence, there was a mood of joyousness amongst the fervent congregation when they were preached to by the kindly Robinson, who had a uniquely paternal relationship with them. Their escape from England with their cherished beliefs and shared poverty bound them tightly together, dependent on one another for support.

With a theologian of the calibre of Robinson at its head the church had an impressive reputation amongst the thinking godly. By 1617 it was no longer a small group of people from Nottinghamshire and South Yorkshire. It had grown to almost 300 people from all over England. Leiden was an international city which the church reflected, and it attracted members of the huge French Protestant or Walloon community. A number became members of Robinson's church, like Hester Mahieu, who was married to an English woolcomber named Francis Cooke. Hester's sister Marie was married to a Jean Delannoy, the ancestor of President Franklin Delano Roosevelt. John Robinson's new brother-in-law, the respected and wealthy English merchant John Carver, most likely had formerly been married to a now deceased Walloon lady. In 1616 Carver married Mrs Robinson's recently widowed sister Katherine. Carver probably had business interests in Leiden in the textile industry and he moved into the Robinson and White family compound. Soon after the Carvers' marriage they buried a child in November 1617. The Carvers had surmounted a great sorrow in their lives, but they were full of robust hope for the future. Robinson described John Carver as someone who had 'always been able so plentifully to administer comfort unto others in their trials'.

And although those trials were many, the community were immoveable about their beliefs and completely unself-pitying. Though their appearance was affected by too much work and poor lodgings, and while they lived on the cheapest cuts of meat from the tripe market and also frequently had no idea where the next penny was coming from, they were nevertheless a joyous community, so much so that years later Edward said 'never people upon earth lived more lovingly together'.

He was twenty-two years old and full of energy. One of his most charming qualities was his enthusiasm. It went with an impulsiveness his family may have rued. Edward was almost overwhelmed by the warmth, kindness and strength of belief of the community he joined. He seems to have lived in a haze of religious excitement surrounded by truly sincere Christians. Even the church's children's names reflected existences lived in the shadow of a demanding God: four of William Brewster's five children were called Fear, Patience, Love and Wrestling, and William and Susanna White's was called Resolved.

Intoxicated by the intense atmosphere, Edward married one of the church parishioners, a devout, gentle young woman named Elizabeth Barker. His parents might have dreamed of their eldest son marrying a daughter of one of Mr Winslow's wealthy patrons, but Edward insisted on being joined to an unknown woman he barely knew. The important thing was that she shared his ideas. By May 1618 they had married in the imposing town hall on the Breestraat, with Jonathan Brewster and Mary Allerton, the wife of the London tailor Isaac, as witnesses.

Elizabeth probably came from East Anglia. There is no mention of her being a cloth worker or weaver, which might suggest that she was a woman of independent means. One of her other witnesses may have been a cousin or niece, suggesting she was part of a family group. On the other hand, it is possible that she was a woman who, like many separatists, was daring in her serious-mindedness, and sufficiently unconventional to travel without a male protector to the United Provinces to join a church in which women had a role.

Edward and Elizabeth Winslow moved into their own lodgings. At much the same time Edward's younger brothers Gilbert and John came to Leiden. The marriage may have been one of the reasons they came, or perhaps they too already intended to emigrate. They probably lodged in the same boarding house with the young couple, for this was a time of little privacy.

The first great mover in the English colonisation movement had been Sir Walter Raleigh. But it was Raleigh's friend the Protestant clergyman Richard Hakluyt the Younger who changed the debate. Hakluyt converted the nation to the need for Protestant colonies in the New World, and made investing in them a patriotic duty. A sense of Protestant mission spread through English educated society, encouraged by a flood of travel books.

As a founder member of the Virginia Company, Hakluyt persuaded James I to grant it a charter to settle on the east coast of America between the 45th and 38th parallels. A major influence on public opinion and policymakers, Hakluyt's travel narratives convinced both Elizabeth and James I it should be national policy to colonise the eastern seaboard of America and promote Protestant settlement as a buttress against the Pope. As a printer, it seems Edward already had considerable awareness of the huge volume of material about the New World. Long before he left England for Holland, exploration and colonisation had been the passion of the day. The French began making settlements in Canada and Acadia, while the Spanish had settlements in Florida and the west coast of America, at San Francisco and Los

Angeles. The Dutch East India Company paid the English navigator Henry Hudson to explore the east coast of America. The Spanish Fleet no longer controlled the world's oceans. The dissolution of the monasteries and the sale of their lands had liberated capital. Gentlemen adventurers and merchants were awash with money. The explorer John Smith was a hero because of the amazing adventures described in his chronicles of Jamestown, the little settlement founded by the Virginia Company in 1607 on the mighty James River.

In the City of London 300 to 400 gentlemen regularly attended the Virginia Company feasts at three shillings a head. It was fashionable to have a sermon after the meal in the way that corporations today might have a well-known speaker. The Dean of St Paul's (the great 'metaphysical' poet John Donne) often obliged, preaching on the need to think about how many Indians were converted before asking 'what trees, drugs or dyes that ship had brought'. The chief glory of colonisation must be the spreading of the Gospel. They would be rewarded by having extended Christ's kingdom to America: 'You shall have made this island, which is but as the suburbs of the old world, a bridge, a gallery to the new, to join all to that world that shall never grow old, the kingdom of heaven.'

Edward's world view was coloured by an anti-Catholic interpretation of global events. In a milieu where Thomas Brewer and William Brewster saw books they printed as 'the chief weapons in the struggle "between the Saints and Antichrist"', his mentality took in the additional strand of the visionary.

Even as he married Elizabeth, plans were made for a small advance party of the fittest of the church community to leave Holland and go to America, to prepare the way for the less able-bodied, wives and younger children. Leaving Holland could not come too soon for some. Many lived in small damp buildings working night and day, contributing to the Dutch Republic's economic miracle. It was a fact of life in seventeenth-century England and the Dutch Republic that children worked, and the lucrative ribbon industry, for example, depended on small fingers. The church were tired of a harsh way of life dictated by others. Their children were becoming 'decrepit in their early youth; the vigour of nature being consumed in the very bud as it were'. For all the intellectual freedom of Leiden, the Dutch were harsh taskmasters.

Some members of the church found work as individual craftsmen – milliners, cobblers, cabinetmakers, pipe makers or stonemasons – but most were forced into the lowest-paid, least-skilled jobs in the cloth industry because they were foreigners. William Bradford, who had owned his own land in England, had to become a serge weaver.

Some were fortunate to live in the odd funnel-shaped weavers' cottages along the canals of Leiden. Whole families lived in one-room apartments such as those in the fourteenth-century house which today is Leiden's Pilgrim Museum. In a typical wooden dwelling, the bed was built into the wall. There was no space for a kitchen, just a fire. In one room families lived, washed, took in piecework and maybe invited a friend to share a bite.

The domestic scenes painted by Vermeer tend to depict a peaceful hall containing a harpsichord, with a young girl being instructed in music by a tutor. In reality the back-breaking work of the wool industry painted by Isaac van Swanenburg was how most members of the church lived. To full or clean the wool, half-naked men trampled on it. The work required brute force.

And the atmosphere was no longer peaceful. The glorious commitment of the United Provinces to freedom of speech was coming to an end. As a condition for James I's allegiance during the impending war against Spain, there was to be no more printing in the Netherlands of material offensive to the English government, and no more independent English church congregations.

The church in Holland had been getting help from sympathetic Puritans back home. The king and the Anglican bishops continued to react against separatist churches and nonconformist clergy, but a very large proportion of the political nation of Jacobean England (the merchants, the magistrates, the MPs, the knights of the shire) were themselves 'godly' – meaning they were Puritans.

Sir Horace Vere, the celebrated English soldier and governor of the Dutch town of Brill, employed one of the many exiled nonconformist preachers, William Ames, as military chaplain. Ames became a close personal friend and religious adviser to Vere and his wife. The protests of the English bishops, once they found out, were ignored by Sir Horace. As the historian Keith Sprunger has pointed out, 'English-language chaplains were needed, and these positions were a God-given blessing for the deprived and silenced preachers from England. The English bishops could exert very little supervision over the English religion of the Low Countries.' One of the soldiers in the regiment in which Ames served was a fiery, impulsive young man from Lancaster named Myles Standish, whose name is one of the best known in early colonial history.

John Carver, John Robinson's beloved brother-in-law, and the articulate and thoughtful Robert Cushman were at court lobbying for a licence to go to America. Various grandees in the Virginia Company promoted their emigration plans, including Robert Rich, the 2nd Earl of Warwick. The sincerity of the group's religious and Protestant beliefs meant that the Virginia Company looked favourably on them because they were going to advance the gospel of the kingdom of Christ. In a letter, John Robinson and William Brewster set out a moving description of their hopes and expectations: 'It is not with us as with other men whom small things can discourage, or small discontentments cause to wish themselves at home again.' The Virginia Company replied 'the thing was of God'.

Helping Protestant colonies became more pressing once the Thirty Years War began. In the great battle against Roman Catholicism already consuming the seventeenth century, it was better to have conscientious Protestants acting as a bulwark against the Spanish in the New World, than being a nuisance in England or Holland.

The dedication of many important government figures – including Sir Robert Naunton, the king's Secretary of State for foreign affairs – to the cause of international Protestantism meant they were willing to help ultra-Protestant communities create colonies abroad. Sir Thomas Coventry was an investor. Naunton tried to enlist royal support, disguising the fact that the Scrooby church were separatists. Sir John Wolstenholme, one of the most important sponsors of exploration of the day and a commissioner of the navy, represented their views to the Privy Council (in an anodyne fashion, glossing over the issue of ordination by bishops). He managed to get the approval of both the king and the bishops by February 1618.

But despite Wolstenholme's sponsorship, nothing moved forward. One of the church's members who was part of the negotiating team was arrested at an illegal meeting.

And then in 1619 Brewer and Brewster ill-advisedly decided to send a sort of ballistic missile from Holland to England, ruining everything. Their campaigning zeal against bishops got the better of them just as the church's negotiations were entering their final phase. It was discovered that they were responsible for publishing an attack on five articles in the new liturgy imposed by James I on the Church of Scotland.

Possibly Brewster and Brewer thought their secret printing would never be found out. Brewer may have become increasingly obsessive.

His wife and two of his children had died, leaving only one daughter named Mercie, and he had been extremely ill himself.

The printed material was a straightforward attack on royal policy, and it was no longer tenable for Sir Robert Naunton to help them. Instead he gave the order to hunt the publishers through the Netherlands. It took six months to track them down, with Brewster being mistaken for Brewer in various semi-comic episodes. Brewster narrowly escaped arrest, fleeing for his life into England. From August 1619 until June 1620 he was in hiding, probably in the north of England among old family friends. Edward was now out of a job. The type had been smashed and the room it was set in was locked by orders of the town government. James I successfully pressurised the United Provinces to stop their support of Puritan printing.

The Virginia Company decided that it was too risky for a patent to be made out in the Leiden congregation's name. The Virginia Company would not trouble them if they settled in Virginia but a patent had to be granted by the company in the name of someone else (all patents had to be made to a person, not a corporate group). It was secured in the respectable name of John Wyncop, a minister in the aristocratic household of the Countess of Lincoln, but he died so the process had to start again. In February 1620 a patent was granted to John Peirce on behalf of the Pilgrims and, though the text does not survive, it is assumed that it followed other patents for individual plantations and was also within the jurisdiction of Jamestown.

The English authorities demanded that Brewer be arrested and sent to London, but Leiden initially refused to yield him up. Their university was mainly composed of foreigners, they said – what sort of precedent would it set? It was agreed that Brewer could go to England to be interrogated about his printing and publishing activities, but could not be tortured or badly treated and must be returned safe and sound to Leiden as a member of the university – as indeed he was.

But now the process of exploring ways to get out of Holland had to be speeded up. The church already had a problem in that one of its most enthusiastic sponsors in the Virginia Company, Sir Edwin Sandys, was a divisive personality, and a suspicious figure for those cautious backers looking for an uncontroversial investment vehicle, as investors tend to. He raised hackles with his independent ways, and his irreverence for James I.

Rumours about the church's seditious nature gave the proposed colony a dodgy reputation, while Sandys' involvement only highlighted the big question mark already hanging over John Robinson's nonconformist head. Most ordinary investors had anxieties about Robinson's fervent beliefs, and these doubts meant that in the end the money to send Robinson to America was never forthcoming.

At this point the chief men of the church – who by now included the energetic Edward – sent a letter from Leiden telling the Virginia Company to stop trying to negotiate with the king's Privy Council. They also gave up attempting to get the Virginia Company to raise funds and instead just accepted any merchants willing to back them.

Small groups of people starting private plantations had become the mode. A number were named after their leaders, such as Smith's Hundred, Southampton's Hundred and Berkeley's Hundred. Over the next four years no less than forty-four patents were issued to private plantations. Among them was Thomas Weston, who began to organise a joint-stock vehicle to finance the Leiden community. An ironmonger turned Merchant Adventurer, Weston and around seventy other investors of various kinds – his business acquaintances, and some connections of some of the colonists – provided the monies which got the church to America.

Investors, or Adventurers as they were known at that time, were looking for new opportunities. Merchants were suffering from administrative changes that brought about a decline in the wool trade in Europe. Fishing and furs from America were becoming new ventures to support with cash and investors were encouraged by the promotional material issuing from John Smith, the Jamestown colonist and celebrity. His vivid writings and genius for self-publicity promoted the colonisation he believed would save the English economy. His tales included an account of being saved from execution by the Virginian Indian princess Pocahontas. The Scrooby church came to regret that he did not come on their voyage, as his experience would have saved them from many mistakes, but the expense of hiring him (plus his lack of religious commitment) meant they preferred simply to buy his maps of New England.

Weston was a typical jack of all trades in the merchant world, perhaps a little like Edward's father in that he could turn his hand to any business, from importing cloth to exporting wool and the carrying trade. He was not a member of the incorporated Merchant Adventurers of London and had been trading unlicensed in the Netherlands, for which he had received an official rebuke from the Privy Council.

His agent in Amsterdam, Edward Pickering, was married to a member of the Leiden congregation. In a becalmed situation, Weston's blind optimism was the breakthrough.

Edward's friend and patron Lord Coventry decided to invest in Edward's project. His name appears on the list of the Adventurers, alongside that of Thomas Brewer, who put money into the common stock. Lord Coventry felt sympathy for these gallant people battling the problems of colonisation with so little experience, and even less money. He was extremely well connected in the City of London both by marriage and by his practice. As legal counsel to both the Skinners' Company and the Grocers' Company, he could make helpful introductions that paved Edward's way to raising money for colonial adventures, both in the short term and for years to come. He may well have lent Edward some of the £60 Edward invested personally in the Plymouth Colony stock.

By February 1620 the church community was agreed. They sold their homes in Leiden and awaited developments. Edward and Elizabeth prepared to emigrate without a backward glance, and Edward wrote about entering on 'this great work'. Gilbert Winslow would accompany them, but John would wait until the following year.

CHAPTER III

Leaving Holland

After many squabbles and anxieties, Carver, Cushman and a third administrator chosen by the Adventurers – a brutal Essex merchant named Christopher Martin – pulled the final details together. The expedition would leave for America from Southampton. The Adventurers had provided extra people who were mainly in practical trades, willing to hazard a go in the New World. To twenty-first-century eyes England's population in 1620 of around 4.5 million seems very small, but it had almost doubled in the previous century, putting pressure on social structures. This was a time of dislocation, when the rich became exponentially richer and the poor exponentially poorer. It was fairly easy to find people who believed they could do better abroad. Half a million acres had been enclosed to make sheep farming more efficient, forcing 50,000 people off the land. The crisis in the countryside was enhanced by inflation from the influx of silver from the New World. Food prices and the cost of living were going up, while wages went down because of the population explosion. Woollen cloth, England's wealth-creating staple industry, was not as secure as it had been, and the international nature of the cloth trade was beginning to be disrupted by the Thirty Years War.

By 20 July 1620 the position had firmed up. A small boat in Holland called the *Speedwell* was bought, which the church intended to keep in America as they would need it for fishing and exploring the coast.

There was not enough money to hire ships to take all the church community. It was decided that the healthiest and strongest of the congregation should go. Hardiness was important. They would need fit young men to hack down trees for houses. The church knew about the Indians' quaint wigwams, made of poles and skins, pictures of which were popularly available in a series of engravings by Theodore de Bry of John White's 1585 watercolours. They had no intention of needing their help.

In the end around fifty members of the Leiden church were chosen to emigrate, mainly families. As well as the original Nottinghamshire/ South Yorkshire contingent there was a cluster of people who had East Anglian roots.* Just as Elizabeth Winslow probably knew Mary Allerton through an East Anglian connection, she probably also knew the two Fuller brothers, thought to be sons of a butcher from Redenhall in Norfolk. Samuel had sufficient medical expertise to be the community's doctor; his married brother Edward brought a twelve-year-old son.

The East Anglians included the Allertons, Mary and Isaac. Isaac had worked as a London tailor but now was more of a cloth merchant. With them was their brother-in-law Degory Priest, a hatmaker who left behind his wife, Sarah, while the Bradfords did not take their young son. Similarly a camlet merchant – someone specialising in a sort of cashmere – Thomas Rogers, originally from Northamptonshire, left his wife and two female children behind, probably because he feared the conditions would be too harsh for them.

Isaac Allerton was not obviously the stuff of which hearty pioneers are made. For all the religious convictions that brought him to Leiden, he could not hear an idea before calculating what was in it for him. It was he who managed to procure the *Speedwell* when all seemed to be failing. William Brewster was friendly with him, though he may have had misgivings. Allerton's cunning made up for there being something a little slippery about him. His dynamism and financial acumen made him an important leader in a church full of devout people who were sometimes a little too meditative for their own good.

His wife Mary, who had been a witness at the Winslows' wedding, was already a member of the Robinson church in her own right when she married Isaac, suggesting she was an interesting, strong-minded and devout woman. One can compare her to Elizabeth Winslow. 'Discreet', 'sober' and 'modest' were Edward's favourite adjectives when it came to women. Elizabeth had all of these qualities, as well as pluck and determination. A number of her friends, including Mary Allerton, were perpetually pregnant and Elizabeth may have had concerns as to why she was not.

William Brewster brought his sons Love and Wrestling. He left behind his daughters Patience and Fear, as well as his eldest son Jonathan. His wife barely concealed her poor spirits at this voyage to

---

* Historians have noted the prevalence of eastern England in seventeenth-century Puritan emigration. When Brewster was at Cambridge, Spanish policies designed to drive out Protestantism in the Netherlands brought Flemish and Dutch Protestant refugees to English eastern coastal towns.

the unknown. She was duty-bound to follow her husband, for whose sake she had left her comfortable life in a manor house in Nottinghamshire.

The Cookes – Francis and his eldest son – were part of the Canterbury group which encompassed Robert Cushman and the separatists from Sandwich (from where Cushman's second wife came). Sandwich volunteers included the outrageous Mrs Chilton, her elderly husband James and their family friend Moses Fletcher. James was not in the best of health (coming home from church one day the previous year, he had been stoned by some youths), but he was determined to go.

A quietly religious type was the well-to-do merchant Richard Warren who had come from Hertfordshire to join the church. An impressive figure who had taken risks leaving England and going to America at quite an advanced age, his experience and good sense meant he was consulted on financial matters. He had a redoubtable wife named Elizabeth, and five daughters aged between two and ten: Abigail, Anna, Elizabeth, Mary and Sarah. They and their mother would be among the crowd of weeping female figures waving off the voyagers at Leiden. But Richard Warren could be sure his lioness-like wife would ensure his daughters were well protected and brought up in a sensible, God-fearing way.*

The young Whites, Susanna and her husband William, took particular care to wrap up their valuable belongings against damage as they were heaved from ship to ship, especially a very pretty writing chest made of black pine which survives to this day. A sort of imitation of Chinese lacquerwork, inlaid with mother-of-pearl, with a door and little drawers for letters, it was a real luxury item.

Everyone assumed John Robinson would be joining the colony, with the rest of the church, once it was up and running. The little community clung to him and his large comforting family. But of course the fact that he was not to accompany them on the initial journey was a subject of grief to many who derived so much from his presence.

There was an emotional gathering at Robinson's house the night before they set off. Robinson gave a memorable sermon, examining how a life in the New World could be reconciled within a historical Christian framework. Robinson impressed himself on Edward in such

---

* When her husband died, most unusually Elizabeth took her husband's place as one of the underwriters of the colony's debts. She died in 1673 aged ninety.

a striking way that years later Edward could remember long passages of his sermons by heart.

Only God knew whether he would live to see their dear faces again, said Robinson. In his unusual and unorthodox way he emphasised they must never make a fetish of his teaching, but seek for guidance in the Bible. At a time when there was much speculative debate in European government circles about the nature of the Indians, Robinson came down firmly on the side of those who believed the Indians had souls.

In late July 1620 the departure began. The whole remaining community – around 200 people – accompanied those who were leaving. They travelled by canal boat to the coastal town of Delftshaven, where the *Speedwell* was waiting to receive them. John Robinson headed the group and gave it dignity.

There were already ructions about the insulting conditions Weston had forced on them. They were furious that, in order to attract investors, the settlers were to work seven days a week and none of them was to own their own home.

Although Robinson admired Cushman because he was a good, thoughtful man 'and of special abilities in his kind', he confided to Carver that Cushman was not the right person to be a negotiator. An odd, intense personality, Cushman's brutal frankness was nevertheless what was needed if the expedition was ever to get off the ground. To the community's frenzied protests about the harsh terms, Cushman responded they must stop thinking about social distinction. To their point that 'All men are not of one condition', he testily replied, 'If you mean by condition qualities, then I say he that is not content his neighbour shall have as good house, fare, means etc. as himself is not of a good quality.'

Weston had been so dilatory and inefficient in obtaining the boats it was felt that – with many people having sold their houses in Leiden – it was better to agree to the conditions or the expedition would never get going. It was now or never. There was still a question mark hanging over their faith. Separatists had a reputation for 'condemning all other churches, and persons but yourselves'. Though they were angry at the hard bargain driven by the Adventurers, there was little that they could do. Bradford, Brewster and probably Cushman owned copies of the English translation of Jean Bodin's influential and wide-ranging discussion of how to govern, the *Six Books of the Republic*, written in the wake of the massacre of the Protestants on St Bartholomew's Day in

1572. Brewster and his protégé Bradford were also aware of – if they had not actually read – the work of writers including Plato, Pliny the Younger and Livy, and Thomas More's *Utopia*. William Brewster was a highly educated man and many members of the congregation were not. Nevertheless, a level of political consciousness existed among them, created by their exiled state. William Bradford, a passionate autodidact whose nose was never out of a book, constantly sought precedents for their new life, not just in the Bible but in classical litera-ture. He would soon be comparing sailing to America to an episode in Seneca, and Plymouth Colony's smallholdings to the early days of ancient Rome.

By now Mrs Brewster was in hiding with her husband, so Brewster asked the Leiden-dwellers to pack up his precious library and bring it to him in Southampton. Over his lifetime he would collect over 400 books, at a time when they were still rare objects. There were many classics, including religious and philosophical works which gave him the stoicism to endure. The leather-bound editions must have been a strange sight amongst the more homely household possessions (brooms, spindles and great black iron cooking pots) on the barges moving serenely from Leiden to the sea, as was William Brewster's chest. Made of Norwegian pine – there was a great deal of trade between Norway and Holland – it can still be seen at Pilgrim Hall in Plym-outh, Massachusetts. About two and a half feet high and four and a half feet wide, with leather straps and made out of six planks, it was used as Brewster's desk, bed and storage unit. It was also the surface on which the first civil contract agreement in New England was drawn up as the *Mayflower* was at harbour in Provincetown, New England.

Some wanted to bring the elaborately turned chairs and bedsteads that were the fashion in England and the Netherlands, but there was not enough room for all their furniture. Many of their last links with their old lives vanished as they left Leiden. Half their furniture was to be sent over later but never arrived.

William and Susanna White already had one child, their son, Resolved. Since Susanna was pregnant – yet apparently unafraid of travel – the Whites commissioned a Dutch cradle for the new baby. This cradle, which rests on oak rockers, was made of wicker, willow osiers or shoots woven in a checker pattern. It was a real souvenir of Holland, where willows were grown along 3,000 polders to help pre-vent flooding.

As the Whites left Holland it was at its loveliest, an orderly man-made landscape. Windmills pumped water out of the saturated earth and the willow trees' trembling branches swayed in the breeze. Did the Whites sigh as they realised what they were leaving behind? Just like other English residents in Holland, Edward Winslow had relished the simple Dutch diet of bread and the local cheeses eaten to this day, including Gouda and Edam. In fact the Pilgrims took so much Dutch cheese with them it would be what they first ate on American soil and offered to the Indians.

Dairy farming was one of the principal occupations. Dutch farmland was the drained soil of marsh and bogs far too wet for crop farming. As Edward and Elizabeth began their great journey into the wilds, a reminder of the Dutch way of life accompanied them: eighty casks of butter, about fourteen hundredweight, made by the church's housewives, including Elizabeth. Stored in firkins, small wooden barrels with lids, it was loaded onto the barges by hardworking Dutch bargemen in their baggy trousers. With their cramped living conditions in Leiden it is unlikely many Pilgrims had gardens in which to tether animals. The huge amounts of butter they made may well have come from paying for the milk of a local Dutchman's cow.

For all those like the ebullient Edward who were eagerly awaiting the future, there were a considerable number who dreaded separation. Mrs Carver had already spent many months apart from her husband John while he negotiated so patiently, despite much exasperation. She found it particularly hard to leave her three sisters and brothers-in-law as she came from a close-knit family who had emigrated to Leiden to be near one another.

Other women were more robust. Mrs Chilton was a forceful, daring person unafraid of censure or unconventionality. She needed to be strong. Unlike many other mothers, she thought her twelve-year-old daughter Mary would be fine in the advance party. Elizabeth Winslow must have liked the fact she was with her good friend Mary Allerton. In that group there was a gently percolating excitement at the thought of a better life. Accompanying them was Myles Standish, a close friend of Robinson, and his wife Rose. As a soldier's wife who moved quarters with each campaign, Rose was perhaps the woman in the party who was most used to discomfort.

Standish was hired for his military experience and expertise to defend the colony from what were presumed to be savage Indians. A small, bristly, red-faced member of the church, he was a veteran of the Dutch wars and had been wounded in 1601. He owned a large number of books on subjects almost as varied as those in William Brewster's library, and was trusted to be the colony's treasurer for a long period. He was very fond of John Robinson and in his will left a sum of money to Robinson's youngest daughter Mercie, in memory of her father. Standish was from a family originally from Lancashire, well known for its Catholic recusant families. Some historians have suspected him of a cryptic Catholicism, but there is little sign of it, especially as he fought for Protestant Holland against Catholic Spain. He took his full armour used against the Spanish with him to America. What had been necessary on the Flanders battlefield seemed absurd against half-naked men armed with bows and arrows. On its first outing his armour became tangled up in the briars and undergrowth of the New England forest.

Edward bought a Spanish rapier in Holland, perhaps as a souvenir of the country he might never see again, but the colonists were short on guns. They were also short of livestock and other animals. The Dutch East India Company provided all Dutch settlers with a herd of cattle, but the Robinson church had nothing like that. They brought their own ploughs, though unbeknownst to them the Indians had no domesticated horses or oxen, only dogs. Everything, including the ploughing, was at first to be done without the help of beasts. (Once they got to England, friends and the new colonists joining them bought pigs and goats to accompany them. On the *Mayflower* there were two dogs, an English mastiff and an English spaniel. Three years after they landed they had fifty pigs, six goats and a large number of chickens.)

There was very little room on the *Speedwell*. Without warning even more of their precious possessions, particularly furniture, had to be left behind with those staying in Leiden. Family tradition had the Winslows bring with them the great carved oak chair which is in Pilgrim Hall Museum, and a table with a walnut top made in Cheapside in 1614. Perhaps Elizabeth also managed to secrete a small set of darning tools and a drop spindle for weaving wool.

After prayers performed by Robinson, those staying in Holland accompanied the colonists to the ship. They were scarcely able to speak to one another because of their emotions. Those who were left behind had to jump off because the tide was running. Robinson himself was on his knees on the quay, barely able to see through his tears. From on deck those departing 'gave them a volley of small shot and three pieces of ordnance'. With this jaunty farewell salute they began their great journey into the unknown.

*

Robinson continued to fret about his flock, either that there might be a collapse of group morale or that they might have trouble mingling with the non-church members who would be joining them in Southampton. With such a mixed bag of settlers, all kinds of fights might break out. The ways of the church were different from others, but they must try and see other people's point of view, 'with brotherly forbearance'. Speaking of his pain at being separated from them he asked, 'Let every man repress in himself . . . as so many rebels against the common good, all private respects of men's selves not sorting with the general conveniency.' In all new enterprises, like new houses, the parts must be firmly knit and 'not shaken with unnecessary novelties or other oppositions at the first settling thereof'.

He wrote several letters to give them some useful pointers, reminding them of the importance of obeying those they elected to govern. Now they had made themselves into 'a body politic, using amongst yourselves civil government', the fact that they did not have any 'persons of special eminency' meant that whatever their social position, office-holders should be given their full loyalty. He reminded them that the image of the Lord's power and authority 'which the magistrate beareth, is honourable, in how mean persons soever'.

The Pilgrims clearly felt a difference between themselves and the new arrivals, many of whom were to give practical help. They were not members of the Leiden church and a good many were not even religious. The Billington family, for example, were a wild bunch. But recent research shows that some of the new people had sympathy with Puritan aims, and may have been members of other separatist churches in London. Some even had Leiden links. The businessman William Mullins had shares in the Adventurers' company. Previously he was thought to have been a shoemaker because he brought 250 pairs of shoes on board the ship. His house in Dorking, Surrey, shows he was well-to-do. He had been hauled before an ecclesiastical court for erroneous opinions. He decided he needed to make a fresh start, and shoes were an easily transportable form of capital. He also brought with him a son, Joseph, and his daughter, the pretty eighteen-year-old Priscilla.

Stephen Hopkins was a promising addition: a merchant and tanner, he is believed to have previously travelled on the *Sea Venture* to Virginia. He was chosen to be on all embassies to the Indians and probably knew the explorer John Smith. He had two servants, and had developed a taste for a new life where he made his own rules. His first wife had died, and his second, Elizabeth, was heavily pregnant.

A rugged, confident fellow (whose love of good living would later get him into trouble with the colony government), he was a reassuring man who did most of the looking after of his two elder children, Giles and Constanta, and his little daughter by Elizabeth, Damaris. Stephen was not religious but he had the sort of robustly individual temperament common to the Leiden congregation. As a result of having already been in the New World, Hopkins had some experience of the Indians and possibly could speak a little of their language. His knowledge put him ahead of everyone else on the voyage.

Edward felt truly sad to leave his mentor John Robinson, yet the happiness of youth bubbled over contagiously. For all the difficulties they faced, the entire group was full of excitement: something was happening at last. Optimism, burning faith and the group spirit of the church carried them on until the *Speedwell* reached England several days later. When they arrived at the port of Southampton, a ship called the *Mayflower* was waiting at the quay.

The *Mayflower* was a cargo ship of about 180 tonnes, which had travelled regularly between England and Bordeaux, mainly bringing cloth from England in return for wine.* She was not an ocean-going vessel, but she was the best they could find for the money. One quarter of the *Mayflower* was owned by its captain, Christopher Jones, a good-hearted and sympathetic fellow. (The Pilgrims named one of the two main rivers in the colony after him.) When not in use the ship was kept at Rotherhithe on the Thames, where the eponymous pub now stands not far from where Captain Jones is buried. *Mayflower* was a popular name for ships at this time. In this case it was apt. 'Mayflower' was another name for the hawthorn, the plant which, as legend has it, sprang from a drop of Christ's blood on the crown of thorns at the Crucifixion. These passenger pilgrims certainly suffered for their beliefs.

The *Mayflower* was not in good shape. (In 1624, two years after Jones died, she was sold for scrap.) So we may imagine a rather battered-looking wooden ship with three central masts, and high sails or shrouds, waving above the sailors. The Pilgrims were to live on a deck one level above the hold where the foodstuffs were kept amidst

---

* A good strong ship was 300 tonnes (according to the Pilgrims' contemporary Reverend Francis Higginson) and thus the *Mayflower* was quite small. Higginson called a ship of 120 tonnes 'neat and nimble'.

the livestock. The ship was around one hundred feet long, and about twenty-five feet wide. Families had to build their own little living areas with their bags for screens. They used their chests as beds. It was airless and stuffy, and let in the water when the ship pitched in gales. Every male passenger was meant to bring a gun.

Before they could set sail, there was a frustrating period of waiting for their leader William Brewster, who was still in hiding. In the weary days to come, Weston produced four children aged between four and eight. Their Puritan father, Samuel More (from a Shropshire family), was disinheriting them because of their mother's adultery.

According to court documents, 'upon good and deliberate advice' Samuel More thought it better to 'provide for the education and maintenance of these children in a place remote from those parts where these great blots and blemishes may fall upon them'. Though his ex-wife tore her clothes and begged him to reconsider, it was agreed 'to transport them into Virginia and to see that they should be sufficiently kept and maintained with meat, drink, apparel, lodging and other necessaries and at the end of seven years they should have fifty acres of land apiece in the country of Virginia'. They were to be looked after by John Carver, Edward Winslow and William Brewster, who were paid for their pains. Their father had also taken shares, and it was not a time to refuse investors.

We do not know what condition the children were in when they came on board, but they perhaps caught, even if they did not fully understand, some of the whispers which must have circulated about them. Elizabeth Winslow, not yet having children of her own, might have found it a fulfilling enhancement of her mission to try to make life kinder for Ellen, the six-year-old girl entrusted to Edward and herself.

Sometime towards the end of July, Brewster reappeared and fired up the faint-hearted with his usual enthusiasm.

After much hanging around, the *Mayflower* and the *Speedwell* finally departed on 5 August. What could have been a peaceful sailing was marred with bitter exchanges. The Adventurers refused to pay the last £100 to clear the Pilgrims' debts and the colonists had to sell a good many of the provisions they had intended to take with them to pay the harbour master's fees. They also lacked some of their armour and swords, having sold them to the beady and not very charitable people of the port.

The governor of the group of passengers on the *Speedwell* was the bullying Christopher Martin, whose purchase of foodstuffs was not satisfactory – £700 seems to have vanished into thin air. One of the small-time adventurers representing the merchants who had bought a few shares previously in the Virginia Company, Martin made life intolerable for everyone, being especially unpleasant to the least powerful passengers.

As the reality that they were leaving England dawned on Robert Cushman, he began to suffer from nervous palpitations. He now understood the more anxious of the Leiden church's protests about the way they were being treated. Cushman wrote that Martin 'so insulteth over our poor people, with such scorn and contempt, as if they were not good enough to wipe his shoes'. Even John Carver, one of the leaders, was anxious about managing the expectations and destinies of so many personalities. John Robinson sent a last note of encouragement to Carver – he had always been good at comforting others in their trials. They would never think him negligent in his duty. It was a farewell to a brother-in-law who had been more like a brother, and his comrade-in-arms.

In theory the delay was a good thing. According to contemporary lore it was better to come to America in the autumn than in the summer so the colonists could plant their food for the next year. Most people tended to arrive in poor condition after three months at sea. If they arrived in the spring, the swampy summer heat of Virginia exacerbated matters, and could be disastrous, making even the healthy sick. If they came in early autumn the climate was much more pleasant. The cool killed off bugs such as those that caused diarrhoea, which was life-threatening in the seventeenth century. The ships had only got as far as the Devon coast when the *Speedwell* started leaking. They went a further hundred leagues (about 300 miles past Land's End), but by then the *Speedwell* was taking in so much water that she had to return to Plymouth. The captain said it must be that the timbers were rotten, for she was filling up. The only answer was to get rid of the *Speedwell*, and put those who were prepared to continue onto the already crowded *Mayflower*. Unfortunately they included Martin. Among those electing to stay behind was Robert Cushman, who was afflicted by poor health and (Bradford thought) nerves. He returned to Leiden to await developments.

On 6 September 1620 the *Mayflower* finally set out for America alone. All the delays meant that the Pilgrims would arrive in the winter, not the autumn. The wind was 'coming east-north-east', as recorded by the journal of the expedition, most of which was written by Edward.

Edward Winslow possessed an almost muscular competence and self-confidence. He could not help but rejoice in his ability to work well, to make things happen. He had a sense of his own powers that only grew stronger through the years in America. The decades surviving in the wilderness saw him become quite a different person from the provincial Englishman he was born.

As the *Mayflower* set sail Edward felt the future beckoning. He was not a poetic man but a curious and thoughtful one. There is no evidence he revisited his old haunts in England, yet his earlier existence did not altogether leave his thoughts. He took away a civic sense which was Droitwich's legacy to him, as well as a determination never to be disgraced as his father had been. He was a man continually looking forward, never back. Yet when he built a permanent home in America, he named it Careswell after the home the Winslows once owned in Worcestershire.

CHAPTER IV

The Voyage

In so far as they could – with 102 passengers on board – Edward and Elizabeth Winslow kept their cramped living quarters tidy and orderly. They were squashed into an area about eighty feet by twenty, and five feet high, known as the 'between decks' or gun decks where cannons were kept. In such a small space, divided by the masts and the cargo hatch, the heap of luggage surrounding them looked like a gypsy encampment.

On board was William Brewster's feather bed, mentioned in the inventory made after his death, with its bolster pillow, as well as an 'old white Welsh blanket' – which may be another expression for flannel as Welsh farmers seem to have specialised in a soft woven fabric brushed for greater comfort. He took items useful for farming, as well as leather drawers, canvas sheets, a lamp, a burning glass, a dagger and knife, a pistol, bellows, a chamber pot. A 'silver beater and a spoon' reminds one of his gentry origins and his days as an Elizabethan diplomat. He was now a tired elderly man of fifty-six.[*]

There could be no greater contrast: he had passed his glamorous youth in a world of great houses and state secrets, of extravagant clothes so studded with pearls and gold thread that they were stiff enough to stand up by themselves, and now he was surrounded by chickens, hogs, smoked herring, vinegar, cheese and salt beef. Yet every piece of evidence suggests he never lost his affability and cheerfulness, and that flowed from his absolute conviction that his course was right. A tiny notebook of Brewster's has survived to the present, and the pages of notes give the feel of this orderly and sensible man. It contains a copy of the licence to Thomas Weston, directions for

---

[*] Few in the early seventeenth century reached their biblical three score years and ten. Average life expectancy for English people in the late sixteenth and early seventeenth centuries was forty.

transporting passengers to New England, and lists of articles necessary for fitting out a fishing vessel for a transatlantic trip.

The Leiden church believed they had a covenant like the Jewish people of old. Their constant comparison and justification was the Bible's description of the Jews' search for the Promised Land. America was the new Promised Land.

The Winslows' bedding was trussed up in bales with spare clothes, and somewhere at the bottom of the bags were the precious books which would make them feel civilised in the face of considerable indignity. For Edward the voyage had an extra dimension, a secret rapture at the thought of the New World which he viewed romantically through the popular sixteenth-century prisms of a new Arcadia and Utopia, vaguely intermingled with a New Israel. He had the sort of enthusiastic temperament which was attracted to ideas. Being a printer requires a fascination with the written word.

Edward's world view was mistily framed by a sense of universal reformation, the dominating intellectual Puritan idea of the period. He maintained contact with John Durie, the Protestant ecumenical clergyman, who had been educated at Leiden in Edward's time. Durie's father, Robert, the exiled Church of Scotland clergyman, had been a minister to various congregations in Holland.

Edward's millenarianism was of a mild but constant kind. He was not one of the New England settlers who experimented with alchemy. The Leiden church did not consist of full-blown 'typologists' like the more learned clergy of Massachusetts who compared episodes in the Bible to life in the colony in order to reveal the working out of a preordained holy destiny. But most of the church, including Edward, wanted to model their lives on the Israelites. The Bible would be consulted for solutions as frequently as the few law books they took with them. One of the most touching relics of William Bradford is his revelation on the front leaves of *Of Plimmoth Plantation* that he is applying himself in extreme old age to study Hebrew: 'Though I am grown aged, yet I have had a longing desire, to see with my own eyes, something of that most ancient language, and holy tongue, in which the Law, and oracles of God were writ; and in which God and angels, spake to the old patriarchs, of old time; and what names were given to things, from the creation.' One senses in him an almost palpable yearning.

Edward and Elizabeth were also at a very emotionally intense moment in their lives, in the middle of an enthralling love affair. It is generally assumed that Puritans disapproved of sexuality. In fact Protestants disliked the celibacy revered in the Roman Catholic Church, where all sexual intercourse was to some degree sinful. The Puritans emphasised the importance of close relationships between men and women. The future founder of the New England colony Connecticut, the clergyman Thomas Hooker, preached a famous sermon celebrating conjugal love. He wrote romantically, 'The man whose heart is endeared to the woman he loves, he dreams of her in the night, hath her in his eye and apprehension when he awakes, museth on her as he sits at table, walks with her when he travels and parlies with her in each place where he comes.'

The journey lasted just over two months. From between decks where the passengers lived they could see and smell the sea, and hear the dash and smash of the waves. Most of the couples were close. To travel on such a perilous journey required the greatest trust and confidence in one another. And Elizabeth trusted her husband absolutely.

There was exhilaration for Edward and his church in moving to a newer, purer, better world knowing that in America their descendants would no longer be liable 'to degenerate and be corrupted'. Among many of the Leiden Pilgrims was a yearning for the pristine and innocent New World, a common theme in the work of authors of the day including Francis Bacon, whose writings were well represented in William Brewster's library. Brewster was contemptuous of those who became haughty, 'being risen from nothing and having little else in them to commend them but a few fine clothes'. It confirmed Francis Bacon's description that 'All rising to great place is by a winding stair.'

Against a background of European cynicism, religious wars and Tudor and Stuart despotism, America offered escape. Against tyranny, even the wildness of the New World's inhabitants seemed attractive. In his startling essay 'Of Cannibals', the sixteenth-century essayist Michel de Montaigne favourably compared the 'natural' New World to 'civilised' European society: 'The very words that import lying, falsehood, treason, dissimulations, covetousness, envy, detraction, and pardon, were never heard of amongst them.'

The settlers made a strength of the simplicity their poverty imposed upon them. They were disapproving of frivolous adornment, in speech or in diplomatic relations, and impatient with the pomposity and corruption of the European past. When the nineteenth-century New England transcendentalist philosopher Henry David Thoreau wrote, 'one piece of good sense would be more memorable than a monument as high as the moon', he reflected a mindset that remains powerful in America even today. Lives driven by moral imperatives meant the Pilgrims rejected pretension in anything. What was wanted in the New World, wrote Thoreau in *Walden*, was not noblemen but 'noble villages of men'. There was real excitement about leaving the wicked old world behind. The historian Samuel Eliot Morison called the Pilgrims 'the spiritual ancestors of all Americans, all pioneers', because of their 'ardent faith in God, a dauntless courage in danger, a boundless resourcefulness in the face of difficulties, an impregnable fortitude in adversity'. Edward's writings show they believed they had embarked on a unique enterprise, and William Bradford would write with conviction and strange prescience: 'Thus out of small beginnings greater things have been produced by His hand that made all things of nothing, and gives being to all things that are; and, as one small candle may light a thousand, so the light here kindled hath shone unto many.'

New England became noted for its settlers coming in family groups, which is believed to have been a key element in its stability. Edward's ebullience was enhanced by his brother Gilbert, a carpenter, who sailed with him on the *Mayflower*. Edward's three other brothers would also emigrate to America, and eventually settled in a little town named Marshfield founded by Edward himself, overlooking the dunes by the great ocean on which they had all ventured with such high hopes.

Edward and Elizabeth had assistance from their two indentured servants, George Soule and Elias Storey. At the end of seven years' training, both servants were expecting to get land from Edward's own holding. Indentured servants made up one-fifth of the voyagers.

However, like all capable seventeenth-century housewives, Elizabeth and her friends were able to manufacture just about anything themselves, from clothes to soap to candles. Their skills in identifying the best plants for salves or cold remedies were to help them find on the American continent plants they were familiar with for cures – from feverfew, to turpentine, to sassafras. Indeed in the future the redoubtable ladies of Plymouth Colony soon observed from the Indians that they cut strips of wood from the pine trees referred to as 'candle wood' which was full of sap. That made a quick and useful light, obtainable at all times from the vast forest that surrounded them.

Puritans were people of the book who believed in prescription. They spent much time defining husbands' and wives' roles, and many of the

Pilgrims took etiquette books with them on the long voyage, including the Bradfords and the Brewsters. William Brewster had at least two: one was the fashionable poet Richard Braithwaite's *Description of a Good Wife* (1618), a witty description in verse of the best feminine qualities. The other was the English translation of the Italian bestseller Stefano Guazzo's *The Civil Conversation*, which addressed the reforming of Italian manners.

Sadly there would not be much time for refined discussions in the months ahead. Good manners would be the least of their problems. In fact all their preconceptions of leading a civilised life were to take an almighty hammering. Etiquette books seem curiously touching and optimistic. Building a colony would be yet another sacrifice they would make for their religion.

What they did not need to read was how important it would be to be able to comfort one another, even if it were just with the warmth of their bodies. Although they set off from England in golden September days, they arrived in America at the darkest and least prepossessing time. The Pilgrims had not anticipated that the ground froze in mid-November, making planting impossible until the spring. In fact they had scarcely anticipated anything in the rush to get away, including that they would need fishing rods. They especially had not known that snow from the Arctic would suddenly sweep in, which made New England impassable unless one had snowshoes, like the Indians.

Although Edward and Elizabeth were on a holy mission, they were also Europeans, used to permanent buildings and a certain way of life, with a sense of history. The merchant community had been involved in the fish trade off the Newfoundland coast for over a century. Edward and Elizabeth knew that they would have to be entirely self-reliant. They would have no friends to welcome them, and no inns to offer warmth and shelter. There were no towns. But despite all the warnings it was very hard for the settlers to get out of the habit of thinking secretly that 'civilisation' would suddenly materialise. Once the Pilgrims got off the *Mayflower* they described looking for Indian 'towns', not aware that the Indians lived nomadically within their territories. Edward was to write sarcastically: 'Can any be so simple as to conceive that the fountains would stream forth wine or beer, or the woods and rivers be like butchers' shops or fishmongers' stalls?' Eight years after the *Mayflower* sailed the philosopher Blaise Pascal was born. One of his most famous sayings was 'The eternal silence of these infinite spaces terrifies me.' Deep down in the Pilgrims there must have been an almost overwhelming fear of the infinite, countered only by the thought of their God protecting them.

The Pilgrims were lulled into a sense of false security on a journey that began in warm sunlight. They gathered on deck and marked the bells for 8 a.m. and the noon watch with Psalms and prayers. The sea voyage suspended life. As David Cressy has written, 'the ship became a liminal space, floating free of conventional considerations'. Voyagers bonded in the cramped space and emerged ready to face change and a new beginning. In some ways it was like a form of birth, as it is for immigrants everywhere.

The image the Leiden church had most readily to hand was the crossing of the Red Sea by Moses to bring his people to the Promised Land. The sea as providential metaphor would be one of the constant themes in the Puritan sermons preached to the 20,000 English immigrants who arrived in America over the next twenty years. Surviving the dramas of the ocean confirmed the Puritan sense that God was looking after them. The verse in Psalm 107 – they 'that go down to the sea in ships, that do business in great waters, these see the works of the Lord and his wonders in the deep' – became one of their favourites. The Reverend Francis Higginson, who followed the Pilgrims ten years later, wrote that those who stayed in 'their own chimney corner' and 'dare not go far beyond their own town's end' would 'never have the honour to see these wonderful works of Almighty God' which were an instruction and a delight.

Elizabeth was fortunate in having several good female friends on board. Though the two women with whom she had travelled from England to join the church remained in Leiden, she was close to Mary Allerton which must have been comforting.

Mary had three children with her, Bartholomew, Remember and Mary (another child had died in Leiden), and she was pregnant again. In fact no fewer than three of Elizabeth's fellow wives were pregnant. Labour could begin at any time. The women huddled together, longing intensely to see land. Although giving birth was then very much a public event for women, even the most elementary hygiene considerations could not be provided on board. Hot water was hard to guarantee, while keeping linen dry and sanitised was an impossibility. Every surface could be invaded by seawater at any time. Three hundred years before flush toilets, life's lowlier details were something everyone had to deal with.

Those unused to ships found it overwhelming. Travellers could be ticked off for being 'very nasty and slovenly', while 'beastliness' 'would much endanger the health of the ship'. There was constant scrubbing and perhaps some discussion with the ship's surgeon barber, young Giles Heale, who had just got his licence from the College of Barber–Surgeons. The Pilgrims also had their popular and courageous medical man Samuel Fuller to rely on for minor aches and pains. One of the Leiden church's deacons, he was a self-taught medic specialising in herbal medicine, who may have attended medical lectures in Leiden. But Samuel and Giles would not be nearly as important as the female community when it came to childbirth. All grown-up women had to know about midwifery.

One day on the ship, it suddenly became clear that Stephen Hopkins's wife Elizabeth was going into labour. While Stephen hustled his children up the other end of the boat, Elizabeth Winslow helped the more experienced married women rig up some kind of curtain for privacy. Amazingly, despite the conditions, a little boy was safely delivered. In wonder his parents named him Oceanus.

Although Oceanus had been safely delivered and the baby was the source of much joy, the pregnant Mary Allerton and Susanna White remained of special concern. The Pilgrims had anticipated nausea but not the poor health a voyage at sea produced. They were wearing all the clothes they possessed for warmth, but they were constantly wringing wet. Sunny days were longed for to hang the clothes out to dry but nothing stopped mould from forming. Some passengers were beset by intense fears which they had found hard to fight against but which they tried to conceal. They were not helped by the ship's crew, who were irreligious and offensive. The *Speedwell*'s alarming leak was believed by many to have been intentional. One group of sailors had lost their nerve about landing on the unknown shores of America.

The absence of Dorothy and William Bradford's three-year-old son left behind in Leiden may have contributed to Dorothy's increasingly desperate mood. There were lots of children on board to remind her of him. The Hopkins children were mainly clustered round Mrs Hopkins in her makeshift bed and delighting in the tiny baby at her breast. Doubtless playing together were Mary's daughters Remember and Mary, six and four, and Love and Wrestling, ten and six, children of the Brewsters.

While Elizabeth Winslow looked after Ellen More, her special charge during the voyage, Edward and the rest of the more articulate church leaders struggled with the problems of how to organise the disparate colony. Coordination was made more difficult by Christopher Martin's unsympathetic manner and bullying ways. When the Pilgrims arrived there had to be some rules of a self-evident kind – crimes like murder and theft were obviously forbidden. Transgressors were tried in a simple procedure by the governor and his assistants sitting in a makeshift court, with a number of freemen (as people who held stock in the colony became known) entitled to vote.

Because there had been so many stops and starts, the Pilgrims were worried that their victuals would be half eaten up before they left the coast of England. The excitement began to become more a mood of endurance as the weather set in the nearer they got to America. After 1,500 miles of good weather, storms suddenly blew up. The boat pitched continuously as they were attacked by fierce cross-winds, and the top sails started to shake, a danger signal. One of the main beams in the midships cracked. If something was not found to hold it up, the ship would not complete the journey. As the passengers crouched in semi-darkness beneath battened hatches there was a parley by the leaders and ship's officers about whether they should return to England. But it was decided that the mast could be replaced by a great iron screw the Pilgrims had brought with them.

In the past scholars believed the iron screw was part of the old Leiden printing press rescued from William Brewster's attic, but the historian Jeremy Bangs suggests it was probably a house jack used to raise heavy timber frames for houses. It held the boat together for the next 1,500 miles, and the crew caulked any holes with pitch.

The weather grew worse, with storms so violent the swell rose to a hundred feet. As the ship was tossed on mountainous waves the passengers thought the wild sea would drag them to their deaths. The men held on to their wives, and the wives sheltered their children as they were thrown backwards and forwards. Water was everywhere, soaking their hair and in their mouths. The sails were taken down and the masts lashed to the ship. The Pilgrims' Ark had simply to trust in being borne by the waves. In the hold they prayed God would make the storm calm and the waves still, as Psalm 107 said He would, and bring them to their desired haven. And they were preserved, despite conditions so appalling they could hardly see for the spray in their faces.

At one point John Carver's servant John Howland, a lively, chatty young man, fell overboard but was rescued when the sailors fished him out with a boathook. And in what was for once a clear demonstration of the Almighty's providence, a haughty and brutal young seaman who had tormented the poorer passengers was suddenly struck by a terrible disease. He had been cursing them to their nervous faces and delighting in his own good health, saying he hoped to throw half of them overboard before they reached America. Instead it was his body, wrapped in a white winding sheet, which would be the first to be thrown overboard. A detailed description of crossing the ocean in the autumn, written in November 1619, reveals how the mood of emigrants veered between annoyance at being becalmed and terrible anxiety when storms lasted all day 'in the surging and overgrown seas'. Women were the ones who suffered most because, believed to be more delicate, they tended to spend most of the voyage cooped up under the hatches. What calmed the Leiden people, as it had done for the past twelve years, was their faith, and their habit of praying together and fasting to 'seek the mind of God'. We know from Edward that many of the congregation were very musical. As the storms subsided and the ship sailed on, contrapuntal melody rose faintly from the decks, as the Pilgrims sung their Psalms.

Later emigrants would note the increasing cold as they neared America. All who were strong enough to go up on deck felt the touch of a sharper climate on their skin, and a brighter, stronger, harsher light in their eyes which was quite different from the soft tints of rain-washed England. Edward thought other people thinking of emigrating should profit by the experience of the *Mayflower* passengers and in 1621 sent the following advice back to England: 'Be careful to have [on board your ship] a very good Bread-room, to put your biscuits in.' On the *Mayflower* they became soggy. The casks for beer and water must be iron-bound so that they did not rot. Passengers should not do the dry salting themselves – no one could do it better than the sailors. Meal, i.e. flour, should be tightly packed in a barrel and in an accessible place for the journey so passengers could take it out for pancakes and pasties. Travellers must also bring plenty of lemons. Edward does not mention it by name but he was aware of scurvy, a terrible disease which could wipe out whole navies. They should 'bring juice of lemons, and take it fasting; it is of good use. For hot waters, aniseed water is the best; but use it sparingly.' Would-be colonists should build their cabins on the between deck as openly as possible, for conditions became fetid. They must take a 'good store of clothes and bedding'. On a journey over two months everything became wet, even clothing that was packed away.

There were no glassmakers in America, but a temporary solution was 'paper and linseed oil, for your windows', and cotton yarn to make wicks for lamps. Every man should bring a shotgun, with a long barrel 'for big fowls'. But travellers should not worry about the weight of it because most of their shooting was from stands. If settlers wished to bring anything as a bit of a luxury, butter or salad oil were very good.

Meanwhile the dazed passengers were saddened by the death of Samuel Fuller's apprentice William Button, a youth of about twenty-one. While it did not exactly inspire confidence in Samuel Fuller's remedies, young Button was the only passenger to die on the journey. Three days after his boyish corpse wrapped in a sheet had sunk to the depths of the ocean, the Pilgrims heard birdsong. The sailors told them that was a sign of land even though it might be 200 miles away. On 9 November 1620, with huge joy they saw what they correctly presumed to be what John Smith had called Cape Cod. It looked like 'so goodly a land' which was pleasantly wooded down to the sea.

CHAPTER V

Land

Even then, nothing went straightforwardly, and for two days, the ship was lashed with rain from squalls.

Although the *Mayflower*'s crew were experienced sailors – Captain Jones had spent a lifetime transporting wine, while the two pilots or mates, John Clarke and Robert Coppin, had previously been to Virginia and New England – Jones had never travelled beyond Europe and he became alarmed by the huge waves, roaring breakers and shoals between Cape Cod and Martha's Vineyard. Instead of continuing south towards Virginia, he decided it was safer to turn the ship round and sail back up the coast to Cape Cod. Where Provincetown now stands on a slender peninsula curved round like a lobster claw, the *Mayflower* made anchor at sunrise on 11 November 1620, after just over two months at sea.

William Bradford remembered that the whole congregation, including Elizabeth and Edward, knelt in prayer at having arrived at all. But for all their feelings that God had saved them, the congregation were half-starved. Those who ran ashore and gobbled green mussels contracted food poisoning. The ship's sanitation, always unsatisfactory, was even more of a health hazard at anchor.

Provincetown had trees, which were reassuring to see. The same species as back home grew round the bay in a harmonious way. There were oaks, pines, and sassafras – nowadays the chief ingredient of root beer, but then reputed a medicine – and other sweet wood. Juniper was cut down and taken back to be burnt on deck to fumigate the ship and cheer the weaker passengers shivering with the cold and incessant damp. Two days after the *Mayflower* had landed, the women felt brave enough to disembark. They washed themselves and some of their clothes on the beach in a discreet fashion, holding up towels with relief at having some privacy and being clean at last (which, Bradford remarks in a down-to-earth way, was very much needed).

There was, however, the real problem of order with some of the 'strangers' who had come on board at Southampton. They did not share the Leiden church's unifying sense of purpose. There were mutinous mutterings that since they were not within Virginia, they had no patent and were not bound by anyone or anything. They said, accurately, that when ashore they could do as they pleased. No one could command them.

The Pilgrims' initial problems about permission to depart meant their new colony did not have the advantage of a royal charter. Therefore just before they landed, they decided that they had to draw up an agreement so that everyone would abide by the same laws, which included many of John Robinson's suggestions. This is now known as the Mayflower Compact. By and large the colonists were sensible people who obeyed the rules and accepted that the energetic Myles Standish should be their military leader, as it was obvious that discipline might be needed at first – authority had to be laid down or the colony would not last. Some of their new companions – especially the chaotic, boisterous Billington family and their ringleader, the obstreperous John Billington – were an argumentative and easily aggrieved group, who were perpetually discontented. One Billington son, the mischievous fourteen-year-old Francis, almost killed some of the passengers when he set off his father's gun inside a cabin full of people. Luckily no one was hurt. Billington's troublemaking and his refusal to obey Standish's orders made John Carver, in many ways the kindliest soul imaginable, lose his temper. Billington was called before the whole company and condemned to having his neck and heels roped together in a humiliating fashion, until he begged for mercy and was forgiven. Bradford described Billington as 'a knave'.*

The Mayflower Compact shows that the more educated – including Brewster, Carver and Edward – had some understanding of early seventeenth-century social-contract theory. So long as they were adults, i.e. twenty-one, all males on board were allowed to sign it, including the indentured servants. It bound these forty-one people into 'a civil body politic, for our better ordering and preservation and furtherance of the ends aforesaid; and by virtue hereof to enact, constitute, and frame such just and equal laws, ordinances, acts, constitutions and offices, from time to time, as shall be thought most meet and convenient for the general good of the Colony, unto which we promise all

---

* In 1630, in a characteristic fit of anger, Billington was responsible for the first murder in New England when he killed another settler, John Newcomen.

due submission and obedience'. There was no necessity to be a member of the Leiden church.

The Mayflower Compact has been much romanticised. The signing took place in no special cabin. It is unlikely that women or children were present for it, as many representations suggest. Yet artists are right to depict the scene as a moment of great drama and historical import. The act of creating such a colony was revolutionary. Plymouth Colony was the first experiment in consensual government in Western history between individuals with one another, and not with a monarch. The colony was a mutual enterprise, not an imperial expedition organised by the Spanish or English governments. In order to survive, it depended on the consent of the colonists themselves.* Necessary in order to bind the community together, it was revolutionary by chance.

The Mayflower Compact has a whisper of the contractual government enunciated in the 4 July 1776 Declaration of Independence, that governments derive their just powers 'from the consent of the governed'. It anticipated the eighteenth-century American Republic's belief that political authority was not bestowed by a monarch but a contractual agreement of free peoples, articulated at the end of the seventeenth century by the philosopher John Locke. The eminent American historian George Bancroft has called the Compact 'the birth of constitutional liberty . . . in the cabin of the *Mayflower* humanity recovered its rights and instituted government on the basis of "equal laws" for the general good'.

These ideas were not hashed about all the time in the community. They were simply a consequence of their endeavour. But of course since the Pilgrims were interested in political concepts, devising the rules by which they were to be governed was extraordinarily empowering, especially after all they had suffered. Once the rules were established, the decision-making powers of ordinary people were validated as a way of life.

As the forty-one men lined up to sign, these printers, merchants, serge weavers, wool combers, carpenters, indentured servants, a sexton,

---

* Twenty years later Edward Winslow and William Bradford became less democratic, defeating an attempt to pass a motion allowing freedom of religion to all who would 'preserve the civil peace and submit unto government'. Edward was horrified at the thought of 'Turk, Jew, Papist, Arian, Socinian, Nicholaytan, Familist' or any other being tolerated. William Bradford, by then governor, agreed. He refused to allow the court to vote on it because most of Plymouth probably was in favour.

a hatmaker and a barrel maker had no idea of the future resonance of their act. It was pleasing enough in the present.

Goodwill, religious faith and fellowship, and an agreement setting out codes of behaviour for people with not much formal training, all stopped the colony degenerating into a lawless place. Some of the settlers had been members of guilds and in a couple of cases members of corporations, but most had no personal experience of government except through being persecuted by it. Nevertheless they were eager to learn. As colonists they became agents of their own government, personally agreeing their local administration, land boundaries, systems of government, courts and punishments. They had to set taxes, and make sure they were gathered in. They rose to the challenge of holding office and dealing with an utterly new people, their Indian neighbours.

Fortunately John Carver was now elected governor instead of Christopher Martin. Carver was a natural choice as leader, not only because he had negotiated much of the nitty-gritty of the expedition and because he was ensured support from the community, but also because he was a man of wealth and status. He possessed character, empathy and force of personality, and had been a commanding and well-to-do merchant. The educated and rich were respected. After all, their wealth and their contacts had underwritten the expedition. But people of character and leadership rose by their own efforts. William Bradford and Edward Winslow came into their own when their combination of authority and kindliness were essential features in encouraging confidence in what could have been very alarming situations. During the worst times Carver also seems to have acted as general nursemaid.

Brewster, similarly, was a sympathetic and sensitive figure whose manner was so inoffensive that any criticism 'was well taken from him'. He undervalued himself and sometimes overvalued others' importance, yet he was still very much the spiritual head of the expedition. He did not want to be elected governor, concentrating instead on his religious role as preacher or Elder. He preached twice on Sundays and would like to have been their minister, ordained by the congregation itself, as was their separatist belief. However, John Robinson seems to have felt uneasy about authority for ordination. A minister also needed a university degree, which Brewster did not have. His ordination never took place, and of course the congregation were eagerly awaiting the arrival of John Robinson.

Brewster's ordeal – being hunted through the Netherlands – had changed him and aged him, and his 'humble and modest mind' was not what was really needed. A striving merchant such as John Carver or a young man with pizzazz such as Edward Winslow had the necessary attack. Brewster was longing for his books. He possessed no less than nine copies of a Christian guide of how to interpret the Bible which he may have used for teaching. He was referred to as an old man, but though frail he embraced manual labour, building his own house – as every man and woman in the new colony would shortly find out they had to.

Elizabeth was not quite well. She may have contracted a form of scurvy on board. One can imagine her lying uncomplainingly in damp bed-clothes in the November fog. Presumably Edward was by her side when he could be, but the rest of the time he was exploring with the other men. Whales bumped around the boat every day. There were all varieties, humpback, minke and finback, forty tonnes in some cases. Sometimes the Pilgrims heard the low boom of their whale-song, and the sailors pointed at them excitedly because their oil was extremely valuable. In Europe they were still perceived as half-mythological. In the New World they contributed to Edward's sense of wonder.

Edward was so curious about Indian culture that he would write a detailed account of his Indian friends and their language. Indian culture had been the subject of discussion in the travel literature of the colonisation movement ever since the discovery of Virginia. Shakespeare's play *The Tempest* had been performed as part of the marriage celebrations in 1613 of James I's daughter Elizabeth to the Elector Palatine. It was inspired by the shipwreck off Bermuda which Edward's new friend Stephen Hopkins had experienced. Revelry included a masque put on by two of the Inns of Court on the theme of Indian priests and Virginian life, orchestrated by Inigo Jones. 'The chief maskers were in Indian habits, with high sprigged feathers on their heads, their vizards of olive colour, hair black and large waving down to their shoulders.' Like Edward, the whole company was extremely excited by seeing these legendary Virginian Indians whom they knew through the popular engravings of John White's paintings, which stirred up sympathy and interest in Algonquian customs.

The Pilgrims were still living on the *Mayflower* anchored in Provincetown harbour. While the women remained on board, the men – led by Captain Standish in full armour – marched through the countryside to try to meet some of the Indians. Their pockets were full of Dutch cheese; the odd gulp of aquavit warmed them in the distinctly chilly air. Because Stephen Hopkins had already been to the New World, he was prized for his knowledge of Indian lore. He recognised the bent trees which were Indian traps for deer. One of William Bradford's first encounters in the New World was to have his leg caught in a noose lying in the grass. He spiritedly admired the subtlety of it.

On 15 November, with trepidation and excitement, having been enchanted by their first sight of a canoe, around sixteen colonists on one of these expeditions suddenly glimpsed other people in America. Initially they thought they were sailors whom they knew to be on shore: five or six people were coming towards them with a dog, who then ran off into the woods. The English followed, but the Indians turned down onto the sands and vanished.

The next morning a small party followed the Indian tracks, but 'fell into such thickets as were ready to tear their clothes and armour into pieces'. But they found water and drank it to no ill effect: 'the first New England water they drunk of, and was now in great thirst as pleasant unto them as wine or beer had been in foretimes'.

Meanwhile a small sailing boat or shallop was put together by the *Mayflower*'s carpenter to explore the coast. Provincetown was too small, sandy and exposed to be a main base for a permanent colony. They needed fields to grow corn and other grains, and fresh running water – Provincetown had ponds, not springs. Also important was a good harbour, as survival depended on trading with ships from Europe. There was an additional problem: the shallow bar meant the *Mayflower* had to be anchored quite far away. There was a long shelf reaching out from shore so boats could not get very close to the beach, and passengers had to wade to land. Soaking clothes added to the strain on their constitutions.

The incessant exposure to damp increased the coughs and colds they were already prey to after so long at sea. They were also affected by the dreaded scurvy 'whereof many died', Edward reported in *Mourt's Relation*. Having so many people at such close quarters was a health hazard, necessarily endured during the voyage, but now they needed to get ashore. The leaders were increasingly worried as it was now the end of November. They decided to have another shot at finding a better harbour across the bay.

A group (including Edward) exploring down the inside coast of Cape Cod in their flimsy shallop, led by Captain Jones, had to spend two nights in the open, in snowy weather. They were attacked at what they somewhat euphemistically called First Encounter Beach (now the site of the famous Nauset lighthouse). Their assailants were from a tribe called the Nausets.*

The Pilgrims had tried to speak to some Indians busy on the shore cutting up a grampus, a kind of dolphin, but they ran away. They then built themselves what they called a barricado with logs and boughs to spend the night in. On the second night, still not having found a good harbour, they were lying round their fire when they heard a terrifying sound. Bradford described it as a 'hideous and great cry'. Edward, who would become an expert Indian linguist, carefully noted it as 'Woach woach ha ha hach woach'. The sound stopped when they shot off one of their guns.

The next morning at about 5 a.m. they were debating whether to take all the arms down to the shallop before or after they had decamped, when they heard one of their party bellow 'Men, Indians, Indians', followed by a volley of arrows which came flying in among them. They ran for their weapons, some of which were already in the shallop on the shoreline, and one of the Pilgrims took a log out of the fire and advanced with it towards the Indians. One of the Indians – 'a lusty man and no less valiant' – took up position behind a tree as close as possible and let fly three arrows. He withstood three musket shots, till the bark splintered round his ears, then 'he gave an extraordinary shriek and away they went, all of them'.

Leaving some to guard the shallop, the Pilgrims ran after them shouting and loosing off shots to show that they were not afraid. Amazingly none of them had been hurt, though their coats in the barricado were riddled with arrows. They gathered up the arrows to send them back to England. As they would find out, the Nausets were suspicious of any Europeans because of their horrible experiences with slaver ships. They had additionally been offended because in their explorations the Pilgrims had found an apparently deserted Indian village and had taken some corn they discovered buried in abandoned Indian huts.

Amazingly, they had brought no seed with them on the *Mayflower*. In a gloomy situation, finding this corn was a providential sign. Bradford says: 'here they got seed to plant them corn the next year, or else

---

* Part of the Algonquian peoples, their cousins included the Narragansett, the Niantic, the Massachusett and the Wampanoag, whose nations spread deep into the mainland to the west. Descendants of these Nauset Indians still live on Cape Cod in Mashpee Village.

they might have starved, for they had none nor any likelihood to get any till the season had been past'. Moreover if they had left it any longer they could not have even planted it for, in another week, he reported, 'the ground was now all covered with snow and hard-frozen' and it had to be levered up with their swords.

By early December the rivers froze and snow blotted out the landscape. It was so cold the water froze on their clothes and made them like iron. There was a new soul too in the wilderness, mewling in his mother's arms. The baby was born on the *Mayflower* during the two last weeks of November's winds. Like Oceanus Hopkins, he was given a meaningful name. His proud parents, William and Susanna White, called him Peregrine, which means Pilgrim. Peregrine was the first English baby to see the light of day in New England. Edward Winslow wrote in *Mourt's Relation:* 'it pleased God that Mistress White was brought a bed of a son'. Swaddled as was the fashion, he was placed in the wicker cradle brought out of Holland.*

But at the same time on board there was a passenger who was sinking into a depression under the cold snowy light and the mysterious backdrop of the new continent. She could not find a way back from her despair and she could not talk about it. In all the anxiety about landing and organising arrangements, no one noticed William Bradford's wife Dorothy was becoming unreachable. Had the return to England from Leiden and the weeks in Southampton reminded her too painfully of the hustle and bustle of the fishing port of Yarmouth she lived in as a girl? Was it thoughts of her own young son, left behind? All we can guess is that the thought of the isolation of America terrified her.

The sick and the well lay side by side. There was beginning to be an epidemic of deaths. Funerals became a daily ritual. Jasper, one of the unfortunate More children, died two days after Edward Thompson, a servant with the White family. James Chilton, Mary Chilton's father, followed two days later. That stoning and beating by youths in Leiden had probably weakened an already fragile frame. The closing of eyes, the huddle of anxious women and then the sorrowful turning away when there was no more to be done were impossible to avoid. Burying

---

* Oceanus Hopkins was a less healthy child than Peregrine White, who lived into the eighteenth century, dying in 1704. In 1623, when some of the land acquired by Plymouth Colony was distributed to all the living colonists, Oceanus's name is no longer among them. His parents went on to have seven more children.

former shipmates was a grim substitute for planting new homes, and still they did not know where they should decide to settle.

Perhaps the frightening atmosphere – God was not reaching out His arms to save them – and the tragic deaths were the last straw that tipped Dorothy into preferring to die rather than to live. On 7 December, after some of the men had gone off on another exploring expedition, her body was found floating beside the ship. She was twenty-three.

The circumstances of Dorothy Bradford's death are disputed. There is no evidence to show she committed suicide, but equally no evidence to say that she did not. It is hard to believe she did not plan her death. There were so many people on the small crowded ship. If Dorothy had slipped and fallen overboard by accident, someone would have heard her cry. It seems likely she had taken care to plunge into the water when she knew no one would notice a splash. Nevertheless, whatever the reason, the mysterious death of a lovely young woman married to one of the most trusted leaders of the Leiden community cast another shadow.

What William Bradford felt about this tragedy he does not reveal. Perhaps he could not allow himself to break down when every atom of energy had to be used to survive. Moreover, as a religious man he believed all things were in God's hands. Death – even of loved ones, even of one's own young wife – had to be accepted as part of God's plan. Bradford was to become the official chronicler of the story of the Pilgrims, but any expression in his writings of personal grief was out of the question. Yet in *Of Plimmoth Plantation*, he was to ask himself if people were any worse for their sufferings. Every biblical text told him they were 'the better . . . It is a manifest token (saith the Apostle 2. Thes: I. 5, 6, 7) of the righteous judgement of God that ye may be counted worthy of the kingdome of God, for which ye also suffer.'

For all the women of the expedition, these were hard times. They experienced none of the excitement of exploration of their male comrades, for they remained cooped up in the ship at anchor. The children needed to be got onto land, not just for their health but because they were starting to run amok, especially the Billingtons. Stores were beginning to run out. Though stocks were supplemented by the fowl they shot such as geese and partridges, they could not shoot enough to feed everyone every day. The *Mayflower* remained their only lodging until they built their homes.

One of their pilots, Robert Coppin, had been to New England

before. He suggested heading west and making for a river he remembered being on the other side of Cape Cod. He was convinced that further round the bay lay a bigger, safer harbour, and better land for planting. The cruel weather was making it a necessity to begin building houses fast. As William Bradford would remember years later from his snug New England fireside, it was winter and 'they that know the winters of the country know them to be sharp and violent, subject to cruel and fierce storms, dangerous to travel to known places, much more to search unknown coasts'.

By 9 December, despite appalling winds and snow, an explorer party in the shallop – Edward, Bradford, Mr Coppin and various others – had discovered what became Plymouth harbour. Their mast had broken in three places and the wind made the sea so rough their rudder split, so they had to steer with oars. They landed on Clark's Island, spending the night there. Pausing for the Sabbath the next day, amazed by their survival in the raging seas, they went round the harbour sounding it for depth and shipping and decided it was good. They also went onto the land, which was gently sloping down to the shore with a great hill behind. They were encouraged by finding many former Indian cornfields. Brooks ran down the hill. In the days before piped water and sewage systems, all urban sites needed running water for clothes washing and ablutions, and for taking waste and dirty water away.

On 15 December 1620 the *Mayflower* weighed anchor and set out from Provincetown. But even now the elements were unfriendly: the wind meant they could not get there straight away because of the harbour's protective sandbar. Luckily the next day the wind was fair and they 'came safely into a safe harbour'.

The big issue now was where in the bay they should settle. The paramount needs of a defensive position and paying off their debts to the Adventurers with fish decided it.* It should be on high ground, facing the sea where a great deal of land had already been cleared 'and hath been planted with corn three or four years ago'. There was also a 'very sweet brook' which ran under the hillside, 'and many delicate springs of as good water as can be drunk'. Below them in the bay there were places to shelter the shallop, and the boats they would build in the future. In one field was a tall hill on which they intended to make a platform and mount their cannon. This would command all views,

---

* In fact it would be the fur trade that was their financial salvation.

because from it 'we may see into the bay, and far into the sea, and we may see thence Cape Cod'. The greatest labour was going to be fetching wood, which was far off, although there was plenty of it. Edward wrote optimistically that the soil was thick and good.

The Pilgrims still did not know what people had inhabited their chosen site because they had seen no more Indians. They continued to find Indian graves and untended cornfields. Previously on Cape Cod they had uncovered several items which pointed to Europeans having stayed on this land before. One was their first find, a big ship's kettle; another was an English pail. They also found a large grave which yielded what they believed was the remains of a European, because of his yellow hair. The grave at first appeared to be Indian because of the bow in it and mats and trinkets, but the bones were wrapped in a sailor's canvas shirt and a pair of cloth breeches, and bound up with it was a packneedle that sailors used for mending sails. Mysteriously, too, with the man was a smaller bundle, that of a child bound about with white beads as well as a little bow. Whether they were victims of sacrifice was not known. The Pilgrims were impressed by the good quality of the embalming and they reverently reburied them.

And, alas, burial was to become the activity that occupied the settlers over the next three months, as much as building houses. Their optimistic plans for getting most people other than the sick off the boat to chop down trees were hampered by the dreadful weather. On 21 December twenty people who were exploring were stranded ashore by the high seas. It proved impossible to build a shelter which protected them against the driving rain. For two days they were soaking, freezing and starving, unable to be rescued.

By that time one person was dying every day. There was no time for the sort of pious observances the Pilgrims would have liked to have shown, and little dignity in their deaths. As sleet and snow blinded the mourners it was difficult enough to get spades into the frozen ground to bury their loved ones. The settlers buried their dead quietly on Cole's Hill without headstones, which is why today graves cannot be found even for the most celebrated Pilgrims who died that winter. The burials took place hurriedly because half the colonists had either died or were dying, and at one point they had only five able-bodied people to tend to the sick.

The Indians, regarding the strangers from camouflaged vantage points, were very surprised at the lack of memorialising of the dead by the Pilgrims: 'they marvel to see no monuments over our dead, and therefore think no great Sachem is yet come into those parts, or not as yet dead; because they see the graves all alike'.

Many Puritans hated all manifestations of ritual which they felt were tainted by popery. Back in England, their funerals were notable for their plainness. Even the vicar meeting the corpse at the lychgate, as was the ancient English custom, was thought to be superstitious. Certainly there were no lychgates on Cole's Hill, and there was no church either. The heroism and endurance of the dead were not noted. Their graves were disguised by leaves. The Pilgrims did not want the Indians – whom they felt around them, rather than saw – to know how very few they now were.

Those that had the strength to cut down trees and carry timber began building what they called the Common House. This was a wooden building twenty feet square on the shore which was to be a gathering place. For a while it was also going to be their meeting house (where separatist churches held their services) as well as where they stored the provisions they had brought with them. They began building on Christmas Day, grimly refusing to be put off despite the snow and ice.

From the ship amidst flurries of snow the company could dimly see little black figures against the pale background raising a gun platform on what is now called Burial Hill, which rises 160 feet sheer above the shore. They had cannon to frighten off the Indians and the position commanded 'all the plain and the bay, and from whence we may see far into the sea, and might be easier impaled, having two rows of houses and a fair street'. That was the plan at least, but they remained very short of labour. Some were too ill even to move, and stayed prostrate on the *Mayflower*.

The sailors were restive and anxious to get their passengers off the boat as soon as possible so that they could return to London, even though the Pilgrims had finished only one house. A spark from the thatch almost burnt it down. Some of the shelters were made of little more than branches. Their first homes were very fragile, frame houses filled with wattle and daub. (In February it was so wet that the daub holding these houses together dissolved and fell off the wattle.) The Pilgrims had not yet begun to use overlapping clapboards as a layer against the snow and sleet pouring through the walls as the wind howled round.

Of the original 102 people, 50 did not survive the next three months. About three-quarters of the women died. Not so long after the death of her husband, the daring, opinionated Mrs Chilton succumbed to disease, her forceful personality no match for the insidious invasion of pneumonia and dysentery. That bold presence was silenced, leaving her daughter Mary an orphan. The women were worse equipped for coping with the wintry conditions than the men, perhaps because they took no exercise and were confined to quarters.

In early January the Pilgrims began marking out the family lots, in two rows for safety. But half the plots measured out with string and sticks were never used. Christopher Martin, the aggressive representative of the Adventurers, took ill very suddenly. The colonists had to quiz the dying businessman about accounts with the Adventurers and bills for provisions.

Three out of the four little exiled More children were already dead of the epidemic they called the 'common infection'. Their tiny bodies might have been a reproach to the settlers under other circumstances, but the Pilgrims were too unwell to ponder their sad short lives. The Tilley brothers, John and Edward, and their wives, who were in their thirties, died after they came ashore, though John's thirteen-year-old orphaned daughter Elizabeth survived. Death took the camlet merchant Thomas Rogers, leaving his eighteen-year-old son Joseph to seek other father figures. The Tinkers – he was a wood sawyer or carpenter with a wife and one child – died as did many others, sometimes two or three a day.

So many were ill – even the barrelling Edward succumbed – that there were only about half a dozen people, including Brewster and Myles Standish, who were able to stay on their feet, fetch wood, make fires and prepare what meat they could find. With some danger to their own health they looked after their colleagues, 'washed their loathsome clothes, clothed and unclothed them. In a word did all the homely and necessary offices for them which dainty and queasy stomachs cannot endure to hear named; and all this willingly and cheerfully, without any grudging in the least.'

That prosperous, confident merchant William Mullins of Dorking, who had such hopes of the New World and his stocks in the Virginia Company, faced his death in the efficient way he lived his life. He swiftly settled his affairs formally, and Captain Jones and John Carver witnessed his will.

The colonists had now seen the odd Indian 'skulking about them', though they always ran away when they were approached. But in mid-February they noticed the Indians were becoming bolder in the woods – no less than twelve were seen running by when one of the community was standing near a creek waiting for birds to fly over-head. The next day two Indians appeared on top of the hill. The Pilgrims made beckoning signs, and Stephen Hopkins and Captain Standish laid down one of their guns, but the Indians vanished again. Alarmed and uncertain as to what this meant, Captain Jones and the other sailors came on shore with the several impressive cannons, which they dragged up onto the hill to command the area. The largest was a saker, whose barrel was ten feet long.

At last in March the weather improved. In better health, the Pil-grims began to plant their gardens. On 7 March those who were fit went exploring, and among them must have been Edward exulting at the many excellent fishing places he could spy, and cheered – as were all – that there were paths 'exceedingly beaten and haunted with deer'. They saw a curious 'milk white fowl with a very black head' and 'this day some garden seeds were sown'. Edward remembered that at last the wind stopped blowing from the north and 'birds sang in the woods most pleasantly'.

On 16 March to the Pilgrims' great excitement one of the fabled beings they had read about at last came and made friends. In the most matter-of-fact way – as the colonists were bent over their spades sweating with the labour – an Indian walked out of the forest and up to the Common House. Stark naked except for a leather fringed belt round his waist, to their amazement he spoke in their own language, saying, 'Hello Eng-lish.' His name was Samoset and he was a minor sachem or chief of the Wampanoag tribe but based in Pemaquid in Maine, where Monhegan Island was a rendezvous for English trading ships. Although they did not know it, his arrival signalled that at last the colony's fortunes had begun to turn.

Samoset was chatty and informative and he spent several days in Plymouth. His land was a day's sail away, or five days by land. The area they were living in was known to the Indians as Patuxet. For-merly it had been a thriving village, which was why all the land had been ploughed. The reason there were so many graves, and no Indians, was a plague had devastated the area and killed most of the inhabitants.

Although Samoset spoke good English – he learned from the ships passing his home – it was his friend Squanto who would be the key to the Pilgrims' prosperity. Squanto was the emissary of Massasoit, the head of the Wampanoags. A few days after Samoset had spent time with the Pilgrims – who plied him with food, alcohol, pudding, mallard, cheese and beer, as well as a horseman's coat because the wind was beginning to rise and he was naked – Squanto appeared.

Samoset had already introduced the Pilgrims to five braves – 'tall proper men' as Edward described them – who were just as quiet and well behaved as Samoset despite their savage appearance. They danced and sang 'like antics' or clowns, and they brought back tools they had stolen in the woods. They had deerskins over their shoulders and one a wild cat's skin over his arm. Leather chaps stretched to their groins and their faces were painted black. Edward noted that they had a 'complexion like our English gipsies, no hair or very little on their faces, on their heads long hair to their shoulders, only cut before, some trussed up before with a feather, broad wise, like a fan, another a fox tail hanging down'.

The *Mayflower* legend has sometimes given the impression the Pilgrims were the first Europeans to know about Cape Cod. In fact the part of New England they were in, including this harbour, had already been explored by information-gathering Europeans for nearly a century. In 1602 the English explorer Bartholomew Gosnold had sailed between what he called Martha's Vineyard and what the Pilgrims named Buzzards Bay after its circling birds. Gosnold tried to create a trading post on the island now known as Cuttyhunk, though it was abandoned after some reconnaissance trips into the interior. In search of a passage to the Far East, Giovanni da Verrazzano had given the name Arcadia to Virginia after his voyages in the 1520s (the mythical name was also later used, with a variant spelling, to refer to the French colony Acadia, what is now New Brunswick and Nova Scotia). But diseases to which the Indians had no immunity had spoilt the idyll, killing ninety-five per cent of the inhabitants. Squanto might well have died of measles or smallpox spread by the Europeans but, ironically, his life had been saved through being carried off by a slaver captain named Hunt.

Squanto escaped and lived in Cornhill in the heart of the City of London with a merchant named John Slaney, who was the treasurer of the Newfoundland Company. Slaney sent him to Newfoundland to act as a guide and interpreter to the New World for the company, and he was befriended by another explorer named Captain Thomas Dermer. Previously an associate of the explorer John Smith, Dermer worked for Ferdinando Gorges, one of the keenest early investors in New England colonies. Squanto was hired for Dermer's exploratory expedition which visited what was now Plymouth. He was much needed as the Nausets, the Indians who had attacked the Pilgrims at First Encounter Beach, were still raging against Europeans on account of Hunt kidnapping so many of their clan.

A savage desire for revenge beat in the breasts of the Indians of Nauset, as had been shown by that fight on the beach. Only months before, Dermer had been very nearly killed when exploring for potential fishing settlements. Squanto saved Dermer's life. Now Squanto was to do something similar for the Pilgrims.

However, the really important person was waiting in the wings, to judge the reaction to his messenger. This was Massasoit, king of the Pokanoket tribe, part of the wider Wampanoag federation of tribes whose name means 'the people of the eastern dawn'. Massasoit lived forty miles away at what is now Rhode Island but ruled most of the area from there to the east coast. He was hidden up in the woods above Plymouth with sixty of his men and his brother Quadequina.

Samoset now indicated that the Pilgrims should raise their eyes. Above them on the horizon was the extraordinary sight of the powerful Indian king and his magnificent entourage of braves.

Massasoit in fact needed the bedraggled travellers as much as they needed him. He had some awareness of the English, their tools and their useful guns as he and his brother had met Thomas Dermer a couple of years before. The forward-thinking chief was determined to use an alliance with the newcomers to his advantage against another local tribe, the Narragansett Indians who had escaped the plague that had wiped out so many. To Massasoit's great resentment, now that his people were so diminished and weakened, the Narragansetts who were once his rivals had become his overlords. The Pokanokets had been particularly badly affected by the plague, being reduced from 15,000 to less than 1,000. But for the Pilgrims, this terrible tragedy was a piece of great good luck because it meant that the land was free and that Massasoit was prepared to make an alliance with them.

Massasoit had been spying on the Pilgrims all winter. They had often felt they were being watched when they were alone or in twos and threes in the woods setting traps or shooting birds. The Indians could have attacked but did not do so. The rapid depletion of the numbers of settlers convinced Massasoit that they were not going to harm him and that some kind of treaty could be negotiated. In the past historians tended to believe the Indian populations were innocent dupes of the early English settlers. The development of ethnohistory has shown the Indians had their own agendas to use powerful newcomers against other tribes.

In the same daring spirit that got him to Holland, Edward now volunteered to go up the hill and parley with the Indians. He rushed towards the braves, bearing two knives as a present for Massasoit, as well as a copper chain with a jewel on it, while to his brother Quadequina he gave a 'jewel to hang in his ear', as well as a 'pot of strong water', i.e. alcohol, and a good quantity of butter, all of which were warmly accepted.

Massasoit was 'grave of countenance, and spare of speech', in fact all that a king should be. Fired up by the exciting sense of occasion, Edward made a grandiloquent speech that King James saluted the chief with words of love and peace and did 'accept of him as his friend and ally', and that the governor wished to trade with him. Massasoit listened to this eagerly, although Edward felt his elaborate language was not adequately translated. The king gave him three or four groundnuts and some tobacco.

It was the beginning of years of listening, observing, and trying to keep the peace. Edward's account in *Mourt's Relation* suggests his fascination with this new world, these new peoples so outside his experience – yet for whom he seems to have felt no fear.

After eating and drinking and expressing admiration for Edward's sword and armour, Massasoit left Edward as a hostage with Quadequina, whom Edward approved of as 'a very proper tall young man, of a very modest and seemly Countenance'.

Placing his bows and arrows on the ground, Massasoit and twenty followers set off to parley with Governor John Carver. Despite the Pilgrims' unprepossessing appearance – their clothes were now very raggedy and dirty after their ordeals – they managed to greet the Indians with considerable ceremony and a musket salute. The Wampanoag leaders were led to a green rug with cushions. John Carver's presence was heralded by the blowing of a trumpet and someone beating a drum. He appeared and kissed Massasoit's hand, whereupon Massasoit embraced him.

Then they sat down and had more strong drink, probably aquavit, and a little meat. Observers noticed that Massasoit, who was heavily oiled with dark red paint, trembled throughout the event. In fact, despite the chief's friendliness, there had also been a secret powwow among the Wampanoags to put a curse on the Pilgrims, in case they were not going to be the allies they needed. The Wampanoags had strong suspicions that, as well as firearms, English people carried in their luggage a plague which they could unleash at will – an imaginative theory which had an element of truth.

Nevertheless a glorious and moving peace treaty was celebrated that day between the great Indian chief and his new friends, as the two allies agreed six articles of peace:

I.   That neither he nor any of his should injure or do hurt to any of our people.
II. And if any of his did hurt to any of ours, he should send the offender, that we might punish him.
III. That if any of our tools were taken away when our people were at work, he should cause them to be restored, and if ours did any harm to any of his, we would do the like to them.
IV. If any did unjustly war against him, we would aid him; if any did war against us, he should aid us.
V.   He should send to his neighbour confederates, to certify them of this, that they might not wrong us, but might be likewise comprised in the conditions of peace.
VI. That when their men came to us, they should leave their bows and arrows behind them, as we should do our pieces when we came to them.

Lastly, that doing thus, King James would esteem of him as his friend and ally.

The king approved this and his followers clapped. The simple but businesslike agreement kept the peace for thirty years.

The Indians liked the trumpet, which they took in turns to blow. Edward recorded the king and his men 'lay all night in the woods, not above half an English mile from us, and all their wives and women with them'. The Wampanoags said that within eight or nine days they would come and set corn on the other side of the brook, and stay there all summer. Slightly alarmed by this and not knowing what to make of it, the Pilgrims had various of their number keep watch, 'but there was no appearance of danger'. As another token of friendship, they asked the king to send over his kettle and they filled it full of peas. Squanto ended what had been a most successful day by tickling 'fat and sweet' eels with his feet, catching them 'with his hands without any other instrument', and bringing them to the Pilgrims. Enchanting, unexpected elements of Elysium had begun creeping into the lives of the settlers.

Edward gives us a wonderful description of the Indian king: Massasoit was 'a very lusty man, in his best years, an able body'. A great chain of what Edward called 'white bone beads' hung about his neck, from which at the back hung 'a little bag of tobacco'. Edward did not know that what he was looking at was not bone but the little white shells known as *wampum*, which was the Indians' currency.

Edward's vivid account of these days, *Mourt's Relation*, breaks off on 23 March. He had to face what he had been avoiding and ignoring in the vast forest: his wife Elizabeth would not see another day. Their personal dream was not to be. Elizabeth had been slowly declining for some time but now she was too feverish to take in her surroundings, perhaps mercifully.

She may never really have recovered after the deaths of Ellen More and Mary Allerton. Just before Christmas Mary had been delivered of a son, but he was born dead. Probably weakened by haemorrhaging and what was turning into a multiple epidemic of tuberculosis and scurvy, Mary herself died two months later on 25 February. She was just thirty years old.

Of eighteen adult women on the *Mayflower* only five were left alive at the end of the first winter. Captain Standish's wife Rose died on 29 January. The Winslows' two servants had died very soon after arrival. Having a dogged belief in a better future for themselves and their descendants had taken the colonists through the worst times. But determination, even if heightened by a religious excitement, could not prevail against immune systems too weakened by poor food and weather to make a proper recovery. Among those who witnessed the deaths of their loved ones was there, perhaps, a secret depression at the fear of a wretched future, that would not be worth their sacrifices?

In her last hours did Elizabeth mentally return to Holland and the carefree existence she had there? She had been ignorant then of what the future really held. The longed-for journey – for her – would end quickly. But to someone of her fervent belief, death was not to be feared. She passed away on 24 March 1621 and was buried in another unmarked grave on Cole's Hill.

It may be that one of the reasons Edward threw himself with such abandon into the New World was a determination not to be destroyed by the vanishing of his dear companion in the great adventure.

The last of the *Mayflower* passengers were disembarked three and a half months after they had first made landfall. The next month, April, those who were strong enough were working in the fields to sow the seed for harvest, using rotting fish for fertiliser, as they had been shown by Squanto. Because he came from Plymouth he told them to wait a week until shad came up the town brook.

The *Mayflower* sailors had become very restive and rude. They did not share any enchantment with the Indians or the New World. After showing some interest in exploring the coast they became impatient. To try to avoid disease they had insisted many of the sick leave the ship before they were well, despite the weather and even though some were delicate women and small children. But the sailors themselves could not escape the epidemic. Half of the thirty-five-man crew died of disease. One lay 'cursing his wife, saying if it had not been for her he had never come this unlucky voyage'. It would have been alien to their creed for the charitable Pilgrims not to help them. They nursed the once-abusive dying men in the most thoughtful manner, providing pillows and brewing herbal infusions.

The settlers saw the *Mayflower* depart on 5 April 1621. The surviving seamen had been testy in case they lost the tide. The messages for the Pilgrims' friends in Europe that Captain Jones had stuffed in his canvas pockets sailed with them.

Over two centuries later, Henry Wadsworth Longfellow – descendant of two of the Pilgrims who subsequently married, John Alden and Priscilla Mullins – imagined the secret tears as the *Mayflower* left. It had been bobbing at anchor in the bay so comfortingly. He wrote: 'Long in silence they watched the receding sail of the vessel / Much endeared to them all, as something living and human.' The last glimpse of the *Mayflower*'s departing sail going towards England, 'Sun-illumined and white, on the eastern verge of the ocean', seems 'like a marble slab in a graveyard; / Buried beneath it lay forever all hope of escaping'. Such ideas may have been handed down to Longfellow as historic truths in his family: that many momentarily wanted to abandon 'this dreary land'.

But whatever their material deprivations, and there would be many, returning was not an option for most of the colonists. England had not been home to the Leiden church members for over a decade. Edward himself believed the Pilgrims were being sheltered against God's coming wrath. God had 'brought His people hither, and preserved them from the range of persecution, made it a hiding place for them whilst He was chastising our own nation'. The caves of the misty Atlantic, the 'measureless meadows of sea-grass / Blowing o'er rocky wastes, and the grottoes and gardens of ocean!' were a protective barrier against an unfriendly English state.

Meanwhile there was not the lading that the Merchant Adventurers were expecting. Weston wrote to the settlers that if they did not spend so much time seeking biblical precedent and arguing, they could have filled the returning *Mayflower.*

In fact, there was little time for any sort of philosophical speculation. Their every breath was taken by clearing the land and ploughing fields. It was hard, grinding work without horses or oxen. A third of the indentured servants had died, the tough young men whose strong arms and firm muscles many families were relying on. Most colonists built their own homes with their own bare hands.

Not long after the *Mayflower* left, the gentle governor, John Carver, collapsed. He was in the fields planting – something he had never done before – when he felt a sudden pain in his head. It was the beginning of the stroke that killed him. He had to be carried back home by the stronger men, to his bed in a half-built house where he was attended by his distraught wife. The community was appalled at yet another blow from the blue. His death was 'much lamented, and caused great heaviness amongst them'. But because they were now friendly with the Indians the Pilgrims no longer had to bury at night. Governor Carver was given a proper send-off, with volleys of shot fired over his grave.

Six weeks later his wife Catherine was laid beside him. Close family ties and an affectionate heart had taken her from her Yorkshire home to live with her sisters in Leiden. With the loss of her husband she too collapsed. The very subdued community believed she died of grief.

There was something of a breakdown of spirit. Though William Brewster had been such a force in Leiden, Bradford hints that going to America was almost too much for him physically. Brewster was in no way unwilling 'to take his part' and to bear his burden working in the fields alongside the rest of the colony, but he was too frail to live on what at times was a starvation diet.

William Bradford was now elected governor, a position he would largely occupy for the next forty years.

On 30 June 1621 John Robinson wrote a letter from Leiden to the colony. 'The death of so many of our dear friends and brethren; oh how grievous hath it been to you to bear, and to us to take knowledge of.' He was full of agonising sorrow for the horrendous mortality rate, as well as the great personal loss of his brother-in-law John Carver. He longed to come to them, but he could not desert the wives and children of many of them and the rest of the community until they were all placed on ships with support from the merchants. Trying to boost their morale, he told them: 'Much beloved brethren, neither the distance of place, nor distinction of body, can at all either dissolve or weaken that bond of true Christian affection in which the Lord by his spirit hath tied us together.' He continually prayed for a way to bring the rest of the community over. Nevertheless they should remember that in all battles some must die: 'It is thought well for a side, if it get the victory, though with the loss of divers, if not too many or too great.' He hoped God had given them that victory 'after many difficulties', even though there were more to come.

At a time of such sorrow and anxiety, and in such an isolated situation, the colonists clung to one another for emotional support. Strong relationships formed suddenly. One such was between Edward and the recently widowed Susanna White.

William White had died in late February. An exhausted Susanna was left with two small children, one of them a demanding newborn. Edward and Susanna were married less than two months after Elizabeth's death. Were they in love? Perhaps not in any twenty-first-century sense, but they were a good partnership. Susanna needed male protection. Who was to say affection would not follow, especially with someone as warm and engaging as Edward?

They were married on 12 May by an Elder, as Edward and Elizabeth had been in Holland. The Dutch system of marriage was much admired by the church. Nowhere in the Bible was it shown to be a sacrament or part of the minister's office. It was 'a civil thing' upon which 'many questions about inheritances do depend'. In any case there were no ordained ministers in the new colony.

Edward now had another good woman to look after him and comfort him. And there was another relationship in his life which also offered hope – his growing friendship with the Indian chief Massasoit.

CHAPTER VI

Massasoit

The year before he left for Leiden, Edward had been working in London when Princess Pocahontas and her train were received in great state by James I. Perhaps he even glimpsed her black hair and slim acrobatic figure accompanied by her half-naked retinue. Indians were the most fascinating cultural topic of the day, the vogue in England since the late sixteenth century. Indian relics were collected as excitedly as American plants. American Indians had occasionally been seen in England before, often freed from slavery as Squanto had been. But the arrival of Pocahontas was electrifying. Already a legend, she was the princess who had saved John Smith's life in the early years of the Jamestown colony.

The Tradescants, the father and son who were the most influential English travellers and collectors of the first half of the seventeenth century, had a vast piece of skin said to be the mantle of Pocahontas's father, the emperor Powhatan. It is covered with nearly 20,000 shells forming a design of two beasts of prey and a human. (The Tradescant Collection forms the basis of the Ashmolean Museum in Oxford, where the mantle remains.)

Columbus's discovery of the Americas in 1492 created a flood of fascinated commentary and speculation, and travel books became hugely popular. Like the invention of the Internet, discovering the Americas altered everything. European philosophers, writers and theologians stretched their minds to fit the new continent and its novel inhabitants into a Christian Eurocentric chronology. What had happened to the New World during the Flood? Were the Indians the original inhabitants of the world who had survived it? Such matters were of great interest to Edward. As he got to know the Indians and became Massasoit's personal friend, he believed it was his duty to show they were cultured and moral people.

Whether the Indians had a recognisable 'civilisation' was a question informing the development of colonisation in England and Spain. The growth of the Spanish Empire organised under the encomienda system – where the indigenous peoples were forced into labour in exchange for protection and enlightenment by their Christian conquerors – led to strenuous public discussion. The Valladolid Debate of 1550–1 at the theological college of San Gregorio saw the philosopher Juan Ginés de Sepúlveda defend the right of Conquest over a people whom he defined as natural slaves. Like the Salamancan School philosopher Francisco de Vitoria, Bartolomé de las Casas – the Spanish friar who was Bishop of Chiapas in Mexico – insisted on native rights: the Indians' government and customs showed they were rational beings, whose property and lives should be sacrosanct. Educated English people were aware of these debates. Las Casas's *A Brief Relation of the Destruction of the Indies* (1552) had been circulating in translation in England since the 1570s. It was hugely influential, fodder for the English patriotic legend of the dastardly Spanish.

Amongst most English colonisers in the early seventeenth century it was a given that the Indians descended from Adam. As the Virginian minister Alexander Whitaker put it in 1613: 'One God created us, they have reasonable souls and intellectual faculties as well as we. We all have Adam for our common parent.'

The Renaissance rediscovery of classical texts had profound effects on English colonisers, who adopted views first propounded by Tacitus, that the ancient Britons and Germans provided an instructive lesson in the manly valour, courage, martial vigour and civic virtue that corrupt Imperial Rome lacked. They favourably compared the Indians to the ancient Britons. The other side of the coin was that English colonisers were to be to the Indians what the Romans had been to the ancient Britons, bringing them civilisation and the Gospel. As Whitaker enquired, 'What was the state of England before the Gospel was preached in our country?'

The classical comparisons which colonisers invoked were also made by Edward himself. Were the temples of the Indians not similar to that of Diana at Ephesus? Such ideas of course made the Indians less alarming and more familiar, and suggest why the Pilgrims were unafraid of peoples quite unlike themselves.

Edward's first encounters with Massasoit indicated that the Indian king had the sort of rugged virtue admired by Tacitus. From very first the Pilgrims were impressed by the Indians' valour and bravery. They also hoped that Massasoit might be the key to the fur trade. (From the late sixteenth century technological advances made beaver fur very valuable. It was boiled down to make the felt for hats. Now that they had recovered their health, the Pilgrims recognised the necessity of repaying their backers. The debt was around £1,600 at the time of their departure, but it grew exponentially. The investors proved costive and unimaginative about sending what the colonists needed to support themselves in the early years, such as supplies and draught animals.)

So it was with mounting excitement Edward made the first visit to Massasoit's home, Sowams. A king was a king to these merchants, and indeed to the court of King James I. The historian David Cannadine has shown that when the English first encountered the native peoples of North America, they did not see them as 'a race of inferior savages ... these two essentially hierarchical societies were seen as coexisting, not in a relationship of (English) superiority and (North American) inferiority, but in a relationship of equivalence and similarity: princes in one society were the analogues to princes in another'.

Pocahontas herself had been treated as the daughter of a great emperor on a state visit by James I. She and twelve Indians with her were received by Queen Anne at Whitehall. She attended a masque by Ben Jonson for the king and sat in a position of honour on his right hand. The artist Simon de Passe made an engraving of her, in court dress with a ruff. Round the portrait runs the legend that she is the 'filia potentiss. princ. Powhatani imp. Virginiae' – 'the daughter of the most powerful prince Powhatan, the emperor of Virginia'. Recent historical investigations have countered the long-held assumption that the early British Empire was underpinned by racist assumptions about the natural inferiority of the races they ruled. The English were not racist in the sense that they believed the Indians were really white people. The theory was that the Indians were born white – as is voiced very clearly by John Smith in 1612: they were 'of a colour brown when they are of any age, but they are born white.'

Going to see Massasoit was meant to be an intelligence-gathering operation. The Pilgrims wanted to enquire how to repay the tribe whose corn they had taken on Cape Cod. This had been on their consciences, and they hoped to exchange some of Indians' corn for other seed, to experiment with what suited the ground best. They were curious to find out how great the Indians' numbers were, and wished to indicate they were very much up for trading in skins, in addition to making money by fishing.

As Edward and Stephen Hopkins travelled, accompanied by Squanto as guide and interpreter, Edward mentally noted every detail for posterity. Stephen was a fairly good fellow who was on all the early exploratory expeditions. As he got older, drink made him obstreperous. Pleasant if rather loud company, and one of the leading figures of the colony as a well-to-do merchant, he was unafraid of the Indians. He remained a specialist on trade with them for many years. But he did not have Edward's hunger for knowledge of them, nor was he especially popular. A fondness for getting the better of people meant he had a reputation for dishonesty when he traded in goods and beer (most of the colony sold things to one another). Perhaps the Indians found him too much of a hard bargainer, a little dishonest and a little coarse.

But Edward was not interested in getting the better of the Indians. Of an intellectual bent, he was uplifted to experience at first hand what he had read about these marvellous denizens of the New World. Squanto was used to English ways. As their guide on the forty-mile walk to Massasoit's home, he showed the Pilgrims alewives, a seventeenth-century word for shad or herring, and the best places to catch deer. The Indians had their own agricultural methods: for 5,000 years they had grown beans, squash and maize together and kept the undergrowth down by burning it.

Passing a group of Indians fishing in the Pilgrims' bay, Edward wrote: 'As the manner of them all is, where victual is easiest to be got, there they live, especially in the summer . . . our bay affording many lobsters, they resort every spring-tide thither.' These Indians accompanied the party as they travelled west to Massasoit, who lived near what is now Bristol, Rhode Island. At what they understood to be the Indian settlement of Nemasket (now Middleborough, Massachusetts) the inhabitants entertained them 'with joy, in the best manner they could, giving us a kind of bread called by them maizium, and the spawn of shads, which then they got in abundance, insomuch as they gave us spoons to eat them'.

As the colonists journeyed deeper into the interior, Squanto showed them the tracks through the undergrowth. It became a piece of New England folklore that Indian paths were no wider than a 'cart's rut'. Relaxed by having an experienced guide, Edward took time to itemise the trees – 'much good timber, both oak, walnut tree, fir, beech and exceeding great chestnut trees'. The terrain was well watered, full of meadows and small hills, but rocky too. Though the country was 'wild and overgrown with woods, the trees were not thick, and easy to pass through'. At night, Edward and Stephen slept in the open fields with their Indian friends, wrapping their mantles round them. The two colonists were not soulmates, but Stephen was good company and resourceful.

As they got closer to Massasoit's kingdom, the countryside became more open and flat. Its position inland from Narragansett Bay offered a sheltered respite from the constant wind and spray of Plymouth's seashore, but there were dark swamps with trees twisting out of them, which were hiding places for Indians. They looked as though they could swallow the unwary. For Edward, such an adventure was a diversion from the tedium and back-breaking work of establishing the colony. It may also have been his way of escaping the sadness of Elizabeth's death. It was only a month after marrying Susanna that he had his first proper immersion in the Indian culture. Chopping down trees and dividing small areas of land were not going to be enough to stop him brooding.

The Indians they met were solicitous. Occasionally the colonists shot off a couple of rounds from their muskets to amuse them. They crossed many little brooks, passing Indians fishing. They were offered bass from the Indians' manufactured weirs – stakes sticking up in the rivers – which they had been making for thousands of years. Sometimes the Indians carried the Englishmen across rivers. Edward noted the Indians never drank water except at the source of a river. He was impressed by the 'valour and courage' of two spindly old men, who challenged them as they neared Massasoit's domain: they 'ran very swiftly and low in the grass, to meet us at the bank, where with shrill voices and great courage, standing charged upon us with their bows; they demanded what we were, supposing us to be enemies and thinking to take advantage on us in the water'.

Edward was struck by the way so much of the land along the river approaching Massasoit's territory had been cleared for corn, as well as the visible evidence of the plague that had devastated the Wampanoags. So many had died they had not been able to bury everyone. Edward and Stephen looked with horror at the many places where skulls and bones were still lying above ground. It was 'a very sad spectacle to behold', with 'so many goodly fields, and so well seated, without men to dress and manure the same'. Ahead, notifying them they were drawing near, was a hill called Mount Hope. About 300 feet high, it was an unusual stone outcrop in what was otherwise a flat, lush area. Mainly used as a gathering place for the tribe, it offered unparalleled views over Wampanoag territory which was useful in time of war. It was covered with giant boulders from the glacial period and Massasoit took refuge in its secret caves in times of danger. But with the powerful English on his side, perhaps he would need to do so less often.

There was a warm welcome when they finally arrived at Massasoit's, having eaten roasted crab offered by Indians on the way. The great king was pleased by the gifts they brought, including a horseman's red cotton coat like the one that the Pilgrims had thrown around the naked Samoset. There was also a heavy copper chain, which could be sent with messengers as a sign they came from him, ensuring that the Pilgrims would not be obliged to entertain any Indians except Massasoit's envoys.

Previous explorers such as William Strachey and John Smith had already printed some Indian vocabulary, so speaking to the king was a less daunting obstacle than it might have been. Massasoit was excitingly informal, considering he was a 'great sagamore' and 'the greatest commander'. Even though his tribe had been greatly reduced, he still ruled about 500 square miles from Rhode Island and Narragansett Bay to Cape Cod. The Pilgrims were naturally respectful of rank, and their accounts are littered with expressions of awe for the formidable kings of the Indians.

Massasoit made a rousing speech before a gathering of his men: 'The meaning whereof was (as far as we could learn)', wrote Edward, 'Was not Massasoit commander of the country about them? Was not such a town as his, and the people of it? And should they not bring their skins unto us? To which they answered, they were his, and would be at peace with us, and bring their skins to us. After this manner he named at least thirty places, and their answer was as aforesaid to every one, so that as it was delightful, it was tedious unto us.' After this he lit tobacco for them. Massasoit was just as curious about his fellow monarch in England as was James about Indian kings. After Edward and Stephen revealed that James I's wife, Anne of Denmark, had recently died (in 1619), Massasoit 'fell to discoursing of England, and of the King's Majesty, marvelling that he would live without a wife'. The English must not allow the French to land nearby 'for it was King James his country, and he also was King James his man'.

That night, the two colonists found themselves sharing the royal bed, at the monarch's insistence – Edward and Stephen at one end, Massasoit and his wife at the other. The bed was only planks laid a foot from the ground with a thin mat over them, but it was better than the open fields. They got little sleep because two of Massasoit's men slept alongside them and the Indian custom was to sing themselves to sleep. They were bitten by 'lice and fleas within doors, and mosquitoes without'. But such discomforts were a familiar concomitant of seventeenth-century life in England – even if mosquitoes were a novelty.

The next day, the colonists dined on two enormous fish that Massasoit had shot with an arrow. They were so large that they fed forty. Most of Massasoit's petty governors gathered with their warriors to meet the English. To the Indians' delight Edward and Stephen showed off their marksmanship with muskets.

And a couple of days later they were home, having sent messages that they were on their way in case the other colonists were worried. The two English travellers felt exultant and perhaps relieved. 'God be praised', wrote Edward, 'we came safe home that night, though wet, weary and surbated [bruised].' Despite the fascination and allure of the Indians, they were still an unknown quantity.

The friendship with Massasoit had an immediately helpful effect: his intelligence system located one of the Billington boys who had been missing for five days. The Nauset Indians across the bay at Eastham were said to have seen a child living on berries in the wood. Although the Nausets were the people who had attacked the Pilgrims at First Encounter Beach, Massasoit's system of alliances cast a magic cloak of safety around the settlers. Iyanough, chief of the Mashpee Indians at Barnstable – 'a man not exceeding twenty-six years of age, but very personable, gentle, courteous, and fair-conditioned, indeed not like the savage, save for his attire' – guided them there and back. Massasoit's protection meant that no ill will was directed at them, even though at Barnstable there was a very old woman 'who came to see us because she never saw English, yet could not behold us without breaking forth into great passion, weeping and crying excessively'; her three sons had been stolen by the slaver Hunt at the same time as Squanto, depriving her of the comfort of children in her old age. The Pilgrims told her 'we were sorry that any Englishman should give them that offence, that Hunt was a bad man, and that all the English that heard of it condemned him for the same; but for us, we would not offer them any such injury though it would gain us all the skins in the country'.

On the way home, leading them in the dark, Iyanough took the water he carried round his own neck to give to the thirsty Pilgrims. His tribe provided an escort: the women joined hand in hand, dancing before the settlers' shallop. The Nausets were friendly too: an amazed but happy young John Billington, hung all about with beads, was borne through the water by about a hundred braves.

The great Massasoit was not as powerful as he gave out. His neighbour, the aloof and majestic Narragansett chief Canonicus, was displeased by Massasoit's alliance with the English. On the way back to Plymouth the Pilgrims got word that Massasoit had been kidnapped. Since the strongest men were on this trip, they were terrified that the Narragansetts might attack their own colony while it was weakly guarded.

A sachem from Rhode Island, Corbitant, the head of the Pocasset tribe, was deployed to execute the kidnap. He too was suspicious of the English because he did not like them on Wampanoag hunting grounds. Though he was Massasoit's ally he captured him near what is now Middleborough, hunting with Squanto and Massasoit's brave, Hobbamock. Hobbamock managed to escape with the news. There was a rumour Squanto was going to be executed. Corbitant was related to have said pithily that if Squanto were dead 'the English had no tongue'.

Despite their desire to be peaceable, the anxious Pilgrims felt they must assert themselves on behalf of their ally or they too might be attacked. Captain Standish set out to avenge Squanto. In fact Squanto was alive and he rescued him. The grim spirit in which the Pilgrims attacked meant Massasoit was released. The Pilgrims delivered a firm warning to Corbitant that if he tried this again 'we would revenge it upon him, to the overthrow of him and his' – though they took the wounded home with them to be tended by Samuel Fuller.

Worried that the peace treaty with Massasoit was not enough, the Pilgrims made approaches to other sachems in the area. By mid-September a series of parleys had led to a remarkable treaty between the colonists and the Indian nations nearby. They included Corbitant, who had no wish to be left out in the cold. He asked Massasoit – who bore no malice to him, as kidnappings happened all the time amongst the Indians – to put in a good word for him, and he was one of the nine chiefs who signed the treaty. The Narragansetts retained an enigmatic silence. They would watch and wait.

September 13, anno Dom. 1621
Know all men by these present, that we whose names are underwritten,

do acknowledge ourselves to be the loyal subjects of King James, king of Great Britain. In witness whereof, and as a testimonial of the same, we have subscribed our names or marks, as followeth: Ohquamehud, Cawnacome, Obbatinnua, Nattawahunt, Caunbatant [i.e. Corbitant], Chikkatabak, Quadequina, Huttamoiden, Apannow.

The Pilgrims were on a roll. Nevertheless, there were worrying rumours that the Massachusett tribe to their north were also hostile – yet they had the best beaver skins as they had access to the Indians coming down from Hudson Bay. (The colder the weather, the thicker the fur.) The Pilgrims believed they had to make peace and trade with them. On 18 September 1621 ten of the colonists in the faithful shallop caught the midnight tide north and came upon an immense bay so large it contained around fifty islands. (Ten years later it became Boston harbour.) Led by Squanto, they found a territory in a state of upheaval. They discovered the tomb of the Massachusetts' fearsome leader in the fort he had defended in a recent war. The warriors were nowhere to be seen, though the Pilgrims sent messengers that they meant no harm. The fact the women had pulled down their houses and were surrounded by their corn in heaps suggested the tribe was on the point of fleeing. Squanto urged them simply to seize some skins but the Pilgrims insisted on paying. Edward noted approvingly some of the women tied branches of trees round them having sold the furs from their backs to the colonists. It was done 'with great shamefacedness, for indeed they are more modest than some of our English women are'.

The ladies fed them on boiled cod and eventually some braves appeared. The king's widow, the Squaw Sachem, was nowhere to be seen, but the males agreed to trade and showed them two rivers nearby (later named the Mystic and Charles rivers). They seemed peaceable enough.

Edward's account of the first Thanksgiving in *Mourt's Relation* tells how what he calls the Indians' 'greatest king Massasoit, with some ninety men', were part of the festival. For three days they feasted 'and they went out and killed five Deer, which they brought to the Plantation and bestowed on our Governor, and upon the Captain and others'. He wrote to the investors that though their lives were not always so abundant, 'yet by the goodness of God, we are so far from want, that we often wish you partakers of our plenty'.

It is hard not to feel a sensual, prelapsarian contentment in the accounts in *Mourt's Relation*. When Plymouth Colony began to live intimately with the Indians it was an astonishingly rewarding experience. New England did indeed appear full of enchantments and mystery. On 11 December in a letter home Edward wrote: 'We have found the Indians very faithful in their covenant of peace with us; very loving and ready to pleasure us; we often go to them, and they come to us; some of us have been fifty miles by land in the country with them.' It had pleased God 'so to possess the Indians with a fear of us, and love unto us, that not only the greatest king amongst them, called Massasoit, but also all the princes and peoples round about us, have either made suit unto us, or been glad of any occasion to make peace with us, so that seven of them at once have sent their messengers to us to that end'. As a result there was peace amongst all the tribes. A little over-optimistically, he believed that would not have happened but for the English.

'We for our parts walk as peaceably and safely in the wood as in the highways in England. We entertain them familiarly in our houses, and they as friendly bestowing their venison on us.' The profusion of food and fruit the land suddenly produced that summer, after the ghastly suffering of the first winter, gave America an Eden-like quality. Almost exactly a year to the day after they landed, Edward wrote in high excitement: 'if we have once but kine [cows], horses and sheep, I make no question but men might live as contented here as in any part of the world. For fish and fowl we have great abundance; fresh cod in the summer is but coarse meat with us', he boasts, for 'in September we can take a hogshead of eels in a night'.

There were mussels, and the Indians brought them oysters. 'All the spring time the earth sendeth forth naturally very good salad herbs. Here are grapes white and red, and very sweet and strong too.' There were native strawberries, gooseberries and raspberries, and three sorts of plum – one variety was 'almost as good as a damson' – and there was an 'abundance of roses, white, red and damask; single but very sweet indeed'. The weather was similar to England though it was hotter in summer. 'Some think it to be colder in winter, but I cannot out of experience so say; the air is very clear and not foggy, as hath been reported.'

Edward basked in the Indians' poetic, elemental civilisation. In his second report for investors* he was determined to do his new friends justice, and wrote a long and detailed account of them.

---

* Edward was responsible for most of the Pilgrims' first communication to England, *Mourt's Relation*, which was published in 1622. This was followed by *Good News from New England* in 1624, of which he was sole author.

'The people are very ingenious and observative [*sic*]; they keep account of time by the moon, and winters or summers; they know divers of the stars by name; in particular they know the north star and call it *maske*, which is to say, *the bear*; also they have many names for the winds. They will guess very well at the wind and weather beforehand by observations in the heavens ... Instead of records and chronicles ... where any remarkable act is done, in memory of it, either in the place, or by some pathway near adjoining, they make a round hole in the ground, about a foot deep, and as much over; which when others passing by behold, they enquire the cause and occasion of the same, which being once known, they are careful to acquaint all men, as occasion serveth, therewith; and lest such holes should be filled or grown up by any accident, as men pass by, they will oft renew the same; by which means many things of great antiquity are fresh in memory.'

Edward recorded their customs with admiration: the manhood rituals of young boys; their strong moral code and laws which were strictly enforced against evil-doers and thieves; and their religion. Their god was called Kiehtan 'who dwelleth above in the heavens, whither all good men go when they die, to see their friends and have their fill of all things. This habitation lieth far westward in the heavens, they say; thither the bad men go also, and knock at his door, but he bids them *quatchet*, that is to say, walk abroad for there is no place for such; so that they wander in restless want and penury.' Their deep mourning rituals, when they sang doleful tunes in turn, drew tears from their eyes, 'and almost from ours also'.

Their *wampum*, the strings of shells they used as a medium of exchange and diplomacy, also had a spiritual dimension. Frequently a gift in itself, *wampum* was woven into complex symbolic belts because it had numinous powers, as did everything in the Indians' poetic, mysterious world. A golden place lacking greed or envy and full of naturally civilised and moral shepherds has always had a hold on western European thought. The generous and kindly Massasoit seemed to reinforce the idea that the world could begin afresh in America. The Indians' strange unearthly appearance, the fact they did not seem to feel the cold (whatever the weather they were largely naked), their astonishing eyesight and hearing, their helpfulness and simplicity and lack of guile – all seemed to represent the sort of uncorrupted ideal all civilisations yearn for.

The last half-century has seen a drastic reassessment of historians' knowledge and understanding of the Indians. In the past, the lack of written records meant American history was written largely from a European perspective, but advances in archaeology and ethnohistory have opened up the Indian point of view. They reveal, for example, a sophisticated society with its own methods of warfare and charitable provision, and we now know far more about Indian attitudes to the Europeans.

The Vietnam War generated narratives which saw equivalence between the Americans' brutal treatment of the Vietnamese in the twentieth century and the Indians in the seventeenth century. It is undeniable that the English colonists in America, fearful of losing their identity, defined themselves fighting the Indians in the decades after the landing of the *Mayflower*. The Indians came to represent a satanic degeneracy when the Puritan settlers had started to doubt their own mission.

But when the Pilgrims landed in 1620, their intentions towards the Indians – as outlined by John Robinson and emphasised by Edward himself – were peaceful. John Robinson intended there to be a native church in line with English colonising literature's focus on the intelligence and natural civility of the Indians. Edward's experience confirmed it. In his view there was a solemn pact between his community and the Indians worthy of the name of Covenant. Indians, he said, were rational human beings with whom he embarked on animated religious discussions. Their gods were worthy of comparison to the Greeks' 'of former ages'. They also wished to be close to the earth. They believed her to be a living god – literally their mother earth from whom the human race had been created.

The Pilgrims waited for John Robinson in vain, because the Adventurers remained anxious about the effect his radicalism might have on the reputation of the colony. From the Green Gate in Leiden, Robinson wrote melancholy letters, accurately foreseeing that the backers would never arrange for him to be transported across the Atlantic.

In November 1621, Robert Cushman – who had taken would-be members of the colony off the *Speedwell* back to Leiden – finally made the sea voyage to Plymouth on a ship named the *Fortune*. He brought with him the permission known as the Second Peirce Patent. The First Peirce Patent had given them permission to settle in a different geographical area entirely. If they were going to remain in Plymouth legally, they needed a patent that gave them permission to be there. Cushman also came with his teenage son Thomas, who remained in the colony, becoming the ward of William Bradford, and thirty-five other new colonists. It was with joy that Edward and Gilbert greeted their brother John; while William Brewster and his wife welcomed their son Jonathan. Jonathan was extraordinarily excited to have arrived in the New World, which held such promise to ardent millenarians like himself.

The colonists did not mind sharing their food and clothing with members of their own Leiden community, but the newcomers also included seventeen men who had little to offer. Not only did they have no religious commitment, they put pressure on the already limited accommodation. By December 1621 the Pilgrims had built only seven separate dwellings, and four communal buildings which were probably warehouses. People were already sleeping five to a room in the single-storey houses. Some families were sleeping among the stores in the warehouses, which now also had to accommodate the new arrivals.

In an attempt to improve the atmosphere, Cushman felt moved to preach a lay sermon to the colonists to revive the community-minded *esprit de corps* that had borne them across the ocean. They must stop being grudging about the newcomers. He said this was not a time for self-love, to 'pamper the flesh, live at ease', it was a moment to 'open doors, vessels, chests, and to say "brother, neighbour, friend, what want ye, any thing that I have?"' They should remember Israel was seven years in Canaan before the land was divided into tribes. Cushman stayed only two weeks in Plymouth before returning with a final assent to the agreement with the Adventurers, and the first description of the colony, *Mourt's Relation*.

Whatever Cushman said, the colonists felt it was all very well for him to preach about unselfishness. Many had a distressing sense of impermanence. They could not put down roots when the houses did not belong to anyone. The Pilgrims managed to lay out their plots and gardens, or what they called 'meersteads', but the houses would belong to the company for another seven years until the debts were renegotiated or paid off. This added to the feelings of anxiety.

At least the *Fortune* could return home with an impressive load of 'wainscot and walnut' and 'two hogshead of beaver and otter skin', to convince the Adventurers that the colony continued to be worth supporting. Down in the hold lay heaps of clapboard or planed timber, heaved on board, made from the tall white pines on the rocky coast. In future years they became a superb source of masts for the English. There was probably £500 worth of goods, enough to pay back about a third of the debt. As the ship left, Bradford ruminated on the change that had overcome these former weavers, wool combers and ribbon makers. They had become fur traders. Thinking of the dishevelled, anxious and powerless group that had set off from Southampton, Bradford wrote fondly: 'neither was there any amongst them that ever saw a beaver skin till they came here and were informed by Squanto'.

Disastrously, the *Fortune* steered too near the French coast and the whole cargo was seized. Cushman was allowed to keep only *Mourt's Relation*. The *Fortune*'s capture dealt a fatal blow to the joint enterprise. The Merchant Adventurers could not afford to underwrite a colony and get no returns. They started to pull out.

Then, at the beginning of 1622, the colony began to run out of food. Edward was one of those who headed for Maine, literally to beg for bread from passing ships.

The need for Indian help was paramount as it became increasingly clear that, if they wanted to keep the angry Adventurers on board, they were going to have to go further afield to get fur. Meanwhile the Narragansett chief Canonicus sent a symbolic gift of arrows wrapped in a snakeskin to Plymouth. William Bradford had the witty brainwave of sending the skin back full of powder and shot. No more was heard from the Narragansetts, but it was ominous, especially as in the spring came news that no less than a quarter of the settlers of Virginia had been massacred.

Suddenly anxious, the Plymouth colonists constructed a huge palisade. But the labour of cutting down trees left less time for planting. The colonists were inexperienced with Indian corn, and weakness from lack of food meant they did not tend it as they should have done. The Pilgrims had to ask the still friendly Massachusett Indians to plant some corn for them, and to sell them some of their own corn and beans. The local Indians began to mock them, making insulting speeches 'and giving out how easy it would be ere long to cut us off'. To Edward's chagrin, even Massasoit became distant with them, 'and neither came or sent to us as formerly'.

Squanto's death that autumn shook the colony. He started bleeding heavily from the nose, which the colonists noticed was often a sign of impending death amongst the Indians. According to Bradford he 'desired the Governor to pray that he might go to the Englishman's God in heaven, bequeathing divers of his things to sundry of his English friends, as remembrances of his love; of whom we had great loss'.

Providentially in late August the arrival of Captain Thomas Jones's ship, the *Discovery*, there to map the harbours between New England and Virginia for the Virginia Company, brought the colonists a supply of beads and knives to trade for corn and beaver skins. For all Plymouth's grave situation, one of its passengers, Brewster's old friend John Pory (the secretary of the Virginia Colony), found much to admire. He felt Virginia could have done well to emulate the unique feature of Plymouth, its friendship with all its neighbours. But of that the Pilgrims were becoming less certain.

The short-tempered merchant Thomas Weston had been the driving force behind the Pilgrims actually getting out of England. He had helped obtain their patent and he had hired the *Mayflower*. He had more belief in the potential for colonies in the New World than the other investors, so much so that he decided he should establish his own plantation and come and live there, particularly as the group of Merchant Adventurers had lost faith in the Pilgrims' enterprise and wished to dissolve the company. As part of this plan Weston had sent out sixty young men in the summer without Plymouth's permission and without provisions, at a time when Plymouth itself was running short of food. (Weston himself arrived later that year.) The Plymouth planters shared their increasingly short commons, but the new colonists were frequently seen at night tiptoeing into the storehouse to steal more.

Weston's men – to Plymouth's great relief – removed themselves to a plantation further up the coast at a place the Indians called Wessagusset (now Weymouth). Then they started stealing from the Indians. Weston's men were too idle and feckless to support themselves. At the end of February 1623 they had completely run out of food and were planning to attack the successful corn famers, the Massachusett Indians. Plymouth was also desperate for food, having very little corn left. Living on groundnuts, clams and mussels, they were scarcely recognisable they were so weather-beaten and skeletal.

When Myles Standish went to retrieve corn from a friendly Nauset sachem on Cape Cod, he narrowly escaped being killed in the night. He was troubled by the behaviour of some Massachusett Indians who came calling, particularly one named Wituwamat, 'a notable insulting villain', who liked to boast of the way he had dipped his hands in the blood of the French and English and laughed about their weakness. 'They died crying,' he said, 'more like children than men.' Standish sensed that Wituwamat was up to no good but could not understand enough of what was being said.

*

In March 1623 the Pilgrims heard that Massasoit was dying. Despite relations being less warm than before, they decided they must visit him. They were much influenced in this, Edward wrote, by 'it being a commendable manner of the Indians, when any, especially of note, are dangerously sick, for all that profess friendship to them to visit them in their extremity, either in their persons, or to send some acceptable persons to them; therefore it was thought meet, being a good and warrantable action, that as we had ever professed friendship, so we should now maintain the same by observing this their laudable custom'.

Edward's action saved the colony. At a time of plots and rumour, Indians less favoured by the English were stirring up trouble. Edward brought Hobbamock with him to guide him to the chief's house and to pay his last respects. After Squanto's death, Hobbamock had taken over as the colony's guide in the wilderness. He and his family lived on land between John Howland and the Hopkins family for the next twenty years. He was to be the Pilgrims' faithful friend.

As they travelled Hobbamock became quite unexpectedly over-whelmed with sorrow at the thought of his beloved king's death, and he started a long lament for Massasoit, which Edward recorded: 'My loving sachem, my loving sachem! Many have I known, but never any like thee.' Then he told Edward that 'whilst I lived I should never see his like amongst the Indians; saying, he was no liar, he was not bloody and cruel, like other Indians; in anger and passion he was soon reclaimed; easy to be reconciled towards such as had offended him, ruled by reason in such measure as he would not scorn the advice of mean men; and that he governed his men better with few strokes than others did with many; truly loving where he loved'.

When they arrived they found chanting men and women, rubbing the king's arms and legs to keep him warm. The Europeans had to fight their way through to reach the bedside. Though he was so ill and his sight was gone, Massasoit put out his hand to Edward, saying twice, almost under his breath: ' "Keen Winsnow"* which is to say "Art thou Winslow?" I answered "Ahhe", that is "Yes". Then he doubled these words; "Matta neen wonckanet namen, Winsnow!" that is to say "Oh Winslow, I shall never see thee again." '

One cannot but feel Edward's own emotion and deep attachment to Massasoit at this scene.

---

* Edward remarks here Indians could not pronounce the letter 'l' and said 'n' instead.

The chief had not eaten in two days. To the amazement of those present, Edward managed to get some preserves on the point of a knife through Massasoit's teeth. Edward wrote: 'I desired to see his mouth, which was exceedingly furred, and his tongue swelled in such a manner, as it was not possible for him to eat such meat as they had, his passage being stopped up. Then I washed his mouth and scraped his tongue and got abundance of corruption out of the same. After which I gave him more of the confection, which he swallowed with more readiness.' When Massasoit vomited blood Edward washed his face, 'and bathed and suppled his beard and nose with a linen cloth'.

For two days Edward nursed the apparently dying king, then his health returned. Massasoit now demanded Edward make him some 'English pottage, such as he had eaten at Plymouth'.

Edward had to invent a soup without fowl, 'which somewhat troubled me, being unaccustomed and unacquainted in such businesses, especially having nothing to make it comfortable, my consort being as ignorant as myself; but being we must do somewhat, I caused a woman to bruise some corn, and take the flour from it, and set it over the grit, or broken corn, in a pipkin, for they have earthen pots of all sizes'. Fortunately, or perhaps unfortunately, his invention was such a success that he was called on to cure the whole village. When a messenger returned with chickens from Plymouth for the soup, Massasoit said they should be kept for breeding instead of being slaughtered.

News of Edward's kindness – and perhaps magic powers – spread quickly all over the area because the tribes had gathered at what they thought was the great leader's deathbed. 'To all that came one of his chief men related the manner of his sickness, how near he was spent, how amongst others his friends the English came to see him, and how suddenly they recovered him to this strength they saw, he being now able to sit upright of himself.'

It was proof that establishment of the Plymouth Colony was a good event in the history of the Wampanoag tribe – or so it seemed in the 1620s.

Now that the English had saved his life, Massasoit saved theirs by revealing a plot against them.

On his sickbed he had been encouraged by all the Indians round Cape Cod to rise up and attack the English. The ringleaders were Wituwamat and an aggressive faction within the Massachusetts – who previously had been on such good terms in that they grew corn for

Plymouth and traded with them in skins. The Indians had used many arguments to try to persuade Massasoit to withdraw his affections. But Massasoit said (as Edward put it), 'Now I see the English are my friends and love me; and whilst I live, I will never forget this kindness they have showed me.'

Massasoit gave Edward very pointed advice. The colony was on the verge of being destroyed: if he wanted to save his countrymen they must kill the Massachusetts' leaders in a pre-emptive strike. When Edward protested that their way was not to strike until they had been attacked, Massasoit was blunt: if they waited until the new colonists at Wessagusset were killed, it would be too late to save their own lives because there were so many Indians now hostile to them. He counselled without delay 'to take away the principals, and then the plot would cease'.

With this urgent message for Governor Bradford, Edward set off for Plymouth. The journey was too long to travel in a day, and at the earnest request of Corbitant, Edward and Hobbamock spent the night with him. Corbitant was pleasingly friendly and anxious to interrogate Edward and get to the bottom of the nature of the English. Were they friendly? Were they good? Despite Edward's urgent mission to get back and warn the colony, the night passed in intense conversation:

Amongst other things he asked me, if in case he were thus dangerously sick, as Massasoit had been, and should send word thereof to Patuxet for Maskiet, that is, Physic, whether then Mr Governor would send it? And if he would, whether I would come therewith to him? To both which I answered yea, whereat he gave me many joyful thanks. After that, being at his house he demanded further, how we durst being but two come so far into the Country? I answered, where was true love there was no fear, and my heart was so upright towards them that for mine own part I was fearless to come amongst them. But, said he, if your love be such, and it bring forth such fruits, how cometh it to pass, that when we come to Patuxet, you stand upon your guard, with the mouths of your pieces presented towards us? ... But shaking the head he answered, that he liked not such salutations.

Further, observing us to crave a blessing on our meat before we did eat, and after to give thanks for the same, he asked us what was the meaning of that ordinary custom? Hereupon I took occasion to tell them of God's works of Creation, and Preservation, of his Laws and

Ordinances, especially of the Ten Commandments, all which they hearkened unto with great attention, and liked well of: only the seventh Commandment they excepted against, thinking there were many inconveniences in it, that a man should be tied to one woman: about which we reasoned a good time.

In his account of his adventures Edward was anxious to do justice to Corbitant's sophistication. He was 'a notable politician, yet full of merry jests and squibs, and never better pleased than when the like are returned again upon him'.

As the travellers arrived back at Plymouth, a Wessagusset man ran in. The Indians had moved their encampment right up against their plantation and were creeping all around. They were waiting for the snow to melt so they could fall on Plymouth after destroying Wessagusset. He had pretended to be hoeing to put them off their guard and then spent the next two days dodging them to get to Plymouth.

The plot had been confirmed by another Indian, a Massachusett. The peace-loving community reluctantly decided to attack first. It was grievous to them 'to shed the blood of those whose good we ever intended and aimed at, as a principal in all our proceedings', but there was no other choice. Because of the Massachusetts' large numbers they decided to take Massasoit's advice and cut off the leaders. Wituwamat was the chief troublemaker. He must be killed and his head brought back 'that he might be a warning and terror to all of that disposition'.

Although this has been seen as a barbarous action and a genocidal attack on the Indians, it is anachronistic to view it as such. Even a hundred years later in England, beheading traitors was a commonplace punishment for enemies. In 1745 the Hanoverian government impaled the heads of Jacobite rebels on the walls of the City of London. The year the Pilgrims left Europe Habsburg troops placed the heads of the ten Czech nobles on poles round Prague. It was perfectly normal by the standards of the day and not an example of heinous treatment of the Indians.

Captain Standish went to the territory of the Massachusetts, trapped Wituwamat and others in a room, killed them and brought Wituwamat's head back to stick on the walls of Plymouth. But he did not exceed his orders and did not steal any furs from the Indian women, 'nor suffer the least discourtesy to be offered them'.

The killing of Wituwamat worked as a deterrent. The other tribes which intended to attack them, alongside the Massachusetts, were now frightened of them: Edward wrote: 'if God had let them loose, they might easily have swallowed us up, scarce being a handful in comparison of those forces they might have gathered together against us'. Many of the hostile tribes fled. There were depressing and hideous scenes, as Edward reported: 'they forsook their houses, running to and fro like men distracted, living in swamps and other desert places, and so brought manifold diseases amongst themselves, whereof very many are dead'. Amongst them was Iyanough, the young chief of the Mashpee, who had been so helpful in the search for the Billington boy and was such an impressive figure to the Pilgrims. Before he died he said he thought that the God of the English was offended with them and would destroy them in his anger. Edward reiterated 'for our parts, it never entered into our hearts to take such a course with them, till their own treachery enforced us thereunto; and therefore they might thank themselves for their own overthrow'.

One person, however, was disgusted by his flock's behaviour: John Robinson. He would have been even more displeased had he seen Wituwamat's head on top of the Pilgrims' fort, and the piece of linen stained with his blood serving as a flag. In December 1623 a furious letter arrived from Robinson: 'Concerning the killing of those poor Indians . . . Oh! how happy a thing it had been, if you had converted some before you had killed any! Besides, where blood is once begun to be shed, it is seldom staunched of a long time after. You will say they deserved it. I grant it; but upon what provocations and invitements by those heathenish Christians [i.e. Weston's men].' Robinson pointed out that Plymouth were 'no magistrates over them', they were emphatically not the Indians' rulers.

The dwellers at Plymouth had been called back to the highest standard of behaviour Robinson expected. But Robinson was safely in Leiden, not living in a small and vulnerable town of fewer than 200 people, perched on the edge of the American continent.

Massasoit himself saw no genocidal impulses in a course of action he had urged on the colony. Six months after the killing of Wituwamat, in an extraordinary scene, he danced merrily at Governor Bradford's second wedding 'with such a noise that you would wonder'. Above the settlement walls were the ghastly remains of the head of his fellow Indian. Little did Massasoit or Edward imagine that one day it would be the head of Massasoit's own son which would hang there.

*

Thanks to Massasoit vouching for him Edward was guided by the Indians miles up the coast to eastern Maine, piloted round forests and unknown valleys in canoes. Edward became the chief go-between and negotiator.

At a time of bitter political and religious strife, pastoralism, or the simple life of noble shepherds, had got a hold on the English literary imagination, whether in Edmund Spenser's imitation of Virgil's *Eclogues*, *The Shephearde's Calendar*, or Shakespeare's Forest of Arden. Plymouth seemed to have many of its elements. Yet as the New World historian J. H. Elliott has written, 'The dream was a European dream which had little to do with American reality.' The Indians were not naïve Arcadians in a fairyland idyll. Nevertheless it took some time for the realities of two opposing ways of life to distinguish themselves. There was a uniquely tender friendship between Massasoit and Edward. At the growing settlement above Plymouth shore a warm welcome to friendly Indian visitors was guaranteed.

Nowadays historians including Karen Kupperman emphasise the symbiotic nature of Indian and English life, and talk more of a middle ground than a battleground. Indians are no longer seen as doomed passive victims. They were as cunning as their English neighbours, but lacked their technology – which they were keen to obtain. Some ethnohistorians have seen Massasoit encouraging the Pilgrims to attack Wituwamat as a betrayal of other Indians' interests, questioning whether there really was a conspiracy amongst the Indians. Some believe that Massasoit manipulated the situation for his own ends, exploiting his relationship with Plymouth to escape paying tribute to the Narragansetts, and rebuilding his power. Tribes that had previously strayed returned to his rule. Ethnohistorians have shown that New England Indian power struggles were as vicious as anything at a Tudor court.

Appropriately, when in time the English started trying to make the Indian kings obey them instead of treating with them, the Indians were absolutely furious. They did not regard the English settlers in any way as the equivalent of their own kings. The only person who was their peer, who they would deal with, was the king of England, whoever he might be.

In the south the Virginia massacre changed the Virginia Company's attitude to the Indians. In a dramatic volte-face Governor Wyatt was told to end the policy of peaceful coexistence with what were now described as a cursed people. The settlers should be 'burning their

Towns, demolishing their Temples, destroying their Canoes, plucking up their weirs' and carrying away their corn. It was the end of the literature delighting in their ways and customs.

Yet this made no difference to Edward. In fact, in a show of the mental strength and independence which would become such a beguiling characteristic, in his new pamphlet to investors, *Good News from New England*, he continued to extol the Indians and the highly moral quality of their way of life. He seems to have had an enviable 'judge not that ye be not judged' attitude.

CHAPTER VII

The Building of 'Our Town'

Edward went back to London several times in the 1620s. When the colony found itself in dire economic straits, with its backers in England threatening to pull out, he came to the fore as a negotiator. His deft handling of New England life including Indian relations had charged an already energetic nature with new conviction: bonhomie linked to serious-mindedness won him the confidence of most members of the colony. Increasingly he was looked to for decision-making and was perhaps more sure of himself than many of his fellow settlers. The terrible lives they were enduring made it hard for some less robust personalities to think about anything except whether their fires had gone out.

A great many practical things were needed. It was hoped that the investors would pay for draught animals to till the ground; at present everything still had to be done by hand. They had only goats for milk until Edward returned – after six months of arguing with the wary investors – with the colony's first cattle, a bull and three cows. Horses were supposed to follow but there are no references to them in early colony records. They were either too expensive to send at all or did not survive the ocean voyage.

Many of the Merchant Adventurers were not wealthy. They often had relatively ordinary ways of earning their livings (Weston, for example, was an ironmonger). Although the Adventurers were blamed at the time (and since) for their parsimoniousness, these were agreed terms of what they regarded as a financial investment. The Adventurers did not actually owe the colonists any more funds, but some of them decided to help additionally for humane and charitable reasons.

On 10 September 1623 Edward left for London, though Susanna was pregnant. Her first child with Edward had died not long after it was born, but neither of them saw it as essential that Edward was back for the birth of this baby. It was regarded as the curse of Eve (for her sin) that women endure childbirth, and travelling with him to London and back would have been even more dangerous, especially with her two children from her first marriage, Resolved and Peregrine. Some sensible women friends had just arrived from Leiden, including the efficient and formidable Elizabeth Warren with five daughters in tow, and maybe Susanna felt that her female friends would be better placed to look after her during the birth than a husband. Perhaps he felt safer leaving her now that the settlement was becoming more like home, especially as she was no longer having to share her house with other people.

It had been decided, after harvest, that the communal system had to be done away with. Weston was a rude and difficult man, but as at Southampton, when his energies had made sure the colonists sailed, his information about the Adventurers now enabled the leaders in the colony to act. They made a démarche to Bradford, asking whether each family member could have an acre to cultivate, so that they could see the effect of working their own land. Just under 200 acres were divided between just over a hundred named individuals. Under the new system, yields shot up dramatically. Women colonists who had previously pleaded that they were too weak to go into the fields were now to be seen working there even with their little children. This was a community established to escape oppression, as Bradford wryly remembered. Therefore to have compelled them 'would have been thought great tyranny and oppression'.

The house-building programme went much faster. When Edward left there were twenty instead of seven, and a year later there were thirty-two.

These land grants were temporary, but Susanna and Edward's plot became their permanent home. It was a bonus not to be living hugger-mugger with other families and to have some privacy at last. Francis Cooke, a wool comber from Leiden who sailed on the *Mayflower*, built the house next to the Winslows. His French Walloon wife Hester and children arrived on the *Anne* in 1623.

The erudite, sometimes sardonic William Bradford was becoming one of the major personalities of the colony, and its presiding genius, vitally necessary for their cohesion as William Brewster became more feeble. Bradford kept notes about the colony's progress, minutely detailing what he called 'Increasings' – that is, children born to the colonists – as well as what are some of the oldest written records in America. In his looping handwriting Governor Bradford begins 'The 1623 Division of Land' with the words: 'The Falls of their grounds which came first over in the Mayflower, according as their lots were cast.' Among the names was that of Hobbamock, whose lot was bounded by Town Brook. Further away were the lots of those who had come on the *Fortune* in 1621; they lay closer to the sea. Then came the lands of those who came in the *Anne*; they lay against the swamp.

There was what the settlers called a 'Highway' – a little passage by the edge of all the gardens. Susanna's garden was next door to the Cookes', whom she had had known in Leiden, and just along from the noisy Billingtons'.

Myles Standish's daughter Loara's sampler with silk embroidery still survives. It reads:

> Loara Standish is my name
> Lord guide my heart that
> I may do thy Will also
> My hands with such
> Convenient skill as may
> Conduce to virtue void of
> Shame and I will give
> The glory to thy name.

The words used many different stitches. The intention was for the samplers to be permanent records of needlework stitch which would be passed from mother to daughter. The linen must have been imported.

Making such a sampler would be part of the education of any young lady in a well-to-do family in England. It would be a while before the walls at Plymouth were plastered and ready to hang ornaments. In the very early days, their living quarters were rather incongruously furnished. Silver porringers, linen and china amidst the smoky, rough-hewn interiors were the only visible signs of a former civilised existence in Europe. But the Winslows were only in their late twenties, and they had all the optimism of youth and religious faith that things would be well. Susanna came from the upper middle classes. She was used to a certain standard of living, as fragments from her house show. She could read and write, and so could her genteel friends.

The Pilgrims took pride in the simplicity of their living. Much of their way of life was influenced by a fervent vision of the early church. Like Susanna, Mrs Warren had also been used to a comfortable, cultured and commodious way of life. It is hard not to believe that she did not initially feel a slight horror at the primitive nature of the colony.

Edward would have expected the community to look after his wife. Although childbirth was a feminine mystery, life amongst the Indians was sufficiently open for Edward to see that Indian women were so fit that they gave birth effortlessly. He noted that two days after she had a baby, one Indian woman was 'in cold weather in a boat upon the sea'.

Losing his own child had of course been a matter of great grief. Edward wrote: 'it pleased Him that gave it to take it again unto himself'. The starvation conditions the colony had undergone possibly meant the little baby did not stand much of a chance. This must have given Edward some pause for thought. That winter, in London, he would write about Indians weeping at the death of their children. Christians were taught to accept what God did, whereas Indian fathers cut their hair and disfigured themselves to show their sorrow.

Also recently arrived on the *Anne* with Elizabeth Warren were the two Brewster daughters, Fear and Patience. Mrs Brewster had been pining, and William Brewster had become very worried at what he called his wife's 'weak and decayed state of body'. Now John Robinson also hoped that the safe arrival of the girls, as well as better provisions, would see a revival in his old friend 'the dear lady'.

Mrs Warren had been separated from her beloved husband for almost three years. A most formidable woman from Baldock in Hertfordshire, she had been looking after her five daughters in Holland while her husband built a home for them in the New World. (The redoubtable matriarch probably did some matchmaking on the *Anne* on her way over. In a few years a cooper also on the ship, Robert Bartlett, would marry her daughter Mary.)

Susanna never seems to have been discontented, never missed England very much and appears never to have considered returning, despite her well-to-do background. Nevertheless she had given Edward instructions to contact her father via her uncle. He was also to send his best wishes to her sister and brother.

Edward was away for six months, raising funds on account of Weston's withdrawing his support from Plymouth and putting it in his own colony. While in London, Edward had hoped his old patron Thomas Coventry would help with connections in the City, but Coventry was too busy with his political life. It seems unlikely Edward managed to get an audience with him, though he obtained a patent to fish at Cape Ann from Lord Sheffield, which was perhaps the result of Coventry's assistance.

Then, as now, investors were conservative and highly sensitive to any issues that threatened their profits. Edward's fund-raising efforts were hampered by strange reports about Plymouth. The colonists' outspokenness and honesty gave them a poor reputation; the fact that they lacked a proper clergyman was making them 'scandalous', while rumours circulated that women and children were part of the colony's government (which was simply not true – Bradford wrote that 'they are excluded, as both reason and nature teacheth they should be').

Edward was very keen to impress upon backers how worthwhile it was to interact with the Indians, and wrote his second pamphlet, *Good News from New England*, when he was in London. Perhaps in the cramped streets he was overwhelmed with longing for his extraordinary American life, and remembered the Indians with nostalgia and warmth. He was in a rather triumphant mood because the harvest had convinced him that God was on the colony's side, and he, in turn, wanted to convince investors. As he wrote in promotional material, he really believed Plymouth could be a successful economic venture where 'religion and profit jump together'.

He and Robert Cushman also made compromises: they decided rather unorthodoxly but sensibly that it would not destroy the colony's purpose if the Adventurers sent out an ordinary Church of England clergyman for Plymouth. They chose a clergyman, John Lyford, who had a degree from Cambridge and had recently been minister to a parish in Northern Ireland. It meant the much-needed money for food-stuffs would continue to flow.

However, his arrival caused a great split when Edward returned with him in March 1624 and Lyford baptised the baby of one of the settlers, William Hilton, who was not a member of the Leiden church. It caused an uproar not only amongst members of the original Scrooby church, but also amongst colonists who were ordinary members of the Church of England and who had a less intense view of religion.

Lyford violently took against the separatist nature of the settlement. He wrote rude letters back to the Merchant Adventurers, and allied himself with the malcontents who had always existed in the colony, such as the disruptive Billingtons, as well as discontented rootless newcomers. One such was a Devonian trader named John Oldham, who was determined to make his fortune in America. He arrived with his wife, stepson and pretty sister Lucretia (who married Jonathan Brewster). Oldham was a strong and unusual personality, who, despite prohibition, would soon trade with the Indians, including the Narragansetts' elusive and reserved chief Canonicus.

Oldham was not the only newcomer who did not like the controlling and religious ways of the Leiden church. The discontented included a vigorous young salter named Roger Conant. He was religious enough, but did not care for the strictness of life at Plymouth. The future founder of Salem, Conant had married a woman from a family with many influential Puritan connections but he became alarmed by what he now saw as the narrowness of separatism.

There were ugly scenes when it was discovered that Lyford had been writing letters attacking the colonists with whom he had pretended to sympathise. When the ship that took these letters was about to set off, Governor Bradford rowed out beyond the sandbar to retrieve them, and then put Lyford on trial for treason. Lyford promised not to write such letters again, but when more of them were discovered he was expelled, along with Oldham. It must have been extremely embarrassing for Lucretia when her brother was found guilty of conspiring to overthrow the colony. But Oldham was not a fellow to be kept down by disapproval. In fact the Lyford episode led to about a quarter of the Plymouth population leaving in 1625, with Lyford, Conant and Oldham. They went north along the coast towards Boston to make a small settlement at Nantasket, where the Indians had given them shelter.

The leavers made trouble for Plymouth at a time when they did not need bad opinions and gossip, especially if rumours got back to England. It was now made to seem that the Pilgrim separatists were not only strange – and potentially disruptive and anarchic – but cruel too. From the Pilgrims' point of view it was the right moment to assert themselves. As the historian of Plymouth Colony George D. Langdon junior has written: 'They had thwarted an attempt to overthrow their political and religious control of the colony, an attempt which, had it succeeded, would have nullified the very purpose of their exile. In surviving these first years they had successfully met the greatest challenge of their lives.' The leaders began to think it would be better to replace the Adventurers with other investors. They had had enough to do holding things together 'amongst men of so many humours, under so many difficulties and fears of many kinds'. But the Adventurers would not let them go.

On 1 March 1625, John Robinson died after eight days of illness. He never saw the little colony he had inspired. Despite his illness he had insisted on preaching twice on the Sunday preceding his death. There was some comfort to be found in the fact that the funeral of Robinson, who had been treated so harshly by his mother country, was attended by all Leiden's most eminent intellectuals. His grave is beneath the Pieterskerk, surrounded by the most celebrated professors and powerful members of the town government.

Robinson's wife Bridget, the sister of Mrs Carver, lived for almost another twenty years. One of her sons, Isaac, went to join the pilgrim colony in 1631, while another, John, became a doctor and returned to England. In 1629 a last remnant of the church would make their way over the waters in a ship hired by the powerful Massachusetts Bay Company and then be guided south by delighted members of the church. After that the congregation in Leiden slowly disintegrated. There is a rumour that Bridget Robinson joined the Dutch Reformed Church at Amsterdam and moved there. She made her will in Leiden in 1643, though the date of her death is not known.

Extremely sad too for Edward and the other colonists was the sudden death of Robert Cushman in the outbreak of bubonic plague in 1625. Despite his fussy ways he had been one of the colony's most important figures.

The plague killed 40,000 Londoners that year. Trade was at a standstill, and this stasis may have convinced the Adventurers to rid themselves at last of their investment and release Plymouth to the colonists, who bought themselves out. The Adventurers eventually sold the colony's debt for £1,800 to fifty-eight people, known as the Purchasers, four of whom were the religious London merchants who remained interested. A smaller group (eight from Plymouth, four from London) called the Undertakers 'undertook' to repay the Adventurers within the next six years. The debts in fact would not be properly discharged until 1645 due to inaccurate accounts. Edward and other Undertakers had to give money from the sale of their homes to make up the shortfall. In return for taking on this burden the Undertakers had special rights. They were to have a monopoly on the trade with the Indians, and the rest of the Purchasers were bound to produce annual payments of corn and tobacco over the next six years to help with the debt. Buying out the Adventurers resulted in huge changes for the Pilgrims. The land and future profits would now be divided between the shareholders, who were mainly the settlers themselves.

They were divided into twelve groups, each of which received a cow and two goats. Although all the surrounding meadowland and all

fishing and fowling was free to all or held in common, it was feared
that the colonists might not be efficient enough to make the payments
on the huge debt. Their farming activities would have to be expanded,
but they had come to realise the area around Plymouth had poor soil.
It was inevitable that a small township would no longer contain them.

On 22 May 1627, at the usual solemn and ceremonial court that
marked a Plymouth Colony gathering to deliberate on matters of
importance, it was announced how the assets of the company – 'to wit
the cows and the goats' – would be divided. Still surviving is a list
of the 156 colonists, divided into twelve lots of fifteen colonists each.
Thanks to animals brought on the *Anne* and other ships, by 1627
Plymouth had a herd of sixteen cattle, over twenty goats, around fifty
pigs and many chickens. Sheep are not mentioned but probate inventories show the settlers owned some. Their wool would have been spun
and carded to make stockings and jerseys.

Around this time Edward's brother John married Mary Chilton,
who, legend has it, was the first European woman who stepped on
what has become known as Plymouth Rock. She had got three shares
in the 1623 Division of Land, one for herself and one for each of her
parents, who had died during the first terrible winter.

The Division of Cattle not only gives all the names of those living at
Plymouth in 1627, it also shows how tightly the settlers had to cooper-
ate with one another. The company did not have a huge number of
animals. It was not a parish pump they gathered round, but the
heifers.

The Winslows' house is the best-documented original house of what
are usually called the 'First Comers'. It would last into the 1660s, being
substantial enough to serve as the colony court house. When they sold
it in 1639 to another merchant named Thomas Wallis for £120, the
details of the sale show the first property included land stretching to
the water. There was a barn and stabling for the family's horses (the
subject of much envy to the Wampanoags, who had no horses), a
'backhouse', an outhouse and some fruit trees. Despite the first years
of very hard graft Plymouth people had not lost their taste for the
accoutrements of pleasant English life which they wished to reproduce
in America. When Edward sold the house he uprooted the fruit trees
and took them across the bay by boat. Tradition has it that plants had
come over on the *Mayflower*. Although crab apple trees were native to
North America these may have been cuttings from the renowned pear
trees of Edward's native Worcestershire.

Showing signs of being a careful businessman like his brother John (and unlike his father), Edward retained the barn, stables and fold yard for his sheep, and the right to come and go through his old garden. Locks were itemised as a precious resource and always removed by the vendor, who used them in their next building.

The house was comfortably equipped with wainscoting, and neatly fenced. Recent archaeological excavations have shown that the early buildings in Plymouth Colony lacked stone foundations because the Pilgrims did not have the tools, and wood was plentiful. They were post-in-earth constructions, as were the later grander dwellings at Duxbury and Marshfield.

The Pilgrims soon imported furniture, though iron rusted and material was corroded by the salty winds. Traditionally the bed was the most expensive item of furniture and in the parlour was a 'wainscot bedstead' which would have been built with the house.

Edward's younger brother Kenelm would be one of the key carpenters in the colony. Almost all furniture for the houses of Plymouth was produced by them; and as time went on and better houses were built, carpenters would also be largely responsible for their design.

Edward Winslow's life flipped between England and the wild American frontier, between conducting business with merchants in London and trading with half-naked Indians beside vast unknown rivers. One thing the relationships with Indians and the merchants of the City had in common was that they thrived on trust. Just as much as the keen-eyed merchants (whose grandiose portraits of themselves slung about with gold and ermine hung in their livery companies), the Indians (who were the key to the hugely profitable fur to be got from their connections in Hudson Bay) believed their word was their bond.

Edward spent time in London with Emanuel Altham and with one of the investors, James Sherley. The Puritan Sherley was a man of property with a goldsmith's shop on London Bridge, a villa in Surrey and a house in Crooked Lane. Edward had letters sent there. Since Sherley became an executor of Edward's will, it seems likely Edward stayed there, as well as using it as a poste restante. Over the years, as Edward became one of the chief people going back and forth to London to raise money, he became friends with the other Puritan merchants who had kept faith with the colony. One such investor, a wholesale linen draper named Thomas Andrewes, was one of the greatest financiers of the day. He and his Puritan businessman brother Richard both had shares in the Plymouth Colony.

By 1627 the experiment was regarded as a success. The late 1620s were delightful years. Bradford wrote nostalgically that they suddenly felt the sweetness of the country. Plymouth was a haven for wildlife: to the north were the cranberry bogs, full of fowl, that were the headwaters of the Eel River and its large watershed with its many wild birds and flora and fauna. Plymouth Beach, the sandbar stretching out for three miles at right angles to the harbour and forming a protective wall, was an important nesting point for migratory birds, the piping plover and the tern. The Pilgrims named a section of the coast across Plymouth Bay Brant Rock due to the Brant geese they saw there. Thoreau wrote in *Walden* that the sound of geese was like a 'tempest' when they flew low over his house, 'their commodore honking all the while with a regular beat'.

In a few years the colonists would start farming in the low-lying lush green pastures of the Eel River, inland from the grassy sand dunes and pebbled beaches that formed Plymouth's natural habitat. It was sheltered from the high Atlantic winds. Salt marshes transformed their lives, providing winter fodder for cattle without the necessity of having to prepare the land for hay. Coastal salt marsh in New England opened up great areas of land for profitable farming. No wonder the Plymouth colonists believed at times they were saved from God's wrath.

CHAPTER VIII

Good Farms

Over the next decade, more scattered settlements began to appear forty miles north of the Pilgrims. When news spread in the City of London that people could live there despite the harsh environment, merchants backed a flurry of small plantations, mostly along the coast. The settlers made their living fishing and trading.

English ships left crew behind in an exercise called double-manning. They grew vegetables and caught and dried fish to be sent back on the next ships. Dim smoky interiors sheltered grimly determined people clinging to subsistence.

The haphazard new settlements were a source of some irritation to the Pilgrims. There were no proper maps so the Council of New England often granted licences to huge tracts of land which overlapped with existing claims. Inevitably on an unknown coastline, ignorance of London grants meant fishermen felt free to set up stages in whatever bays they came upon, pitching their tents until their drying frames had enough fish on them to make the return worthwhile.

Nevertheless, the fact that the Pilgrims had managed to survive meant that New England became a plausible destination for the anxious godly. In *The Planter's Plea* the Dorchester clergyman John White described how 'men but of mean and weak estates of themselves' had conceived 'God's Providence had directed them unto that place'. They had sent home tidings of 'the soil and inhabitants ... which occasioned other men to take knowledge of the place, and to take it into consideration'.

Serious-minded Puritans in England increasingly believed the Church of England was under threat from Charles I, who became king in 1625 and was married to the Catholic Bourbon princess Henrietta Maria. Roger Conant's influential Puritan connections meant he was the beneficiary of a new mission to colonise New England and save the Puritan religion, inspired by White and merchants in the west of England. The enterprising White knew Roger Conant's brother, and he now invited the exiled Conant to join the Dorchester Company's little settlement, Gloucester on Cape Ann. Conant gave a description of Myles Standish losing his already short temper with some of the company's fishermen because Plymouth had a patent to fish there. They would have come to blows or worse had Conant not intervened.

Roger Conant was a man of character and integrity. In 1626, after the Dorchester Company went out of business, he founded a settlement at a place the Indians called Naumkeag north of Boston Bay. Two years later the vigorous John Endecott arrived as the representative of a new Puritan colonising entity – the Massachusetts Bay Company. It absorbed both the Dorchester Company and Roger Conant's group. Endecott renamed Naumkeag Salem. It was intended to have the sense of the Hebrew word 'shalom', meaning peace.

At least the small settlements were a source of the goods which Plymouth always needed. When it came to the Plymouth government's ears that the short-lived Monhegan plantation started by West Country merchants was about to break up, William Bradford and Edward Winslow dashed off to see if any goods could be salvaged. What they got there, and from a French ship cast away at Sagadahoc with textiles on board, enabled further trading with the Indians.

The Pilgrims' hope that they were going to make their fortune by fishing had come to an end when the *Little James* sank in 1624. Fishing was never going to be the solution. There were too many professional deep-sea fishing operations to compete with. Plymouth had proved too shallow a harbour for transatlantic trade and had too few ships. Their fish salter burnt to the ground and the experiment ended.

In the forests of the north were the beaver that would bring the profits the colony needed.* Edward did not have all the necessary information, but he was now beginning to make informed guesses as to where they were. After one expedition yielded fur worth £700 (around £70,000 in today's money), it was seen as the best way forward. Fortunately for the Pilgrims, who were always short of the trinkets and tools Indians liked, the tribes of north-eastern Maine wanted the colonists' corn. The recent plague had killed many Indian farmers, whose fields were overgrown with weeds and many were starving. It had been a strange and moving moment for the colony

---

* In the early seventeenth century there were 60 million beavers in North America, which were hunted almost to extinction on the East Coast.

when their own harvest was bountiful, and the pleasure was enhanced because their crop was so valuable.

The Pilgrims' first trading post was by Buzzards Bay on the Manomet River, with another by Massasoit's longhouse in Sowams. They initially believed the best skins were to the west because that was where the Dutch were. But in fact the thickest furs came from the north-east. Europeans were believed to lack the skills and patience to capture beavers, which were the architects of the New England woods. Their lodges dammed thousands of streams and made deep ponds.

The Indians navigated by canoe the many small rivers of the Kennebec watershed, as they did most New England streams and rivers. At a time without horses the innumerable waterways of Maine meant they could travel wherever they pleased. Steeply forested Maine, which lies between Plymouth and Canada, was swiftly traversable in a canoe. Skilled canoeists travelled hundreds of miles a day, utilising the rapids and system of portage routes (carrying the canoe between waterways was called 'portaging') which were thousands of years old. Canoeing was a method of travel all early seventeenth-century travellers took to with delight and wonder. The town of Salem, surrounded by rivers and brooks, was believed to possess more canoes than all the rest of Massachusetts, with every household having 'a waterhouse or two'.

Once the Pilgrims discovered that the best furs came down from Hudson Bay they deserted their first trading post in favour of one miles up the 170-mile Kennebec River. Here, in the echoing Indian hunting grounds of the north, was where Plymouth needed to have agents awaiting the loaded canoes that came south.

The Kennebec was a direct route to the Chaudière River in Canada. Edward became a veteran of journeys towards Canada to meet representatives of the northern tribes. The territory was harsh and bleak. He passed endless middens of oyster shells sometimes fifteen feet high along the riverbanks. Local tribes had eaten oysters for centuries. Two hundred miles from Plymouth the great unmapped tidal river recalled thousands of years of tribal history. The Abenaki people lived on these most important trade routes.

The trading season started in April when the snows melted and the Indians began their helter-skelter ride down through the forests, furs piled up high in their canoes. Observers recounted their amazing ability to live and travel in the wilderness, which Edward himself was privileged to witness. By now he was bilingual, a man with impressive diplomatic skills, picked to be in charge of the two most important trading expeditions to the Kennebec River in 1625 and 1626.

Maine had been the place of the failed Popham Colony of 1607. Even the intrepid John Smith thought it was a country 'rather to affright, than delight one'. Its sublime scenery could be forbidding. The New England winters were sharp enough but in Maine the snow stayed on the ground for two months longer. The densely wooded interior concealed an amazing network of ancient pathways and river routes, and Edward had his first glimpses of the great unbroken pine forests of North America, full of otter, deer and beaver.

Because of his special links with Massasoit, the energetic Edward had found himself journeying to within a hundred miles of the Canadian border. Ten years later most of the local Indians – especially the Massachusetts, after Myles Standish's attack on them – were too scared to trade with the Pilgrims. This made the colonists even more dependent on Massasoit for intelligence and protection, for negotiating the wilderness and for bringing them valuable furs.

For Massasoit's part, being Plymouth's ally meant he profited as a middleman, taking his cut on the *wampum* trade and extracting tribute from local tribes who had to negotiate with him before they could deal with the English. Being allied to the English enhanced his own power amongst the struggling communities who had suffered badly from the plague.

Edward had the goodwill of the Indians to rely on. He portaged the secret single-file paths which the Indians had created with their signs called 'blazes' marked on the trees. Above Cushnoc, the last navigable place on the Kennebec, Indians poled their canoes upriver through multiple rapids till they reached the river's headwaters at Moosehead Lake.

Skowhegan, in the Kennebec River Valley midway between Cushnoc and Moosehead Lake, was part of the 1629 Pilgrim grant made by the New England Council in London. The Pilgrims called a unique inland delta on the lower Kennebec, Merrymeeting Bay. It is a freshwater tidal estuary into which no less than six rivers empty. Thanks to its saltwater tide it never freezes in the winter and is a meeting point for colonies of migrating birds which feed on the migratory fish such as salmon and eels.

As the years passed Edward became the principal go-between for the colony and the Indians. Bargaining with the Indians brought out his exuberance. He showed them beads, and other goods, and England's proudest export, cloth. Indians began to adopt cloth mantles in contrast to the furs they skinned and dried with such skill.

He also enjoyed debating with the Indians. The historian Karen Kupperman has pointed out that Edward and the Pilgrims believed the Indians lived in a 'civil society': 'Indians and English did not come to these confrontations with set, preconceived categories for describing others; both the native Americans and the English were evolving definitions of themselves as groups in this period, so the processes of defining self and other went forward together and were mutually reinforcing.'

It seems likely the widely read Edward was influenced by John Smith's ideas of the moral duty of cultural dissemination to improve the lot of indigenous peoples. Smith believed the English must transmit to the people whose country 'we challenge, use and possess' the civilisation passed on to the English by their own ancestors. In his magisterial *Manitou and Providence*, the historian Neal Salisbury singles Edward out for remaining 'the single exception, albeit a partial and timid one, to the colony's aversion to preaching to Indians'. Salisbury sees Edward's natural tact and diplomatic ability harnessed to make sure the Indians were their friends and allies.

The skilled artisans and radical thinkers who made up the colony at Plymouth had to adapt for any eventuality. When their ship's carpenter died, the house carpenter had to solve the problem of taking corn up rivers in the rain so it was not ruined. In this land of rivers, lakes and bays, the carpenter – an 'ingenious man' – invented a covered sailing ship. One of the shallops had a special deck nailed across her 'and so made her a convenient and wholesome vessel, very fit and comfortable for their use'. She lasted them for seven years, during which she went up and down the rocky coast, and she was shallow-draught so could also go up tidal rivers. The same carpenter probably also built the frame houses carried up the rivers and erected on site at the new trading posts.

By the late 1620s Plymouth had a successful import–export operation of their surplus corn and was also a fierce participant in the territorial wars for control of the lucrative fur trade. With the French in Canada, the Dutch on the Hudson and the English in New England, the European powers began to converge in a deadly combination. In

1629 the mild-mannered Pilgrims seized the French Fort Pentagouet at the foot of the Penobscot River, sending its commander packing. It became their most north-easterly trading post until it was retaken by the French in 1635.

The Pilgrims' main trading post at this time was a strong wooden building on the Kennebec about a hundred miles from the Canadian border at Cushnoc, just below the falls.* They had fifteen miles on each side of the river. Cushnoc had to be manned all year round. John Howland, the young man who had been swept overboard the *Mayflower*, took on this lonely job, protected only by palisades against bears and wolves. A former indentured servant who had the force of personality to become a leading colonist and one of the Undertakers, Howland had a fierce temper, a brave heart and cool nerves. They were needed in the isolated pine forests of north-east Maine where he might not see a fellow Englishman for months (although Edward and other Pilgrims did visit this dramatic spot, sometimes staying for weeks at a time). They were put up in the twenty-foot-square trading house which had been constructed in Plymouth and taken upriver. Here they waited for the Indian canoes to come downriver in the spring. Howland's wife Elizabeth (née Tilley) and their children spent time there too in the summer, fishing and hunting while Howland bargained with the local Indians. Elizabeth may even have given birth there, high up in the mountains.

At some point a serpent was bound to enter paradise. The arrival of many more English from 1630 was the death knell of easy relations between them and the Indians. After John Endecott had settled in Salem in 1629 as the advance guard of the Massachusetts Bay Company, 20,000 people poured into New England over the next decade, the majority of them living in Massachusetts. In 1629 at a great Puritan meeting at Sempringham in Lincolnshire near Tattershall Castle, home of the 4th Earl of Lincoln, some of the most famous names in New England history – Governors John Winthrop and Thomas Dudley, Roger Williams, the founder of Rhode Island, and Thomas Hooker, the founder of Connecticut – took the decision to depart. They knew that they had to have their own way of worshipping in dignity and peace, and left their comfortable homes in the belief that they were

---

* Now designated a national historic landmark. The state capital, Augusta, is nearby, built on land once owned by Plymouth.

imperilling their mortal souls if they stayed. Their most brilliant clergymen, such as Thomas Shepard, were being arrested, expelled from their pulpits and forbidden to preach.

Endecott had the power to organise everything for the patentees, while they tied up details about their charter. In a cunning move, they took the charter with them so it could not be revoked. The aim was that there should be nothing about the colony to which the king could take exception. It was very important they appeared to obey the Church of England so that there would be no excuse for the Crown to send soldiers.

But times were changing at Plymouth. Ever since the Division of Land, Governor Bradford had been distraught that colonists farming far away from the town would unravel the bonds that had tied the settlers together. As Bradford had rightly feared, they would establish their own small churches, and would forget the Covenant. The Pilgrims – and especially Bradford – had longed to banish all the worst elements of human nature in a genuinely utopian fashion; but in practice this was hard. The simple life – once yearned for – governed by very strict laws, began to feel restrictive and oppressive. The leaders had wanted all single men to live in families so they could benefit from the good example of godly older couples, but this custom was soon ignored. Bradford himself quoted Pliny approvingly, that in the virtuous days of early Rome, he was 'a dangerous man, that would not content himself with seven acres of land'; but to the Plymouth colonists, seven acres was now paltry.

One hundred acres was felt to be a reasonable size for a farm for a family of five members. The colonists started to agree territories and fields. Their land stretched up the Eel River with its low green banks and away from the little double street of Plymouth. Inevitably people begin to think about settling across the bay and up the coast, expanding into what became the New England towns of Duxbury, Scituate and Marshfield.

There seems no reason to doubt the colony had bought the extra land from Massasoit or indeed that he had granted the area to them in the 1621 peace treaty. The Aldens and the Standishes were the first to move away permanently. It had become too time-consuming to move backwards and forwards between their land and their old houses in the township. The new settlement was called Duxbury, probably named after Myles Standish's ancestral home, Duxbury Hall, near Chorley in Lancashire. Alden put a wide fence round his property, which had fields and orchards. These first buildings were small and very narrow. As the years went by colonists added porches and elaborate floor plans, but in the earliest days the frame timber houses were probably ten feet wide and around forty feet long, as per the Alden house. Records show how the 'bounds of the land of Mr John Alden at Duxburrow' were laid out or walked by Edward, and other members of the colony. It was an exciting if bittersweet moment. The Duxbury-dwellers were meant to return to Plymouth every week for the Sabbath service, but during the harsh winters travel was impossible – hence they founded their own churches, to William Bradford's great sorrow.

Edward and Susanna were already farming fields they had north of Duxbury. Encouraged by the good corn harvests, they made plans to relocate to what was then called Green Harbour.* As Bradford lamented, the lure of the land was like a magnet pulling the original town apart, an early example of the expansion into new territories that became one of the great themes of American history.

Like all great achievers and leaders, William Bradford was an obsessive. Plymouth Colony depended on his vision and passion. He had thought by giving special 'good farms to special persons, that would promise to live at Plymouth, and likely to be helpful to the church or commonwealth', it would tie their owners to Plymouth. But 'alas', he wrote, 'this remedy proved worse than the disease; for within a few years those that had thus got footing there rent themselves away'. They had gone on and on petitioning to be allowed to leave 'by wearing the rest with importunity and pleas of necessity, so as they must either suffer them to go, or live in continual opposition and contention'. In ten years there was another dispersal of the inhabitants to different parts of the colony. Recalling it, Bradford could not stop a cry of lament: 'and thus was this poor church left like an ancient mother, grown old and forsaken of her children . . . she that had made many rich became herself poor'.

Perhaps it was inevitable once families had adapted to making a satisfactory life in the wilderness they had less need to cling together,

---

* Susanna and Edward did not move out of Plymouth to the house they built, named Careswell, until 1636. They founded a town called Marshfield. Edward received a very large land grant of between 800 and 1,000 acres. The area was a place 'very well meadowed, and fit to keep and rear cattle, good store', and took its name from wide acres of salt marsh. The original records describe it as 'westward upon a marsh called Careswell Marsh follows a small ridge of hills to the great marsh on Green Harbour's River'.

especially as there was so much unclaimed land. The colonists pushed out, buying and exchanging land in an energetic and successful way. Wealth came to Plymouth too with the arrival of the Massachusetts settlers, to whom the Pilgrims provided animals.

During the 1630s seven new towns were created. Each clapboard house stood in its own neatly fenced lot, not far from its neighbours. At the centre of most New England towns, just as it was at the centre of the inhabitants' lives, was the congregational church which also did duty as the meeting house for the town government. Interiors had floorboards sawn mainly from the stately white cedar, which never seemed to warp. Furniture was usually made of black walnut.

And a few Pilgrims moved back to England. One seems to have been Edward's brother Gilbert. The whole New England adventure had been too much for him. Five years younger than Edward, Gilbert was not present for the Division of Cattle in 1627. Sadly life did not go so well for this Winslow. On 11 October 1631 he was buried in Ludlow, Shropshire. It was not far from his old home. He never made a will, though he left an estate valued at £30.

Edward's reaction to everything seems to have been a sort of stubborn patience and an amazing confidence that the Lord would provide. In a couple of years his brothers Kenelm and Josiah appeared in Gilbert's stead.

Plymouth's community ideals crumbled a little more when it was discovered Isaac Allerton was secretly trading for his own benefit. Isaac had married Fear, the daughter of the church's beloved Elder William Brewster. She was much younger than him and had arrived in America in 1623. Being the saintly Brewster's son-in-law had given Isaac countenance. Brewster's wife had died in 1627 and he was considerably more frail after her loss. Perhaps it was the additional strain of Isaac's behaviour that made him seek refuge in the new settlement at Duxbury with his old friend from Leiden days, Myles Standish. There was anger in the colony about Isaac Allerton and, though Brewster remained a hallowed figure, he must have found it upsetting for contempt to be directed at his daughter Fear's family. It turned out Isaac had been abusing his position as the London agent to make deals for himself, even while he was pursuing a new grant at the end of the 1620s. Isaac had always been a slightly slippery character but now it was discovered he was not playing straight with the colony. On his trips to London he was creaming off a personal profit from the goods. He even established a trader and trapper named Edward Ashley to operate solely on his behalf up at Penobscot.*

The colonists' outrage increased when Isaac began colluding with Thomas Morton. Morton had been a sophisticated lawyer, a member of Clifford's Inn. In 1624 he moved from London to what is now Quincy, twenty miles north of Plymouth, with a man named Captain Wollaston and a number of indentured young men. Their employer was Sir Ferdinando Gorges. As far as the royalist Gorges could help it, not all the people settling New England would be rebellious Puritans. Thomas Morton was certainly no Puritan. Under different circumstances Edward, who had a good sense of humour, might have liked Morton, who was as interested as he was in the origins of the Indians and their customs.

Morton had the sort of metropolitan witty temperament that found little to recommend in many Plymouth-dwellers. Thinking their gruff earnestness unsophisticated and tedious, he presumed they were all ignorant men. In fact it was more that they were busy, having to spend an inordinate amount of time in hard physical labour to keep their farms going. Morton found Plymouth's strict laws ridiculous and their military ceremonies foolish. His nickname for Myles Standish was Captain Shrimp.

The sarcastic and dissolute Morton was a difficult neighbour. Antipathetic to its sincere ideals, he saw a great chance for amusement in the democratic way of life at Plymouth, noting with deep irony that what he called 'a Parliament' was called for the most banal occasions. A highly educated man, he was easily bored by the people at Plymouth, whom he called 'the illiterate multitude'. He began secretly (or not so secretly) to refer to the settlers as the Moles.

The Pilgrims had been brought this great distance by the power of their religion but it was neither witty nor sophisticated. Trust in God gave them an inner confidence which allowed them to survive every life-shaking disaster. They took pride in the plainness of their living. Their making of an incorruptible new world, into which all the sinful things such as pride would not intrude, made for a simplicity which could appear dull and dour. Badmouthing them when he got back to London, Morton said the Pilgrims' default position was against learning, an unfair but successful slur. They were 'vilifying the two universities [i.e. Oxford and Cambridge] with uncivil terms;

---

* In the end Edward took over from Allerton as the London agent of Plymouth Colony.

accounting what is there obtained by study is but unnecessary learning; not considering that learning does enable men's minds to converse with elements, of a higher nature than is to be found within the habitation of the Mole'. The Pilgrims' religious scrupulousness meant they were always 'troubling their brains more than reason would require about things that are indifferent'. The Venetian ambassador to England in 1637 read Morton's *New English Canaan* describing his time in New England, and was appalled that 'the Brownists' (i.e. the Pilgrims) thought ignorance the key to heaven: 'For this reason their followers have ceased to associate with others and have withdrawn to New England, which is further north than Virginia, calling it New Canaan, which to the Hebrews was the land of Promise.'

As traders whose hard work had made them masters of the area's fur trade, Plymouth was suspicious of Morton's intentions. But their greatest concern – which other settlements shared – was that he would sell the Indians guns. The cynical and worldly Morton believed, since all European colonists were secretly selling the Indians guns, there was nothing wrong with doing so openly – especially if it gave him and his associates access to the beaver market.

Morton and his men began to have parties with Indian ladies. The Pilgrims were admiring, friendly and fair to the Indians but they were disturbed by the natives' free attitude to sexuality. The licentious Morton relished it. He wrote songs to the squaws, one of which contained what were regarded as infamous lines: 'Lasses in beaver coats, come away, Ye shall be welcome to us night and day'. Such antics infuriated Plymouth, not just because it was dissolute but because Indian men were very possessive of their wives. The Pilgrims feared such abuses might lead them to turn on the English colonies en masse.

To the Pilgrims, Morton did not have the sense of a personal boundary between the colonist and the Indian which they believed was necessary. He hung obscene verses on an eighty-foot maypole which may or may not have been a phallic symbol. Bradford wrote that Morton was celebrating in a pagan fashion – similar to 'the beastly practices of the mad bacchanalians'. Morton's house, Merrymount, was becoming a den of iniquity, but it was only when the Pilgrims became worried about guns, and were asked to get rid of Morton by his neighbours because of people being killed in the woods, that they took action. They could put up with his mockery, but drew the line at weapons.

Most of the little English plantations – especially that of David

Thompson at Piscataqua, on the border between New Hampshire and Maine, and Roger Conant at Naumkeag (i.e. Salem) – asked Plymouth to try to reason with Morton. Twice he was instructed to desist, but Morton would not listen to their argument that trading in guns was against their common safety and indeed the king's proclamation, telling them that the king was dead. Captain Standish was sent to seize him. This was not difficult. Though they were armed, most of his men were too drunk to fight. Morton was put on a ship headed for England.

But he returned, employed as Isaac Allerton's secretary and help-meet, living in his house in Plymouth. Morton had not reckoned with the character of John Endecott, governor of Salem. Endecott took himself and his role very seriously. As hot-tempered as Myles Standish, he not only hacked down the maypole, he took summary action, seizing Morton again, binding him in chains and sending him back to England in disgrace.

Further strain came at this time of change in 1630 when John Billington shot a man named John Newcomen. Anxious about how to punish Billington – they had a horror of shedding blood – the Pilgrims asked the advice of Governor Winthrop, who had just arrived in Massachusetts. Billington and his family were constantly in hot water with the authorities and were one of the 'profanest families amongst them'. Nevertheless, the government was reluctant to execute John. Back came the harsh answer. The Old Testament was unequivocal. Billington had to die so the land could be purged of blood.

Billington's death struck a dark and sombre note. The idyll was drawing to its close. Meanwhile, in England Morton was busy doing damage to the Puritan colonies. Working once more for his old employer Sir Ferdinando Gorges, this time in a legal capacity, Morton stirred up trouble. Nathaniel Hawthorne would later poke fun at the Pilgrims' treatment of Morton, but he represented a considerable threat to their existence by damaging their reputation. Thanks to Morton's information, Gorges denounced the colonists in a petition to the king as treasonously allying with the Dutch, saying they nursed 'disaffections both to his Majesty's government and the state ecclesiastical', including the habit of magistrates (including Edward) performing civil marriages quite illegally. When Edward next set foot in London on business, he was slung into prison.

CHAPTER IX

Massachusetts Begins

Puritan issues – such as their opposition to the English church's practice of making the sign of the Cross – had not gone away after the *Mayflower* left England. The godly had had hopes of reforming the church from within. However, by the end of the 1620s, under the Church of England's rising star William Laud (who became Bishop of London in 1627 and would be made Archbishop of Canterbury in 1633), the emphasis on sacraments, ceremonial, and ecclesiastical hierarchy meant the church was widely feared to be travelling further towards Roman Catholicism. Lectureships – preachers paid for by the community – the solace of Puritans, were stopped. Like the Pilgrims, these immigrants were convinced that a terrible judgement was coming to England, and New England would be a Noah's Ark in which they could shelter.

Edward became a close personal friend of the man appointed governor of Massachusetts, John Winthrop, a thoughtful if somewhat austere personality. Winthrop's yearning for a life of proper godliness meant he had long been considering emigration, though he was a member of a key administrative English institution, the Court of Wards and Liveries, and would have to leave behind his large estate in Suffolk. As part of the local elite he had had aspirations to be a Member of Parliament. Many of the people who settled in the Massachusetts Bay Colony had similar issues. They held important positions in England such as landowners and lawyers, but as serious Puritans their careers were blocked. All were forced out of England by their commitment to their beliefs.

In the intimidating atmosphere created by Laud and Charles I, many wealthy and eminent men – some of whom, such as John Pym, Lord Saye and Sele, and Lord Brooke, were the most vocal of Charles I's parliamentary critics – saw a future in backing godly colonies abroad. Even Oliver Cromwell had feelers out for a place to settle away from the great tyranny,* either in New England or Providence Island off the coast of today's Nicaragua.

Plymouth could not avoid being involved in the changes brought by the thousands of Massachusetts immigrants. Edward Winslow was attracted by their keen minds. Highly educated, they were accompanied by some of the most cerebral of the Puritan clergy who disagreed with Laud. They brought a new element to America.

The Massachusetts Bay Company settled along the broad rivers in the coastal country forty miles north of Plymouth. As they spread out west over the next few years, seeking larger farms in the Connecticut Valley, their original homes were occupied by a continuous flood of new immigrants, particularly from East Anglia. To the poet George Herbert, so large were the numbers leaving England it seemed that 'Religion stands on tiptoe in our land / Ready to pass to the American strand.'

The Salem group's leaders in the summer of 1629 were two pastors, Samuel Skelton and Francis Higginson (who was to be Skelton's assistant). Both had Lincolnshire links. A friend of John Endecott, Skelton had probably once been the vicar of Sempringham, and Higginson was a charmingly enthusiastic Church of England clergyman whose nonconformism was initially tolerated by the bishop. He recently had lost his licence. Since he was about to be prosecuted in the English Court of High Commission, he seized the opportunity to escape on the first ships of what became a mass exodus.

Skelton and Higginson deepened the interaction begun with John Endecott over Morton. They were not censorious about the Plymouth church, and the pastors asked the Pilgrims' advice about how to worship in America. The Plymouth Elders and Salem ministers alike shared the desire to recreate a purified church on the lines of Christ's ancient church – and that drew them together.†

Skelton and Higginson were anxious not to separate from the mother church in England. However, they found much to like and reassure them about Plymouth church's practices. The Pilgrims' church was an inspiration for the system they instituted in America known as Congregationalism. Despite complaints from some of their fellow

---

* Charles I suspended Parliament between 1629 and 1640, a period known as the Eleven Year Tyranny.
† Although Salem was part of the Massachusetts Bay Colony they operated as a separate entity. The second wave of Massachusetts Bay Colony settlers landed a year later in 1630 and settled at Boston and Charlestown. They had a different church to Salem.

colonists who feared being regarded as outlaws (about which the Pilgrims remained highly sensitive), Skelton and Higginson decided to abandon the English Book of Common Prayer at Salem. Such practices would eventually become known as New England Congregationalism, or the New England Way. Their decision to make a covenant with God and one another gave the congregation the lead role in deciding the way of the church. After some debate, this got the approval of the Salem community.

The Reverend Higginson enthused about the country: the curious flies named 'musquetos', and the rattlesnakes, bears, and a moose. He reported there were said to be lions at Cape Ann – although he had no evidence for their existence, whereas he had seen the skins of all the other beasts. He discoursed on the 'fat black earth' round Massachusetts Bay and Charlestown, and the good stone, slate, limestone, ironstone and 'marble stone also in such a store, that we have great rocks of it, and a harbour hard by. Our plantation is from thence called Marble Harbour.' There were wonderful roots and berries. The Indians dyed their clothes what he described as 'excellent holiday colours that no rain nor washing can alter'.

Higginson reported that he had not gone without a cap in the daytime for many years due to ill health, but now wore only a nightcap. 'And whereas beforetime I clothed myself with double clothes and thick waistcoats to keep me warm even in the summer time, I do now go as thin-clad as any, only wearing a light stuff cassock upon my shirt and stuff breeches of one thickness without linings.' One of his children who had suffered from scrofula, a tuberculotic inflammation of the lymph nodes, seemed almost cured because 'the very wholesomeness of the air' was 'altering, digesting and drying up the cold and crude humours of the body'. The sharp invigorating climate meant 'a sup of New England's air is better then a whole draft of old England's ale'.

He also cautioned that the average colonist – unless he was sufficiently wealthy to have servants to send ahead to build for him – was going to have to build his own home.* Not only were there 'no taverns nor alehouse, nor butchers, nor grocers, nor apothecaries' shops to help what things you need', there were 'neither markets nor fairs to buy what you want' – especially 'all manner of carpenters' tools, and a good deal of iron and steel to make nails, and locks, for houses, and furniture

---

* Higginson wrote that he and others had assumed that they would arrive to live in houses already built by the colony and felt they had been misled.

for plough and carts . . . and many other things which were better for you to think of them than to want them here'.

In fact this portrait was extraordinarily rosy. New England was far harsher than they had expected.

An emigration process of such large numbers required a businesslike and sensible approach with proper records kept. John Endecott was instructed to make detailed notes as to who was arriving off the various boats, and who intended 'to remain in the country; as also a note of the cattle and all manner of goods, of what kind soever, landed out of them, with the several marks, and names of the owners thereof'. A register was to be taken by an overseer and paper books filled in.

When the first four ships of the Winthrop Fleet landed at Salem in 1630 they 'found the Colony in a sad and unexpected condition, above eighty of them being dead the winter before; and many of those alive weak and sick'. Despite his reports of his own health, the Reverend Higginson was dead. The deputy governor, Thomas Dudley, reported they scarcely had enough corn and bread for a fortnight. Other than a lucky few, most of his fellow shipmates found themselves living in tents, cellars or in the open air, ravaged by sickness, pneumonia and scurvy.

The colonising organisers were overwhelmed by the amount of labour needed to build a settlement for such numbers and could not cut down enough trees or make enough wattle. Wolves were always trying to kill the weaker specimens of cows, hogs and goats which had come on the *Arbella*.

Dudley's daughter Anne Bradstreet, America's first published poet, wrote that when she first came to America 'I found a new world and new manners, at which my heart rose' (meaning it rose in horror or anger). However, 'convinced it was the way of God, I submitted to it and joined to the church at Boston'. During her cultured adolescence the learned Anne had had access to the magnificent library at Sempringham, the seat of the Earl of Lincoln, for whom her father was a steward. She was conversant with all kinds of poetic forms and Renaissance high culture, as was common in sixteenth- and seventeenth-century England for women of the educated classes. Now her friends in America had scarcely enough to eat and slept on the beach amidst their drenched belongings. Trunks of books were either ruined by seawater or never arrived.

Not impressed by the look of Salem, and anxious about a future which now seemed far from what they had imagined, they set about exploring to find other places to live. Time was short, as Thomas Dudley put it, 'lest the winter should surprise us before we had builded our houses'. As the death toll rose, a hundred people lost their nerve and returned to the ships going back to England. Half the cows and almost all the mares and foals had died on board. The horses ordered from Ireland never appeared at all. It was such a cold winter that the Charles River froze. The only good thing about that was settlers could travel from plantation to plantation on the ice, instead of waiting for the boats which in future became town ferries.

The exhausted settlers could not agree as to where their main town and church should be planted. The leaders moved the capital to what they called Boston and built the first church there because of better water supplies, yet many preferred to live along the Charles River in the area now called Charlestown. Others thought Newtown, which became Cambridge, was better. Thomas Dudley had moved there with many of the more socially prominent settlers, who created the streets around Harvard.

The unfortunate Dudley was publicly excoriated by John Winthrop for trying to build a mansion at a time when no one should crave personal distinction. Dudley told his patroness the Countess of Lincoln that he had 'yet no table, nor other room to write in than by the fireside upon my knee, in this sharp winter'. All he wanted was the elaborate wainscoting which he had enjoyed at home. But it was wrong and embarrassing in a new colony where it was important for there not to be too many social differences between the colonists. John Winthrop rolled up his sleeves with the best of them: he was 'a discreet and sober man, wearing plain apparel, assisting in any ordinary labour, and ruling with much mildness and justice'.

The Massachusetts settlers decided they must secure the eastern seaboard, and they fanned out. After five years there were small plantations at Dorchester, Roxbury, Watertown, Lynn, Newbury, Hingham and Weymouth – Weston's old colony. Concord, twelve miles west of Watertown, was noted for being 'right up into the woods' (which might have amused its future resident Thoreau).

Three hundred people died in the first winter. They included the Earl of Lincoln's daughter, Lady Arbella (after whom Winthrop's ship was named), and her husband, Isaac Johnson – one of the colony's wealthiest men. Both died only three months after their arrival. People who came from wealthy backgrounds were simply not used to living in such conditions. Instead of farming their new land, they were buried in it. It forms the site of the first cemetery in Boston (now known as the King's Chapel Burial Ground on Tremont Street).*

The Pilgrims' doctor, Samuel Fuller, tended to the camps of new immigrants. If he could not stop them dying, he could at least make their passing more comfortable and less frightening. Edward Winslow was at Salem with Fuller tending to the sick when John Winthrop wrote despondently that the hand of God seemed to be against them at Charlestown, 'in visiting them with sickness . . . not sparing the righteous, but partaking with the wicked in these bodily judgements'. This was a bad omen for a company which believed God was on their side. To try to regain His all-powerful favour, a message was sent to Plymouth asking them to take part in a day of prayer. If it worked, it did not do so for long.

In 1633–4 smallpox carried away many of the old Leiden community, including Thomas Blossom and Richard Masterson. It also killed William Brewster's two daughters, Fear and Patience. Nor could his medical skills save the sympathetic Samuel Fuller; he who had held the hands of the dying now expired himself. In a cruel blow William Brewster was left quite alone except for his son Jonathan – who was usually lost in his books.

Once more the Leiden Pilgrims sought God and humbled themselves. At least this time their friends died with their families round them, amongst their possessions and in their own sheets, even if they were worn and patched. Ten years previously they were living twenty to a room. The dead were buried in the peaceful graveyard overlooking the great blue ocean.

Edward was relieved that Plymouth's separatism was not held against them. And to the Pilgrims' awe, Governor Winthrop and other Massachusetts dignitaries condescended to visit Plymouth. It was a considerable occasion when the new Bostonians walked along the Indian ways to Plymouth. They had sailed to Wessagusset in Winthrop's boat *The Blessing of the Bay*, were guided through the forests and the swamps, and then carried across the cold rushing waters of the North River. The governor sternly rechristened what was known to Edward

---

* In the next fifty years some of the most celebrated figures in early New England history would be interred there, including John Cotton, John Wilson and John Winthrop.

and his friends as Hugh's Cross, Hugh's Folly. (Winthrop had been worried that it 'might give the Papists occasion to say that their religion was first planted in these parts'.) Edward was impressed by the sombre Winthrop's sense of history. Here was the sort of defined man of strong opinions Edward could not but admire and aspire to. Winthrop had the magistrate's sense of order imported from old England and a supple legal mind, as well as the sort of decent common sense Edward himself possessed.

The Massachusetts settlers had no experience of the local tribes. They were by turns alarmed and yet fascinated by the Indians who surrounded their settlements. They were everywhere: dark, enigmatic figures in the forest, observing the English in the fields or removing fishes from the spikes of their weirs which showed at low tide all over the bay. The Indians delighted in English technology, especially the cloth, the tools and the guns. They slipped in and out of the market near Boston harbour.

Dudley built a 1,000-foot palisade round the houses at Cambridge, but Plymouth's good relations with the Indians encouraged the Massachusetts colony to keep an open mind, especially once they realised that Plymouth controlled the fur trade because of their network of Indian tribal friendships. They saw that the Pilgrims, especially Edward Winslow, frequently stopped by Massasoit's longhouse to hitch a lift home in a canoe or to be guided back by a friendly Wampanoag. John Winthrop recorded with some amazement an example of Indian humour:

> One pleasant passage happened which was acted by the Indians: Mr Winslow coming in his bark from Connecticut to Narragansett and he left her there, and intending to return by land, he went to Osamequin [another name for Massasoit] the Sagamore his old ally, who offered to conduct him home to Plymouth. But before they took their journey Osamequin sent one of his men to Plymouth to tell them that Mr Winslow was dead and directed him to show how and where he was killed: whereupon there was much fear and sorrow at Plymouth. The next day when Osamequin brought him home, they asked him why he sent such word, etc. He answered, that it was their manner to do so, that they might be more welcome when they came home.

By the end of the 1630s *wampum* became one of several official currencies of New England. The others were silver pieces of eight captured from the Spaniards, as well as corn and cattle, which were barter, and not very portable. *Wampum* was given an exact official equivalent value in English shillings and pence and adopted by every colony. All arriving English colonists who wished to join in the lucrative fur trade handled this curious shell currency so valued by the northern Indians. It was measured in fathoms, strings of beads about six feet long. *Wampum* gave an air of novelty to every transaction, as of course did the presence of Indians wearing it. Naked other than for leather breeches, often holding large stone pipes which were purchased by the tobacco-mad English, they sported belts and necklaces covered with the famous shells.

Edward's friendship with Massasoit continued to be warm and playful. Edward and the other Pilgrims encouraged Massachusetts to treat the Indians as they had done, by having the leaders stay in their houses and introducing them to Puritan ways. The Massachusett chief Chickatabot, who lived nearby, came with his chiefs and squaws, and presented the governor with a hogshead of Indian corn. He, one squaw and one chief stayed the night. Winthrop gave them some clothes. As a man used to the formalities of life in a manor house he was not tolerant of the Indian tradition of wearing very little. Once Chickatabot was 'in English clothes, the governor set him at his own table, where he behaved himself as soberly . . . as an Englishman. The next day after dinner he returned home, the governor giving him cheese, and pease and a mug, and some other small things.'

Narragansett leaders including Miantonomo, the rising power in the tribe – nephew of the brilliant grand sachem Canonicus (who had sent the arrows wrapped in a snakeskin to the Pilgrims in 1622 but who had since been friendly) – visited and spent the night. Gifts of skins were exchanged with pewter pots. Miantonomo visited with his squaw in August 1632, and listened to a sermon. However, some of the twelve exuberant warriors whom he brought with him broke into a house during the sermon. But it did not stop Governor Winthrop entertaining another Narragansett tribal leader and making 'much of them', as he wrote in his diary.

Amongst the more highly educated, the fascination with Indian culture and ethnography first encouraged by the Virginia Company had not gone away. It was an appetite which grew as the American colonies attracted larger numbers and could report on the reality of life amongst the Indians. Edward's own interest had produced an ethnographic study. His fondness and admiration for the Indians meant he had wanted to do them justice by being accurate in his representations of them. Now that the English were living amongst the Indians, European correspondents could write for corroboration about signs of similarities between the Indians and the Jews that fitted the theory they were the Lost Tribes of Israel, which was exciting in those millennial times.* In 1635 one of its most vocal theorists, the Norfolk clergyman Thomas Thorowgood, wrote to Roger Williams asking him for his observations. (By 1650, Thorowgood had published his thesis affirming that the Indians were, as he titled his work, *Jews in America*.)

The Indians were kindly and well disposed. They were constantly called on to guide the colonists: 'when the English have travelled forty, fifty, or three score miles into the country, they have entertained them into their houses, quartered them by themselves . . . not grumbling for a fortnight or three weeks' tarrying'. John Winthrop was not above staying the night when he got lost amidst the immense forest, although he was once embarrassed when it turned out he was occupying a squaw's wigwam. William Wood, a clergyman visiting Massachusetts in 1633, wrote down his observations of the symbiosis between the Indians and the English, and noted that for 'these ranging foresters' it was as easy for them to find their way around 'as the experienced citizen knows how to find out Cheapside Cross'.

Wood himself and two companions attempting to reach Plymouth were misled by what appeared to be a broad path to follow. They assumed it must be made by their fellow English because the one thing they knew was that the Indian trails were practically invisible. In fact it was a path taken by some Narragansetts specialising in trading their goods for English shoes, which they had worn home, making the track look like it was made by the settlers. Wood and his two companions travelled in circles, never reaching the ocean. Fortunately in the depths of the forest they found a wigwam – a 'homely lodging' where they were fed 'with the haunch of a fat bear'. The next morning, for a piece of tobacco and a fourpenny whistle, the son of their friendly albeit naked host conducted 'us through the strange labyrinth of unbeaten bushy ways in the woody wilderness twenty miles to our desired harbour'.

---

* This theory was of immense fascination to serious Puritans who believed in the Apocalypse because it fitted in with the prophecies of the Book of Daniel. The Second Coming was to be preceded by the conversion of the Jews. The theory had currency for around fifty years.

Indian braves rescued injured people from the snow. They took one man home on their bare shoulders to their wigwams in which Wood rapturously claimed they rested better and more securely than some 'blind obscure old England's Inn'.

Wood wrote admiringly about the Indians. Perhaps he did not reflect the views of all settlers, but warmth towards the Indians was fairly widespread. It was thought they would soon learn 'any mechanical trades, having quick wits, understanding apprehensions, strong memories, and a quick hand in using of the axe or hatchet or such like tools'. For their part the Indians remained enthralled by the colonists' technology such as iron tools like ploughs, as opposed to the shells they used or 'flint-tipped shovels'.

In terms of relations between the colonies, inevitably the new arrivals clashed with Plymouth over the beaver trade, but on the whole they were friendly. Massachusetts needed Plymouth's crops and animals to keep them going until their own farms were established. Plymouth did very well from the agricultural trade, which enhanced Edward's opinion that there must be closer links with the businessmen in the north.

One person who did not share Edward's view was the ascetic Bradford. He was far from delighted by the wealth that started to flow into the country. He was not interested in greater comfort, he did not care whether settlers could swap agricultural goods for English manufactures such as cloth instead of having to weave it themselves, as they become better off. This was not the vision for which he had sailed on the *Mayflower*. Secretly he feared it would be 'the ruin of New England, at least of the churches of God there, and will provoke the Lord's displeasure against them'. (At the end of his life Bradford would say that Plymouth had been a small candle to light a thousand, which had 'shone unto many, yea in some sort to our whole nation'. Massachusetts was the beginning of the many.)

Edward had a more outgoing nature. As he had correctly predicted, in New England religion and profit could jump together. He grew to profoundly admire Winthrop. Always intellectually curious, as he became older and more self-confident through his work for the colony, Edward found the sharp and authoritarian people in Massachusetts stimulating, and was impressed by their sense of civic purpose. He was an ambitious man, not just a utopian. He became a frequent visitor to Boston for both business dealings and social interaction.

John Winthrop reinforced Edward's sense of mission, buoying up a new tendency to grandiosity that increasingly impelled him through life. He had heard that Governor Winthrop had bucked up the nervous settlers on board the *Arbella* as they crossed the Atlantic, telling them the eyes of all people were on them, 'For we must Consider that we shall be as a City upon a Hill'. That appealed.

Edward developed a warm friendship with Winthrop, for whom he raised cattle. This may have begun through Susanna knowing a number of the Lincolnshire settlers, as her uncle's family had professional connections with the Earls of Lincoln. Edward's letters show a sort of hunger for Winthrop's approval; he wished for 'the whetting of and quickening of our affections towards each other'. Edward's own strong character and convivial ways, which were able to handle Indian chiefs as easily as Puritan grandees, stood him in good stead. The friendship which developed meant that within a few years Edward was trusted to represent Massachusetts as well as Plymouth on his business trips back to England, of which he had many in the 1630s.

Edward was now forty and had come into his own. He was rightly confident of his powers of leadership. In the wilderness a can-do mentality allied to a natural charm went a long way, and it got him to prominence in Boston. Edward was always 'employed for the Colony in occasions of great weight'. He seems to have enjoyed being a representative and public figure, who had the ability to put into words many of the aspirations of the colonists.

His path to becoming a trusted envoy for the Massachusetts colony began with an embarrassing and regrettable episode in 1634. Men from the Piscataqua colony – which had been taken over by a new colonising entity, the Saybrook plantation, which itself had links to English investors in the Massachusetts Bay Company – clashed with John Howland during one of his stints in the trading house up on the Kennebec. Trappers led by a man named John Hocking tried to sail further upriver into Plymouth's territory. There was an altercation and Hocking refused to leave, so Howland sent two men out into the middle of the river to cut the cables to Hocking's boat's anchor. Hocking shot at one of the Plymouth men and killed him, whereupon his friend shot Hocking dead. This was exactly the sort of thing no one wanted to happen, especially when the New England colonies were at such a fragile stage. John Winthrop wrote that it had 'brought us all and the Gospel under a common reproach of cutting one another's throats for beaver'.

Archbishop Laud had got wise to his enemies hiding in New England, practising their illegal religion, and in 1634 he had set up a Commission for Regulating the Plantations to prevent it. He was looking for excuses to withdraw the charter on any pretext, and especially from those colonies where men were being killed.

For this reason Massachusetts dealt peremptorily with the Pilgrims who had been on the Kennebec. John Alden was arrested and the Massachusetts Council demanded to see the Kennebec patent. Plymouth was outraged but listened to reason, and Edward was sent to England with letters of apology from Winthrop and Dudley to Lord Saye and Sele. It was at this moment that Thomas Morton and his employer Sir Ferdinando Gorges saw their chance.

In the midst of Edward's audience in the Privy Council, the mocking figure of Morton appeared, attacking the seditious way of life at Plymouth. Ever since Morton had been expelled he had been looking for vengeance, while Gorges' plan was to dissolve the New England Council. He aimed to make himself governor general of the area with the power to go to America and reform the Puritan settlements.

Morton accused Edward of illegally preaching in church and illegally marrying couples. Edward replied that the absence of a minister made it necessary. Had he not preached, 'we might have lost the life and face of Christianity'. As for marrying couples, he believed it was 'a civil thing, and he found nowhere in ye word of God that it was tied to ministry'. After all, he himself had been married that way in Holland. As far as the English authorities were concerned, however, conducting marriages while not a member of the clergy was a crime. Edward was immediately sent to the Fleet prison.

For around six months Edward languished in jail, leaving Susanna to be supported by her friends. She had very little idea whether her husband would survive the squalid conditions. It was then that Lord Coventry came to the rescue.

One of the attorneys of the Court of Wards was John Winthrop's brother-in-law Emmanuel Downing, a future immigrant to New England.* He found out Edward had been released because of the influence of Lord Coventry. Lady Coventry had heard her old friend's son was in prison and told Edward to petition her husband, who was

---

* The husband of Lucy Winthrop, Emmanuel Downing emigrated to New England in 1638. His son Sir George Downing was an important financial minister in the Restoration and built Downing Street in London.

now Lord Keeper: 'Mr Winslow, being my Lord Keeper's countryman, whose father also his Lordship loved very well, his Lady sent last night to Mr Winslow to give him notice of her husband's affection to him, and willed him to petition his Lordship for the furtherance of his freedom out of prison: the which he hath now done.'

Only a month before, Downing had been asked to help smooth over reports that John Endecott had cut out the red cross of St George in the royal ensign on the grounds that it had been given to England by the Pope and was thus 'a relic of Antichrist'. Charles I's attitude to the New England colonies became markedly more aggressive. Ships began to be prevented from sailing from London ports without licences for the passengers, in case they were hiding Puritan subversives. The Boston leaders were acutely worried and they fortified Castle Island in Boston Bay because Laud was rumoured to be dispatching soldiers to seize back the company charter. But at least Edward had escaped.

In September 1633 John Cotton, fleeing persecution, arrived in Boston on the same ship as his equally charismatic fellow minister Thomas Hooker, the future founder of Connecticut. They both had a genius for popular preaching. A couple of years later around 120 people from Newtown departed with Hooker as their leader. They had come out from East Anglia specifically as part of his congregation. They went west along Indian trails, following what is now called the Old Connecticut Path, and founded Hartford. Mrs Hooker lay on a litter as they stumbled through the woods in the shadow of towering trap rock formations. The settlers drank milk from the 160 cattle they drove before them.

Meanwhile a brilliant young clergyman named Roger Williams had declared the Massachusetts charter invalid. Drawn to the Indians, whom he got to know at Plymouth, Williams' fertile mind decided the king of England could not grant land in New England as it belonged to the native inhabitants. Nothing could have been more disastrous – or more typical of its author. The charming but completely unorthodox Williams had a new idea every two minutes. One saying of the time was that the inside of his head must be like a windmill.

A follower of Thomas Hooker, he found his way to Plymouth shortly after arriving in Boston in 1631. He was accompanied by his heavily pregnant twenty-one-year-old wife Mary. It was to be the story of her life in America that no sooner had she moved into lodgings than she had to move on. Williams was meant to be a minister in Boston but, oblivious to anything other than the pursuit of truth, and with his usual impulsiveness, he announced that the church in Boston was corrupt because it was still linked to the Church of England. He preferred separatist Plymouth.

Roger Williams described himself as a 'Seeker', searching for 'soul liberty'. Although to our ears this may sound attractive, to the early settlers he was too disruptive. He had not been in Plymouth for very long before ideas began to proliferate. He profited from Plymouth's unusual openness to Indian culture and developed a very warm relationship with Massasoit.

By Massasoit's own account he and the Wampanoag Indians were curious about Plymouth's religion. They assumed that anyone who preached was a sachem, and attended services in the meeting house to hear them. Almost fifty years later Roger Williams realised how unusual he himself was in that God had furnished him 'with advantages . . . scarce any in New England had. First a constant zealous desire to dive into the Natives language. Secondly God was pleased to give me a Painful, Patient spirit to lodge with them in their filthy smoky holes . . . to gain their tongue.'*

His wife gave birth to their first child at Plymouth, and the Williams and Winslow families were thrown together in its tiny society. Edward and Roger became close friends, sharing a deep feeling for the Indians and ethnographical fascination with their lives. In Williams' case the kindness of the Indians to him created a burning passion that never faded. He became their devoted champion for the next forty years.

John Winthrop appealed to Edward's need for a father figure providing order and stability. Roger Williams appealed to Edward's emotional and romantic side. Williams' sensitive and unorthodox personality set up an echo in Edward's faith in the New World. Even though Edward thought Williams was wrong about many issues – especially the subject of authority – there was a warmth and and

---

* William Wood referred to Williams in *New England's Prospect* as a clergyman who was very popular with the Indians because he could speak their language: 'One of the English preachers in a special good intent of doing good to their souls, hath spent much time in attaining to their language, wherein he is so good and proficient, that he can speak to their understanding, and they to his; much loving and respecting him for his love and counsel. It is hoped that he may be an instrument of good amongst them.'

fearless logic to him that Edward found irresistible. He would describe him as 'the sweetest soul I ever knew'.

The issue of the charter and land compact had begun when Williams was living at Plymouth. The leaders asked him to write a treatise on the matter, which he sent on to Boston. Winthrop reported in his journal that it 'disputes their right to the land they possessed here and concluded that claiming by the king's grant they could have no title: nor otherwise except they compounded with the natives'.

Williams also criticised the system of government. It had struck him that magistrates had no right to administer oaths or punish people for not observing the Sabbath. In 1636, having been asked to retract his views and refused, Williams was about to be arrested and shipped home. But he was warned in advance – probably by John Winthrop, who retained great fondness for him and his real godliness. The only place where Williams could find safety was with Massasoit. He escaped and lived in the Indian chief's winter camp.

For much of his time at Plymouth, Williams had preferred to be alone with the Indians: 'My Soul's desire was to do the Natives good, and to that end to learn their language (which I afterward printed) and therefore desired not to be troubled with English company.' Now he had the opportunity. He bought land from Massasoit with the permission of Massasoit's overlords, Canonicus and his nephew Miantonomo. His long-suffering wife Mary duly joined him, taking the fifty-mile path through the forest with their two-year-old daughter Mary, and a baby named Freeborn. Edward came to Providence in person and put a piece of gold into Mary's hands. He also warned Roger to move to the other side of the water because he was within Massachusetts' bounds.

In the late 1630s the most bitter row erupted in Boston over the teachings of Anne Hutchinson, darkening the already stormy atmosphere.

Anne was the strong, clever wife of the prominent Lincolnshire merchant William Hutchinson, who was a deputy to the Massachusetts governing assembly in Boston, the General Court. The charismatic midwife daughter of a clergyman, the scholarly Anne soon had around sixty men and women coming to her house twice a week to discuss Scripture. In England, Scripture discussion groups were illegal; this was what they had come to New England for. At Mistress Hutchinson's Bible classes, conversion frequently occurred. She was inspiring, stimulating and reassuring. The problem was that her ideas undermined the authority of the clergy in Boston, and thus the whole Massachusetts colony.

The Hutchinsons' house was directly opposite John Winthrop's and he became alarmed by Anne's large public meetings criticising John Wilson, the chief minister of the Boston church. Winthrop disliked her intensely: she was 'a woman of a ready wit and bold spirit' who had brought over 'two dangerous errors' from England, namely that the Holy Spirit was dwelling in a saved or 'justified' person, and that good works were not a sign of being saved or sanctified. Winthrop wrote: 'From these two grew many branches.'

According to Anne none of the ministers except John Cotton were sealed by the Holy Spirit. Anne was one of Cotton's most devout parishioners and a personal friend. In England she had often travelled twenty-four miles several times a week to hear him preach. Cotton's revelation – that spiritual conversion (known as Free Grace) was needed, not works – struck Anne with such force that she began to give lectures on the subject assisted by visits from the Holy Spirit. Cotton preached a covenant of grace but the other ministers preached a covenant of works.

Anne's view was that the saved (or elect) would know they were saved or 'justified' from their own feelings of spiritual conversion. As her exciting reputation grew, more would have attended her meetings, had she the space.

The complicated subject of grace had generated quarrels between Protestant theologians for the past hundred years. It caused mayhem in New England because so much was at stake. Massachusetts was no ordinary colony as far as its members were concerned, but a key element in the struggle against the Antichrist.

Worse still, the recently arrived new governor, the young and emotional Henry Vane, was a great supporter.* The sensitive Puritan son of one of Charles I's most trusted courtiers, to his family's surprise Vane had abandoned court for a godly life in New England. His long hair and elegant clothes were met with a certain amount of surprise, but he was a popular and accommodating soul. It was hoped his election might end talk of the charter being removed.

Anne and her supporters were so many that they threatened the

---

* Henry Vane the Younger became a Parliamentarian MP who helped draft the Root and Branch bill to get rid of bishops with Oliver Cromwell and Sir Arthur Hesilrige, a dedicated member of the pro-war party against Charles I. A close personal friend of Roger Williams, Vane supported freedom of conscience after the Civil War.

theocratic colony and its magistrates. The clergy were a key part of the political system, and the Boston church became agitated. They emphasised the covenant of works and the need for ministers to interpret the word of God to the laity. The colony divided between Anne and the orthodox led by John Winthrop.

Anne's brother-in-law John Wheelwright, another minister who had recently emigrated to Massachusetts, sided with her. He was just as fiery and sufficiently popular for supporters to sign a petition on his behalf, and he was made the chief preacher at Mount Wollaston or Quincy.

Many feared the divisions could herald the end of the plantation. It was already overwhelmed by extra immigrants who arrived without stores to support them and at the wrong time of year to secure a harvest the next. This very public spat would be a perfect excuse for Charles I to rescind the charter. In the houses spread out round the Shawmut peninsula there was anxiety lest the dangerously outspoken Anne spoiled everything with her message that they were the elect and the clergy were no longer to be listened to. Anne and her followers began to be called Antinomians (a Lutheran term meaning people who were against the law), or Familists. If a sense of the Holy Spirit was relied on too much it could lead to anarchy. It did not privilege biblical learning and law as laid down by ministers and scholars.

The emotional and idealistic Vane wept at the anger unleashed in Boston as he was forced to return to England. John Wheelwright preached an alarmingly inflammatory sermon against the Boston church, calling the clergy who did not agree with him Antichrists. Convicted of contempt and sedition, his behaviour was deplored because it increased the corrosive bitterness in the colony, and he was banished. Those who petitioned in his favour had their weapons confiscated because it was feared they might use them against the government.

Anne continued to defy the authorities, saying she was receiving instruction from the Holy Spirit. She was arrested and two trials followed, one in 1637 for sedition, one for heresy a year later. It was a very painful experience. Staring angrily at Anne and her brother-in-law during their trials were former friends and colleagues, including Governor Dudley, Governor Winthrop and Simon Bradstreet, who had been part of her Lincolnshire community in England. She and others of her views were evicted from Massachusetts. Insulted but unashamed, they made their way to the Narragansetts where, with land from their sachems, they too founded a new colony in Rhode Island at Aquidneck, the island below the Mount Hope peninsula. To many of the profoundly religious colonists, the division Anne had caused suggested satanic influences were abroad.

Anne did not help matters by pronouncing the colony cursed if it did not listen to her. After her devastating trial she shouted that God would deliver her out of their hands, 'Therefore take heed how you proceed against me; for I know that for this you go about to do to me, God will ruin you and your posterity, and this whole state.'

Sadly John Winthrop could not let this rest. And in the hysteria about the colony's future he and his orthodox friends did not behave well. As the shattered Anne Hutchinson was leaving the church after having been excommunicated, a woman named Mary Dyer emerged from the crowd and took her hand. Feelings were running so high that Winthrop was delighted to hear that someone asked was that not the woman 'which had the monster'? It emerged that during Hutchinson's trial Mary Dyer had given birth to a misshapen stillborn child. On John Cotton's advice it had been buried at night by Anne and her friend Jane Hawkins, another midwife. Cotton believed the foetus had served as divine instruction, but only for the parents. Unfortunately in a tense and overwrought atmosphere, to John Winthrop and his friends it was proof of devilry, so much so that it would be the subject of an essay sent to London. It was recalled that when Mary Dyer had given birth the baby had strange features which were regarded as signs of evil. By an 'unexpected providence' this had taken place when its father was being questioned in the church for 'monstrous errors'. Winthrop insisted on having the corpse exhumed and the midwife Jane Hawkins questioned. She was expelled from the colony with the Dyers and Hutchinsons.

Winthrop and many other leaders were obsessed with the idea that wickedness could become physically manifest in the world. The miscarriage Anne Hutchinson herself suffered not long after she moved to Rhode Island was the subject of a lecture in the Boston church. The apparently misshapen foetus (in fact a mass of cells which had never developed into an embryo, what is known as a hydatidiform mole) was used as evidence of Satan at work.

She had given birth to a monster. To her former friend John Cotton her 'unnatural birth' symbolised her errors 'in denying inherent righteousness'. The clergyman Thomas Weld went further: 'the wisdom of

God fitted this judgement to her sin every way'. Anne had 'vented misshapen opinions, so she must bring forth deformed monsters'.*

What were the views of the Winslows and the rest of Plymouth of this scandal? Perhaps like many women of the time Susanna Winslow thought the analysis of a miscarriage was a great deal of nonsense. However, it is true to say that from this point on Edward's happy-go-lucky ways became coloured with a more troubling eschatological sense.

---

* Not all Puritans agreed with this analysis. John Wheelwright had a more commonsensical approach. He wrote that this was a 'monstrous conception of his [Winthrop's] brain'.

CHAPTER X

The Pequot War

For years Plymouth had heard rumours about an immense river stretching to the northern hunting grounds. Beginning on the Canadian border and emptying into Long Island Sound, it runs through five states, but in the seventeenth century its origins were known only to Indians and trappers. Edward's ceaseless exploring meant that he was the first Englishman to see the 400-mile stretch of water called Quinetucket, 'the long tidal river' – Connecticut, as it became anglicised. His jerkin and breeches constantly wet from undergrowth and streams, he had pushed past foliage to be shown the great river, whose headwaters rise in a hidden lake.

By the early 1630s – thanks to Edward's network of Indian friends – Plymouth had been contacted by a group of river Indians seeking protection against the most powerful tribe of the area, the Pequots, who had expelled them from their territories. The river Indians were probably linked to the Narragansetts of Rhode Island who wanted to disrupt the Pequot system of alliances with a tributary system of their own.

To have access to a new area held considerable attraction for Plymouth, whose trading posts in north-eastern Maine were coming to the end of their natural life because of competition. In the summer of 1632 the French raided the Penobscot trading house and carried off a very valuable quantity of furs. They claimed the territory as part of Acadia in the Treaty of Saint-Germain-en-Laye, signed that year, which returned control of the French colonies to France after the British had seized them three years earlier.

Edward and his brother John continued to have dealings with the Abenaki Indians on the Kennebec River valley for another twenty years, but the Connecticut River valley offered a chance to break away from an area which was becoming crowded. Plymouth was invited by local Indians to have a trading house there and help the Connecticut Indians to re-establish themselves. Edward led the expedition. He was in the mood for adventure and new vistas. Since around 1628 he had been farming land at Marshfield, twelve miles from Plymouth town. It lay north of Duxbury and he had plans to move there.

Unfortunately the invitation to trade had unwelcome consequences. The countryside seemed deserted but the river valley, which had huge agricultural potential as well as being a conduit to furs, was about to become a battleground for trade rivalries between not only the English and Dutch but also between the Narragansett Indians and Pequot Indians. The great river would be the scene of converging and conflicting designs as the English and Dutch competed to trade with Indians whose lives had been dramatically changed in so many ways by the coming of the Europeans. It would also be the site of a horrible war.

The rivalry was exacerbated by a relentless new smallpox epidemic in 1633, heralded by what Bradford described as 'a great sort of flies, like (for bigness) to wasps, or bumble bees'. They came out of holes in the ground and were probably some kind of locust which stripped all green leaves from the trees. Plymouth's Indian friends told them sickness would follow, and it did. What they did not appreciate was that this plague made not only the colonists ill, but it would go on to kill a staggering eighty per cent of the southern New England tribes in the next fifteen years. The Narragansetts had escaped the earlier plague which had depleted Massasoit's men, which was how they had become his overlords. But now the Narragansetts and the Pequots suffered hideously. Vast numbers of Indians died and Bradford described how 'they lie on their hard mats, the pox breaking and mattering, and running one into another, their skin cleaving (by reason thereof) to the mats they lie on; when they turn them, a whole side will fly off at once'.

The Narragansetts' chief Canonicus correctly attributed the coming of smallpox to the English, as did the Pequots, although he was thinking in terms of powerful magic or a manitou, rather than it being another of the many contagious European diseases to which the Indians had no immunity.

The net effect of disease was to increase pressures on the Indian leadership, which was already searching for responses to the English settlements. It made the tribes unsettled and insecure, as did the threat to their territories when the English and Dutch began to move into the valley. The Narragansetts were proprietorial about the lower reaches of the Connecticut River because the shells from which *wampum* was made proliferated there. Being the manufacturers of *wampum* made them the most wealthy and powerful tribe in New England. They were, as historian Karen Kupperman has described them, the 'mint-masters of New England'. Just as the Europeans needed the Indians to reach the furs of the interior, the Indians needed European manufacturing skills: the use of iron tools had already speeded up the production of *wampum* unquantifiably.

Although the Narragansetts were the most numerous tribe, they were also the most peaceful and Canonicus was determined to keep relations with the English amicable. He spread the word of peace amongst the New England tribes who were his tributaries, partly because he realised that a struggle with the English would be unequal, and partly because he had the natural confidence of a member of the royal family of the area, and assumed that life would continue as it had for many centuries. The fact the Narragansetts escaped the first plague which hit Massasoit so badly was believed to be due to their superior priests' burning ritual in a great temple hidden in the depths of their territories in Rhode Island.

However, the Pequots had become powerful middlemen, frequently insisting on a cut on transactions, to the Narragansetts' indignation. Moreover, the 1633 epidemic made the Narragansetts less confident about their powwows' magic as their numbers rapidly declined from over 30,000 to 4,000 in the next fifteen years.

In 1633 some Pequots spotted a group of Narragansetts tracking towards the new Dutch trading house north of Hartford: they took the quickest method of prevention and murdered two of them.

The Pequot attack on the Narragansetts was dealt with harshly by the Dutch traders. With no possibility of help from Holland thousands of miles away, these hard men living in the forest were not going to have the Pequots dictate who they traded with. The Narragansetts were especially valuable to them as the manufacturers of *wampum*.

The Dutch kidnapped the Pequot chief, Tatobem. Anguished and alarmed, the Pequots spent the equivalent of millions on *wampum* to pay the ransom on him. But the Dutch showed the utmost contempt for regional custom. They kept the ransom, handed up by the Indians from their canoes where they were patiently waiting their leader's release. Then they threw out the dead body of the Pequots' mighty chief.

Thanks to their good relations with Massasoit the Pilgrims had never experienced Indians on the warpath. But now blood called for blood.

Washing Fleece and Sorting Wool, Isaac Claesz van Swanenburg

Leiden Town Hall

John Robinson's home in Leiden, the Groeneporte or Green Gate on the Kloksteg

The Mayflower carrying the Pilgrim Fathers across the Atlantic to America in 1620, Marshall Johnson

Illustration of the signatures of the Pilgrim Fathers, from *Hutchinson's Story of the British Nation*

The Signing of the Mayflower Compact, Edward Percy Moran

Princess Pocahontas on her visit to
England, Simon de Passe

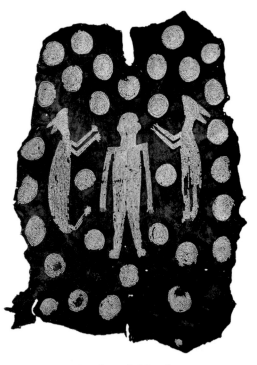

Powhatan's Mantle

Pine writing cabinet with
mother-of-pearl inlay, believed to
have been brought on the *Mayflower*
by Pilgrim William White

The Brewster chest

Mary Chilton Winslow's will

Peregrine White's cradle

First American sampler, made by Loara Standish

The Winslow joined chair

'Inhabitants of Virginia', from *Admiranda Narratio*,
Theodore de Bry

Plimoth Plantation

Massasoit,
Cyrus Dallin

William Bradford,
Cyrus Dallin

Roger Williams Leaving Salem Under Obloquy, H. Brackner

Beaver hat

John Winthrop

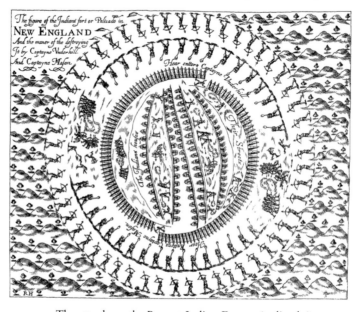

The attack on the Pequot Indian Fort or 'palizado'

Anne Hutchinson,
Cyrus Dallin

John Cotton,
artist unknown

Site of the original 1636 Governor
Winslow house, Careswell

Miantonomo Monument

The Isaac Winslow House in winter

Edward Winslow, artist unknown

Josiah Winslow, artist unknown

Penelope Pelham Winslow, artist unknown

Penelope Pelham Winslow's embroidered silk shoe

Monument to Sir William Waldegrave, his wife Elizabeth and his ten children in St Mary's Church, Bures

Smallbridge Hall, home of the Waldegrave family. It was visited twice by Queen Elizabeth I

Penelope Winslow's deposition about her Waldegrave grandfather

Ferriers

(Top left) Philip, King of Mount Hope, Paul Revere

(Top right) Algonquian bowl of carved elm burl, known as King Philip's bowl

(Above) King Philip at Mount Hope

(Left) *The Bible* in Algonquian, commissioned by John Eliot showing the first page of Genesis

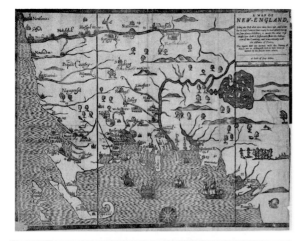

A Map of New England,
John Foster

Weetamoo, J. Andrews
& C.A. Jewett

*The Captivity of
Mrs Rowlandson*

Captain George Curwen

Wheeler's Surprise: Nipmuck Indians attack Brookfield, Van Ingen Snyder

Col. *BENJAMIN. CHURCH.*

Benjamin Church, Paul Revere

Elizabeth Paddy Wensley, artist unknown

The death of King Philip

King Philip's Seat, Mount Hope, Bristol, Rhode Island

The slate tombstone showing the Winslow and Pelham coat
of arms made in Boston, commissioned by Isaac Winslow

Shortly afterwards a disreputable alcoholic English privateer trader named John Stone outrageously kidnapped two western Niantics – a tributary tribe of the Pequot – and forced them to show him the way to the Connecticut River. Unlike the Wampanoags and other coastal Indians, the Pequots were not used to differentiating between European nationalities and assumed that Stone was the same nationality as the Dutch murderers. They killed him in direct revenge for the murder of Tatobem. Stone was a drunken good-for-nothing, an adulterer and possibly a thief – but he came from Massachusetts, and his murder could not be allowed to pass.

Tatobem's successor, Sassacus, attempted to placate the Bay with a huge gift of beaver and *wampum*. More importantly he offered access to Pequot areas of the Connecticut Valley, and his blessing to establish a plantation on Pequot land. The Pequots would thus have a good new defender against the Dutch, and indeed against the Narragansetts. But this was not part of the Bay's plan. Winthrop insisted they would not be the Pequots' protectors, though they would trade with them. To the Bay's intense annoyance, meanwhile, the Pequots refused to hand over the murderers. Inconclusive negotiations proceeded between the Pequots and Massachusetts for two years. In the meantime, increasing numbers of English settling in Connecticut ramped up the unrest amongst both Narragansetts and Pequots. In today's terms of immigration, the flood of English into the Connecticut valley was small, but it was threateningly large for the Indian tribes.

Into their hunting grounds came the settlers for Hooker's new town at Hartford, as well as Plymouth's trading house at Windsor under William Brewster's son Jonathan. The Puritan rebels Lord Saye and Sele and Lord Brooke had also planted a fort at the mouth of the Connecticut River. Called Saybrook after its owners, the fort was designed and manned by a caustic but commonsensical engineer named Lion Gardiner who had worked for the House of Orange in the Thirty Years War.

In the mid-1630s, the new colonies of Massachusetts and its satellite Connecticut leapfrogged the longer-established but tiny Plymouth to become the dominant English power in the region. They changed the Indian/English dynamic. By the end of the 1620s, Plymouth's population was officially estimated at 300; ten years later it was around 2,000, but Massachusetts had thousands more, and their colonists were very different people who saw things in categorical and absolute terms. For them the plague was another clear sign that their God wanted the country to be free of Indians.

Previous generations of historians assumed that the Pequots were attacking the English as a first act in a deliberate war. But modern authorities are now convinced that the Pequot attack was a knee-jerk reaction without thought of its long-term consequences. Official Pequot policy towards the Europeans was peaceful. The Indian tribes and their leaders were just as anxious to use the Europeans' technology as the Europeans were anxious to gain access to the Indian fur trade. Pequot numbers meant they could have attacked various European trading posts at any time in the early 1630s, but it was not in their interest. Most historians today believe the Pequots could easily have destroyed the vulnerable new settlements on the Connecticut River had they wanted to, likewise Plymouth's trading post. They did not.

The Pequots were legendarily fearsome warriors. The Massachusetts government, on the other hand, had only been in America for a few years and was ignorant of Indian behaviour, unlike Edward and the Plymouth colonists, who were well used to the manners of the New World. Aggressive behaviour did not necessarily mean the Indians had any intention of launching a full-scale war against the English. The male Indians were a sporting, heroic, warlike people who, like the Spartans, trained their young people to be fit for battle. Being on the warpath was an activity they enjoyed. Like their athletic competitions, it gave them an opportunity to demonstrate their powers.

Aggressive stand-offs were second nature to the Indians. As Roger Williams, who had studied the Indians and lived among them, put it, Canonicus, 'the great Sachem of the Narragansetts', and Massasoit, 'the great Sachem on Plymouth side', were 'at deadly feud and enmity'. Williams' need for shelter in the disputed lands meant he had been forced to win the 'agreement of these two great mortal foes'.

The Massachusetts Bay Colony felt acutely vulnerable. Their settlers were surrounded by Indian tribes as far as the eye could see. Analytical and learned, the people of the Bay were not open to the wilderness. They were also determined to impose their own ideas on its inhabitants.

As Plymouth's destiny became more closely linked with Massachusetts, the cordial relations between the Pilgrims and Indians came to an end. Even the weather seemed menacing. On 15 August 1635 there was a great storm followed by an eclipse of the moon. Thousands of trees were uprooted. The sea below Plymouth swelled to twenty feet high.

Into this highly combustible mix came the ambitious and opportunistic figure of Uncas, a minor chief of the small Mohegan tribe, a subset of the Pequots. For some time Uncas had had his eyes on Pequot territories. The other Indians considered him an upstart; he had been exiled for attempting to seize land from the Pequots, though he was married to the sister of the new Pequot leader Sassacus. The cool-headed Uncas saw his chance. Hungry for power, in effect a poor relation, he was looking to make trouble for the Pequots by stepping into their territories under English protection.

Uncas's scheming helped destroy not only his kin, the Pequots, but the peaceful relations of the Narragansetts with the English. From 1637 onwards Uncas became the favoured Indian ally of the English. For the next forty years, in order to make himself the dominant Indian leader in New England, he created a situation of perpetual anxiety. Thanks to the stories of Narragansett treachery with which he perpetually provided the Massachusetts government, all tribes other than the Mohegans seemed dangerous. Only Uncas was to be trusted.

The Mohegans' territories centred on a fort at Shantok, near the small settlement named Windsor which Jonathan Brewster had founded and which now had a number of settlers. Among them was a recently arrived soldier, Captain John Mason, who had eight years' experience in the brutal Thirty Years War and was now a representative to the General Court. Mason was a man of energy and determination who had recently put paid to the depredations of a pirate named Dixie Bull on the north-east coast. The charismatic Uncas struck up a friendship with the mystical Jonathan Brewster, who had a passion for alchemy and astrology. Both Mason and Brewster found Uncas fascinating and intriguing. Perhaps they were flattered to be taken into his confidence; perhaps Brewster saw him as a mythical figure come to life. Mason became Uncas's close friend and defender.

The Pequots had found many excuses as to why they had not handed over Stone's murderers to Massachusetts, one of them being that the killers had recently died of smallpox. It was the perfidious Uncas who assured the Bay that the murderers were alive and the Massachusetts leaders became increasingly nervous about the Pequot obduracy. They now regarded their insubordination as dangerous, rather than merely a disagreement.

Uncas's machinations were brilliantly successful. In June 1636 he told Jonathan Brewster that the Pequots were sure the English all along the river were going to attack them. Therefore the Pequots were going to attack first. This devastating news terrified the vulnerable new English communities in Connecticut. Intensely alarmed, Massachusetts summoned the Pequots to Boston. If Stone's killers were not delivered, along with the *wampum* tribute, the colony would no longer be at peace with them. They would 'revenge the blood of our countrymen as occasion shall serve'.

As bad luck had it, a few weeks later, there was another death and it was of grave moment to Jonathan Brewster: on 20 July Indians killed his wife Lucretia's brother, John Oldham. Oldham had become wealthy and respectable. Settling at Watertown, he had been a representative to the General Court at Boston. He was on a trading voyage when Indians boarded his ship. They had cut off his head and were sawing at his hands and feet when an English scout discovered them. The deck of the ship was glistening with Oldham's blood. It gave Uncas another perfect opportunity to raise the ante with his outraged friend Brewster. Oldham's murder was a game changer as far as the Bay government was concerned, that they should be on their guard against the Indians.

In fact this murder had absolutely nothing to do with the Pequots. It was the work of the Block Island Indians, allies of the Narragansetts (and at their chiefs' direction). The Narragansetts believed that Oldham was on a voyage to trade with the Pequots. The murder was not intended to bring on a war with the English. The Narragansett chief Canonicus and his stern, proud nephew Miantonomo wished for their friendship. A quick killing was to make it clear that they did not wish English traders to work with the Pequots, though they denied it to the Bay's messengers – and were believed. The messengers observed in Canonicus – 'the conqueror of all these parts' – 'much state, great command over his men: and marvellous wisdom in his answers'. Nevertheless the Boston leaders were becoming very jumpy about dealing with the Indians.

To Plymouth's alarm the Massachusetts government decided their best hope of safety lay in pre-emptive action. In August, amidst an atmosphere of undisguised anxiety, an expedition under John Endecott, who had been so rough with Thomas Morton, set off to Block Island in Narragansett Bay. They were to retrieve Stone's killers and put all the braves to death, sparing the women and children but burning their homes and fields. Then they were to go west along the coast to an important Pequot village near the Saybrook colony fort and demand tribute.

Unfortunately Endecott's adventure had the worst outcome, without achieving very much. It put the Pequots into a fury as they were not guilty of Oldham's murder. Their demand for a parley was rejected. The commander of Saybrook, Lion Gardiner, accurately forecast that the Pequots would now be buzzing like angry wasps round him in his exposed situation while Endecott retreated to the safety of Boston, a hundred miles away. For the whole of the next winter and early spring the Pequots not only imprisoned Gardiner and his fellow colonists in their fort but roamed up and down the Connecticut River attacking the new English towns, killing over thirty people.

The raids on remote settlements alarmed not only Lion Gardiner but other colonists now beginning to spread into outlying towns. The whole of New England felt in danger. The risks especially annoyed Plymouth – Edward wrote that the war 'did not concern them, seeing the Pequots had not killed any of theirs'.

The Winslows were peculiarly vulnerable, exposed in the newly built town of Marshfield above Duxbury Bay. They had taken the decision to move permanently out of Plymouth that very year. Edward was entirely reliant on his good relations with Massasoit's Wampanoags. To get to Plymouth and its protective fort, Edward and his family would have to go across the marshes or via Brant Rock out to sea. The Winslows' new home was built on a peninsula at the edge of a salt meadow backing onto the northern part of Plymouth Bay. Although today the land is flat, then it was more of a bluff. Like those of other early settlers, the house was probably positioned for defensive purposes, especially in light of the rising tensions in New England. The creek which lay at the end of the garden was a navigable waterway, providing a sure escape for Edward, Susanna and their children: Edward's two stepsons Resolved and Peregrine, and his three children, who included the eight-year-old Josiah and his five-year-old daughter Elizabeth.

There was a distinct possibility the besieged Saybrook garrison could starve to death. Those manning the fort built to house the flower of the exiled Puritan nobility watched as the bloated bodies of their fellow English floated by. Master John Tilly, the operator of a small sailing vessel, was murdered in a particularly grisly fashion. On his way back to Boston from Connecticut he made the mistake of stopping to spend a pleasant afternoon 'afowling' near Saybrook. As he ambled about with his piece resting on his shoulders, the Indians rose up from the long grass. He did not stand a chance. He uttered not a word as he was tied to a stake and flayed to death, having first had his fingers and toes cut off in front of Saybrook fort. The Indians admired his courage and shouted that he was a stout fellow.

In the late summer came news that the unthinkable had happened: the Pequots' bitterest enemies, the Narragansetts, were thinking of joining their side. Roger Williams had been on Narragansett land at Providence for less than a year but he had become very close to their leadership. The magnificent Miantonomo frequently dropped in without warning, accompanied by his warriors, and spent the night. Such was Roger Williams' popularity that chief Canonicus himself had measured out the width and depth of his trading house. In old age Williams remembered how 'I never denied him [Canonicus] or Miantonomo whatever they desired of me as to goods or gifts or use of my boats or pinnace, and the travels of my own person, day and night'. He was often seen transporting fifty Narragansett warriors in his large canoe.

Williams was trusted to be the Narragansetts' 'councillor and secretary in all their wars'. Nothing could have been more crucial. When the English corn was ready for harvesting the Narragansetts told him 'The Pequots and Narragansetts were at truce'. Miantonomo revealed that the Pequots 'had laboured to persuade them that the English were minded to destroy all Indians'. If the Narragansetts did not join and fight with the Pequots, they would be attacked next.

Determined to stop this alliance, hardly telling his wife what he intended, Williams jumped into his canoe 'to cut through a stormy wind, with great seas, every minute in hazard of life, to the sachem's house'. He stayed three days and nights with Miantonomo, side by side with ambassadors from the Pequots whose hands and arms he thought 'reeked with the blood of my countrymen, murdered and massacred by them on the Connecticut River, and from whom I could not but nightly look for their bloody knives at my own throat also'.

Williams' invaluable diplomacy that long autumn and winter meant the Narragansetts were persuaded to remain neutral – though it was touch and go.

With the careless self-confidence of those who for centuries had been born to rule, the Narragansett leaders dismissed the Pequots' warning. At this point the Narragansetts saw the English as people they could do business with, and assumed they would be able to carry on their usual way of life. It did not mean that they would not enforce their own punishments on English people not abiding by their laws – the Narragansetts were used to having their own way in their dominions.

Miantonomo was summoned to Boston, where, as he had done before, he made a speech protesting his love for the English and pledged loyalty to the Bay. As proof, he offered firstly a great deal of *wampum*, and secondly – the unambiguous sign of loyalty as far as the Narragansetts were concerned – a severed Pequot hand.

Had the Pequots and Narragansetts combined at that date, it certainly could have meant the end of the English colonies. The Pequots could raise around 4,000 warriors. The Narragansett numbers were declining because of the smallpox, but in 1636 they were still a tribe numbering nearly 30,000. At least a quarter were braves who could have fought. The combined English colonies' official fighting force was under 200 soldiers. Even with Roger Williams' urgent representations, the New England colonies stood in great danger in the winter and spring of 1637. Pequot ambassadors continued secretly to visit the Narragansetts to urge them to come over to their side, repeating their warnings: if they did not rise against the English now, they would be rooted out of their own land.

New England's majestic rocky terrain could always assume a stern and threatening aspect. That spring it seemed additionally unsettling. Its high cliffs were the vantage points of hostile Indians. The settlers laboured under an oppressive mood. There was bitter friction between the supporters and enemies of Anne Hutchinson. Many began to question what had seemed the certainty of their mission. The continuous attacks from the Indians meant the settlements were on constant alert. It was no longer clear which Indians could really be trusted, other than Massasoit and Uncas.

When the siege of Saybrook was finally lifted after some difficulty in March 1637, the Pequots simply went upriver. To the colonists' horror, on 23 April the riverside settlement of Wethersfield was attacked. Founded only three years before, it was at a fragile stage of development. A local tribe had been angered by Wethersfield occupying land they viewed as theirs. Wethersfield's citizens had not realised the depths of their resentment and trusted them. Nor did they recognise that their Indian neighbours were affiliated to the Pequots. The settlers had gone out to their fields to work in their usual way. Indians rose up from the shadows, their tomahawks poised to scalp. They killed three women and six men and carried off two young girls. Escaping by water, their canoes with a hundred warriors and the captive girls passed Saybrook fort. The Indians shouted and jeered at the English; imitating the English Puritan custom they used the word 'brother' sarcastically.

Plymouth reluctantly came round to Winthrop's warnings that the whole English presence in New England could be wiped out. The colonies were now in agreement that an 'offensive and defensive' war had to be made against the Pequots. By this stage, Massachusetts was not in a state to be very considered in its responses to the Indians. It now appeared to many colonists that Satan was operating against them, both inside the colony and in the wilderness surrounding them. The Anne Hutchinson affair had been the first sign. The presence of many soldiers who had been involved in the religious battles of the Thirty Years War in Europe exacerbated the colonists' tendencies to encase the conflict with the Indians in eschatological terms, and allow it more menace than it deserved. The learned clergy searched Holy Writ for guidance. In sermons the Indians were portrayed as instruments of Satan and the difficulties the colonies were facing in terms of a struggle between God and Satan. The struggle against the Pequots became a holy war. The New England colonies officially declared war against them on 1 May.

On 10 May John Mason left Hartford, Connecticut at the head of the militia with sixty Mohegans from Uncas to rendezvous with John Underhill, coming from Boston. They were to meet in Pequot country. The path to the Pequot fort lay through Narragansett territory. It was a thorny wild landscape, covered with scrub and undergrowth and completely unknown to them. Mason was courteous and formal, apologising for coming armed onto Narragansett territory. But the Indians were angered, especially since English troops surrounded the Narragansetts' fort for the night and said anyone passing in or out would be killed. The English were worried the Narragansetts might leak their plans to the Pequots.

The Narragansett leadership viewed an English army on their territory with dismay. Many years later Roger Williams would recall how 'that old Prince Canonicus who was most shy of all English to his last breath' had been wary about allowing any English to settle on his land. Williams was only welcomed by Canonicus because he was a friend and because he spared no cost in plying the Indians with gifts. Williams related how Canonicus was not only shy but canny: he was not to be stirred with money to sell his land to let in foreigners. It was true that he 'received presents and gratuities many of me' but it was not thousands of pounds or even tens of thousands that 'could have bought of him an English entrance into this bay'.

Thanks to Williams, Miantonomo gave them crucial information. The key to success was to attack at night. It would take too long to reach the Pequots' main fort, Weinshauks. They should head for the Indian fort at the mouth of the Mystic River, a rocky eminence dashed by the roaring surf about twenty miles from Saybrook. Miantonomo insisted the Pequot 'women and children be spared'. There were rumoured to be about 700 Pequots in the fort. Miantonomo said rather slightingly he thought the English numbers 'too weak to deal with the enemy, who were (he said) very great captains and men skilful in war'.

Sparing the women and children was the last thing on the colonists' minds. After the attack on Wethersfield none of the English felt very merciful. Moreoever it was unclear how reliable the Narragansetts were – or indeed the Mohegans. Both tribes were rumoured to have Pequots in their ranks. The unaccustomed heat made several English soldiers faint. Although some of Miantonomo's men accompanied the English towards the Pequot at Fort Mystic, the body of the Indian troops were the Mohegans.

The assault was an almost total success, from the Puritan point of view. A dog barked as they approached. The Indians woke up and shouted 'Owanux! Owanux!', meaning Englishmen. But it was too late. Creeping up to the top of the hill, the colonists rushed in and set fire to seventy wigwams. The whole fort started to blaze, in the process killing between 400 and 700 people. John Underhill reported 'many were burnt in the Fort, both men, women, and children, others forced out, and came in troops to the Indians, twenty, and thirty at a time, which our soldiers received and entertained with the point of the sword'.

Mason and Underhill had worried unnecessarily about the untried nature of the militias. Their novice soldiers had been guided by God Himself. The Mohegans provided cover for the English to run back to their boats at Pequot harbour. Meanwhile the Narragansetts hung back and did not really fight – which made the English very suspicious.

In fact the Narragansetts were horrified by what they saw, and expressed the deepest disapproval of the mass murder of civilians. Underhill reported with some amazement how upset the Narragansetts were watching the Mystic Fort burn with the Pequots inside. They shouted, 'It is naught, it is naught,' meaning it is wicked or evil. Miantonomo told Underhill that he disapproved of 'the manner of the Englishmen's fight' because it 'slays too many men'. Despite their fondness for torture, low population levels meant the Indians did not go in for pitched battles. Mason described how Indian war confrontations were for display: 'they might fight seven years and not kill seven men' because they did not come near one another. They shot randomly with their arrows. 'Then they gaze up in the sky to see where the Arrow falls, and not until it is fallen do they shoot again, this fight is more for pastime, than to conquer and subdue enemies.' Indian tactics were far closer to guerrilla warfare. Miantonomo might have suggested that they crept up on the Pequots, but he had not anticipated the wholesale slaughter and was amazed that they were not negotiated with, as was customary. All of this was outside the Narragansett rules of engagement.

In the Thirty Years War, it had been usual to burn fields and towns, and kill women and children. Now the slaughter of the Pequots had more than a whiff of genocide, even though the English had felt it was a question of 'us' or 'them'. Captain Underhill was asked 'why should you be so furious' and 'should not Christians have more mercy and compassion?' Unsurprisingly his response was to seek biblical example: 'sometimes the Scripture declareth women and children must perish with their parents; sometimes the case alters: but we will not dispute it now. We had sufficient light from the word of God for our proceedings . . .'

Via Roger Williams the Narragansetts sent messages urging clemency, but the remaining warriors of the vanquished Pequots were killed. A final group was rounded up in a swamp near the Quinnipiac River where the men made a last stand and the women and children surrendered. The leader of the Pequots had fled desperately to the Mohawks, but they killed him and sent his scalp to Connecticut to show their friendship was not with the defeated Pequots. Miantonomo expressly asked that the Pequots who surrendered should not be enslaved. But this was not to be: the women and children were rounded up and sold into slavery in the West Indies or became servants to the English. The name of the Pequots was officially extinguished.

Many historians have seen this as an alarming portent of a future where African Americans were enslaved for two hundred years. Although amongst the Indians slavery of defeated tribes was a consequence of battle – the victors enslaved the defeated – it had a pernicious effect between Indians and English. The Pequots were a different race and different civilisation from the English. Enslaving them entrenched differences between the two peoples, enhancing a superiority complex amongst the English. Indian leaders who were not Pequots took away the lesson that, deep down, the English were not their friends.

Miantonomo was immensely offended by the aftermath of the war. He had expected far greater rewards. The Narragansetts assumed they would take over much of the territory of the Pequots, and become the dominant tribe of the area. Thanks to Uncas this did not happen.

Uncas's close relationship with John Mason lasted for the rest of their lives. The portly captain had warmed to him for fighting so bravely during the expedition. In return, Mason was rewarded by much Mohegan land in what had been Pequot territory. Though Mason's troops became notorious for brutality to the Pequots his ties to the Mohegans were different. By 1671 he had tied up 20,000 acres for the Mohegans in such a way that he believed it could never be touched by other land-hungry English settlers.

After the war even Plymouth no longer acceded to what has been called 'the Indians' persistent expectations of equality and reciprocity'. Instead the English dictated. Miantonomo would later say, 'Did friends ever deal so with friends?'

By the Treaty of Hartford in 1638 most of the Pequot territories went to the Connecticut river towns. Owing to the alliance between Uncas and Mason, the Mohegans received much of the Pequot territory east of the Connecticut River. The Narragansetts got nothing and were forbidden to go anywhere near the old Pequot area. The favourable treatment of the Mohegans was one more insult to Miantonomo. He regarded the Mohegans 'but as a twig' in comparison to the Narragansetts: 'we are as a great tree,' he said.

Hartford was isolated and had tremendous anxieties about its security. It remained distrustful of the Narragansetts. The fact that the Narragansetts had been in conference with the Pequots the whole winter of 1636–7 contrasted poorly with Uncas's protestations of devotion. The famous diagram of the war to accompany John Underhill's 1638 book *Newes from America* shows the fort surrounded by two rings of soldiers, the inner ring being English, the outer being the enthustiastic Mohegans. The Narragansetts were thought to have held back.

Miantonomo was now not permitted to wage war against Uncas without the permission of Massachusetts (which was an attack on the Narragansetts' cultural traditions and way of life), while his tributary system was already threatened by Plymouth's protection of the Wampanoags and the loss of the Block Islanders. It enhanced his sense of the shrinking population of the Narragansetts. Uncas, meanwhile, continued to profit from being the official frontier scout against the Narragansetts.

Letters to John Winthrop show that during the war Edward came to feel bound in what had become perceived as a Christian crusade. John Robinson had hoped for a native church. But Edward became increasingly orthodox under John Winthrop's influence. It seems he began to adopt the learned Boston clergy's hostile views, to believe that the testing of the 'Saints for Christ' in the wilderness was to be by the Indians.

The Pequots were the 'accursed seeds of Canaan', said one of Boston's most celebrated new ministers, Richard Mather. Edward began to reinterpret relations with the Indians. After a winter of horror he commiserated with Winthrop for Massachusetts' nightmare. He hoped God would 'sanctify His hand and fit us for such trials as He hath appointed'. He signed his letter passionately. He was 'yours till death'.

In the past Edward had been happy to engage in religious argument with the Indians. He had called their leaders 'discreet, courteous, and humane in their carriages', 'scorning theft, lying and the like base dealings, and stand as much upon their reputation as any man'. He had reported back to England on correspondences between Christian worship and the Indians' religion, and had been at some pains to describe their moral sense. Now a passion for typology (looking for events in the Old Testament which foretold events in the New, or indeed by extension in the present day), combined with sermons and very real danger, radicalised Edward, whose own certainties altered. There was an impatience which had not been there ten years before.

Even though Plymouth saw the war as entirely created by Massachusetts, and even though Hobbamock continued to live at Duxbury with Myles Standish, the trust between Plymouth and the Indians began to trickle away. For all their bluff spirit even Plymouth could not dismiss the memory of Indian attacks during the recent war and current prickling anxieties about their survival thousands of miles from England.

Only Roger Williams resisted. In this context it is mournful to read some of his testimony about Plymouth in the past. According to Williams, Massasoit himself often professed 'that he was pleased that I should here be his neighbour, and that rather because he and I had been great friends at Plymouth, and also because that his and my friends at Plymouth advised him to be at peace and friendship with me and he hoped that our children after us'.

The person now more in touch with Indian communities was Jonathan Brewster. But he was under the spell of Uncas, the aggressive new actor upon the stage, whose rise to prominence was regarded at first with amazement then indignation by the rulers of the better-established tribes.

Perhaps Edward became alarmed by the very customs he had once found enchanting or perhaps the growing hostility on the part of other Indians began to prey on him. Perhaps he regarded his former attitude to the Indians as not zealous enough, indicating sinfulness. His roaming life meant he was uniquely well informed because of his networks amongst Indians and their English scout and trapper friends who lived deep in the woods. He had detected a level of hatred and defiance that could not be denied. Describing Pequot preparations to defend themselves, he wrote to Winthrop on 22 May 1637: 'They profess there you shall find them, and as they were there born and bred, there their bones shall be buried and rot in despite of the English.'

Edward was spending an increasing amount of his time in Boston, where the strenuous sense of mission affected him. An autodidact who was thirsty for knowledge, and slightly in awe of the more sophisticated colonists, Edward was increasingly drawn to Winthrop. In the same letter to Winthrop, Edward wrote that the older man's 'many and undeserved kindnesses . . . especially at my being last with you, tie me if possible yet nearer in heart and affection towards you and yours'. Perhaps Winthrop made him think he had had a naïve view of the Indians. Winthrop was quite categorical in his warning to Plymouth: they must look at 'the Pequots and all other Indians, as a common enemy' whose intention was 'the rooting out of the whole nation'.

Edward was a man of strong and independent views, but he was also easily influenced. He was forever being seized by enthusiasm – first in London, then in Holland, then in Plymouth, and now in Massachusetts.

Massasoit himself became more subservient to the English in this new atmosphere. He had lost much of his confidence. On 21 April 1638, in an uncharacteristically late winter when snow was still masking the trees, Massasoit made his way from Sowams to Boston on snowshoes. Behind him on a sledge was the tribute of eighteen beaver skins from himself and various sachems under his rule. He had heard that the Bay was angry with him, because he had sold land at Aquidneck, Rhode Island, to what were evidently their enemies – Anne Hutchinson and some of her supporters. He came to make sure Boston realised he wanted peace. He also asked for Winthrop's help with the Connecticut magistrates. A letter was duly given.

In 1640 Massasoit repeated the submission to Plymouth he had made so solemnly when they first met in 1621, lest Plymouth should doubt his loyalty. Was it because he was alarmed by a new coldness between himself and Edward that when three Englishmen were arrested and tried for the murder of an Indian boy, Massasoit wanted one of the men to be let off? He 'must not die for he was Mr Winslow's man: and also that the man was by birth a Nipmuck man and so not worthy that any other man should die for him'. John Winthrop noted in his diary that Indian witnesses were required, but such was the effect of the war that they were terrified of coming forward 'for they still feared that the English were conspired to kill all the Indians'. The government of Plymouth insisted justice be done, otherwise it would start another war. William Bradford reported with satisfaction the trial and hanging of English ne'er-do-wells for murdering a tragic Indian boy for his *wampum* and three coats of cloth. Yet quite a number of the English at Plymouth agreed with Massasoit that it was very severe to hang three men for one Indian.

A careful study by the leading expert on land deeds, Jeremy Bangs, has concluded that 'the barbarous cruelty of the English retaliation' was not forgotten. Bangs demonstrates that in the years that followed the war, Indians in Plymouth Colony sold off 'tract after tract of land, even when there was no apparent immediate pressure to sell, leaving themselves in the end, almost nothing to call their own'. Plymouth's old scrupulousness about land ebbed away, encouraged by Massasoit himself, who was eager to sell to remain in favour. He clung on to good relations with Plymouth even though as the years passed the treatment of the Wampanoags by the English became increasingly oppressive. Over the next decade Massasoit and his family and tributary sachems disposed of colossal amounts of their ancestral lands. This was the background against which Massasoit's sons Wamsutta and Metacom grew up.

There is something inexorable about the march of English towns across the Indian countryside and the records of what they paid for Indian land. In 1637, moving south and west, William Bradford and partners bought the acreage which became the town of Sandwich for £16 19s in commodities. The next year Yarmouth, formerly the Wampanoag area called Mattacheese, was settled. It was acquired for 'six coats, six pair of small breeches, ten hoes, ten hatchets, two brass kettles . . . and one iron kettle'. In 1643 Edward and John Brown bought the westerly part of Rehoboth for ten fathoms of beads. Plymouth's settlements were creeping perilously close to Mount Hope, Massasoit's ancient home.

In his classic account *The Pequot War*, Alfred A. Cave summed up its effect in one sentence: 'Although the Pequot War was a small-scale conflict of short duration, it cast a long shadow.' Many historians concur with his view, that the image of 'brutal and untrustworthy savages plotting the extermination of those who would do the work of God in the wilderness became a vital part of the mythology of the American frontier'. After the Pequot War the English emerged not only as victors but more powerful than the Indians. As the celebrated historian Alden T. Vaughan has written, 'The destruction of the Pequots cleared away the only major obstacle to Puritan expansion. And the thoroughness of that destruction made a deep impression on the other tribes.'

The Narrangansett leadership came to the conclusion that the Pequots had been right when they had told them the English wanted to drive them out of their ancestral homes. Many contemporary descriptions, including Edward's, make a point of Miantonomo's ambition. Whereas Canonicus had decided not to engage in any struggle with the English, his nephew was made of different stuff. The English did not like Miantonomo. He was a man 'who could not be trusted', according to William Bradford. Edward Johnson called him 'of great stature, of a cruel nature, causing all his . . . attendants to tremble at his speech'.

Edward criticised him for being a 'great aspiring sachem' and 'very proud'. Edward had formed a high opinion of the Indians' natural nobility and leadership qualities when he arrived in America. When push came to shove, though, in reality he preferred an Indian king like Massasoit who was under his control.

The aftermath of the Pequot War set off a slow but unstoppable reaction. It would not make itself properly felt for thirty years, but when it emerged it was an uncontainable and furious tsunami, the rebellion of Massasoit's son Metacom, or 'Philip' as he was by then also known. It is no exaggeration to say that in 1675, King Philip's War was the direct descendant of the Pequot War.

The only Englishman of influence who represented the Indians' point of view was Roger Williams. He would continue strenuously to fight their corner.

CHAPTER XI

The Pan-Indian Conspiracy

As the Indian population dwindled, that of the English expanded. Their hogs spoilt the Indian hunting lands and their fences stopped the running of the deer. The country rang with the sound of loud confident English voices as they hammered and chopped and split rails in what had been silent places which knew only Indian hunters. They set to work building more small churches. With some relief their wives and daughters could spread out bedding to air. Around 200 houses went up on the Connecticut's banks amongst its graceful trees.

Uncas, meanwhile, constantly suggested to his English neighbours in Connecticut that Miantonomo was really on the Pequots' side and would one day attack them. He was right.

On 29 April 1640 Bradford sent a secret message to John Winthrop. He had heard there was to be an uprising by the Narragansetts with help from the Mohawks. No threat could have been more alarming. The Narragansetts had 'sent a great present, both of white and black beads to the Mohawks to entreat their help against you, and your friends, if they see cause. And the Mohawks have received their present and promised them aid, bidding them begin when they will, and they will be ready for them, and do encourage them, with hope of success.' Bradford could not reveal his source, or it would cost him his life. He feared that laziness about allowing the Indians guns meant 'they are too well furnished with pieces by too much remissness'.

The Mohawks or Maquas, reportedly flesh-eaters, lay to the Narragansetts' west and were the most feared of the Iroquois confederacy, the Five Nation federation of the Indians of western New York which also consisted of the Oneida, Onondaga, Cayuga and Seneca peoples. The Mohawks were known as the Keepers of the Eastern Door and historically they were the habitual enemies of the Algonquian Indians, who included the Narragansetts and the Wampanoags. Although they were based in the Hudson Valley to the west of Connecticut, the fearsome Mohawks ranged widely, collecting tribute from as far east as the interior of Maine and what is now New Hampshire and Vermont up to the Great Lakes. One of the reasons the Connecticut River Indians had encouraged Plymouth to have a trading house near them was so that their guns would stave off the Mohawks.

Now there was a chance the Indian tribes might unite against the settlers. All over the Narragansett country below the circling flights of the great blue heron, Miantonomo's most trusted officials were speeding up the production of *wampum*. This honing of the shells generally took place over the long cold winters. Picking it from the black rocks in the sparkling waters of Narragansett Bay was the Narragansetts' pursuit all the long summer days, as it had been since time immemorial. Now it had to be swifter.

But despite the whispers there was no proof. In 1640 the Narragansetts did not, in fact, revolt. Yet the rumour mill did not stop, fed ceaselessly by Uncas. Miantonomo was summoned to Boston to answer questions. He vehemently denied he was planning anything. He was not pleased to be told that he could not bring Roger Williams to translate for him because Williams was banned from Boston. The Indian prince never moved without a train of attendants and warriors for security and as a sign of his status. Roger Williams described the great pride and splendour of Miantonomo, who kept his 'barbarous court' at his house with fifty warriors in attendance. But when the Indian king was met at Roxbury, Governor Thomas Dudley did not treat him with the courtesy he was expecting. When the English insisted on a Pequot interpreter, who was also a woman, it further infuriated Miantonomo. He thought it an insult to provide a woman and also feared the Pequots would deliberately misinterpret what was said. Dudley thought it a 'dishonour to us' to give way so much to them. At this Miantonomo stormed out, 'departing in a rude manner, without showing any respect or sign of thankfulness to the governor for his entertainment', as John Winthrop noted in his journal. But the Indian king had not departed before the former articles of peace between the two peoples had been read to him, and once more agreed.

In 1639 after the Pequot War, Lion Gardiner, along with some of the other Saybrook soldiers, had bought what is still called Gardiner's Island in East Hampton. He became friendly with the Montauk Indians. The Long Island chieftain Waiandance had long been warning Gardiner that Miantonomo planned to leave the English alone only till they had got rid of Uncas, then they 'with the Mohawks and Maquas and the Indians beyond the Dutch, and all the Northern and Eastern Indians, would easily destroy us, every man and mother's son'. Gardiner passed this information on to Boston and the leaders of the river towns. In the spring of 1641 Waiandance told Gardiner there was a specific plan to attack along the Connecticut River. The Montauk sachems had been told to watch for 'three fires that will be made forty days hence, in a clear night'. The following day with the aid of a party of 300 Narragansetts, the Montauk Indians must fall on 'men, women, and children'. They were not to touch the cows 'for they will serve to eat till our deer be increased again'.

Although it is plain that many minor sachems such as Waiandance were reporting on Miantonomo in order to further their own interests, it is equally clear that the charismatic Miantonomo was stirring up the Indians to make a last stand, visiting Indian camps and having secret meetings all over southern New England. He warned his Indian allies that if they failed to unite as the English colonies had done 'we shall all be gone shortly'. The Narragansetts in the past had received presents, in their progresses; now Miantonomo gave the gifts, 'calling them brethren and friends, for so are we all Indians as the English are, and say brother to one another'.

In a speech that was a lament for the passing of Indian supremacy, Miantonomo warned that while their fathers had plenty of game to live on, now the English had got their land 'their cows and horses eat the grass, and their hogs spoil our clam banks, and we shall all be starved; therefore it is best for you to do as we, for we are all the Sachems from east to west, both Moquakues and Mohawks joining with us, and we are all resolved to fall upon them all, at one appointed day'.

On 22 June 1642 Winthrop reported to his diary with some alarm that there had been an assassination attempt on his new trusty friend. Edward had been attacked at Plymouth's trading house in Maine. It appeared 'the Indians at Kennebec, hearing of the general conspiracy against the English, determined to begin there'. One of them, knowing that Edward liked to walk outside the trading house, 'within the palisades, prepared his piece to shoot him, but as he was about it, Mr Winslow not seeing him, nor suspecting anything, but thinking he had walked enough, went suddenly into the house'. God had preserved him. Edward himself must have relayed this failed attempt with its frightening implications when he returned to Plymouth via Boston, having taken a boat down the coast. Meanwhile, information was coming in thick and fast about a rising from 'testimonies of the Indians many hundred miles asunder from each other'.

Connecticut's colonies were vulnerable and isolated. The planters constantly sensed Indians 200 feet above the valley floor watching them from clefts in the traprock. When a new warning appeared of Miantonomo's plans to attack Connecticut after the harvest, their magistrates demanded a war. The Indians intended to go in small groups 'to the chief men's houses by way of trading, etc and should kill them in the houses and seize their weapons'. But Winthrop and his fellow Bay magistrates were loath to go to war again: 'Although the thing seemed very probable, yet we thought it not sufficient ground for us to begin a war.'

They would have to stand continuously on their guard. Unable to venture out beyond their palisades they would be prevented from attending to their farms or continuing to trade with the Indians. The Bay disarmed important chiefs: Cutshamekin at Braintree and the celebratedly long-lived Passaconaway, chief of the Pennacooks, who lived by the Merrimack River. Once again Miantonomo was hauled in to be questioned. At his examination at Boston he insisted on having several councillors with him, for as Winthrop noted, Miantonomo was 'a very subtle man'. He wanted witnesses to confirm what he had said. He denied all manner of conspiracy and asked for those accusing him to be present and do so to his face. He said the accusations were mere rumours set about by Uncas – whom he said was treacherous to the English. Miantonomo was fed up of having to keep his men at home and not allow them to go out hunting.

By the end of October the Indians' guns were handed back, though most of New England's small settlements remained tense and on edge. The winter of 1642–3 saw extraordinary snowfall, reducing communication between settlements to the advantage of the Indians. It was decided that every town must be furnished with powder out of the common store. Guns must be provided, as well as military watches and alarms.

The citizens found it hard to contain their anxieties. The town records show their fears about Miantonomo were so great that colonists travelled in convoys. The Indians' mastery of woodcraft and ability to move silently through the forests in their moccasins meant the colonists were constantly on edge.

The farmers were sitting ducks. Some said that Pequots were now part of Miantonomo's force prepared to burn homesteads and scalp the inhabitants. Edward was one of the chief architects of a plan to join the separate plantations into an overarching organisation for their protection, so the colonies could coordinate troops and act at short notice. The English government could not help because their soldiers were occupied on English Civil War battlefields, and in any event they were too far away. Putting aside their differences and jealousies over land patents, an inter-colonial organisation called the New England Confederation was established. The more far-sighted, including Edward, believed it was all too possible for the Dutch and French to be drawn in on the Indian side, not to speak of the Mohawks. The United Colonies created on 19 May 1643 were a 'perpetual league of friendship for offence and defence'. Each colony sent two commissioners and no colony was to declare war without consulting the others.

Plymouth, Massachusetts, Connecticut and New Haven* were thus drawn together. Rhode Island, however, was regarded as being full of dangerous heretics – like Roger Williams, plus Anne Hutchinson and her supporters – and was not allowed to join. Nor were its idiosyncratic settlers interested in doing so. Anne Hutchinson and her husband and followers were in exile at Aquidneck, Rhode Island, on land sold to them by the Narragansetts and the Wampanoags. The Narragansetts' decision to sell land to the Bay's enemies of course did not improve their standing in Boston. In addition it had become clear that the land round Narragansett Bay was some of the most fertile in New England with potential for a superb harbour.

Most Plymouth colonists fatalistically buried themselves in the hard work involved in just getting by, raising enough pigs for the winter, chopping enough trees for the stove. They did not want to think about war. Edward, one of the two commissioners representing Plymouth in the confederation, spent far more time in Boston. His fierce devotion to John Winthrop continued. He hero-worshipped Winthrop as he had once hero-worshipped William Brewster and John Robinson. It had altered him, making him more zealous and less open-minded. Moving in the company of Bostonians gave him more of a sense of a New England that was not just a loose collection of small settlements, but a place growing up into a godly nation.

Immigrants fleeing Charles I's reforms continued to arrive. Perhaps they had no idea of quite how disturbed the situation was. They were

---

* New Haven, another theocratic state, had been founded in 1638 by 500 discontented settlers from Massachusetts, headed by Theophilus Eaton and Reverend John Davenport. The land on the Long Island Sound had been granted by the Quinnipiac Indians.

just anxious to get out of England. In the August of 1638 twenty ships and at least 3,000 persons 'of good quality and estate' came through the port of Boston. Many were enterprising and zealous Puritan gentry who had no faith in the king's promises. Amongst them was a small party of East Anglians, connections of the Winthrops headed by Herbert Pelham. His wife Jemima (née Waldegrave) had died on the voyage, but Herbert sailed on. The Pelham family would play a big part in the Winslows' lives. Amongst the arrivals, no doubt bewildered by their mother's sudden death, were Herbert's four young children, including the five-year-old Penelope, Edward's future daughter-in-law. Their maternal grandfather, Thomas Waldegrave, had pooled resources with Herbert Pelham, investing early in the Massachusetts Bay Company, so they were entitled to at least 800 acres once they got to America.

Like many of the gentry passengers who came off the boats in their heavily embroidered and expensive fabrics denoting their status at home, the Pelhams were damp and anxious. Accompanied by their beautiful and elaborate household objects they lumbered down the rough gangplanks onto the mud of the Boston wharves in their dainty shoes, clutching their cloaks tighter against the sharp air. What had started out as an exhilarating adventure in a large family party had gone tragically wrong already. They were perhaps a little fearful, but the Pelhams had powerful connections in colonising circles, as well as family in Boston. Herbert's brother William and sister Penelope were there and could look after Herbert and his motherless children. William Pelham was one of the first planters at Sudbury – he had secured land there for Herbert and the Waldegraves.

Despite the storm of the Anne Hutchinson affair, the settlers at Boston had not lost all their human qualities, including the governor, Richard Bellingham. He had been not only the recorder of Boston, Lincolnshire, but also its MP before emigrating in 1634. Herbert's sister Penelope caught his eye. She was already promised to a young man lodging in the governor's house, but the forceful Bellingham, who was one of the most powerful politicians of the day, soon got her to prefer himself, and they married in 1641. In Boston in New England Bellingham had a large country house on the marshes at what is now called Chelsea, where he hunted. He owned the ferry between Boston and Chelsea, across the Mystic River.

Fortunately for Herbert and his motherless brood an intimacy sprang up between himself and Elizabeth Harlakenden, the young

widow of an admired and very orthodox Boston magistrate. She may
have felt sorry for a man struggling with small children, as she was in
a similar position herself, and they probably had friends in common.
Herbert and his former wife Jemima had been close neighbours of the
family of Elizabeth's husband Roger, living a couple of miles away
from their manor house at Earls Colne in Essex. By 1638 Roger had
died of smallpox. But he left a wealthy widow and by 1639 Herbert
had married her, adding a New World fortune to his already sizeable
portfolio (he owned at least 800 acres of Lincolnshire and had great
expectations of his father-in-law Thomas Waldegrave's estates in
Suffolk).

But many immigrants were not in his fortunate position and had to
travel to found new towns. Freshly arrived from England, the less
well-to-do inhabitants of Massachusetts had little idea how to survive
in the wilderness, let alone how to combat their Indian neighbours.
There were few horses and they were no good in forests. To get to the
new towns they had to travel through watery swamps with all their
luggage, walking on tree trunks in thickets which sometimes gave way
to 'an uncertain bottom in water'. Once they emerged from the forest
they met 'a scorching plain'. Sometimes the sun was so strong and the
fern undergrowth smelt so overwhelming that folk whose stockings
were already cut to pieces fainted, yet on they went, carried by their
pastors and their faith.

Once they found a place to plant their church, near water, it was
thin times bartering with the Indians for flesh, including an animal
none of them had seen or eaten before, a 'rockoon' or raccoon. And
'instead of apples and pears, they had pompkins and squashes of divers
kinds'.

It was hard to get a herd established; often after one or two years
the cattle died, wolves still took the pigs, and the sheep did not thrive
unless they were farmed with cattle. Horses also did not do well,
'which made many an honest gentleman travel a foot for a long time,
and some have even perished with extreme heat in their travels'. The
lack of English grain – wheat, barley and rye – 'proved a sore affliction
to some stomachs'. Those who survived best were the ones who could
live 'upon Indian bread and water'.

Emigration ceased abruptly when the English Civil War began, and
with it the specie that came with immigrants. Prices plummeted: cows
and corn lost three-quarters of their value. The New Englanders could
not pay their debts in England for commodities they had already

imported. There were gigantic economic problems as well as the fear of the Indians.

A weary Edward was permanently in the saddle on the trail through briars and undergrowth that lay between Marshfield and Boston. Nowhere was safe. Even the most trusted Indian guide might turn out to have Pequot sympathies or have a relative who was a Pequot or a Narragansett. Now that the colonists had essentially become an occupying force, it was hard to make a distinction between friendly pro-English Indians and those full of hatred for these newcomers. The wrong guess could mean death. Edward was no longer their champion and perhaps no longer even really their friend. His admiration for the exotic ways of the Indians had been replaced by fear.

He now believed there was a 'deep conspiracy against all English in the land', a conspiracy his knowledge of the Indians convinced him the Indians could win. Pamphlets written by Edward in the 1640s show his belief in the necessity of patrolling all Indian alliances, particularly anything to do with Miantonomo and the Narragansetts. Writing for an English audience to defend the way of life in New England and convince the English government not to interfere in it, Edward was mindful of London friends who asked why the colonists kept needlessly engaging 'in the troubles between the Indians'. Attempting to convey the intricacies of life surrounded by the tribes, Edward told them that in New England it was fantastically important (even if unimaginable to an English person) to know what was going on amongst the Indians. He wrote: 'if we should not here and there keep correspondence with some of them, they would soon join all together against us'. A couple of marriages could link dynasties and armies in the twinkling of an eye.

At the height of the threat of war, a mystical free spirit called Samuel Gorton – a man regarded as a heretic by most of the New England leadership, including the 'heretical' Rhode Islanders – chose to befriend Miantonomo. Gorton and his family refused to obey the laws of Plymouth, and moved from settlement to settlement managing to offend everyone with whom they came into contact. Gorton challenged William Coddington for the leadership of Newport. The Rhode Island settlements found him insolent and intolerable. Roger Williams thought he truly deserved the name of 'familist' and refused to have him causing trouble in Providence. Taking pride in not being book learned and saying the first thing that came into his head, Gorton had a genius for putting people's backs up. (In fact he shared many of the traits of Puritan settlers – self-belief and a conviction that he knew best about God.)

In the winter of 1642 Miantonomo sold Gorton land at Shawomet, now Warwick, Rhode Island (no colonist would sell him land). Miantonomo's right to do so was forcefully challenged by the English, and he was yet again summoned to court in Boston. Not only was the Narragansetts' freedom of movement curtailed, Miantonomo's right to deal with his family's land how he pleased was now denied.

Samuel Gorton had considerable sympathy with the Narragansett royal family, who were astonished not to be treated as if they were the Bay's equals. To the colonists' intense annoyance, Gorton started to tell Miantonomo that the Indian's peer was Charles I. Lion Gardiner heard from his sachem friends that Miantonomo told his chiefs not to give any more *wampum* tribute to the English, 'for they are no Sachems, nor none of their children shall be in their place if they die; and they have no tribute given them; there is but one king in England, who is over them all'. Gorton's friendship with Miantonomo made him a traitor when the New England colonies were in a state of siege.

Gorton was encouraging Miantonomo to resist the main power in the land. In Edward's view Gorton and his friends had acted as the Narragansetts' 'tutors, secretaries and prompters to suggest their greatness and our weakness to them'.

Feeling so outnumbered in the huge foreign land, and under pressure to save their lives that winter, the New England colonies resembled military garrisons. Loyalty was everything. Fiercely independent views had taken the Puritans to America, but now they were living in a state of siege there was no room for quirky individual thought. At a time of hysteria exacerbated by the Indian threat, and when the success of New England was believed so much to depend on fulfilling the terms of its godly covenant, Gorton could not be viewed rationally. He was perceived as posing a huge danger to the New England mission, though in fact his way of treating Miantonomo as an equal and great chief might indeed have been a better way forward.

For his part Miantonomo was assaulted by angry feelings of grievance. Around thirty years old and at the peak of his powers, in every way he was hemmed in. He kept the peace, although he was said to have hired an assassin to kill Uncas. In fact, had Miantonomo's life been less circumscribed, his all-consuming antagonism might have come to an end. It is not clear that he still planned to enact a conspiracy against the English – his real focus was on Uncas, whom he was determined to murder – but most colonists believed Miantonomo was continuing to send secret signals to allied Indian tribes that they should be prepared to rise, and that payments to the Mohawks had not ceased.

Edward and the leaders at Boston and Plymouth felt as frustrated as Miantonomo. The New England magistrates wondered who would rid them of this troublesome sachem. The answer was not long in coming.

As Uncas schemed how to accrue more territory and power via the English, fate rolled the dice in his favour. A sachem of Connecticut and a cousin of Miantonomo, Sequasson, was involved in a skirmish with Uncas and the Mohegans. At a time of maximum tension, what was just one of the many little border fights which were part of the Indian pattern of life made the Connecticut settlers fear for their lives and their cattle. Sequasson asked Miantonomo for help. Maddened by not being able to hunt or even move in the country of his ancestors, Miantonomo leapt at the chance to attack his hated rival.

As much as he disliked rules, Miantonomo was nevertheless careful to appear to abide by them. He asked for Boston's permission – as he had been constrained to by their treaty – to go to war against Uncas. Boston did not veto it. The answer came: it was up to him. Miantonomo did not approach Connecticut. He may have felt such anger at the Treaty of Hartford, which had removed the Pequot country from him at a stroke, that he elected to ignore it. Perhaps tired by treaties which he could not read, he thought one English group's permission was enough.

In the summer of 1643, with 1,000 men he went after Uncas, who he knew had only 400 or so warriors, pursuing him to the edge of his fort at Shantok, situated between two rivers. The rival chiefs met on the plains below the fort by the Thames River. Throughout the hot August night Uncas's scouts watched the palisaded fort. The moonlit plain seemed empty, but Miantonomo's men were hidden in trees and rocks, their faces painted black.

When Uncas saw that he was heavily outnumbered, he asked for a parley. It took place before both armies, which were drawn up facing each other. Uncas asked for single combat. When, as Uncas had predicted, Miantonomo rejected this, Uncas dropped to the ground as if he had been attacked. It was a secret signal. The Mohegans let fly with their arrows, and the unprepared Narragansetts fled. Many of them did not know there was a bend in the river close by. The path unexpectedly came out onto cliffs and a gorge through which ran swirling rapids. It is said hundreds of Narragansetts perished when they fell to their deaths in the foaming Yantic Falls.

While the Narragansett braves were in their usual leather breeches, Miantonomo himself was weighed down by the suit of English armour lent to him by Gortonists who naturally had taken the Narragansetts' side. He was unaccustomed to wearing heavy armour, which prevented him from escaping quickly. According to John Winthrop, two of his captains saw he was struggling. Hoping to save their own lives, the traitors dragged their leader to Uncas. The ruthless Uncas rewarded them by dashing out their brains.

Witnesses said Miantonomo stood mute and Uncas jeered at him: 'If you had taken me . . . I would have besought you for my life.'

Unable to resist causing mischief and genuinely sorry for Miantonomo, Samuel Gorton added his usual inflammatory ha'p'orth to the stew. He sent a message to Uncas as if from the Boston government, saying Miantonomo must be released. He had considerable sympathy for the magnificent chief who had been personally generous to him. Instead, Miantonomo was borne in triumph to Connecticut by Uncas. On the march to Hartford an exhausted Miantonomo made one final attempt at a pan-Indian rising. He offered a blood alliance to Uncas, the tie which was valued above all others by the Indians. He would marry Uncas's daughter, and proposed his brother Pessicus should marry one of Massasoit's daughters to unite all the Indians against the English invaders.

According to some accounts Uncas did briefly pause and think about it before he pressed on to Hartford cunningly to ask the magistrates' advice as to what should happen to his captive. Miantonomo was interested in religious questions. In conversation with his braves on the issue of where heaven was, he had said that it was not clear – was it to the south-west? Now he might find out for himself.

A hundred miles away at Boston, the commissioners of the United Colonies met to decide what should be done. They included Edward, who had ridden over from Marshfield. They were all of the same opinion as John Winthrop, who frankly admitted to his diary regarding Miantonomo 'that it would not be safe to set him at liberty, neither had we sufficient ground to put him to death'. They decided to take advantage of the General Assembly of Elders to ask what they should do. Without any qualms the clergymen ordered death.

This conference met in the utmost secrecy because they worried that if word got out to the Narragansetts, they might kidnap some of the commissioners on their way home and use them as hostages to bargain for Miantonomo's life. The Mohawks were reported to be within a day's journey of Hartford waiting for Miantonomo's signal. It never came.

The commissioners asked Uncas and his men to take Miantonomo away from Hartford jail, where its governor, John Haynes, was holding him, and execute him themselves. They phrased it thus: 'These things being duly weighed' they believed that Uncas 'cannot be safe while Miantonomo lives' and that by secret treachery or open force his life would still be in danger. Uncas could 'justly put such a false blood-thirsty enemy to death, but in his own jurisdiction, not in the English plantations'. Because Uncas had shown himself a 'friend to the English, and in this craving their advice, if the Narragansett Indians or others shall unjustly assault Uncas for this execution, upon notice and request the English promise to assist and protect him, as far as they may against such violence'.

There were many stories about how Miantonomo met his end. One had Uncas's brother step up behind him unexpectedly on his march to Uncas's territory and bury a tomahawk in his head. Edward insisted Miantonomo had been put to death in a formal fashion in a house. The death was 'one blow with an hatchet on the side of the head as he walked easily in the room (expecting no less) which fully dispatched him at once'. There were two Englishmen there to ensure there was no torture, as was the Indians' usual custom. They were required by the commissioners 'to give him honourable burial, which they did and had thanks returned by the Narragansetts for those particulars'. How very far Edward had come in twenty-three years to describe the end of the pride of the Narragansetts. Samuel Gorton would muse how peculiar it was that Christian clergymen found it so easy to give the death penalty to an Indian. He wrote sarcastically that Uncas 'murdered him in cold blood, according to the direction of his Christian advisers'. Most historians nowadays see Miantonomo's death as judicial murder. The United Colonies got Uncas to do their dirty work and he was more than happy to comply.

The English had not felt safe while Miantonomo was alive, yet they were no more secure after his death. Miantonomo's pan-Indian uprising had been thwarted, but the Narragansetts were doubly determined to destroy Uncas. Wild with the desire to avenge their executed leader, they brought New England to the brink of war periodically for many years thereafter. Their heartbreak created a burning hostility to the English that lasted for decades.

A month after Miantonomo's death scouts and trappers in the woods told the petrified towns they needed to be on permanent professional Indian watch. They braced themselves for bloodthirsty attacks. In Marshfield at a town meeting run by Edward the townsfolk were told to sleep in their clothes with arms ready by their beds on account of 'imminent danger near to the whole body of the English in this land'. There was to be a watch against the Indians in four parts of the town. The Winslows' home had a permanent sentry on duty to raise the alarm: one shot meant a neighbouring township had been attacked; two, that the Indians were attacking Marshfield. On the Sabbath all those able to bear arms had to bring them to the meeting house. They begged the colony government for a new barrel of gunpowder.

To Romantic nineteenth-century writers searching for heroes after the American Revolutionary Wars, Miantonomo was a sympathetic figure. His fate reminded the historian Samuel Drake of Napoleon: 'We do not say that the English of New England dreaded the power of Miantonomo as much as those of Old England did that of Napoleon afterwards; but that both were sacrificed in consequence of the fears of those into whose power the fortune of wars cast them, will not, we presume, be denied.'

Today a cairn of stones marks the spot where Miantonomo died. One of the most important authorities on the period, Neal Salisbury, believes that Miantonomo's peaceful prior record and his friendship with Roger Williams indicate that if Uncas had agreed to a pan-Indian front, as Miantonomo had requested on his last journey, there could have been an effective institutional counterweight to expansion by Connecticut and Massachusetts Bay. It would have stabilised 'Indian–European relations in and around what was soon to become Rhode Island'. Handled more thoughtfully after the Pequot War, Miantonomo might have behaved differently.

Roger Williams at the time believed that there were 'some sparks of true friendship' there. Miantonomo had just needed to be convinced that 'the English never intended to despoil him of the country'.

Gorton seems to have been genuinely sad. He reported that the Narragansetts mourned for a year and a half because of the enormity of the crime of executing a great prince. Although Edward disputed this because it reflected so badly on Massachusetts, there was no question that the Narragansetts were devastated. As Edward himself had reported many years previously, mourning was a huge part of Indian culture – it was so heartfelt it drew tears even from the English.

After a while the Narragansett women removed the black from their faces, and came off their knees. They had been wailing night and day. In the royal temple the Narragansett priests spoke continually of their loss.

Narragansetts remained dedicated to avenging his murder. If they did not do so, it would so 'lie upon their own heads, as to bring more miseries and evils upon them'. It was religiously ordained that they avenge their prince.

In the autumn Miantonomo's brother Pessicus sent huge amounts of *wampum* to John Winthrop as a gift, intended to allow them to attack Uncas. Winthrop kept the *wampum*, but sent back a message that the Bay and all the United Colonies were Uncas's friend, and vowed to protect him.

In the spring of 1644 Boston demanded the presence of Canonicus, Miantonomo's uncle, to make it clear that the Bay would take severe measures if the Narragansetts attacked the Mohegans and did not stop sending *wampum* to the Mohawks. But old Canonicus refused to come to a meeting. Uncharacteristically – for he had always been a man of courtesy – he kept the Massachusetts messengers waiting outside the wigwam in the rain. He did not care if they were insulted. He wanted them to know how grief-stricken the tribe was at Miantonomo's death. Canonicus was a man of intense emotions. When his own son had died he is said to have burned down his palace. After his nephew's death he could not bear to meet with the English. It was clear to him that Miantonomo had been right. The English were determined to wipe them out. But the Narragansetts had a wily friend in Gorton.

In the winter of 1643–4, shortly after Miantonomo's death, Gorton and his associates had been evicted from their homes at Shawomet by the Bay government. They were convicted of sedition and blasphemy – in a court that had no jurisdiction over them, in their view – and sentenced to hard labour in towns nearby. Fears that their anarchic ways might be contagious – as well as many colonists' considerable disapproval of their persecution – got them released. But worried that their title was still in doubt, Gorton escaped to England. Furious at the way he had been treated, he approached the English Committee for Foreign Plantations to ask that he and his fellow planters be reinstated at

Shawomet. Lord Warwick was the friend and sponsor of Puritan colonies, but he also believed in freedom of religion. He told Massachusetts that they must leave Gorton's settlement alone. As a gesture of gratitude, the Gortonogs – as the Indians called them – renamed it Warwick.

Gorton saw parallels between the oppression of the Narragansetts and his own. He told the Narragansetts they too should put themselves under the protection of the English government. The Puritans were in bad odour back home. He reported, Edward wrote, 'us to be base and low, out of favour with the king and state'. Gorton played on the fact that any court cases in New England had a higher legislature in the shape of Charles I, a notion that was to become an important part of Indian political thinking. He and his friends drew up a document on 19 April 1644 for the Narragansetts: 'The Act and Deed of the voluntary submission of the Chief Sachem and the rest of the princes, with the whole people of the Narragansetts, to the government and protection of that honourable state of Old England.' In theory that meant other colonies must leave them alone. Roger Williams also successfully appealed to Warwick on behalf of all the plantations on and round Rhode Island for a special patent to protect them against Massachusetts.

When the Bay ordered the Narragansetts to court once more to lecture them about attacking Uncas, the tribe responded in writing that they still intended to wage war against Uncas to avenge the death of Miantonomo and others of their people whom he had slain. If they had problems with this, the matter should be referred to Charles I. The letter was signed not with signatures but with symbols: Canonicus's was a hammer, described as 'The mark of that ancient Canonicus protector of that late deceased Miantonomo during the time of his nonage [minority or youth]'.

The Narragansetts could not know that Charles I was about to be defeated and would be in no position to defend them. They remained recalcitrant and defiant. Around the same time the Powhatans in Virginia launched a final attempt to drive the English out of their lands. It seemed as if all the English colonies were at risk of perishing.

Anne Hutchinson's husband had died in 1642. Worried about her own position vis-à-vis an expansionist Massachusetts, she decided to move from Rhode Island to New York state, into remote territory disputed between the Dutch and Indians. But there she and all but one of her children were surrounded by Indians and scalped.

This was interpreted as God's judgement on her. Thomas Weld, the revered minister at Roxbury, wrote he had never heard of the Indians in those parts attacking like that, 'therefore God's hand is the more apparently seen herein, to pick out this woeful woman, to make her and those belonging to her an unheard of heavy example'.

After a year of skirmishing and raids, the Narragansetts surrounded Uncas in his fort at Shantok, intending to starve him out. A messenger was sent to Pessicus, Miantonomo's successor, to tell him to move away. Loath as they were to go to war again, the United Colonies felt duty-bound to defend what Edward described as 'Uncas our confederate'. The Narragansetts received the messengers from the commissioners with contempt. They said there would be no peace without Uncas's head. The English should not try and assist Uncas or they would 'procure the Mohawks against them'. They threatened that 'they would lay the English cattle on heaps as high as their houses, and that no Englishman should stir out of his door to piss, but he should be killed'. Canonicus remarked fatalistically that 'the young Sachems, being but boys, will need war, and so set all the country in Combustion'.

An army of 300 men assembled at Boston. It was the last military outing for peppery Myles Standish. Amongst the fray were Massasoit and his men. It was a fearsome-looking troop commanded by Edward Gibbons which made its way west to meet the men of Plymouth, Connecticut and New Haven.

Just before the Massachusetts troops arrived Myles Standish saw the Rhode Islanders take the Indians into their houses even though they were armed. He sent Roger Williams a furious message which 'required them to lay aside their neutrality, and either declare themselves on the one side or other'. But the Narragansetts lost their nerve at the thought of such a great army coming against them. They sued for peace.

At Providence, however, the tender friendship between Roger Williams and Canonicus continued. Williams was particularly distraught about the treatment of the Narragansetts. He continued to see them as peaceful people, as he would report in a book written for the English market. *A Key into the Language of America* was a study mainly of the Narragansett tribe and the Algonquian language intended to show the humanity of the Indians. Written on board ship on his way to England to get his charter, and published in 1644, the book became a bestseller in the England of the Civil War. The reason he could be so empathetic with the Indians was that they were descended from Adam. For him, it was 'admirable to see, what paths their naked, hardened feet have worn through the wilderness, even in the most stony places'. He could not help contrasting the Indians' kindly treatment of him with the colonists': when 'the hearts of my countrymen and friends and brethren failed me' God stirred up 'the barbarous heart of Canonicus to love me as his son to his last gasp'. As far as he was concerned, 'Nature knows no difference between Europe and Americans in blood, birth, bodies etc.' But that was increasingly not the position of the English.

The fact that the Indians were barbarians did not matter – Roger Williams had concluded, after much soul-searching, that the true uncorrupt church had vanished with the Apostles. In his 1645 tract *Christenings Make Not Christians*, he wrote how his friendship with the Indians meant he could have converted the whole country. But to convert them 'from one false worship to another, and the profanation of the holy name of God', was pointless. In his view man had to wait for the next Revelation, whenever that would come.

In *A Key*, trying to demonstrate the Indian word *wunnaumwayean*, meaning 'if he say true', Williams wrote:

'Canonicus . . . once in a solemn oration to myself in a solemn assembly, using this word, said, "I have never suffered any wrong to be offered to the English since they landed; nor never will". He often repeated this word "*wunnaumwayean*": "If the Englishman speaks true, if he means truly, then shall I go to my grave in peace, and hope that the English and my posterity shall live in love and peace together". I replied, that he had no cause (as I hoped) to question Englishman's, "*wunnaumwauonck*", that is faithfulness, he having had long experience of their friendliness and trustiness. He took a stick and broke it into ten pieces, and related ten instances (laying down a stick to every instance) which gave him cause thus to fear . . . I satisfied him on some presently, and presented the rest to the governors of the English, who I hope will be far from giving just cause to have Barbarians question their "*wunnaumauonck*".'

In 1647 when Canonicus was dying – perhaps of a broken heart – he sent for Williams 'and desired to be buried in my cloth, of free gift', and so he was. Williams saw Canonicus as a great man. On 5 October 1654, when once again Massachusetts was threatening war against the Narragansetts, he reminded them of the persistent loyalty of the statesman who ensured his people had never shed English blood. To him the Narragansetts' 'late, famous long-lived Canonicus', 'their prudent and peacable prince', had qualities comparable to Boston's 'prudent peace-maker, Mr Winthrop'. Canonicus's funeral was celebrated with the same 'most honourable manner and solemnity, (in their way)', as the English laid Winthrop to sleep.

The days of trustful intimacy had passed. The rising power amongst the Narragansetts was Ninigret, the chief of a smaller tribe closely linked to the Narragansetts, the eastern Niantics.

The only existing painting of Ninigret shows a childlike figure in a headband and a pair of red shorts. But nothing about Ninigret was childlike. He was cunning personified. Recognising the inferior size of his tribe, his attitude was to play for time. While appearing to agree pleasantly with all points of treaties at the moment of making them, in practice he completely ignored them. Hostages were sent who were not royal children; the *wampum* was never delivered. Ninigret was not in the same heroic mould as Miantonomo. As a result he was a good deal more successful.

In behaviour recognisable 300 years later to leaders such as Gandhi who had no political power but the support of their people, the Narragansetts embarked on what has been described as passive resistance. A pattern developed: troops were sent and at the last moment the Narragansetts appeared to capitulate. A cold war developed and continued for over two decades with the English threatening war, but never having to wage it.

New men such as Humphrey Atherton, whose name was to become notorious for illegally taking Indian land, treated the Narragansett leaders discourteously. On one occasion Atherton stormed into Pessicus's wigwam, held him by the hair and demanded *wampum* holding while a pistol to him. It was a different era.

Passaconaway, sachem of the Pennacook people by the Merrimack River, made a point of paying tribute and submitting to the Bay. In 1660 he gave an apocalyptic warning to keep the peace with the English. 'Hearken to the words of your father,' he said.

'I am an old oak that has withstood the storms of more than a hundred winters . . . I who have had communion with the Great Spirit dreaming and awake – I am powerless before the Pale Faces . . . I commune with the Great Spirit. He whispers me now – "Tell your people, Peace, Peace, is the only hope of your race. I have given fire and thunder to the pale faces for weapons. I have made them plentier than the leaves of the forest, and still shall they increase! These meadows they shall turn with the plow – these forests shall fall by the axe – the pale faces shall live upon your hunting grounds, and make their villages upon your fishing places!" The Great Spirit says this, and it must be so! We are few and powerless before them! We must bend before the storm! The wind blows hard! The old oak trembles! Its branches are gone! Its sap is frozen! It bends! It falls! Peace, Peace, with the white men – is the command of the Great Spirit – and the wish – the last wish – of Passaconaway.'

In 1646 Penelope Pelham was a thirteen-year-old girl a little worried by the Indians but not much. The possibility of sinning was much more alarming, as her stepmother Elizabeth, now married to her father, Herbert Pelham, was very godly and a little stern. The family lived in Cambridge on the corner between Dunster and South streets with a view to the marshes and the Charles River. Her father's land was near the new towns of Sudbury and Framingham, named after their home towns in East Anglia.

The Civil War in England had caused the economy of New England to go into free fall. The intricate web of debts and bills of exchange which reached across the Atlantic very nearly disintegrated beneath the onslaught of falling prices and foreign commodities becoming unaffordable. Elizabeth and Herbert Pelham went back to East Anglia. Herbert needed to attend to his inheritance from his first wife's family, the Waldegraves. He had a lawsuit pending against his brother-in-law, who had moved into his property, the manor house Ferriers at Bures St Mary. Most likely he was excited because his father-in-law, Colonel Godfrey Bossevile, was on a number of important committees in the new regime. That might advance his fortunes.

Herbert may have always seen New England as a speculative venture and never intended to live there forever. But for his teenage daughter Penelope, who had left England when she was five, Massachusetts was home. An atmosphere of submission to the Lord who held the colony in His mighty hand was the background to her upbringing. For the old and the scholarly, Satan was always lurking. New England could be a harsh place for anyone with ideas of their own after the horror of the Anne Hutchinson scandal. Public learnedness in women fell under suspicion for a generation. At her trial Anne had been told: 'you have stepped out of your place; you [would] rather have been a husband than a wife, and a preacher than a hearer'.

Along with her brother Nathaniel – who was to be educated at Harvard before looking after the Pelham estates – Penelope elected to remain in Boston. They were to reside at their aunt Penelope Bellingham and Governor Bellingham's house while the rest of the family took a ship back to England. Penelope liked being part of a close-knit community in Boston, privileged and protected by her position as Governor Bellingham's niece.

CHAPTER XII

Leaving for London, 1646

New England had narrowly escaped another war with the Indians. But Massachusetts faced a continuing crisis about competing ideas of political authority. Although the town deputies now had their own separate assembly, their growing numbers demanded greater powers from the magistrates. Many were discontented with the churches excluding newcomers who, in a challenge to the old order, were demanding civil rights.

Those who were not members of the covenanted Puritan churches were barred from political and commercial life, effectively second-class citizens. To vote you had to be a freeman, and to be a freeman you had to be a member of a church. And you still had to contribute to your local church even if you were not allowed to belong to it. Under threat of a severe fine, every Lord's Day you were obliged to appear at your local congregation. Many simply moved on to the greater freedoms of the Rhode Island plantations – heretical or not – to live under less oppressive rules.

The orthodox party at Boston headed by Governor Winthrop was furious. Edward took it personally, as did Governor William Bradford, and they tried to tighten up the rules. In the summer of 1645 Boston's General Court attempted to persuade the other New England colonies to introduce legislation to make church membership even more exclusive, such as allowing baptism only to church members and their children. These measures were intended to suppress any settlements which opposed and undermined the Scriptures – such as Anne Hutchinson's – 'under a deceitful colour of liberty of conscience', as the United Colonies commissioners put it.

To Edward's outrage his close neighbour William Vassall was one of the pro-toleration party. Vassall had drafted a bill for freedom of religion at Plymouth. Most of the deputies backed Vassall, but Bradford refused to allow the matter to come to a vote, and Edward concurred. Today what Vassall wanted sounds innocuous enough – 'full and free tolerance of religion to all men that would preserve the civil peace, and submit unto Government' – but to Edward and Bradford that would put an end to a New England built on churches which had covenants with God. For some time Edward had been infuriated by Vassall's attempt to disseminate what he regarded as the 'spirit of division ... creeping in amongst us'.

But William Vassall's point was that he had left England for freedom of conscience. If he could not have that in New England, where could he have it? In May 1645 he asked a local minister, Ralph Partridge, 'Shall we never be at rest, nor suffered to worship God according to our consciences?' More poignantly, he also wanted to know 'how is it that the persecuted have become persecutors?'

In 1646, amidst mounting tensions as the lower house of deputies flexed their muscles and demanded a legal code not at the discretion of the magistrates, rebels upped the stakes. Vassall had already secretly appealed to the English government to intervene when Winthrop waded into the election of a militia leader in the small town of Hingham. Winthrop was forced to defend himself in court against the charges of arbitrary government. Vassall and the other merchants now presented a highly critical Remonstrance or petition to the General Court. It accused Massachusetts of extreme cruelty to those who were not members of the independent congregational churches. But as far as Edward and his friends were concerned, this was not England and English laws should not have to apply. By criticising membership of the independent Puritan churches, the Remonstrance undermined the whole basis of the New England experiment.

William Vassall had a powerful brother, Samuel, who was an MP in London. He had been on the committee which was behind the recent granting of freedom of religion to Bermuda. If Bermuda, why not Massachusetts?

Massachusetts moved to defend its privileges in the way it knew best – with extreme severity.

Although the Remonstrance was in the name of an English merchant – Dr Robert Child, who was visiting Boston to explore the manufacture of iron – Vassall was one of its most important authors. Most inconveniently for Edward, Vassall was the father-in-law of Edward's beloved stepson Resolved White (Susanna's son by her first marriage), and lived far too close – at Scituate, the next town to Marshfield. Although in the past they had been friends Vassall was now hated by Edward, who regarded him as being behind the dangerous unrest. Vassall's 'busy and factious spirit' made him a threat to civil authority. Edward was a kindly man but his anger led to disdain. In what was to become a pamphlet war in England and Massachusetts, Edward described in biting words how Vassall had encouraged the others: Vassall knew better 'how to ripen such fruit than all the coster-mongers in London'.

Vassall came from a highly respectable family and was extremely wealthy, with property in London as well as New England, Barbados, Marshfield and Scituate. An early member of the Massachusetts Bay Company, he had moved to Plymouth because it was less oppressive than the Bay. In 1640 Resolved married Judith Vassall, a marriage which at the time had seemed appropriate and pleasing. The young Whites farmed at Scituate and then Marshfield until 1662 when Judith died. They also had a farm on the North River. Resolved was given one hundred acres bordering his father-in-law's land – a generous bequest. Resolved had grown into a thoughtful young man who also helped farm Edward's land at Marshfield. Edward had brought him up as his own son. Josiah, Edward's son with Susanna, who was almost a decade younger, regarded Resolved as his brother, as his will makes clear. The dispute with Vassall was not only intensely inconvenient – it was also very sad.

The Winslows and Vassalls, two well-to-do and godly families, had once been on cordial visiting terms. Edward was pleased to meet a neighbour with an interest in political ideas in a place where many of his relations were good people but not intellectual. (Edward some-times felt starved of learned company, hence the frequent visits to Boston and his fascination with the cultivated John Winthrop.) Edward therefore initially enjoyed long discussions with Vassall over haunches of venison or hunched against the wind along the pale Atlantic shore as the two men walked together. Vassall pressed on Edward what to him was now a blinding necessity, and he tried to draw his friend over to religious toleration. But Edward was immoveable: the covenant with God through their New England churches had preserved them in the wilderness.

However, Vassall's ideas about a more inclusive religion were wel-comed by some of Edward's own family. Parish records show that Josiah and Edward's nephew Kenelm joined the liberal church Vassall founded at Scituate, which was not particular about allowing Com-munion to those who were not church members. Some were even members of the Church of England. Vassall insisted it was no crime:

'that sweet communion of souls, the love of brethren, so highly com-
mended to us by the Holy Ghost is not broken but for great failings'.
Perhaps even Susanna attended services there, possibly believing that
Edward had become rigid and too much under the influence of the
severe John Winthrop. She may have disapproved of the reaction to
Anne Hutchinson and her terrible death. (One of the accusations
against Jane Hawkins, Mistress Hutchinson's friend and fellow midwife, was that she had given women herbs for fertility. This was a
charge which the commonsensical Susanna may have viewed with
some contempt.)

The busy, bulky figure of Edward, who perpetually had business on
hand, who always had time for everyone, had changed. He had become
much harsher in his judgements. In 1644 he personally approved
the extradition to Massachusetts for adultery of Mary Latham, the
eighteen-year-old wife of a Marshfield farmer. The tragic girl was executed, and died 'very penitently'. In a pathetic speech from the scaffold
on Boston Common she urged 'all young maids to be obedient to their
parents, and to take heed of evil company'. (Massachusetts enforced
the death penalty more rigorously than Plymouth, where, although
it was on the statute books, it was never implemented.) Of course
Edward was not alone in demanding strict rules. Parts of his community
remained harsh. Even his own dear stepson Peregrine and his wife
Sarah were convicted of premarital fornication in 1648–9 (though
their sentence was commuted to a fine).

The anxious scrawny youth who had scrabbled for shellfish by the
sea fresh off the *Mayflower* had gone forever. Edward was now a man
who owned 1,000 acres and his figure reflected that. The body that
had once survived on Indian rations had swelled into luxuriant folds,
enjoying a superb diet he shot for his family on his estate. But he
increasingly felt he was not living amongst kindred spirits. Perhaps
he was too successful. In December 1639 he wrote of how 'Malicious
and slanderous persons' were defaming him 'with impudent, false and
shameless reports to my no small grief and trouble'. He now spent
more time with the people of Massachusetts than those of Plymouth.
Far more hardline in every way, he had drawn much closer to Boston,
especially once Vassall began operating in his neighbourhood. As a
United Colonies commissioner he had to spend the night in Boston on
a regular basis. Edward had become sufficiently close friends with the
merchant Robert Keayne, one of Boston's most notorious figures, to be
made an executor of his will.

Edward had a confessional relationship with John Winthrop in Boston which he does not seem to have been able to replicate in Marshfield. In the winter he often felt marooned in his home. Paths became impassable in December, and the sea dangerous. The weather forced Edward to kick his heels at Careswell, missing 'many godly and precious friends and brethren I have both in Boston and elsewhere amongst you'. Perhaps he and Susanna also drifted apart when one of their sons died in 1640 (it is not clear whether this was Edward junior or John, who are mentioned in the Division of Cattle in 1627 but of whom nothing else is heard). Edward saw it as God punishing him for his pride. Susanna may have concentrated on her loss.

Plymouth did not have the overseas merchants and their capital which Edward and his brother John needed. It did not have the contacts in English commercial circles which were so important for success. Boston had those connections naturally, and the ambitious Winslows gravitated there.

Soon after its founding Boston became the main seat of importing, followed by Salem. And with that came all the little seedlings of culture and information that accrue to a big port town – whether they were ideas, or news, or foodstuffs, or articles of manufacture. Plymouth harbour was unsuitable for transatlantic business as it could not accommodate deep-water vessels. The presence of the Massachusetts colony thirty miles north stymied Plymouth's development. The first ship had been built in what was to become Boston port in 1631, and a shipbuilding industry rapidly followed. The Winslows became very much part of the bustling Boston scene, a city growing with extraordinary speed from the village of farms with which it began. It is unsurprising that John Winslow, who became one of Boston's wealthier merchants, should choose to move there in 1656. He had started trading with the West Indies via Boston when the English Civil War and Royalist warships made English seas too dangerous for commerce.

Edward's friendship with Massachusetts leaders and his openness to other colonies – like many other elements in Edward Winslow's variegated life – were not perceived with unalloyed approbation by Plymouth. In the spring of 1645 the United Colonies suggested Plymouth became a partner in the fur trade with all the other colonies. But this offer was firmly turned down. There was such 'a disproportion in our estates to theirs' that they would not do well as a poor relation against much wealthier partners. What Plymouth did have was excellent trade up the coast. The towns on the north-eastern sea-board depended on Plymouth to provide things they lacked: tallow, pork, beef, hides, oil from whales, hemp, tar and timber.

As a Plymouth farmer Edward was preoccupied with everyday decisions about trading (in one letter he says he had to send cattle to the Boston market but 'the weather is so hot, the fly so busy and the woods so thick' he decided to send them by water). But what got him out of bed in the morning was the thought of 'that great and weighty work which doth so much concern the glory of God in raising up his church among us'. And like all the New England politicos of his day, Edward was fascinated by the godly revolution in England.

Success beyond the wildest dreams of the Puritan party had begun with the extraordinary spectacle of Charles I invading Scotland, to impose the Anglican prayer book on the Scottish church. The defeat of local English militias left the Scottish army on the English side of the border at Newcastle, and Charles I had to call the Long Parliament in late 1640, to pass finance bills after the Bishops' War with Scotland had bankrupted him. Within a week, in return for granting money for an army and to the amazement of the New England Puritans, their great enemy William Laud, the Archbishop of Canterbury, was impeached.

Edward found it hard to keep his thoughts from the maelstrom blowing through the mother country. He badgered John Winthrop for information and lamented news of his old friend Lord Coventry's death. Since his spell in prison Edward had got to know John Winthrop's brother-in-law Emmanuel Downing. He and his wife, Lucy Winthrop, had moved to New England in 1638 and were in touch with informed opinion in London. In a letter to John Winthrop that summer Edward asked to be remembered to them: 'what will be the issue of these sore beginnings the Lord only knoweth, but it concerneth us deeply to be affected with them as a people that must share with them in weal and woe'.

The Long Parliament got all Laud's reforms thrown out, and the 'papist' altar rails destroyed. The Court of High Commission which had terrorised Puritans was no more. There were riots in London against bishops. John Winthrop's contacts in high places meant information about the dramatic changes in England arrived by every ship. One in four New Englanders who returned to England to fight in the Civil War or participate in the Republic were from Massachusetts.

*

Edward's brothers, whose farms surrounded him at Marshfield, had none of his ambitious interests. There was now quite a number of houses scattered all over the marshes with fine views out to sea. By 1640 Marshfield had its own church and was officially incorporated as a town. Josiah, Edward's brother, was town clerk for many years. Always present at the meetings held in the Marshfield church, he was a little slow at writing and rather disorganised. The same brotherly spirit that had got Josiah employed for Plymouth's trading company meant the impatient Edward shrugged his shoulders as papers cascaded to the floor. Josiah's disorderliness may have been the reason it took well over a decade to get permission for a town corn mill on the South River.

As governor in 1636, Edward had been the driving force behind getting a legal code for Plymouth that year. He was a man with a flair for organisation and had a passionate energy which meant he could never be still. For periods, that ardent fervour burnt low like a pilot light; but with the Remonstrance it flared up again. When New Englanders first started going back to England, Edward also felt a yearning to return. At the end of December 1646, he got his chance.

Although Vassall's associate Robert Child had been imprisoned, Vassall himself had escaped with a copy of the petition. It was thought the petitioners intended to demand a governor general to enforce Presbyterian rule and revoke the charter. It was very important that someone went to Old England and put the case for New England.

In a public-relations disaster that August, Samuel Gorton had done just what Edward feared: published an account of being persecuted at Shawomet, and manhandling and vicious treatment by the Bay's commissioners. Even the Indians, he said, were treated nastily. The Narragansetts had asked 'how we could live, seeing the Massachusetts had not only taken our estates from us in goods and chattels, but also our houses, lands and labours, where we should raise more, for the preservation of our families, and withal told us that their condition, might (in great measure) be parallel with ours'.

Roger Williams, meanwhile, had written a devastating account of how he and other dissidents had been persecuted, to accompany his own petition for a royal charter for the Providence plantations.

Child's carefully itemised and reasoned Remonstrance was the third denunciation of the New England way of life. Thanks to its well-connected petitioners, it had the potential to do real damage.

With the confidence of a man who had been a grandee in Suffolk,

Winthrop believed Massachusetts would not be 'condemned before we are heard'. Edward was more suspicious. He had long feared Gorton spreading prejudice against New England. They needed to be better prepared in regard of the petitioners and many others who were very busy, and who 'insult and boast as if the victory were attained'. One of Edward's aims was to try and overturn the patent Lord Warwick had given allowing Gorton to settle at Shawomet and make sure Gorton was not allowed to return.

Edward urged Winthrop to send someone with the status of a professional diplomat to England to give the Privy Council the right information. He should be a man 'of wisdom and courage'. It was a 'common error' to have these affairs taken care of casually by colonists who happened to be over on business. As Edward told Winthrop severely, this issue was 'of such consequence' that if he failed to grasp the nettle he would repent it.

John Winthrop may have smiled to himself. That man of wisdom and courage, to beard the Committee of Parliament in its den, had better be Edward himself. Winthrop wrote a rare compliment in his journal: Edward was 'a fit man to be employed in our present affairs in England, both in regard of his abilities of presence, speech, courage, and understanding'. He had also become well known to the London commissioners over the years.

Despite it being late in the winter season for sailing, Edward departed for England in a mood of excited anticipation, even though one of the Child party said the mission was cursed because Edward's horse had died under him as he rode to Boston. And he had taken that seriously. But he was buoyed by what he saw as providentially good winds. As he got older Edward was apt to see providential interference where in the past he assumed human agency was the more probable explanation. Plymouth's and the other Puritan colonies' success against the odds made God's permanent intervention in human affairs demonstrable.

With the same zest with which he abandoned London for the Leiden church, he was to throw his energies into attacking the colonies' enemies in London, convincing the Committee for Plantations why it was so deleterious for them to interfere in New England and alter its way of life. A natural fighter, he thrilled to be in the thick of great events.

For as well as arguing on behalf of New England, he was also going to a place which seemed to bode great, even apocalyptic, times. The effective imprisonment of the king in the spring of 1646 after he surrendered to the Scottish army, and in October the abolition of episcopacy (insisted on by Parliament's Scottish Presbyterian allies), corresponded to the prophecies in the Book of Daniel taken so seriously by many New Englanders. Finishing his account of the colony's history full of pride in its extraordinary events, William Bradford wrote in 1650: 'Full little did I think, that the downfall of the Bishops, with their courts, cannons and ceremonies, had been so near, when I first began these scribbled writings.'

Edward took with him a series of letters he intended to publish about Massachusetts' new project of converting the Indians to Christianity. In 1644 a few Indians had submitted to the Massachusetts government and indicated some interest in learning something of their religion. These were regarded as 'hopeful signs', and John Eliot, a minister at Roxbury and close friend of Edward, had begun to preach to the Indians at Nonantum. Whether the chiefs who submitted really wanted to be Christian, whether they thought they would have greater power because the Christian God was powerful, or whether they were fearful of what would happen if they did not convert, Eliot's mission and that of the Mayhews on Martha's Vineyard from 1643 were astonishingly successful.

At first Edward was himself doubtful about the conversion of what he had come to think of as the Indians' frozen hearts. But as the evidence piled up, he began to think these Christian conversions might be a sign of the Second Coming.

Every bone in Edward's body was set to resist the imposition of English rule. The colonies must be allowed to rule themselves. If they had to wait until 'we have leave from England, our throats might be all cut before the messenger would be half seas through'.

In later years Edward was compared to Hercules for his work defending New England's independence. He had no premonition that he never would see again the country he helped create.

He exchanged a land with dramatic waterfalls, whose rivers, 'having their Originals from great lakes', were hastening to the sea, for the homeland he had not lived in for over a quarter of a century. There were no tobacco pipes of stone with imagery upon them, and the quills of the porcupine were not an adornment. The land he had helped fashion became a dream of the past. The deer carried by Indians past his windows or spotted far away in the distance amidst the pine forests were replaced by their cousins in the deer parks which his new circle owned.

Did he take a final voyage in the creek at the foot of his house across through Duxbury Marsh to Plymouth? He may have said an ordinary farewell as people do before the start of a long journey. William Bradford was displeased by the amount of time Edward spent on Massachusetts business and his going to England for Plymouth's sister colony. Perhaps Edward decided instead to have a quiet drink with Myles Standish, whose house was closer. He probably asked Standish to keep an eye on Susanna and Josiah, who was now nineteen, and his daughter Elizabeth, who was fifteen.

The Indian threat was over, at least for the time being, and no more guns were taken to church. Many of Edward's relations lived just a few fields away. The cattle on the salt marshes below Careswell were mostly descended from the three Edward had brought across the ocean. Peregrine had planted apple trees on the land Edward had given him. A young man of twenty-six when Edward departed, Peregrine was a common sight riding across the country in a coat with big buttons the size of a silver dollar, to visit his mother.

There must have been some kind of farewell between Edward and Massasoit. If not as tender as in the past, their relationship had the comfortable quality of long association. Edward needed to make sure his family was protected by the Wampanoags since his long-term views about Indian treachery were so pessimistic. But the Indians seemed well under control, and he would soon be back.

In April 1644, two years before Edward left for England, William Brewster had died. William Bradford wrote how fortunate he was to die in his bed, in peace, given that so many of the early settlers met violent deaths. The gentle Brewster died in the midst of his friends 'who mourned and wept over him, and ministered what help and comfort they could unto him, and he again, recomforted them whilst he could'. He still managed to be up and about even on the day of his death: 'His speech continued till somewhat more than half a day, and then failed him; and about 9 or 10 o'clock that evening he died, without any pangs at all . . . he drew his breath long, as a man fallen into a sound sleep, without any pangs or gaspings, and so sweetly departed this life unto a better.'

Brewster was borne to his final rest on the shoulders of the younger men of the colony, as well as his son Jonathan and his grandsons who had come from Connecticut. The boon companions of Brewster's *Mayflower* youth were gnarled men approaching sixty, an age that was positively elderly in the seventeenth century. William Bradford recalled Brewster's grand origins, heroic life and death on the American frontier. Bradford wondered whether Brewster had been tested too harshly: had his friend been the worse for his sufferings? No, he was the better, Bradford concluded, and they only added to his honour. Brewster could be sure of his heavenly reward. Relishing the simple grave they dug for Brewster at Duxbury, Bradford dismissed Brewster's lack of 'the riches and pleasures of the world in this life, and pompous monuments at his funeral'. He wrote defiantly in his diary that 'the memorial of the just shall be blessed, when the name of the wicked shall rot (with their marble monuments)'.

Edward was not at all ready for such peaceful oblivion. The momentous events taking place in London were an irresistible magnet.

As time passed, Bradford regarded Edward's absence as an act of desertion. He later wrote sourly: 'By reason of the great alterations in the State, he was detained longer than was expected; and afterwards fell into other employments there, so as he hath now been absent this four years, which hath been much to the weakening of this government, without whose consent he took these employments upon him.'

CHAPTER XIII

Republican England

In New England, as a commissioner for the United Colonies, a former governor at Plymouth and a founder of Marshfield, Edward was a person of importance with a large estate. In London he had to re-establish himself. Life in London was always beset with problems for New Englanders because of a lack of cash, but discomfort had never put him off before – and neither had his pride. The same trust in God buoyed him up as it had all his life. He said of Gorton, 'He can act no more than God hath determined'. The belief that everything was in God's hands led to a wonderful confidence.

England was almost unrecognisable after four years of war, polarised as never before. Brothers had fought against brothers. Parliament had taken over all Charles I's functions. Quite unthinkably the monarch was a prisoner of the Scots. About 100,000 people had died, amongst them Archbishop William Laud, the chief reason so many colonists had left for New England, who had been executed on Tower Hill in 1645. Many survivors suffered from terrible injuries. The countryside had been ravaged, and the agrarian poor were starving. Most Royalist land was in the process of being confiscated. Many of the more ordinary gentlemen from old families were penniless. The landscape was transformed by officious Parliamentary soldiers who occupied county towns as garrisons. Edward had serious worries about the condition of his sister Magdalen and her family.

The ancient Dorset family she had married into had suddenly found their world turned upside down. In the great upheaval Anglican clergy were expelled from their vicarages in counties controlled by the Parliamentary armies. The Wake family were one such casualty. Edward's brother-in-law, a parson with a robust temperament, was as Royalist in his sympathies as Edward was Parliamentarian. Despite their religious differences Edward had strong family feelings, and his brother-in-law was a fine man.

Although Edward's purpose was to lobby Westminster and make

sure New England was not interfered with, he was also determined to find his sister. He had written to her at the charming, pale stone vicarage in Wareham on the coast. It was no longer her home.

Magdalen and her family had suffered horribly during the war. Her Royalist husband had been singled out for punishment. The Reverend Wake's preaching made him a man of huge influence in the surrounding area. He was accounted the reason for the town all being 'dreadful malignants'. When a Parliamentary local declared he had the authority to fortify the town, the fiery Wake challenged him in the marketplace. He was shot twice in the head and carried home by members of his flock (one of his loyal workers in the vicarage's fields challenged the Parliamentary soldiers with her spade). Wake was imprisoned for a year in Dorchester, in agony from his wounds.

Magdalen and her three children were turned out of doors. All their possessions had been looted in front of them. Wake's assets were seized and his estate was forfeit for being a rebel.

Not at all in good health, the parson next joined the Royalist army. He was at the siege of Sherborne Castle when he was paraded naked through the town. Then, in a prisoner exchange, he was one of the defenders during the legendary siege of nearby Corfe Castle, where Lady Bankes held out for three years. Because Wake's money had been sequestered, Magdalen – who had been a considerable figure in Wareham as the vicar's wife – was destitute as well as homeless. She and her daughter worked at humble jobs to put food in the mouths of the younger children.

On arriving in England, Edward probably gave Magdalen and her younger children a home, while one of her sons became involved in some of Edward's business ventures.

It may have been Edward's influence that helped the Wake children to get back pay for their father from the Dorset county committee in 1648. Like many New Englanders he had powerful friends amongst England's new rulers. Despite her strong character Magdalen seems to have had a nervous collapse and was unable to petition herself. Her children succeeded: the Reverend Wake's successor was ordered to pay Magdalen £15 for the year, starting with the arrears to provide for herself, her mother and her siblings. There were further orders for later years.

Edward now turned his attention to the onerous task for which he had been sent over. Gorton's, Vassall's and Child's fierce critiques had to be argued against immediately. His great anxiety was that the Parliamentary Committee for Plantations might not see Massachusetts' point of view. Edward could not rely on his oratory to sway the Earl of Warwick and his friends. He had not forgotten his earlier experience as a pamphleteer for the young colony of Plymouth. Written submissions were needed. Upon arrival he published an attack on Gorton, *Hypocrisy Unmaskd*.

Edward's dander was up. He wanted to take on all enemies of the New England way of life. Yet he was anxious not to insult Roger Williams, of whom he was so fond. Despite Williams' attempts to damage Massachusetts, Edward felt he remained 'a man lovely in his carriage, and whom I trust the Lord will yet recall'.

On the committee there were many Presbyterians – who were pro-toleration – but there were also representatives of the Independent party. Sir Arthur Hesilrige, for example, was sympathetic to the vision of Massachusetts that Edward put forward. Edward knew several of the commissioners, including George Fenwick, who had actually lived at Saybrook in Connecticut and had briefly been the fort's commander after the Pequot War. Fenwick and Edward had both been commissioners for the United Colonies. Fenwick was now the MP for Morpeth and Edward immediately got in touch with him to deliver a letter from John Winthrop.

London was in a poor state in 1647. Though it had never been attacked, it was surrounded by ugly earthworks, which had been thrown up for eighteen miles round the city for its defence. Trade was only starting to revive. Nevertheless, for all its ragged state the capital required more formal clothing than Plymouth or Boston. Edward led an expensive life, wining and dining the influential. By the time he died he was hundreds of pounds in debt. Perhaps he was careless, living in lodgings away from his family, initially with his old friend James Sherley, the goldsmith who had been an original investor in the Plymouth colony. He may have taken larger premises to house Magdalen and her children. Perhaps everything in London cost more than he had anticipated.

But he also had a benevolent new friend in the shape of Herbert Pelham, who made his life more pleasant and introduced him to some important politicians on the Plantations Committee. Edward and Pelham had got to know one another in Boston when they sat as United Colonies commissioners. Now back in England, Pelham knew several important Independent politicians. He introduced Edward to Sir Arthur Hesilrige, to whom he himself was connected.

Pelham was alarmed at the low financial state Edward found himself in. Many of Pelham's relations and friends, including his own father-in-law, Colonel Bossevile, had been involved in Puritan colonisation projects with the Earl of Warwick. It was in front of Warwick in the Parliamentary Committee for Plantations at Westminster that Edward was to appear to make the case for leaving Massachusetts alone.

Herbert took an interest in the warm, energetic Edward, who had arrived with not much more than his courage and commitment. He opened doors for him and had him to stay in his house in Suffolk, Ferriers. Herbert had returned to England to sort out various conflicts with his former in-laws over their mutual Waldegrave inheritances – a number of manor houses in Suffolk with thousands of acres attached, and his own patrimony in Lincolnshire. Doing so had additional interest because his fellow Puritans were now in the ascendant. There was no longer a reason to be absent from England.

Pelham's second marriage to Elizabeth Harlakenden (née Bossevile) had also given his fortunes a tremendous boost. In the post-war world her father, Colonel Godfrey Bossevile, the MP for Warwickshire, was an important figure. He had raised a troop for Parliament in the war and was a member of the Independent party. Bossevile was a vehement man, who had pressed for the destruction of the bishops to 'cleanse the house of God' when MPs were faltering. He talked language Edward was comfortable with. Bossevile's half-brother Robert, the 2nd Baron Brooke, who died in 1643, was the celebrated Parliamentarian, and one of the chief investors in Saybrook.

And it was now discovered that Edward Winslow, Herbert Pelham and Arthur Hesilrige were cousins.* In letters of 1647 Edward was referred to as 'my cousin Winslow' and 'my honoured cousin' while Hesilrige's wife Dorothy addressed him as 'good cousin' and signed her letter 'your loving cousin, D. H.' Edward had known Elizabeth Bossevile in Boston, but there does not seem to have been a recognition of their relationship then. But now, her father, Colonel Godfrey Bossevile, sat on a parliamentary committee with an old Worcestershire connection, John Wilde, so that may have been the link. The association

---

* Hesilrige and Pelham were further connected: Hesilrige's wife, Dorothy Greville, was Lord Brooke's sister. She and Pelham's mother-in-law, Margaret Bossevile, were both half aunt, half niece, and close cousins. It seems one of Edward's grandparents was probably a Greville. For some reason the families had lost contact in the past – perhaps because the Winslows had not flourished.

may also have been made via the new MP for Droitwich, Thomas Rainborowe, a man with many New England connections. Somehow someone put two and two together.

Though she was a shy and religious person, Elizabeth Bossevile was not an insignificant girl when it came to that all-important seventeenth-century gentry family background. She belonged to the powerful and influential Greville clan through her mother Margaret. Greville cousinship did Edward proud, catapulting him into the group of Puritan colonising aristocrats who were also at the heart of the English revolution.

Once Herbert Pelham discovered Edward was related to his wife, what had begun as natural liking for his earnest and enthusiastic friend – and amazement at Edward's heroic activities as an early colonist – became a positive duty of care for someone in his kinship circle. In a few years Edward's son Josiah would marry Herbert's daughter Penelope in New England. The two families would become completely enmeshed.

But even before this marriage, Herbert kept a friendly eye on a man who could be disorganised and chaotic but whom he admired for his godliness and willingness to take on difficult challenges. Herbert was one of the very few Puritan aristocrat investors in the Saybrook group (George Fenwick was another) who had put his money where his mouth was and actually taken up land in New England. He knew from experience what it meant to settle because he had done so himself.

It worried Herbert that there was no proper financial provision for Edward's role. Interested in money and land – of which he had quantities on both sides of the Atlantic – Herbert was secretly moved by Edward's unwavering belief that funds would appear like manna from heaven. He became his champion, frequently lobbying John Winthrop to make sure the Massachusetts government supported his friend financially.

Herbert had to point out to Winthrop that in England expenses were 'greater than happily you can conceive'. Letters from Herbert to Winthrop claim it was impossible to shake Edward from faithfully discharging 'that trust you have reposed in him', and his 'care and diligence in improving every opportunity, and his many wearisome journeys and attendancies for the despatch of the business he came about'.

Hesilrige and Edward took to one another. Edward embarked on an elegant way of life, doubtless visiting Sir Arthur Hesilrige's fifteenth-century manor house, Noseley Hall in Leicestershire, where Oliver Cromwell spent the night before the Battle of Naseby in 1645. Legend has it that Cromwell stabled his horses in the thirteenth-century chapel. Even if Edward found Hesilrige a little loud, he was in awe of him. He was staying with a legend of the Civil War. Hesilrige's high colour and prominent eyes spoke of a vigour Edward found very appealing. His regiment were known as the lobsters because of their heavy three-quarter-length armour. They were an alarming sight as they advanced. Sir Arthur was a member of the Independent political faction. More fundamentally religious than the Presbyterians, the Independents had widespread support in the army. A large number of them were fervent nonconformists, and often members of sects. Their most important leader was Oliver Cromwell. They were in some ways similar to New England churches in their championing of congregational churches. Unlike the orthodox party in New England, they believed in religious liberty for Protestants. But their passionate godliness was to Edward's liking.

It was hard to get Parliament to concentrate on the New England colonies. Charles I remained a prisoner. Normal authority had disintegrated and the sense of events rushing out of control increased when the New Model Army kidnapped the king.

When push came to shove, Edward swiftly disposed of the accusations against Massachusetts. With so much at stake he was a little economical with the *actualité*. New England was a kindly place. If there were problems, he hoped God and Christ would 'discover, pardon, and reform what is amiss amongst us'. With some exhilaration he explained their way of life, how the New England colonies were 'growing up into a nation'. But the settlers might as well return to England, if they did not have 'the power of government, and cannot administer justice seasonably on all occasions'. The colonies were not very old, they were up against constant internal and external danger. For Parliament to rule on the New England colonies when they had no MPs was not in the English Parliamentary tradition.

Some 130 years before the American Revolution, Edward wrote: 'if the Parliaments of England should impose laws upon us having no burgesses in their House of Commons, nor capable of a summons by reason of the vast distance of the ocean being three thousand miles from London, then we should lose the liberty and freedom I conceived of English indeed'. Every shire and corporation with their knights and burgesses consented to their laws, and opposed 'whatsoever they conceive may be hurtful to them: but this liberty we are not capable of by reason of distance'.

Vassall remarked sardonically that if the New England colonies were given such independence, Ireland would be next. But the Plantations Committee backed off. There were many listeners sympathetic to Edward's views, especially when he reminded them of the colonists' noble struggle, what they had fled England to avoid – 'the hierarchy, the cross in baptism, the holy days, the Book of Common Prayer, etc.' In the next ten years, England herself moved towards a way of life predicated on ideas of a godly reformation very similar to New England's. Edward's listeners liked his sincerity.

Edward won the war but lost the battle: the Earl of Warwick and Samuel Vassall insisted Gorton's settlement must continue. Freedom of religion remained an unbreakable principle for them and for Sir Henry Vane the younger.

Less than six months after he arrived, Edward had achieved victory against the Remonstrants, and had got a reputation amongst Independent politicians. He thrived in the electric atmosphere. One of the most powerful of the new men, the lawyer William Steele, talked of 'the integrity, abilities and diligence of the said Mr Winslow being well known . . . as also his great interest and acquaintance with the members of Parliament and other gentlemen of quality in the respective counties of the commonwealth'.

Edward had assurances from the Plantations Committee that the English government would not interfere in local justice, nor retrieve the Massachusetts Bay charter, nor send over a governor general. The commission left them 'all that freedom and latitude, that may, in any respect, be duly claimed by you', and recognised 'that the limiting of you in that kind may be very prejudicial (if not destructive) to the government and public peace of the colony'.

Strictly speaking Edward had no pressing reason to remain in London. And yet he did, carried away by the unrolling of an extraordinary revolution. It was astonishing to be in London after the reforming Confession of Faith had been produced by the Westminster Assembly of Puritan divines advising Parliament. London was thronging with New Englanders whom Edward knew. An astounding number – probably a quarter of its inhabitants, many of them young men who came as soldiers – returned to the old country. The New

England divines Thomas Weld and Hugh Peter had been sent to offer advice on the new church discipline, as well as representing Massachusetts' business interests. Peter, who had been an army chaplain in the Netherlands, became the most celebrated New Model Army padre and a close companion of Cromwell. He was even voted a salary by Parliament. Young George Downing, the son of Edward's friend Emmanuel, came to work for Hesilrige. The Boston magistrate Israel Stoughton and John Leverett, a future governor of Massachusetts, came back to England at the behest of the celebrated siege captain Thomas Rainborowe. The Rainborowes were a commercial clan with strong links to New England. Edward and Susanna knew Thomas's sister Martha, who lived in Charlestown from the 1630s with her first husband. Later she married John Winthrop a couple of years before his death. Susanna may have urged Edward to be in touch with the Rainborowes, but he disliked the anarchic side of the Levellers – a movement coming to the fore as he arrived. Rainborowe was their hero, but they reminded Edward of Gorton.

Hesilrige became Edward's patron and Edward's fortunes rose with the Independents. In later July 1647 the army occupied London, bringing them to power. Their ranks included Puritan merchants in the City who had been involved in New England for the past quarter of a century. Edward had dealt with them for years, especially the Andrewes brothers who were investors in Plymouth and Massachusetts. Thomas Andrewes became the first lord mayor of the Republic after the execution of Charles I. London MP Matthew Cradock had been a founding member of the Massachusetts Bay Company and its first governor. Cradock never went out to New England, but he had an estate and shipbuilding interests there. John Endecott was his wife's cousin.

Many of the more regicidal Independents worshipped at certain City churches: St Stephen's in Coleman Street was a centre for political radicalism and Independent Puritanism, and members of its congregation found their way to North America. In 1638 one of St Stephen's most famous pastors, John Davenport, founded the colony of New Haven in Connecticut.

Specialising in trade in North America and the Caribbean, they came to power after the Civil War. Over the years Edward had become personal friends with a number of them. He had bought goods from them or convinced them to lend more money to the struggling colony.

One of the things which made Edward particularly appealing to the Independents was his promotion of the new mission to convert the

Indians, which had some astonishing successes. John Eliot, back in New England, believed that total acculturation of the Indians must be achieved by placing them in Praying Towns, the first of which was at Natick near Roxbury. Their conversion to Christianity caught the imagination of the lobbyists, politicians, merchants, clergy and intellectuals milling round Westminster because of the biblical prophecy that the Conversion of the Jews would precede the great day of Christ's return.

The downfall of the king was also believed to be ushering in the Second Coming. Many soldiers had millenarian expectations, and Cromwell himself had become increasingly convinced that he was fulfilling a providential destiny predicted in the Old Testament. Edward was living in restless anticipation of something amazing, heightened by the abolition of the bishops and the imprisonment of the king, which lent events in London an extraordinary quality.

The second Civil War broke out in June 1648. Scottish troops invaded and Oliver Cromwell's generalship was decisive. In late November, masterminded by Cromwell and Ireton, the army sent a Remonstrance to Parliament demanding that Charles I be put on trial. When Presbyterian MPs refused and voted to continue to negotiate, Colonel Thomas Pride and his soldiers marched to the House of Commons and threw them out. In January 1649, to the horror of many fervent Parliamentarians – including Hesilrige – the king was put on trial. On 30 January he was executed.

On the whole Edward was a very conservative man. But as the revolution spiralled, his religious convictions meant he parted company for a while with Hesilrige, who did not accept the trial and execution of Charles I as legal, and refused to serve as a judge in the trial. Like many members of the House of Commons and House of Lords, he retreated to his country estate. They had fought against the king, and in theory liked the idea of a republic, but shied away from the deed.

Edward, used to taking quick decisions in the rough-and-ready arena of New England, did not have the same anxieties and scruples. And there were people who shared Edward's hungry impatience, religious radicals who had no qualms about executing the king. For them, Charles I was merely a figure in an apocalyptic narrative.

We do not know for certain whether Edward was present at the execution, but it is unlikely he would have missed being amongst the crowds thronging Whitehall waiting for the king, who wore an extra shirt so as not to be seen to tremble with cold, to come out onto a platform outside Banqueting House that grey day at the end of January. Edward might have heard that strange cry, almost as if the whole country was in pain, when the king's head fell with a thud to the sawdust. A great groan of regret and dread ran through the crowd after the head was raised by the masked executioner.

To the majority of the English nation, regardless of their politics it was a dreadful and upsetting event. Even those Independents who had agreed to be judges were so agonised by executing an anointed king that out of 135 commissioners, only 59 could bring themselves to sign the death warrant. Herbert Pelham's neighbour, the clergyman Ralph Josselin, wrote: 'I was much troubled with the black providence of putting the King to death, my tears were not restrained at the passages about his death.' He hoped the Lord would not see it as a sinful action of the country.

Most New Englanders, however, had a different view of the king. There were no groans from them. Perhaps the emotional and psychological changes wrought by the process of emigration involved cutting themselves off from their roots. Living away from England for so long made Edward unsentimental. Perhaps he had been brutalised by life on the frontier. By April 1649, as much of England was still reeling in an atmosphere of horror and disbelief, the regicidal Republic appointed him as one of the twelve commissioners to auction Charles I's goods like those of a common criminal. They included the Crown jewels, the king's sceptre and orb, and his outstanding art collection. It was stated that most of the goods had belonged not to the royal family but to the Crown, and were now therefore the property of the Commonwealth. They could sell anything to pay the mutinous soldiers. And, to the shock of the polite world, they did.

Carts loaded not only with paintings torn from the walls of the palace of Whitehall but royal pots and pans processed through an amazed London to be auctioned at Somerset House. The commissioners made themselves thoroughly unpopular with their search warrants which enabled them to go anywhere. It is not clear if Edward bought anything. There is no record of his doing so. Perhaps he regarded them as tainted. His fellow commissioners bought priceless paintings and even the Crown jewels. Titians were sold for £10 apiece, Van Dycks for rather less. They were seized on by many Parliamentarians. Charles very quickly became a royal martyr. Ten days after his death the holy king's apparently autobiographical memoir, the *Eikon Basilike*, relating his mental sufferings and spiritual strivings, was published. It became a bestseller.

But Edward viewed the king not as the Lord's anointed but as the last piece in an eschatological drama, and won golden opinions as the sort of man needed for the transformation of society. He was attractive, zealous and enthusiastic. By 1650 he had been appointed to one of the most important committees in the revolutionary government: the Committee for Compounding with Delinquents, as Royalists were known. Edward was one of only seven members, a position of considerable power. Every day he dealt with angry Royalists, many of whom had lost everything. Edward's great enthusiasm for the godly experiment of New England made him the perfect Puritan revolutionary.

Edward's lightning ascent of the political greasy pole came at a unique time when those who agreed with the idea of a godly commonwealth were favoured. It was during the year of the execution that Edward proved his credentials as a man wanting to bring in Christ's kingdom on earth with his successful sponsorship of the Act to establish a corporation to convert the Indians of New England. It was one of the first actions of the Republican Parliament to help bring on the millennium.

Along with Herbert Pelham, Edward was on the board of this New England Corporation. The aim was to raise money for missionaries and teachers to civilise the Indians as well as sending goods for them. Raising hundreds of pounds in country collections, the Corporation bought goods for the Indians. The company sent books including 200 English Bibles, cloth, clothing, medicine, tools, seeds, spindles and needles.

The twentieth-century historian Gerald Aylmer's examination of the personnel who made up the Cromwellian regime includes a long entry for Edward. Aylmer noted that, since the Commonwealth was a revolutionary regime which came to power through civil war, its 'legality was not universally recognised in the country' which put a premium on ideological reliability. In general it was personal recommendation which got the man the job. Edward most likely was helped by his friendship with the wealthy Puritan merchant Thomas Andrewes. Andrewes had been one of the commissioners of the High Court who was named to try Charles I – and he had no qualms about doing so. The fact that one of Andrewes' chief business partners in international trade, Samuel Moyer, was on the Committee for Compounding suggests that Andrewes may have recommended Edward. Andrewes had a drapery business which was so successful it helped finance the Parliamentary side. Edward by this time was exporting cloth probably as part of the activities of the New England Company. One of the Winslows' backers, Richard Ffloyd, was the treasurer of the New England Company, and sufficiently close to Edward to be made an executor of his will. Ffloyd was another Englishman who had lived in Boston for over a decade, and returned when the war began.

Many at Boston had no wish to pay for the project to convert the Indians. Edward's personal finances were strained, and Plymouth was not supportive. He was in low spirits, and at the beginning of 1650 he wrote to Massachusetts and asked that they 'send over some other in his place'.

It was not only financial concerns that had contributed to Edward's dark mood. In late February 1649, the sixty-two-year-old Governor Winthrop had suddenly become very unwell. He was tended to anxiously by his new wife, Martha Rainborowe, who was expecting a baby. His son Adam wrote uneasily to his brother John Winthrop junior that their father had kept to his bed for over a month, a highly unusual state of affairs.

The great founder did not live to see the birth of his last child. On 26 March 1649, after several weeks of fever and the cough of consumption, he finally passed from life. John Cotton asked for prayers from the congregation for whom Winthrop had been a friend, a brother and above all like 'a Mother, parent-like distributing his goods to brethren and neighbours at his first coming'. Governor Winthrop was buried in great state in what is now King's Chapel Burial Ground, Boston. The day of his funeral was made a public holiday so that as many people as possible could attend, and it was delayed a week so that all could gather. Edward must have wished he was there to pay his last respects to the man who had been such an influence in his life. Perhaps wistful, on 26 April 1649 he gave a piece of land for a new meeting house in Marshfield.

Edward had had enough. He very nearly got onto Captain Hawkins's ship which was sailing for New England, but William Steele, who was now president of the New England Company, insisted he remain. Edward was 'of absolute necessity for the carrying on of the work'. As it was acknowledged that 'it is uncomfortable to him to be so long from his family and personal occasions', it was agreed they 'must see he be no sufferer'. The compromise seems to have been to get a member of his family to join him in London.

It was probably at this point that arrangements were made to pay for his nineteen-year-old daughter, Elizabeth, to come over from New England and look after him. And thus Edward stayed on.

CHAPTER XIV

Hercules

Reverend Wake, the husband of Edward's sister Magdalen, was a great friend of the poet Mildmay Fane. The king was godfather to Fane's eldest son, and Fane had married into the celebrated military Vere family. Despite six children and a life managing a great estate, Mereworth Castle in Kent, Fane (now Lord Westmorland) had not lost his affection for his old friend. Nor had the Reverend Wake lost his love of poetry. But now Wake had fallen on very hard times, and Fane was helping out his old friend by paying him to make fair copies of Fane's poetry in his prison cell. Poignantly one such poem was Wake's own Latin translation of the best known of Fane's verses, 'A Happy Life'.

Magdalen was a spirited person who had the courage of her strongly anti-Puritan convictions. She had once been 'a very active industrious woman' who 'did many services to the King in the time of the Civil Wars'. But now – despite the protection of Edward – she was perpetually anxious about her husband, who was in extremely poor health, and one of her sons, Captain William Wake, who had also been captured and imprisoned.

Throughout Edward's time in London the Wakes were at the centre of Royalist rebellions. Captain Wake boasted that he and his father had been imprisoned over twenty times. Twice Captain Wake could have been executed. Edward's natural kindness came to the fore. The Royalist connection had the potential to embarrass Edward but he refused to let it – years later Captain Wake described how what he called a 'rebel uncle' saved him from the gallows. To his colleagues, Edward's Wake relations were simply traitors, the enemy – in the term of the day, 'delinquents'.

Once Edward was employed by the well-paid Cromwellian bureaucracy as a member of the Committee for Compounding, his money worries eased for a time. His salary of £300 a year solved the issue of Plymouth or Massachusetts funding him in England. He was several times also appointed to committees to judge treasons against the

Commonwealth. He could now support his daughter Elizabeth and his sister Magdalen Wake in pleasant lodgings, though the latter spent much time in the West Country tending to her imprisoned husband.

Elizabeth was a bright and determined character. She was amazed by London's grandeur: despite the war the new squares and streets designed by Inigo Jones round Covent Garden and the Strand were still standing.

And she enjoyed meeting her Wake cousins. Magdalen's second son, Edward, was less hot-blooded than his brother, Captain William. Edward Wake was interested in business, perhaps because of seeing the effective ways of his uncle, whose City connections probably helped his nephew to set up the Corporation of the Sons of the Clergy in 1655. Existing to this day, it was begun by merchants of the City of London to raise funds for the children of indigent clergy, such as Edward Wake and his siblings, who had been dispossessed during the Commonwealth. Certainly his mother found him a great comfort. Many years later she would insist on being buried in his tomb, 'as she had devised in her lifetime'.

Magdalen and her family were Edward's flesh and blood. With his own eyes he had seen how a whole generation was traumatised by being on the losing side.

At the beginning of February 1654, on one of his outings from prison, Captain William Wake married the daughter of a rich Dorset farmer neighbour, Amie Cutler. Rather curiously the wedding took place in London in the Church of St Bartholomew the Less in Smithfield. This was almost next door to Edward's office at Haberdashers' Hall in Smithfield. Had it all been arranged by Edward? Normally Amie would have been married from her home parish, Stourpaine in Dorset, but these were not normal times. Perhaps her parents thought that, as she was marrying a dangerous Royalist, it was sensible to have the blessing of a government figure.

Amie had been brought up in a conventional and genteel fashion. But at the wedding ceremony, out of earshot of the guests – including her distinguished uncle by marriage – she gave a vow to her husband: 'if there should be any opportunity given or methods used to restore the King, my father should be at liberty to return to his arms for that purpose'. He soon did.

When Captain Wake came out of the king's army, he used her dowry to help set up his family in the clothing and stapling trade. This was business which brought raw wool from the Dorset countryside to towns such as Wareham and Dorchester which had exclusive royal charters for sale and export – trade with which Edward most likely helped. But Wake was soon back in prison.

Whatever Edward's fondness for his sister, helping the Wakes over and over again was a big ask.

Edward's meteoric rise continued, however, as did his friendship with Herbert Pelham, whose daughter Penelope had married Edward's son Josiah, probably in New England sometime around 1651–2. Edward also resumed his friendship with Sir Arthur Hesilrige (who had reconciled with Cromwell and taken his seat in the Rump Parliament and on the Council of State). Fortunately, in what seems to have been a genuine love match in New England, Josiah now ticked all the boxes as far as the Pelhams were concerned. Josiah was doing well in business with his father, exporting iron along with beaver and sugar from Barbados to England, and importing clothing.

Edward was riding high in his own right, a considerable figure in London. His work on the Commmittee for Compounding involved eyesight-destroying paperwork determining who owned what sequestrated estates. People queued to beg for their property. Defeated Royalists appeared amazed to be asked to lay out their possessions and plead for them, paying a fine which was generally a year's assessment of a third of the estate's annual worth. The concentrated work it required – going through petitions, land deeds, subsidiary leases, women's portions, minors' trusts – might have killed anyone who was less of a workhorse than Edward. It may have contributed to the loss of the ox-like strength which had taken him through years of deprivation in New England.

Edward enjoyed the perks of office, but also continued to run up debts, including celebrating his new importance by commissioning a coat of arms. That was not cheap. Arthur Squibb the Younger, who was related to one of the heralds at the College of Arms, was also on the Committee for Compounding. Perhaps Squibb arranged for the coat of arms to be commissioned. Edward was evidently very proud of his new status, having his coat of arms engraved on a gold signet ring used to seal documents, including his will. In future years Josiah united the new Winslow arms (seven silver lozenges on a red background) with his wife's aristocratic Pelham arms, adding the Pelham strap and buckle on the crest, which were then engraved on pewter plates by the English pewterer at Bristol, John Batchelor.

Edward's thoughts could not be on the Second Coming all the time. The lure of luxury shops reopening in the West End could not be resisted. By the early 1650s the seas were clear for ships from the East India Company to berth in the London Docks. The East India factories had produced cotton, silk, tea and saltpetre (a crucial element in gunpowder), food preservatives and fertiliser since the beginning of the century. Now they could be landed again.

Edward enjoyed spending money in places such as the reopened New Exchange, with its dazzling textiles. It is no surprise that Edward also had his portrait painted. Not only was it another symbol of his status, it may have been prompted by his new alliance with the Pelham family. To mark the occasion, either Edward or Herbert Pelham, in a spirit of lavish celebration, also commissioned portraits of Josiah and Penelope in what may have been their wedding finery. Penelope wore a green satin dress with a salmon pink stole while Josiah had a festively gilded necktie similar to his father's. They must have had these likenesses painted in Old England and subsequently shipped over to New England to hang on the walls of their home at Marshfield. (Today they are in the Pilgrim Hall Museum.)

There is no evidence that Josiah's sister Elizabeth, now living in London as her father's companion, was ever painted, which may indicate the grand portraits were Herbert Pelham's idea to ensure his daughter did not forget the position she had been born to in England.

Edward's portrait is the only one that exists of any of the *Mayflower* passengers. To their contemporaries in Plymouth, portraits would have seemed an extraordinary extravagance. But Puritan London was less austere. There has been much discussion about how the Roundheads and Cavaliers differentiated themselves through dress. Black is always assumed to be a Puritan colour, but in fact it was popular to be painted in black at court before the Civil War as it gave the subject status, since black dye was the most costly. Puritanism was a demanding way of life, but the court Cromwell presided over exulted in the display of magnificence, which made his regime seem legitimate and confident.

Edward's new friends' houses were full of portraits. In response to the elegant life of the English gentry perhaps he thought he too should have a portrait made of himself to hang in his own home at Careswell. There had been many letters from Careswell asking him what he thought about the price of cattle, how he was doing, when he was returning. But it is tempting to believe that Edward's choice to be painted holding a tenderly signed letter from Susanna was a symbol that his wife was never far from his thoughts.

Despite earning around £300 a year for at least five years, Edward's debts amounted to £500. Many of Herbert's letters warn about Edward's carelessness: Edward must not use his 'own credit' on behalf of New England when he should be demanding supplies from the Massachusetts government. But Edward not only had a fatal but good-natured inability to separate his personal finances from business expenses but also rather extravagant tastes and not much interest in balancing his account book, if such a book existed.

Although he was fitted by temperament and belief to be part of the Puritan revolutionary cadre after the Civil War, ideological purity did not trump his human qualities of loyalty and friendship. He used his position to do a good deed to the children of his old benefactor Lord Coventry.

Lord Coventry's son and grandson were Royalists. The final battle of the Civil War in 1651 was a close-run thing and alarming for the Parliamentarians. The future Charles II and his army of Covenanter Scots marched to the West Midlands and met no opposition until they came to Worcester, where battle was engaged amongst Edward Winslow's boyhood scenes. Charles commanded operations from the top of Worcester Cathedral Tower, next to Edward's old school. He was eventually defeated and went into exile.

The republican victory at Worcester was an event of the greatest providential magnitude for Edward. He personally superintended a hundred narratives of the battle to be sent to New England with 'Acts for a day of thanksgiving'.

However, Lord Coventry's son and grandson were accused of having sent £1,000 in gold, horse and arms to Charles II shortly before the battle. Their entire estates, even their lives, could have been forfeited for treason. But the case against them mysteriously collapsed. In a strange twist of history, Edward was able to repay his old patron Coventry for all his help over the years. A key event was Edward's interrogation of the Royalist general Edward Massey in the Tower of London as part of a deputation from the Committee for Compounding. Massey's interrogation was supposed to strengthen the case against Lord Coventry, but in a dramatic development on 25 February 1653, the Committee for the Advance of Money, of which Edward was also a member, declared 'on hearing the depositions, it is resolved, *nem. con.*, that he [Coventry] is not guilty of the charge'. They ordered 'that the seizure of all his estates in cos. [counties] Worcester, Gloucester, Warwick, Oxford, &c., be taken off, and his bonds and securities restored'. John Lyne, the secretary who had informed against him, was arrested instead. Coventry's sons, whom many a witness had seen riding by the side of Charles II before the Battle of Worcester, also got off scot-free. By March 1655 all the Coventrys' estates had been returned to them.*

Edward did not slacken doing what he could for the New England colonies in the continuous battle to establish land rights in the great American continent. He was the go-to person for colonists with contacts in London to promote claims, whether in contentious Rhode Island, or Maine or New Hampshire. Despite his grand life in London he never bought any property in England, assuming he would soon return to Careswell. He kept in close touch with Plymouth. William Bradford still entrusted him with attempting to obtain Plymouth's claim to the whole Kennebec River. In 1653 he once again put to Parliament the point of view of the congregational churches, which was beginning to be known as the New England Way. He proudly published the Cambridge Synod's Platform of Church Discipline in New England.

Edward continued to fight his friend Roger Williams in London. They had a new disagreement: the need for the Praying Towns, intended for converted Indians. In letters Williams talks of the Indians' fear at being oppressed into becoming Christian. Williams was always fond of those he disagreed with and Edward was warm-hearted, even if disapproving. Williams met Cromwell several times to discuss the Indians and the millennium.

There were other New Englanders in town with whom Edward was more in sympathy, such as Edward Hopkins. Hopkins was a good friend whom Edward particularly admired because he was 'a man that makes conscience of his words as well as his actions'. One of the earliest settlers of Connecticut, a governor and United Colonies commissioner, Hopkins returned to London in 1652 and became a

---

* They were officially exonerated, but their innocence was clearly taken with a pinch of salt. The year after their protector Edward died, they were slapped with the so-called Decimation Tax – ten per cent of their property – which was imposed to punish Royalist rebels. The Committee for Compounding, now minus the noble Edward, acidly noted that they were satisfied 'that Lord Coventry is within the orders for the tax by the Major Generals, and instruct them to proceed accordingly'.

navy commissioner and an MP. Living without his wife, not always satisfied with the company of his daughter and her youthful friends, Edward had found solace with Hopkins.

Hopkins' wife Ann suffered from appalling depression. It was Mrs Hopkins of whom John Winthrop wrote in his diary – to what many regard as his shame – that this 'godly young woman of special parts' was 'fallen into a sad infirmity, the loss of her understanding and reason, which had been growing upon her divers years, by occasion of her giving herself wholly to reading and writing . . . Her husband, being very loving and tender of her, was loath to grieve her; but he saw his error, when it was too late. For if she had attended her household affairs, and such things as belong to women, and not gone out of her way and calling to meddle in such things as are proper for men, whose minds are stronger, etc., she had kept her wits, and might have improved them usefully and honourably in the place God had set her.'

It is hard to believe Edward or indeed his feisty daughter Elizabeth agreed with this narrow view of women. In the future Elizabeth would show she was afraid of no man, including her stepson, the Salem Witch Trial judge Jonathan Curwen, who tried to bully her into handing over guardianship of her younger daughter after her husband's death. Since we know Susanna could read and write, she too must have found Winthrop's view of the education of women preposterous.

In 1652 a trade war between Holland and the Commonwealth broke out, making the Dutch and English official enemies in New England. Many of the exiled English royal family were living in Holland, which lent the struggle additional importance. That July, ships including a ketch named *John's Adventure* (which may have been owned by John Winslow – there was a ship by that name in his will) were sent to New England carrying one tonne of shot, 156 barrels of powder and 1,000 swords, 'for increase of their present store'. Edward was pleased to note the damage done to the Baltic trade in masts, as he had long suggested that Baltic pines could be replaced with those from New England.

Cromwell dissolved the Rump Parliament in April 1653. Edward bravely joined Thomas Andrewes and forty other City figures in a petition to recall Parliament. Rumours went around New England that Edward had been imprisoned. This is unlikely, but Edward did lose the office that gave him his very pleasant income. Nevertheless within a year he was back in favour, reappointed to the Committee for

Compounding and named by Cromwell as a member of his new High Court of Justice for treason.

Many thought revolution had gone far enough. The forced dissolution of the Rump by Cromwell and the army was a sticking point for Arthur Hesilrige. He became a leading member of the opposition to Cromwell's Protectorate, which he regarded as a dictatorship.

Edward and Hesilrige came to a second parting of their ways – this time a permanent one. Edward had approved of the new version of Parliament at Westminster, an assembly nominated from members of congregational churches – the Praise-God Barebone's Parliament, as it was nicknamed.

Its elevated agenda of godly reformation was what Edward wanted. Cromwell told the Barebone's Parliament in July 1653: 'You are as like the forming of God as ever people were ... you are at the edge of promises and prophecies.' Such a speech was balm to Edward's soul.

Letters show Edward's admiration for Oliver Cromwell. He always had a tendency to hero-worship, and here was a man after his own heart, strenuously trying to make a better world. In his tongue-in-cheek poem 'An Horation Ode upon Cromwell's Return from Ireland', Andrew Marvell wrote of ruining the great work of time and casting the 'kingdom old / Into another mould'. But for Edward that was a worthy aim.

As part of the Anglo-Dutch peace treaty, Edward, who had excellent Dutch, was tasked with assessing the price of English ships taken by the king of Denmark. Amongst the Winslow family papers lies a certificate, showing Cromwell and the Dutch States General had made him a member of the arbitration committee created by the Treaty of Westminster to agree on issues arising after the First Anglo-Dutch War.

Edward was brought into contact with the poet John Milton, who was the Latin Secretary responsible for diplomatic correspondence with foreign countries. During Charles I's trial, Milton had boldly published *The Tenure of Kings and Magistrates*, which argued it was lawful and acceptable 'to call to account a Tyrant or wicked King and after due conviction, to depose, and put him to death'.

By June 1654 Edward was a member of a High Court convened to try a conspiracy against Cromwell. Three Royalists – John Gerard, Peter Vowell and Summerset Fox – were accused of plotting to assassinate Cromwell and install Charles II. Increasing numbers of more moderate politicians wished to return to a system similar to the monarchy before the Civil War in which there were checks on the executive power, but Edward was not of their number. He did not object to the written constitution, the Instrument of Government, in which Cromwell adopted a quasi-monarchical role as Lord Protector. He was the only one of the original seven Compounders reappointed to office. No theoretician, Cromwell's ideas chimed with Edward's deepest convictions about conforming to God's will. And perhaps the funds were useful to a man permanently short of cash.

On 21 February 1654 Lorenzo Paulucci, the Venetian ambassador, sent a description of Cromwell's visit to the City of London. 'At seven in the evening he returned to his dwelling in the same pomp, with the addition of three hundred lighted torches and all the outward signs of respect and honour, but with very scanty marks of goodwill from the people in general.' Paulucci thought the rancour and hostility of the people increased daily because Cromwell had 'arrogated to himself despotic authority and the actual sovereignty of these realms under the mask of humility and the public service'. Cromwell lacked 'nothing of royalty but the name' – though in fact Cromwell made it known he wished to be addressed as Highness.

Prophecies were rife. People were talking about the tide in the Thames protracting its ebb and flow for two hours longer than usual. Credible witnesses declared they had seen the ghost of the beheaded king in the former royal palace. Paulucci believed 'it is impossible for this kingdom to remain long quiet without the sceptre of its legitimate king . . . the majority of the people sigh for him, though threats and fears induce silence and resignation and prevent them from speaking out freely or complaining of the present yoke'.

Not content with banning plays, in July 1654 racing was banned for six months. Enemies of the Commonwealth had been ready 'to take advantage of public meetings, and concourse of people at Horse-races, and other sports, to carry on such their pernicious designs, to the Disturbance of the Public Peace, and endangering new troubles'. The pleasure-loving English did not take kindly to this.

The constant attempts to enforce a cultural revolution by the godly reformation of the English way of life which began in 1647 by banning Christmas and Easter was hugely unpopular and largely ineffective. To Edward's eyes, of course, such reforms were simply logical. Since the beginning of the colony such festivities had never been part of Plymouth life.

Edward's burning desire to be of service had not gone away with office, neither had the fervour that had taken him to the New World and back. In December 1654, as the Republic took on fresh labours to reform the world, Edward could not resist volunteering for a great expedition to the West Indies.

The plan, known as the Western Design, was meant to give a base to England in the Caribbean to thwart the Spanish Empire and attack the shipments of silver which regularly crossed the sea to get to Spain. Hispaniola (the island which is today shared by the Dominican Republic and Haiti) had great resonance because it was where Christopher Columbus first raised the Spanish flag on the American continent. The Western Design was another fulfilment of millennarian prophecies. Throwing the Spanish out of America could be viewed as the drying up of the Euphrates predicted in Revelation 16:12, 'that the way of the kings of the east might be prepared'.

Edward was to be the chief of three civil commissioners in charge of planting these new colonies. He was also substantially remunerated. In December 1654 he was awarded £1,000 as salary, with £500 to be paid in advance.

Two well-known officers of the Civil War were in charge of the military side of things: Admiral William Penn, the father of the founder of Pennsylvania, and General Robert Venables, who for good or ill had successfully commanded the siege of Drogheda, which had ended in a massacre. Unfortunately they loathed one another, and squabbled continually.

Edward performed a last good deed in December 1654. He wrote to the navy commissioners to ask if they could release a boy named William Lygon who had been press-ganged out of a coal ship and put on board a warship, 'as he is the chief support of his mother'.

Edward had laboured for the Commonwealth without a break for days at a time. His strenuous soul was pining for real action after the grinding days in his office at Haberdashers' Hall. The physical side of him was yearning for the liberation of a sea voyage. He made his farewells to his daughter and sister, and the rest of his friends. His brother John was over from New England as he departed, and it is likely that John's son had a place on one of the ships. (A letter from Roger

Williams suggests that a couple of months later, Susanna went to London; perhaps Elizabeth was lonely and asked her mother to visit.)

The fleet left from Portsmouth for Barbados. As long letters written at sea reveal, Edward was desperate for the Western Design to be a success. The two principals were at daggers drawn, but Edward was determined everyone should get along. His optimism and enthusiasm meant he wanted to give the expedition its all. In beseeching letters he badgered John Thurloe, the Secretary of State for Foreign Affairs, for information to see how the great republican experiment in London was faring.

Edward was not especially well when he set sail to Hispaniola. He had cancelled a visit to a friend a few weeks before, and had insisted on an apothecary being on board. He may have felt the need for someone who could deal with stomach ills. One possibility is that he suffered from some hereditary ailment, perhaps a weak heart. It is also possible that he had picked up a virus or some kind of bacterial infection in London. The Great Plague of 1665 is believed to have started because of the poor housing round the areas Edward frequented. Slums lay cheek by jowl with the elegant new facades. The Fleet River was choked with the waste from Smithfield Market. Westminster itself was built on unhealthy marshes.

As an expert transatlantic traveller, Edward noted they made the crossing amazingly swiftly, in an unprecedented five weeks. But in spite of its distinguished military leaders, the Hispaniola expedition was a badly planned disaster, which might have been predicted from the outset. It had only 1,000 veteran soldiers. Most of the troops, including the 1,500 new English soldiers and 4,000 colonial conscripts raised in Barbados, had neither seen action nor had much training. Edward's knowledge of the West Indies was ignored. Most of the food was inedible. More importantly, the planners had not included vessels to store water, and 200–300 men were to die of thirst. The apothecary never arrived. His ship was becalmed along with the food-store ships, and was then blown to Ireland. Almost a third of their stores were lost at sea and never reached the West Indies.

Nevertheless when Edward arrived in Barbados in mid-January he was full of excitement, anticipating a swift victory. Via John Thurloe, Edward entreated Cromwell to remember 'that the settlement of the Protestant religion is one of the grounds he goeth upon'. The government should send out some 'very able ministers'. He was critical about the low standard of public life in Barbados and the levels of corruption: 'all places of trust are disposed of by favour, and not by a sound judgement, for few active able men are in power, that may prevent such a mischief'.

In mid-April the English ships left Barbados and set out for Hispaniola. They passed St Vincent, and dropped anchor at St Lucia for a council and to give orders. Then they streamed past Martinique (a new French colony) and Dominica (where they were becalmed), Guadeloupe, Montserrat and Nevis. When they made St Kitts, the French fired off thirty shots as a salute. After St John's they were hovering off Hispaniola, a mass of white sails crowding the sea.

But nothing went as it should. The expedition was supposed to be top secret but because it was planned for so long, the Spanish had known about it for months. The 4,000 troops raised reluctantly by the Barbadians either could not or would not obey orders. There was no central command. The land and sea generals had to confer not only with one another but with the three civilian commissioners. Once the ships arrived off Hispaniola and the land army was dropped off, time was lost in endless consultations. Lieutenants rowed backwards and forwards to get each commander's opinion. It was not clear who had precedence. Edward angered the rank and file by proclaiming death to any soldier who plundered, with what one witness called 'his always unresistible affirmative'. This was announced as the men landed, which 'proved fatal to the army' in the view of another witness. But Commissioner Winslow would not be contradicted. The most he would agree to was to 'give them their six weeks pay when they had taken this place' – which was decent enough.

There was a superstition in the navy that women were unlucky on ships, and General Venables was not only resented for bringing on the expedition his new wife but also despised for meekly bowing to her domineering ways. A complaining Mrs Venables frequently disembarked and went on shore into the war zone, distracting her husband.

Years as a colonist had made Edward very aware of the weather. He pressed for the expedition to get going because they would otherwise lose the dry season and be at the mercy of hurricanes, storms and disease, but the high command continued to prevaricate.

Eventually, when the store ships had still not arrived, the leaders decided to cast themselves 'into the arms of Almighty God, whose

Providence we trust will be forever good, and will own us as instruments in his right hand' to exercise vengeance on the Spanish.

The Almighty was not in a receptive mood. They had left it too late. The rains created landslides and turned much of the lower ground to mud. Sanitation problems meant disease spread like wildfire, and the army was attacked by dysentery and fever. A third of the men died and rotted where they lay. Some 3,000 men were sick. Horses got bogged down in the swampy terrain. They were swiftly eaten along with the dogs because of the lack of food.

Forty Spaniards defeated 400 English troops in one mortifying battle. The rest were taken off the island by Penn, a humiliation felt by all, especially Edward. Offers by Penn to have his ships bombard the main fort were rejected by Venables. By now Edward had lost faith in Venables' judgement. One memoir has Edward trying to force the soldiers back for a last attempt on the citadel, to no avail.

Eventually Edward and the other commissioners pressed Venables to give up Hispaniola as a bad job. On board the *Swiftsure* on 28 April they wrote to the governor of Barbados saying that they had had to abandon the attempt because of 'the cowardice of our men' of which they were deeply ashamed. All stores which should by then have arrived at Barbados were to be sent on to Jamaica, where they were going next.

Edward had survived the *Mayflower* but he had been only twenty-five then. Although he had made many, many sea journeys, his previous transatlantic voyage had been almost ten years ago, when he was in his prime. Now he was almost sixty. He was not wounded but, like many of the soldiers, became very ill of the flux, as well as a despair which exacerbated his fever. The conservative herald Sir William Dugdale heard that Edward, whom he called disparagingly 'a Committee man', had raved 'of Haberdashers' Hall in his sickness'.

Edward had expected so much of this expedition. His letters had been full of an almost hysterical exaltation. In rapturous tones he had written: 'Oh! what would we give, and how do we long to hear from England of the conclusion of the Parliament with his highness; and so what settlement is made in the nation. I beseech you, when you have occasion to write and send to us, let us not be strangers to England's condition; but impart such news to us, as the time affords.'

As well as suffering from a fever which in the past he might have shaken off, there was also a psychological problem that no ship's doctor or apothecary could alleviate: the Hispaniola debacle showed that

God was no longer on his side. The expedition's success was going to be yet another sign of God's favour. Such failure was a sign the regime was cursed. Edward was so grief-stricken by what had happened it dealt him a mortal blow.

On the evening of 5 May Admiral Penn noted: 'This evening we set sail and stood off the land all night south. The next day we stood westward, and kept between SW and NW. Mr Winslow began to grow bad in health, having complained a day or two before; taking conceit (as his man affirms) at the disgrace of the army on Hispaniola, to whom he told, it had broken his heart.'

On the 8th a fast was kept on board to seek the Lord's favour. Edward, who had come up on deck to feel the breeze on his face, suddenly 'fell very ill'. He was carried down in the afternoon to his cabin and 'deceased in the evening'.

Penn wrote that it had pleased the Lord to call Mr Winslow away. Another observer, Henry Whistler, recorded in his journal that 'some did say it was with grief, but he had a strong fever on him when he died'. Whistler also noted it was 'fair weather and the wind at east', and they steered away west. The next morning they arrived at the westernmost part of Hispaniola, very high land. On 9 May the burial of Commissioner Winslow was performed 'as solemnly as might be at sea'. His body was put into a coffin with two cannon shot at his feet to weigh him down. His corpse was 'held forth to the sea with ropes over the ship's side ready to lower down. Command being gave they all let go. Our ship gave him twenty guns, and our vice admiral gave him twelve and our rear admiral ten, and so we bade him adieu.' Edward's linen was packed up, along with his watch.

The ships sailed on to capture Jamaica, leaving Edward Winslow behind. There he lies to this day.

Someone on board ship was making notes. Possibly it was Edward's nephew John, or Henry Whistler. Whoever it was, the notes were later worked up into a poem, printed in *New England's Memorial*.

> The Eighth of May,
> West from 'Spaniola shore,
> God took from us our Grand Commissioner,
> Winslow by Name; a man in Chiefest Trust,
> Whose Life was sweet, and Conversation just;
> Whose Parts and wisdom most men did excel;
> An honour to his place, as all can tell.

Penn abandoned Jamaica without permission to return to London, and Venables followed shortly after. They were both arrested on suspicion of deserting their post, in Penn's case of being a secret Royalist. Both were imprisoned in the Tower for not obeying orders. Cromwell was reported to have shut himself into his room for a day to discover 'what "accursed thing" had provoked God's wrath'. John Milton had to write an explanation of why the expedition should not be regarded as the judgement of God.

On 11 May 1657 Resolved White, Edward's stepson, was in Barbados on family business: his sister-in-law was selling off part of the Vassall plantation. On the way his ship would have passed very close to the coast of Hispaniola where Edward lay on the ocean floor. Was past bitterness forgotten when Resolved remembered the larger-than-life character who had been like a father to him?

In the circles of the seventeenth-century Massachusetts colonial elite, Edward Winslow was regarded as a hero. He was a 'Hercules', wrote Cotton Mather, 'From his very early days accustomed unto the crushing of that sort of serpents' which got Massachusetts 'deliverance from the designs of many troublesome adversaries that were petitioning unto the Parliament against them'. To give a proper account of what Edward did for the New England colonies would take so long it might not be 'expected until the resurrection of the just'.

But in the here and now, his family had to suppress thoughts about why Edward could not have remained in London, rather than embark on another adventure. Perhaps ultimately Susanna herself did not disapprove. She had known her husband longest and had put up with so much, but she also understood the forces that drove him, because she shared his beliefs. They had also driven her to seek a new world. In his will Edward wrote proudly of being 'now bound in a voyage to sea in the service of the Commonwealth'. For thirty years his life had been voyaging backwards and forwards across oceans for those dreamed-of commonwealths. Now it was time to rest.

CHAPTER XV

Generational Change

As the news spread, there was consternation amongst Edward's friends. Roger Williams was still grieving for him twenty years later. For all his long absence, Edward was an irreparable loss to New England. As well as representing them in the councils of power in London, he had been a living link to the glorious past.

In London, however, Elizabeth and Susanna were discovering that a life lived on a heroic scale had its financial cost. Shell-shocked by his death, they found out that Edward still had huge unsuspected debts 'to the value of £500 and upwards unsatisfied at his departure from England'. Edward's 'great disbursements' buying provisions for himself and his servants for the voyage to Hispaniola had been very expensive, and most of the goods had been lost. The matriarch of a leading family in New England, Susanna was now stranded in London with little cash while she sorted out his affairs. In a petition to Cromwell and the Council of State, she said she was 'in a low condition having little else to subsist on but the expectation of his salary'. She asked for the balance of £500 that he was owed for the Hispaniola expedition.

In the previous nine years Edward's absence had thrust considerable responsibilities upon Josiah, who was approaching thirty years old. A soldierly man who, aged twenty, had become insignia-bearer and captain of the Marshfield militia, he had risen to the challenge. Now he had to rush to London, to ensure the English side of the family business continued.

Tradition has Josiah as a gentleman farmer who was devoted to Plymouth, serving the colony in many official capacities. But documents show he was also just as much a merchant involved with sugar plantations in the West Indies, as well as exporting iron and cloth on a large scale. His uncle John had paved the way, but being married to Governor Bellingham's niece Penelope drew Josiah even more tightly into the heart of the Boston merchant elite, a financially innovative and daring community.

Bellingham had taken the opposite view from Josiah's father and the orthodox party on most of the issues of the past. He saw nothing wrong with the Child petition, and no reason to discriminate against non-church members and members of the Church of England. Unlike John Winthrop, who believed in the discretion of the magistrate, Bellingham wanted a body of laws, which he helped draw up in 1648. Josiah seems to have discreetly come over to Governor Bellingham's side. While many Plymouth farmers proudly farmed their own land and were dependent on no one, especially not the slick city folks of Boston, Josiah had a more outgoing and ambitious stance. The fact that he was amongst the earliest students at the new Harvard College was another sign of the Winslows growing apart from the rest of the Old Colony. Since Plymouth did not have a proper grammar school until the 1670s, let alone a university, it was only natural to seek out education elsewhere.

Susanna got her money. At the bottom of her petition was written in Cromwell's now shaky handwriting: 'Oliver P. We refer this paper to a Council April 18 1656'. What was described as 'compensation' to Edward's wife and children was paid forthwith.

Cromwell had once stated he 'had rather have a plain russet-coated captain that knows what he fights for, and loves what he knows, than that which you call a gentleman and is nothing else. I honour a gentleman that is so indeed.' Edward had been such a man. However, Cromwell might have been less generous had he known about the Winslow connection to the Penruddock Uprising, the most important insurrection of the Republic. Josiah arrived to find his cousin William Wake in prison at Exeter, having been captured during the rebellion. Wake was part of the Royalist secret resistance movement, the Sealed Knot, and faced the possibility of execution for high treason.

In the past, having Royalists for cousins could be shrugged off – almost everyone in the Civil War had relatives on different sides. But the Penruddock insurrection had been such a challenge to the regime that having William's brother, Edward Wake, as a major investor in the Winslow business was potentially very embarrassing. So dangerous was the situation that Cromwell had brought in the Major-Generals. For the first and only time, England was ruled by martial law. Josiah had at least two ships in which Edward Wake had investments. The Winslows – now just Josiah – had been importing clothing to New England on a large scale, getting several hundred pounds of kersey, cotton, penistone, serge and linens by one ship alone. It seems likely that some was manufactured by William Wake and his wife Amie's clothing business in the West Country, in which she 'was a great help to him; and brought him a considerable portion in money to enable him to carry it on'. Josiah needed to fill those ships regardless of the cloth's provenance.

'Cuz Ed Wake', as Josiah called him, may have been the middle-man dealing with Josiah. Probably Edward Wake, as well as Josiah, thought William Wake was a damned fool. Certainly, the imprison-ment of William didn't stop the cousins doing business. A year later Ed was expecting a £30 return – that is interest on ventures – which may have originally been several hundred pounds (tens of thousands today). Josiah, like his father, simply ignored the potential difficulties of being linked to Royalists.

The Sealed Knot had ordered their followers to seize power at the beginning of March 1655 when Edward Winslow had been in Bar-bados. William Wake was part of the little group captured at South Moulton in Devon. Colonel John Penruddock had his head cut off inside Exeter Castle on 16 May, and his gentlemen associates were hanged in the market square, which could have been William's fate. Very fortunately for William, his captor, Captain Unton Croke, had offered articles of surrender that included his not being executed. Wake and six others were pardoned by Parliament and eventually released. William had a very narrow escape.

But being married to a rebel took its toll on Amie. Her first son had been born when Wake was still in prison. Continuous anxieties through the Interregnum shortened her life, and ten years after the Restoration she was dead, aged just thirty-two. Captain Wake outlived her by thirty years.

Though Josiah had arrived back in England with cash and the expertise to deal with his father's probate, the family still had a large hole to plug. The sums owed suggest that it was not only Edward's life-style which was the problem – perhaps he had bought shares in other ships going out from London, and perhaps those investments had made losses. Whatever the reasons, Susanna had need of money. She also had the sudden expense of a wedding.

In the way of the world when an energetic unattached female is in the vicinity of a successful male, her attractive and strong-willed daughter Elizabeth had formed an attachment to the Winslows' London business partner, a substantial merchant named Robert Brooks.

On 9 March 1656 they married at the tiny fifteenth-century City church St Olave's in Hart Street near Tower Hill.*

Brooks' family was sufficiently eminent to have a coat of arms, and probably ran a cloth-manufacturing business. To be flourishing at this time they were most likely of Puritan sympathies. Brooks dealt in iron hardware and ammunition – he sent powder, shot, nails and scythes to New England – and he was also a considerable importer of sugar, arranged by Josiah's contacts and paid for by Brooks, and of beaver fur, also sent by Josiah. Brooks was a tough-minded businessman who fought his corner to the last penny. There were the inevitable tensions between partners about charging interest and credits. In a memorandum to himself Josiah noted he must examine the accounts more closely to 'find how my debt as by his account current the last year could be so much'.

But Susanna approved of the wedding. Elizabeth also found her husband's painstaking counting of the pennies and pounds sensible and reassuring. Enmeshing these various in-laws in a tight family net was very helpful for their commercial activities.

Herbert Pelham sent the young married couple a silver candlestick to celebrate the birth of their child John Brooks. It was a handsome gift costing far more than pewter.† Elizabeth had a taste for material gifts, and lots of them, as a list of her special possessions shows. She had grown accustomed to sophisticated objects and the new luxuries of the period. She owned elegant furniture which would not be manufactured in Boston for another thirty years, including the wicker-backed chairs which were then fashionable. Her pomander baskets made with oranges and cloves kept away bad smells. Even in New England it was beginning to be the fashion to be more ostentatious. Before a wedding, bride gloves were often sent to new relations. Pieces of cake followed. Her wedding probably featured sugared almonds. Sack posset would have been served to jolly up spirits. Music played while the families got to know one another. Some New England weddings had psalms sung throughout the evening, but Elizabeth may have preferred a quartet. The Winslows did not want to be sneered at

---

* St Olave's was where Samuel Pepys worshipped when he was at the Navy Office, and he was buried there. The Winslows were probably living nearby.

† Silver objects were at a premium after the Civil War because so much family silver had been melted down to provide coins for the war, especially in Royalist families. In at least three sieges in the Civil War citizens were asked to bring in their silver spoons to be made into coins to pay the troops.

by Londoners for being uncouth. There were all kind of rumours about strange New England customs: in the Connecticut Valley, for example, young people whispered to one another in full view of the family through what were called courting sticks, and it was said that engaged couples were allowed to share beds divided by a bolster or a sheet, a custom known as 'bundling'.

In godly London the Puritan leaders enjoyed display. A wedding was a time to show off. Cromwell at his daughter Frances's wedding in 1657 wore 'a rich suit of uncut velvet' made up of a doublet and breeches 'of the Spanish fashion', as well as 'lace trimmed fine linen, silk stockings, black Spanish leather shoes and gold buttons'.

Elizabeth's ceremony was very different from what Susanna's wedding on the shores of the Atlantic had been like, when a simple joining of her hand to Edward's had sufficed. It fitted the Pilgrims' mood in the wooden meeting house they had built with their own hands. But this was a different era. The couple received lavish gifts: Elizabeth describes a 'large tankard' made of silver 'with our arms'. The tankard sounds as if it was a present celebrating the union of the two families, as does what she described as a 'plate sugar box given me per Governor Winslow'. Sugar boxes held personal portions cut off the big sugar loaves, which is how sugar was sold in the seventeenth century. They were a recent novelty, and proliferated amidst the wealthy merchants of New England because of their close links to the new West Indian sugar plantations and the sugar trade. An excuse for craftsmen to show off their talents, these boxes were pioneered by the celebrated Boston gold- and silversmith John Hull, who made the first coins in Boston in the safety of the Interregnum (it was illegal to make coins anywhere other than England).*

Susanna and Elizabeth probably kept the lodgings on where Edward, Elizabeth and Magdalen had lived reasonably well for the past few years. Magdalen was now in the West Country helping soothe her daughter-in-law's fears. Much in London was more pleasing to Susanna than when she was last there decades before, especially its godliness: since 1642 the last Wednesday of every month was meant to be a fast day.

---

* One of New England's first silversmiths, another Edward Winslow, born in 1669, was Elizabeth and Josiah's first cousin once removed. His rare rococo trifles in silver, chocolate pots and sugar boxes are treasured by museums, especially one made in 1702 now at the Winterthur Museum in Delaware. Its elaborate chasing explores themes such as courtly love and chivalry, which would have been regarded as highfaluting by the earlier settlers.

Susanna now had the melancholy task of sorting through Edward's things and taking what she could home to America. She left most of his household goods with Elizabeth to form the basis of her new married life. Edward's will gave his linen, 'which I carry with me to sea, to my daughter Elizabeth'. The heavy, expensive suits were sent back to New England, one to each brother. The rest of the goods went to Josiah.

It seems likely Josiah took Susanna to stay with his father-in-law, Herbert Pelham, before she began her long journey back to Marshfield. It would have been a relaxing sojourn at a time of grief. When the New England Winslows visited the manor house Ferriers, the peace of East Anglia formed a striking contrast to their own beautiful but dangerous countryside. The sixteenth-century Waldegrave memorial in St Mary's in Bures was a marvellous sight: a kneeling Sir William Waldegrave with his six sons behind in descending order of size, and Dame Elizabeth with their four daughters. Susanna may have been shocked to see that the arms of all the figures had been sliced off during a visit from the Puritan soldier and iconoclast William Dowsing. He went to over 200 churches in East Anglia carrying out the Parliamentary army's order that 'all Monuments of Superstition and Idolatry should be removed and abolished'.

Herbert Pelham had slotted back into a society in which a number of the Puritan gentry had links with New England. Susanna knew many of them. She probably visited the Gurdons, cousins of the Waldegraves who lived at the magnificent Assington Hall nearby, where Cromwell had stayed during the siege of Colchester. It was now inhabited by the MP for Suffolk, John Gurdon, who knew Edward from the Council of State. The family had considerable interest in the Puritan experiment in New England. Gurdon's half-sister Muriel had married a Saltonstall and lived in Ipswich, Massachusetts.

Funeral sermons did not become fashionable reading matter in New England until later in the century but they were beginning to have a vogue in Old England. Susanna's hostess, Herbert Pelham's wife Elizabeth, may have given the bereaved Susanna Ralph Josselin's poignant sermon on the recent death of Mrs Smithea Harlakenden. William Harlakenden – who was a cousin of Elizabeth's first husband, Roger Harlakenden, whom Susanna had known twenty years previously in Boston – had the sermon printed at his own expense in 1652. He and Josselin had thought the words might also be a comfort to other bereaved and 'their damped, grieved spirits'. Such was its success it was published in a pamphlet containing John Donne's great funeral sermon on the death of Lady Danvers, the mother of George Herbert. That had become a staple of mourning literature in England over the twenty-five years since it was printed.

Perhaps Susanna was comforted by Josselin's idea that it was God's Providence that allowed people to forget the dead, so that time digested 'those bitternesses of Spirit that are like death itself'. The forgetfulness was not of the 'graces and virtues of the dead'. In that respect saints lived, 'but it is of their persons which in time pass from us, and we scarce retain their image in our mind; and indeed how should we, when we forget our own face even before the glass is set aside'. God allowed men to mourn, but He also put a limit to their mourning: it must be remembered 'your friends shall return again, they are not buried in the dust for ever, believe it, dwell upon it'. The bereaved must 'but consider they are but gone before on the same way, in the same journey thou art travelling, and all the Saints are following'.

It was indeed a very long time since Susanna had seen her own dear traveller. She would never see him again, on this earth at least. For Josselin the Resurrection made the dead 'our comforts, so that when others go to the Tombs and Graves to mourn, Christians go to the graves to rejoice'. Alas, poor Susanna could not visit a tomb for Edward; she could only think of him lying offshore hundreds of feet below the surface of the sea.

But now it was back home for her. With her dead husband's possessions in the ship's hold, she made the long and uncomfortable journey back to America. She could have remained in England with her daughter but – despite all its dangers and difficulties – New England was her home. Her three sons lived there. Elizabeth, meanwhile, was so homesick for tastes of New England that Josiah sent her a barrel of cranberries which he called 'a token to my sister'. As early as the 1650s, to the first generation born in America the sour taste of the unique New England fruit had become the taste of home.

Susanna was a woman who embraced the new. Like her daughter-in-law Penelope, she never became disenchanted with the colonial life. Even if she occasionally found fault with New England severity there was satisfaction in the orderly ways of the tiny God-fearing piece of civilisation that was seventeenth-century Marshfield. The marsh was full of creeks, channels of water. Edward and the rest of the community had deepened them into what they called Green Harbour Canal, thereby creating a continuous waterway from Plymouth to Marshfield. One of the creeks came up to the house and a boat was kept there. The branches and delicate leaves of silver birch trees today almost hide the spot, but the mighty view ahead remains spectacular.

Susanna had helped forge it. By the end of the century the town had two grist mills, one saltworks, by the North and South Rivers, and a herring fishery. Cordwood was being exported to Boston by the Winslow and Baker families. The North River became important for shipbuilding owing to the oak trees in the area.

Susanna was not lonely because Penelope and Josiah lived across the way. She and Penelope felt safe at Marshfield surrounded by the many Winslows and their multiplying offspring on neighbouring farms up amongst the green hills where the forests had been cleared. She was proud of Josiah, who from a young age had demonstrated a strong service ethic.

On the whole Plymouth Colony was a kinder place than Massachusetts. It lacked Boston's harshness and what today we would think of as misogyny. Ever since the Anne Hutchinson episode, it was a given that sensible women in Boston guarded their tongues. But Anne Hibbens – the wife of William Hibbens, the Massachusetts ambassador to the Long Parliament – refused to do that. A dispute with lazy workmen who were defended by a church member resulted in her being called before her church for criticising Brother Davis. The case segued into criticism of her dominating her husband. She was expelled from her church for refusing to apologise for her remarks and for being a contentious woman.

Once her husband was dead, the sharp-tongued ill-tempered Mrs Hibbens was easy prey for the malicious. Old age made her angry and not quite in control of her emotions. Hibbens had lost a great deal of money through bad investments. Accused of witchcraft, she was executed against the will of the Court of Assistants around the time of Susanna's return from London. Years later John Norton, the minister who succeeded John Cotton as teacher at the First Church of Boston, said privately that Mrs Hibbens was 'hanged for a witch only for having more wit than her neighbours'. The horrible treatment of a respectable old woman was a terrible warning to young women like Penelope and Elizabeth about the dangers of being outspoken. It may have been a reason for Elizabeth to enjoy London. Despite the Interregnum it was a less rigid society.

Anne Hibbens's punishment contrasted with attitudes to Susanna's old friend, the assertive Elizabeth Warren. Force of personality, and the need for funds, meant that after her husband's death she became a Purchaser of Plymouth Colony's debts. A woman who brought her servant to court for profanity, she defeated her own son Nathaniel and his manipulative mother-in-law, who had tried to obtain land she had gifted to her two sons-in-law. Nathaniel was told to 'forever cease all other or further claims'.

Yet Susanna was all too conscious that the older generation were passing, that the once boisterous male comrades of the *Mayflower* were fading away. Stephen Hopkins had been in his grave for thirteen years. Loara Standish, Myles's daughter who made the first sampler at Plymouth, had grown up, but never married. She died in 1655, as did her new sister-in-law, soon after her wedding. A heartbroken Myles asked to be buried beside the both of them. A year later he was.

On 9 May 1657 William Bradford suddenly fell down dead in his garden. To the inhabitants of Plymouth he had been a revered, fragile old man for a number of years. But Susanna had known him in his passionate youth. He had played a fatherly role in Edward's absence. Susanna was pleased that Josiah wrote a tender acrostic poem on Bradford's death.

Generational change even affected the extraordinarily youthful Massasoit. Two of his children, Wamsutta and Metacom, who had been boys at Edward's departure, were now strong young men. In the time-honoured way of aristocratic elites, by the mid-1650s Massasoit had married them to the daughters of the head of an important local family, the Pocasset chief, Corbitant. Corbitant had been hostile in the early days of Plymouth and his eldest daughter, Weetamoo, who married Massasoit's eldest son, Wamsutta, was a strong independent personality. She was an Indian princess who was said to have too much character for her own good. She was not happy with the increasing land sales. A very formidable young woman who married five times, she was anxious to protect land opposite Rhode Island at Pocasset. She succeeded her father Corbitant as chief as there was no male heir.

The year after Edward died, his brother John moved to Boston with his wife Mary. While Susanna was away there had been a great scandal with their daughter and son-in-law, Susanna and Robert Latham. Marshfield was shocked when their fourteen-year-old servant John Walker died of serious mistreatment. A whipping had broken the skin. The Lathams were accused of felonious cruelty. Robert was taken to

Plymouth prison and convicted of manslaughter. He was allowed to plead benefit of the clergy, a legal loophole which meant first-time offenders could be treated leniently.* Plymouth Colony records show he 'desired the benefit of law, viz, a psalm of mercy, which was granted him'. Though he and Susanna had not shown much mercy to John Walker, Latham intoned: 'Have mercy upon me, O God, according to thy loving kindness: according unto the multitude of thy tender mercies blot out my transgressions.' Sentence was now pronounced: 'that the said Robert Latham should be burned in the hand'. This was the branding on the thumb sometimes with an M for manslaughter or a T for thief which meant he could not plead mercy twice.

The townsfolk believed Susanna to have been equally culpable: the jury presented her for being 'in a great measure aguilty . . . in exercising cruelty towards their late servant'. She had not given him proper food, clothing or lodging and 'especially in her husband's absence, in forcing him to bring a log beyond his strength'. The presentment remained live for three years but she was never brought to trial. It was then ordered to be struck from the record.

Some New England jurisdictions like Connecticut and Massachusetts exempted women from being tried for capital crimes such as perjury and idolatry. It may be that Susanna's fellow citizens ultimately believed that a woman's weaker nature meant she must have been overborne by her husband. Or it may be that no one wished to offend the powerful Winslows.

The Lathams spent the rest of their lives in East Bridgewater. It seems likely that they moved from Marshfield after their humiliation (although Susanna Latham remained in her mother's will).

As well as doing business in Boston, Josiah spent time there because Penelope was close to family members: Governor Bellingham and his wife, her aunt Penelope, and her father's other sister Elizabeth, who had brought her up. Governor Bellingham was an outrageous and thunderous character, an impulsive and rather fierce man moved to great acts of kindness and used to having his own way.†

---

* By the seventeenth century, capital punishment was the penalty for many felonies. One way round this was that a member of the clergy was defined as anyone who could read. Reciting the first verse of Psalm 51 was regarded as proof of this, even though it was easily memorised. It was known as the 'neck verse'.

† Governor Bellingham left thirty acres of his land to Angola, a respected member of the small African community in Boston, who had saved Bellingham's life when he had fallen into the Charles River.

Susanna visited Boston several times a year. There were always pots and pans which needed replacing by English manufactures. She was on visiting terms with Governor Winthrop's children and families such as the Dudleys and the Bradstreets, elite families who had emigrated with the Winthrop Fleet.

Governor Bellingham was one of the last living people who were patentees of the Massachusetts charter. Most of the major figures in the founding of New England, such as Thomas Hooker and Thomas Dudley, were dead. In 1649 – the year when both John Winthrop and Cambridge's inspired preacher Thomas Shepard died – it had looked like winter even in springtime because a plague of caterpillars ate all the leaves off the trees. The beginning of John Cotton's terminal illness had been marked by a comet in the heavens. Appropriately its light slowly faded, getting dimmer and dimmer until it was quite extinct. People said God had removed a 'bright star' to glory above.

But Josiah and Penelope were young, and had their lives ahead of them. They also went to England on at least two occasions. Marriage and trade brought them renewed acquaintance with Penelope's father and a number of siblings, step-siblings and English relations. Penelope might also have been seeking a professional opinion from the medical experts New England lacked about why she had problems having children. It was almost a decade after her wedding that Penelope gave birth to another Elizabeth Winslow, probably named after her sister-in-law.

The later 1650s were not especially happy for Penelope. Her elder sister Jemima died after only three years of marriage to the exciting soldier chaplain Samuel Kem. In Bristol, Kem was said to have preached in a scarlet cloak with pistols on the cushions beside him. But in peacetime there was too little to occupy his strenuous energies. He was good friends with the hermetic philosopher and alchemist Thomas Vaughan, who died in Kem's house after one experiment too many. Jemima seems to have been estranged from Kem at the time of her death, as she was buried at Ferriers. Perhaps Kem did not have the strength of character to nurse her through a long and painful illness. Ralph Josselin came to comfort her at a time when she was afraid of dying. He noted on 7 May 1657: 'preacht this day at Bures, the Lord touch hearts, I was with Mrs Kem who is under fears, and endeavoured to persuade her to roll her soul on God in Christ'.

More heart-rending for Penelope even than the deaths of Jemima and her stepmother – who died shortly after – was that of her cherished brother Nathaniel that November. He had been her companion and friend growing up in Boston after her family returned to England. Nathaniel was one of the 'persons of great worth and virtue' drowned when the magnificent 400-tonne ship of the highly reputable Mr Garrett sank with all hands on board. It was never recovered. The sinking was a national tragedy: a large number of New England's most promising young people had been on board. They included the missionary Reverend Thomas Mayhew the younger, whose work among the Indians on Martha's Vineyard and Nantucket Edward had been at such pains to describe.

Josiah too knew Nathaniel well. By this time Josiah was a trusted agent for Herbert Pelham, looking after his hundreds of acres in New England.

To add to her low mood, what Penelope perceived as ill treatment by her father overshadowed these years. Herbert Pelham had gone out of his way in England to be courteous to Josiah's family, and he was warm to Penelope and Josiah themselves. At first Penelope had looked forward to getting to know her father better. But at some point she learnt that she was owed a legacy from her grandfather, Thomas Waldegrave. Penelope may have accompanied Josiah to England when he went to discuss what should happen to Herbert's land in New England now that Nathaniel was dead. She may have come to Ferriers when she knew her sister Jemima was dying, and stayed to nurse her sick stepmother.

News of the legacy came as a complete surprise. Penelope had only found out by chance, probably at a wedding or a funeral with a large gathering of relatives. Someone – a cousin, perhaps, or one of her sisters or half-sisters – may have asked her if she had received the £450 'in trust for them payable as they respectively came of age or at day of marriage'. As Penelope put it in her own witness statement some years later, 'Your said orator, having lived at the time of the making of the said deed [1640] and ever since in New England was for a long time wholly ignorant of what her said grandfather did in the premises'. Penelope had never received the money. Taken aback, she asked her father what had happened to her legacy. At first he said that her grandfather Waldegrave had not been in a financial position to make such a disposal.

When Penelope was tipped off – perhaps by the same relation – that her father was farming the land which was meant to fund the legacy, Herbert Pelham said the deeds did not exist. A bitter row took place. Herbert continued to make what Penelope regarded as feeble and ultimately criminal excuses. Suggesting a series of furious face-to-face discussions as well as demands by letters over the years, Penelope described how her brother Waldegrave 'did often persuade and advise the said Herbert to pay the same as what was in equity due . . . by virtue of the said deeds'. Waldegrave himself had seen the deeds and knew 'in whose custody they are or hath formerly been'. To Penelope the idea that the estates of her grandfather were in no condition to support such inheritances was a lie. Her father lived in great style in a magnificent manor house.

At first glance the delicate little face of Penelope in her portrait, with huge soulful eyes, makes her appear fragile. Her actions, however, show she was a forceful character. It was brave of the young Penelope to challenge her father. Speaking out in New England could be positively dangerous, especially criticising a man and even more importantly a father, but Penelope refused to button her tongue. And she had her husband's support.

Herbert Pelham was a formidable figure who had held office in Boston and England. He had held a raft of county offices in Suffolk and Essex in the Interregnum, including being commissioner for expelling scandalous ministers, as well as joint treasurer for the charity for maimed soldiers. Penelope was proud of her family's past and pleased by a sense of family history. She reproduced her Pelham coat of arms on many of her possessions. Her son had it etched on the tombstone over the family vault. But her keen sense of injustice overrode awe of her father.

Staying in Suffolk, the young Winslows found out that Herbert Pelham had a reputation for being a little sharp when it came to property. Penelope's aunt – the joint heiress with her mother to Thomas Waldegrave's property – and her husband, Isaac Wincoll, had taken a case against Herbert about other Waldegrave inheritances. The issue there also concerned Thomas Waldegrave's will. Had he intended Penelope's branch of the family, the Herbert Pelhams, or the Wincolls, to inherit Ferriers and two other Waldegrave houses, Ravensfield and Payton Hall?

During Herbert's absence in New England all these properties had fallen into the hands of his brother-in-law, Isaac Wincoll. Brampton Gurdon, the father of the present inhabitant of Assington Hall, was chosen to arbitrate. An award was made which gave Herbert Ferriers, the largest Waldegrave manor house. The Wincolls refused to accept the ruling and moved into Ferriers. They also seized Herbert's extensive inheritance in Lincolnshire. Sir Matthew Hale, the author of the Hale Commission, had been brought in to see whether it could be dealt with amicably. Isaac Wincoll died before the case was wound up, probably of stress. Although the outcome is not recorded directly, a later deposition and other sources indicate that the Essex lands were partitioned between the two families. The legal issues and payments of fines, to enter into binding agreements with one another, had only recently been resolved at the south porch of St Mary's Church in Bures, as was customary. The whole subject was so painful that the Wincolls were not on speaking terms with their Pelham first cousins for the rest of the century.

All this gave the young Winslows a sense that Herbert was not quite straight. Although Penelope did not go so far as to sue her father for the money, years later she did sue her brother.

For the present there was nothing Penelope and Josiah could do about the situation. They did not want to alienate Herbert and he did not want to alienate them. Common sense and family feeling prevailed, and there was no permanent estrangement. It was important for the wily Herbert to remain on good terms with the conscientious Josiah, so Josiah could supervise Herbert's land in America until Herbert's son Edward was old enough to do so himself. Herbert kept a close eye on his New England property. In 1648 he successfully petitioned the Massachusetts General Court for 800 acres. His own investments and marriage to Elizabeth Harlakenden had made him what one nineteenth-century authority called 'one of the largest landed proprietors in Cambridge'.

Josiah and Penelope had no wish to get on the wrong side of a respected New England figure who had so many influential friends.

Penelope chose to make her life in New England. The rows with her father and brother may have convinced her to focus on her Massachusetts and Plymouth family. The links with England were something from which she deliberately distanced herself. Anne Bradstreet's poem 'A Dialogue between Old England and New' on the eve of the English Civil War reflects a sense of difference between the two societies. For Bradstreet New England was the more vibrant. 'You are my mother, nurse,' she wrote. Perhaps that expressed Penelope's own feelings. She and Josiah, who were very close, were different from their kin in England. Life was harsh, but it was what they were used to. Penelope's reality was the Winslow family home at Marshfield where her mother-in-law Susanna lived and farmed, and a neighbourly way of life, in which each villager had to do their bit to protect the community from the two main dangers: Indians and wolves.

Josiah's life was physically daring and adventurous. There were days at a time when he went up the Kennebec River looking for fish and furs, which he sold at the port of Boston amongst the other merchants. Since 1657 he had been a deputy to the General Court. He was military leader of the colony by 1659 and remained so until he became governor in 1673.

Josiah's disciplined dutifulness made him a popular local figure. As well as being a trader and a magistrate, he was also a surveyor, and sometimes rode for days looking for fast water for sawmills, marking bounds, or working out who could be relied on to oversee the plans for a house of correction attached to the prison. Colonists trusted Josiah's considerable administrative abilities.

At a time when all colonies were jockeying for precedence and territory, Josiah's standing as a wealthy man and son of Governor Edward Winslow made Plymouth feel it was still an important colony that could punch above its weight.

In 1660 Charles II was restored to the throne. The Puritan experiment in England came to an end, with ruinous effects for many – especially those who had speculated in land confiscated from Royalists or the Church of England, which had to be returned. Governor Bellingham had four unfortunate nieces, the Misses Goodricke. During the Interregnum when all the royal palaces were sold off, their father, Colonel William Goodricke, bought the royal palace of Richmond as part of a syndicate. It seemed a marvellous bargain at the time.

But Goodricke had backed the wrong horse. At the Restoration Richmond Palace was confiscated with immediate effect. The family was left in terrible straits. In May 1662 his daughters wrote Governor Bellingham a piteous letter. Their father had asked them 'to let you know by these that he and [his wife] are yet alive, though much troubled both in body and spirit through old age and many infirmities and trials arising from the present times'. They hoped he would continue to pray for them and that one day they would meet in heaven. In 1668 the most enterprising Miss Goodricke decided Boston was easier to achieve than heaven. She tried unsuccessfully to emigrate to live near the Bellinghams as her circumstances and security began to crumble. Her husband, a gentleman's son who had once had an estate in Yorkshire, was reduced to keeping a 'Scrivener [printer's] shop near the Pump in Chancery Lane'. She was grateful that when every house round them was visited by the plague they were spared, but it was a depressing situation. She felt surrounded by signs of God's displeasure. By 1672 Governor Bellingham felt so worried about his nieces that he left them the rents of two of his farms in New England.

Elizabeth's Royalist aunt Magdalen briefly returned to the gracious, light-filled rooms of her rectory in Wareham when her husband was released from prison. But he was so unwell he died the next year. His health had been permanently damaged by his ordeals. Magdalen returned to live with her sons. She lived at Shapwick House in Dorset, the home of Captain William Wake, until her death just short of her ninetieth birthday.

Elizabeth and Robert Brooks were much better off than the penniless Goodrickes. But Restoration London was an uncomfortable atmosphere to live in. By the Act of Oblivion the past was forgotten for most who had served on the side of Parliament in the Civil War. But anyone who could be linked to the execution of Charles I was not allowed oblivion. What were later called regicide trials began six months after Charles II's return. Many escaped death for political reasons or because they had friends in high places, but several people who were part of the Pelhams' and Winslows' circle were executed in grisly ways. Hugh Peter was amongst them.

There were attempts to crack down on the administration of the English colonies in America, especially New England. Even in faraway Boston there were rumours of future changes, that the free and friendly intercourse between New England and the motherland would be a great deal less favourable. It was regime change with a vengeance, and vengeance was the operative word for returning Royalists.

Elizabeth had bad luck with raising children. Three sons were buried in the graveyard of St Olave's in Hart Street, where she had married; none of them lived to be older than two and a half. The only survivor was John, which may be the reason that his fond family showered him with gifts – he was the recipient of much christening booty, including twelve silver spoons. One of them came from Lord Mayor Andrewes, who perhaps sentimentally wanted to send a little something to the son of his deceased friend's daughter. Josiah and Penelope sent a porringer.

The parish registers of St Olave's show that by April 1663 the Brookses had moved to a less prosperous area, Gravel Street in St Botolph without Aldgate. Life was now not quite so easy for Elizabeth. The Restoration made doing business more difficult. For Puritans associated with the old regime, much of their comfortable way of life fell away.

The New England Corporation was reconstituted with different personnel. It continued to support John Eliot's missionary work, but the republican merchant element was allowed to retire. As the clergyman Richard Baxter put it, 'we all agreed that such as had incurred the King's Displeasure, by being members of any Courts of Justice, in Cromwell's days should quietly recede'.

Elizabeth's husband Robert Brooks died, probably of the last major outbreak of the plague which ravaged London, during the very hot summer of 1665. It is unsurprising that she then decided to return home to New England.

In July 1669 she married the richest entrepreneur in New England, George Curwen of Salem. Curwen was one of the most dynamic and extraordinary of Salem's merchants. It was an amazing coup for a widow in her thirties with a young son who had travelled from London to New England in not very good financial shape.

Herbert Pelham remained not only financially interested but emotionally attached to the colony he had played such a role in establishing. Massachusetts was still the place where God's kingdom was earnestly being created on earth. He made himself a first port of call for cash-strapped delegations from the colony of Massachusetts.

In the mid-1660s Penelope's teenaged half-brother Edward, Herbert Pelham's third son, came to live in New England and was supervised by the Winslows. It was sensible for at least one member of the Pelham family to escape what was not a favourable period for any family identified with the Interrregnum.

Young Edward went to John Eliot's Latin School and attended Harvard University, matriculating in 1673. He probably lived with Josiah and Penelope in the holidays. He would eventually inherit the land he was being trained up to look after. Josiah in his responsible way took Edward under his wing just as he had looked after Edward's elder brother Nathaniel. Herbert's will shows that he expected Josiah to handle financial affairs for Edward. (It also states grudgingly that Josiah was to be paid back money 'in satisfaction of a debt which (he says) my son Nathaniel Pelham owes him'.)

The cattle brand with the initials HP on it found by archaeologists in the ruins of Josiah and Penelope's house suggests Herbert Pelham had a herd which Josiah managed. But despite Penelope and Josiah's kindness to Edward, of whom Josiah was clearly fond (he would leave his brother-in-law 'a young horse for his own riding'), over the next twenty years relations between Herbert Pelham and the Winslows became increasingly distant. Josiah no longer had a reason to travel to England and he had other preoccupations, such as the rising disquiet about the Indians.

The Puritan impulse had been faltering for a while. In 1657 the Half-Way Covenant was drawn up by a ministerial convention. It slackened the rules for membership of the churches. Previously, members of the congregational churches who were baptised but had not given an account of their own conversion, as was the custom, were not allowed to baptise their children. Now they were. The children could proceed to full membership and not lose their political rights. It was hoped that falling membership might be halted.

In 1669 Half-Way Covenanters in the First Church of Boston broke away to form the Third Church, now known as the Old South Church. John and Mary Winslow became members.* But Governor Bellingham became upset that the covenant was being diluted, and tried to have the seceders arrested.

The Quakers refused to compromise. Their insistence on listening to their inner voices, their refusal to swear oaths, their pacifism and their individualism made them alarming. In Boston, the reaction was explosive. The hanging of four Quakers known as the Boston Martyrs – one of whom, Mary Dyer, was a supporter of Anne Hutchinson – reinforced Massachusetts' reputation for severity. Charles II himself was shocked by their execution. He intervened in 1661 and banned the death penalty being applied to Quakers; he allowed William Penn, son of Admiral Penn, to found Pennsylvania as a refuge for Quakers. Nevertheless thousands of them were imprisoned and several hundred transported.

The Quakers' sincerity made these new fugitives from England the subject of curiosity amongst leading families of the Pilgrims who had

---

* The Half-Way Covenant created new churches for those who felt unsure about their own regeneration experience. Mary Winslow was one of them. No longer the little girl who legend has it was first off the *Mayflower*, she was unsure whether she had experienced feelings of salvation. She was one of twenty-eight members of the First Church (along with her husband John Winslow) who retreated to become members of the Third Church of Boston.

their own history of religious individualism and separatism. Plymouth's official policy was to ban Quakers. The death penalty was passed against them, but unlike in Massachusetts it was never used. Plymouth Colony inhabitants were interested in hearing what the Quakers had to say. Governor Prence imprisoned Arthur Howland for holding a conventicle, but seven years later his own daughter married Howland.

There were some overzealous characters in Plymouth but nevertheless it was the one New England colony where Quakers were allowed to preach. They were not allowed to vote but, as Josiah himself reported, the Quakers 'are not disturbed except they disturb the peace'. Peace was what Josiah was determined to safeguard, wherever the threats came from.

CHAPTER XVI

The Coming of War

Massasoit died around 1660, leaving a great void. The older generation of colonists and Indian leaders who had mutual respect for one
another were dying out. The Wampanoags were becoming less friendly.
They could not help but be affected by the way the Narragansett royal
family had been treated. Meanwhile English nerves had been set on
edge by disturbances on the frontier. There were constant rumours
that the Narragansetts might be aligned with the Dutch, made more
serious in 1654 when their leader Ninigret spent the winter in the New
Netherland colony. The Dutch produced special light weapons for the
Native American market. When Ninigret attacked the Long Island
Indians, settlers in Massachusetts thought they would be next. Another
war threatened.

Praying Towns began to mushroom all over New England, a development which alarmed the Narragansetts, who begged their faithful
friend Roger Williams to present their petitions to 'the high sachems of
England that they might not be forced from their religion'. They had
been told by other tribes who lived nearer Massachusetts 'if they would
not pray they would be destroyed by war'. Williams asked Boston to
think the best about the Narragansetts, not the worst. The Indians had
been 'more friendly in this wilderness than our native countrymen in
our own land', and had entered what he called 'Leagues of love' with
the English. English families and towns had grown up in peace
with them.

But twenty years of skirmishing with Indians since the Pequot War
had had a corrosive effect. New Englanders had more brutal attitudes
to the Indians. Many, including Josiah, believed they were essentially
treacherous.

Equally for two decades Ninigret enjoyed playing with the colonists. The Narragansetts were the largest tribe in southern
New England. They had been terribly reduced by smallpox – and
the demographic balance of power had shifted decisively to the

English* – but they were still believed capable of putting warriors into the field. Ninigret constantly brought the two peoples to the brink of war. There were isolated attacks, which resulted in fines, which were never paid. Such behaviour increased the colonists' perceptions that the Narragansetts were a dangerous enemy who would one day fall upon them with the help of the Dutch and the Mohawks. Josiah became convinced the Wampanoags, too, had to be kept under control; it was always possible the tribes could join together and pose a real danger to Plymouth.

Uncas continued to be a source of instability. He and his neighbour Jonathan Brewster remained close. Brewster provided arms, and encouraged Uncas to defend their mutual interests on the frontier.

When a Narragansett killed one of the Brewsters' Mohegan servants at the feet of Jonathan's wife Lucretia, this was regarded as 'a breach of etiquette in the eyes of the English that could not go unpunished'. Another huge and unpayable fine was demanded, or else the United Colonies would go to war. In an act then and now regarded as sharp practice, a group of New England entrepreneurs – the Atherton Company – said they would assist the anxious Narragansetts with paying the fine. The Atherton Company demanded a mortgage over 400 square miles of Narragansett land, much of the tribe's total territory. If the Narragansetts failed to repay over 500 fathoms of *wampum* in four months, the company had the right to foreclose on this land. In England at this point the law of the equity of redemption prevented mortgagees from closing on the indebted – generally land-rich country gentry like Herbert Pelham. But there was no such help for the Narragansetts.

By 1662 the land had fallen into the hands of the Atherton Company. In order to outwit Rhode Island's stringent laws about land purchase from Indians, the company's leader, Humphrey Atherton, cunningly wrote loving messages into contracts, implying that they were gifts. The Narragansetts were already close to bankruptcy because of the previous fines imposed for their wars against Uncas. Although Humphrey Atherton was the managing director, John Winthrop junior was also heavily involved. He was also the commissioner of the United Colonies who imposed the fine.

The Narragansetts soon understood the land was no longer theirs. In 1664 Charles II's Royal Commissioners reported: 'These Indian

---

* By 1675 there were around 60,000 English and 20,000 Indians.

princes gave a long petition complaining of violence and injustice from the Massachusetts', who 'had caused them to be fined, and then took their whole country in mortgage, according to the remonstrance sent to his Majesty'. Atherton had violently tried to extract the *wampum* fine from Pessicus (the Narragansett chief who had succeeded Miantonomo) by dragging him out of his wigwam with a pistol at his throat.

The Narragansetts wished to be allowed to live in their own way. They felt oppressed by the English, as did the Wampanoags. The punishment of Ninigret for continuing to avenge the death of Miantonomo was regarded as another nail in the coffin of the Indian way of life. Wampanoag anxiety began to reach new heights.

The English were intruding on every aspect of Indian life. Praying Towns, in which Indians lived after the English fashion and prayed to the English God, were growing up across the country, a sign of colonial authority. There was constant pressure to sell land to which the Indians yielded because the English had been indisputably proved to be more powerful than them. But that was resented. Tribal land was shrinking, though many Indians continued to assume that they still had hunting rights, which was an additional source of tension. As they were driven inland from their fishing grounds by the new English coastal towns, the Indian fever for guns grew, because they were a more effective method of hunting.

Some historians have blamed Massasoit for selling so much of the territory that was his birthright. Others argue it was for the Indians' benefit that there was a technology transfer. The Indians were indeed extremely excited by advanced European tools. But there was no equivalence. Like other chiefs all over southern New England, Massasoit sold miles of land for objects which would have made Englishmen laugh: a few hatchets, trousers, cloth.

As early as the 1640s and 1650s the Indians were complaining about the haemorrhaging land sales to the English. But after Massasoit's death the Plymouth colonists' acquisition of land increased six times as fast as before (although his sons cannily insisted on cash). The scholar Jeremy Bangs puts it dryly. It was a process which was 'the erosion of the possessions of the five or six major landowners, Wamsutta and his brother Metacom, Quachatassett the sachem of Manomet, Tispaquin the Black Sachem of Namassaket, Charles Ahaz alias Paupmumit, and Josias Wampatuck alias Chickatabut'.

At the Restoration, *wampum* was demonetised. It no longer had an official value in English pounds and ceased to be the currency of New England, emphasising the waning power of the Indians. Since beaver had been hunted to near extinction and the little shells were worthless, it was now almost impossible for Indians to pay for English goods, especially the tools they craved. Like the other Indian tribes the Wampanoags had nothing the Europeans wanted – except their land. So they traded that.

In this uneasy atmosphere, in which all Indians were suspect, Massasoit attempted to pour oil on troubled waters and remind Plymouth of the goodwill of the past. Before he died he had taken his two sons, Wamsutta and Metacom, to his neighbour John Brown, who lived near Mount Hope. He said solemnly he hoped 'there might be love and amity after his death, between his sons and them as there had been betwixt himself and them in former times'. On Massasoit's death, Wamsutta confirmed the peace treaty with Plymouth. He asked Plymouth General Court to confer English names upon himself and his brother. He was to be known as Alexander, and his brother Metacom as Philip.

Yet as Alexander, Wamsutta had no intention of being dominated by Plymouth. He and his brother were less in awe of the English than their father had been. They saw that Massasoit's technique of using the English as a shield against the Narragansetts had become a harmful pact that was destroying their patrimony. The nineteenth-century historian Samuel Green Arnold put it brutally: Massasoit's 'fatal alliance which had released him from his recent subjection to the Narragansetts, was destined to place a severer yoke upon his own neck, to weaken, instead of strengthening, his influence over the subordinate tribes, and finally to effect the extermination of his race'.

Alexander attempted to turn back the clock, and he stopped the transfer of land that Massasoit had agreed to sell to the new town of Taunton. Unlike his more emollient father, Alexander was insulted that new laws meant all land sales should go through Plymouth General Court for its approval. He took issue with the number of land sales, but he also wished to be able to sell where he pleased as the Wampanoag chiefs had always done.

Plymouth now took a more aggressive stance. In 1662 it was decided that Alexander was behaving in a rebellious and potentially dangerous fashion. Alexander had not only sold more land without permission to Plymouth's unpopular neighbour Rhode Island, he was also said to have visited the Narragansett country. Alexander was sent for, a command he regarded as disrespectful. And thereupon a major tragedy unfolded.

Although there are several versions as to what happened, what is known for sure is that Alexander refused to attend court. By now the Indian royal families had a sense of their own difference from mere elected English officials and did not see why they should obey them. A party of officials, including Josiah, went out to bring him in. The minister who wrote a contemporary history of the war, William Hubbard, described Josiah as a 'prudent and resolute gentleman' who was neither afraid of danger, 'nor yet willing to delay in a matter of that moment'. He set out, 'taking eight or ten stout men with him well armed'. One story had Josiah drag Alexander by the hair out of his wigwam holding a pistol to him, as his friend Humphrey Atherton had done to Pessicus.

Hubbard could not believe that someone with the manners and 'so noble a disposition' as Josiah would allow anyone to ill-treat or be uncivil 'to a person allied to them by his own as well as his father's league'. But when it came to dealing with Indians Josiah had a short fuse. Like many of the leading members of the government he expected the Indian chiefs to be under the control of the English bureaucrats.

Alexander asked to go home, leaving his son as a hostage. Halfway there, he fell sick. Hubbard dismissed the rumour that Alexander had been made to walk too fast behind the English and that he was subsequently badly treated by the local physician. Nevertheless Hubbard had Josiah saying that if Alexander stirred or refused to go, he was a dead man, surely uncivil behaviour in itself. Hubbard thought that it was 'the pride and height of his spirit' which made Alexander so angry and indignant at being arrested in such an insulting fashion as to bring on a fever.

Other near-contemporary accounts insist that Alexander came along quite happily with the Plymouth party. They had found him on a hunting expedition at Munponset River eating breakfast. Having denied any involvement in any plots, Alexander set off west to Sowams.

What can be said for sure is that in the middle of the journey home Alexander felt unwell. He turned back to Careswell, Josiah's house at Marshfield, where he became extremely ill. From there the sachem was taken by canoe along the rivers leading to Narragansett Bay. A few days later he died at Mount Hope, surrounded by his people.

The Wampanoags were horrified by their leader's death. His brother

Philip's accession was marked by the wild dancing that usually preceded an attack. A suspicious number of Indians were reported to be
gathering at Mount Hope.

Whatever the reasons for Alexander's death, three crucial events
emerged from it. First, Philip became king; secondly, Josiah was
believed by Philip to have poisoned his brother; and thirdly, Alexander's widow, Weetamoo, queen of the Pocassets who controlled an area
opposite Rhode Island, became immensely distrustful of Plymouth –
although she concealed her feelings.

Philip had known Careswell when he was a child, accompanying his
father and brother to Edward's warm house in Marshfield. They had
been an honoured delegation inside its thick walls. Now Philip had a
particular animus against Josiah. Contemporary accounts of Alexander's death stress that the story circulated that the English had
deliberately poisoned him. Whether these rumours were true or not,
Alexander's death, and a much harsher policy towards the Indians,
hardened Philip's heart. He was made angrier by being hauled into
Plymouth Court in 1662 to take a vow of loyalty in a humiliating fashion. From then on it seems that Philip began privately to think that he
could defeat the English only with a major extirpative war. And he was
not alone. Many of the other Indian tribes coexisted with what were
now their overlords in a tense way. The Indians remained superficially
friendly, but secretly they festered. They seemed calm, but it was the
calm of a people biding their time. The new generation of English were
becoming associated with nothing but trickery, as far as the Indians
and their land were concerned.

Life in Plymouth was becoming far more comfortable for the English. But for their Indian neighbours the reverse was true. Philip's
proud nature made it impossible for him to overlook the past. Alexander's death, and the punishment of the Narragansetts, were still raw.

As one of the magistrates formulating Plymouth's responses to
Indian aggression, Josiah believed firm handling was the only answer.
Josiah was a more tolerant man than his father when it came to religion and was regarded as far less rigid as a governor when it came to
the Quakers. Where he *was* rigid was with the Indians. If Plymouth
could not have her will done because of affection, it must be done by
fear. And with the proud and ambitious brother and son known as
'King' Philip, that was utterly the wrong tactic. English observers
thought Philip was too haughty. Yet what they had forgotten – though
it clearly was not forgotten by Philip himself – was that he had been

brought up to live as an exalted member of the ruling family. The English had already made the same mistake with the Narragansetts' proud chiefs.

As a fine educated gentleman with elegant clothes, grand tastes and illustrious connections in England, Josiah considered himself above the Indians. Huge technological advances underlined that difference. Josiah was highly conscious of the rapidly expanding body of scientific knowledge in England and Europe which had practical applications. Merchants were importing manufactures of an extraordinary quality into New England. The inventions of the seventeenth century – the telescope, pocket watch, stocking frame, barometer, air pump – arrived at Boston and Salem just as the great continent seemed to be yielding to men of vision. Josiah could not but be impressed by medical instruments and the precision-made farm tools.

Josiah resented anything that smacked of familiarity on the part of the Indians, which in the past had been an attractive feature of relations between Plymouth and the Wampanoags. He had told John Winthrop junior in a letter in 1660 that he keenly felt 'the insolencies and affronts done to any of yours (as if to ourselves) and do the more clearly see their pride and malignity, in that they strike not only at more obscure persons, but have been injurious to some of the most eminent amongst you'. Such was 'the lowness and baseness' of the Indian mentality that our 'clemency and gentleness is but abused and condemned by them'.

It was a very different attitude from that of the first generation, including his father, who had been so attracted by what he saw as the Indians' natural nobility. Commentators such as William Wood thirty years before had praised the Indians' loyalty and bravery: 'Such is their love to one another, that they cannot endure to see their Countrymen wronged, but will stand stiffly in their defence.' But that was no longer a reason for admiration. Although their fortitude was still remarked on, it was no longer of interest, now that it was part of a disobedient mentality.

Perhaps dealing with the West Indies, where African slaves were used as labour in the manufacture of sugar products, hardened Josiah and made him more callous. Like many New Englanders since the Pequot War, something harsh had entered into him when it came to dealing with the native population. Indians as servants who had as few rights as slaves had become fairly commonplace. In 1638 the first recorded evidence of African slaves from Barbados was noted by John Winthrop in his diary. They came on a ship called the *Desire*.

Edward and Susanna had an Indian servant, a man named Hope. In 1648 Hope was 'put off and sold' to a Mr John Mainford, a Barbados merchant. Although Hope's term of servitude was limited to ten years, he was in effect a slave. Edward's brother John had a slave, 'my negro girl Jane', whom he freed (albeit rather grudgingly in his will) 'after she hath served twenty years from the date hereof . . . and that she shall service my wife during her life and after my wife's decease she shall be disposed of according to the discretion of my overseers'.

Edward and the other first colonisers had been more interested in the Indians' magicians and powwows than disturbed by them. Josiah was not a bad man but he did not have his father's intellectual curiosity. Lacking the early settlers' sense of wonder at the New World, he simply wanted to organise it. From a young age his family's position and his crisp logical mind meant he was revered at Plymouth. He had the same kind of determination as his father. All who knew Josiah described him in admiring terms. It seems that he had much of Edward's charisma and warmth as well as leadership qualities. Then as now that was perceived as the habit of command. The reverse of that coin was a certain kind of arrogance. Josiah lacked the appealing earnestness of his father, who at his age had a more open mind. Josiah was succumbing to the spirit of the age. But there were others, notably a Plymouth farmer named Benjamin Church who was about ten years younger than Josiah, who retained a warmth towards the Indians and sense of the need for justice which Josiah forgot.

If Josiah had lived in England he might have been an excellent magistrate. He was kindly, responsible and public-spirited. He was a loving husband, a devoted son, a good father, but he lacked a larger sense of connection and sensitivity.

Like so many Josiah feared creolisation – degeneration to a more primitive level through living far from English civilisation. The empathy with the Indians which made Plymouth so unusual was completely absent in him. Roger Williams had insisted that Indians and English alike were all descended from Adam; but history had moved on. The English no longer tried to see the Indians' point of view, and their lives no longer depended on the Indians' help. They were simply alarmed by them. The mode was less religious, more scientific. With the old generation dying out, even Plymouth had forgotten how much they owed to the Indians who had saved the first colonists from starvation. The Indians remained mysterious but they had lost the cachet of earlier times. The 'Lost Tribes' theory evaporated when the Restoration punctured millennial ideas. Puritans no longer thought they were living in the last age of history.

The commonsensical, sharp Josiah believed in progress. Amongst the circles of Boston's most influential merchants – in which Josiah now moved – land speculation was the new buzz activity. They wanted to expand the New England economy, to get their hands on the acres of fertile country surrounding them. Boston was full of energetic entrepreneurs who devoured information such as the new scientific kind of farming being practised in England, including the draining of the Fens.

By the early 1660s Josiah was one of many named in an English government report as an associate of the Atherton Company who made such a fortune out of the Narragansetts. Josiah saw nothing wrong with wanting to be part of the ferociously rapid infant American capitalism. Those directing its process had no time to think about anything that got in the way, especially Indians. Josiah had become close friends with George Curwen, the fabulously wealthy New England merchant who arrived at Salem in 1638 and who was one of the most innovative businessmen of his day. Josiah's sister Elizabeth's marriage to him in 1669 marked the fact that the Winslow family were a significant cog in the transatlantic businesses expanding so dramatically. The last inventory of her uncle's goods in 1674 mentions money received from Curwen. Curwen had the advantage of having remained in New England during the Civil War and Interregnum. He was on friendly terms with Sir William Peake, an important figure in the City of London who visited New England in 1664.

Kinship networks in seventeenth-century New England were as far-flung as any of today's international corporations. As Josiah knew well, a New England merchant could write a bill of exchange in Boston and his cousin or father or brother-in-law could honour it in London. Since the English Civil Wars, when goldsmiths acted as banks issuing promissory notes for gold on deposit, there had been a tradition of paper cheques on both sides of the Atlantic. In 1691, three years before the Bank of England was founded, Massachusetts created an official paper currency. This made trade far easier in New England, where specie had always posed a major problem.

After the Restoration, trade resuscitated even though most of the New Englanders had been outright Parliamentarians. Vast fortunes were being made. The early settlers' Puritan fears about importing corruption to a purer New England had vanished. Merchants such as George Curwen and Josiah used the old country for credit to expand their businesses in a pragmatic fashion.

The New England colonies were a secure, stable financial destination which could be trusted. The original settlers were educated and commercial contracts were enforced thanks to a rigorously observed rule of law. All was orderly. The Indian threat was played down by new settlements needing workers.

Because its members were often abroad, the merchant community not only had to stand surety for one another, but also help out in frequent crises. Josiah's uncle John, for example, testified he had stood in as *loco parentis* in a court case taken on behalf of a merchant friend's orphaned son suing for a missing sugar cargo. Merchants were manufacturers and moneylenders. George Curwen was a polymath. He came from Worksop, and his family were gentry in Cumberland, but he was an entrepreneur, not a man to look backwards. He revolutionised the fishing industry which saved the New England economy as the beaver population declined. Initially a shipbuilder, he was soon running an international business penetrating the cod markets in Spain and the West Indies. He also relied on close client relations, weaving local farmers and fishermen into a complex web. The fishermen's problem had been organisation. Hard men doing tough physical jobs, taking the nets out early, often away for days at a time, they were too busy to plan ahead and were sometimes in debt for years. Curwen lent them the capital for boats on generous terms. They owed him everything and he extended a long line of credit to them, so long as they purchased food, tools, waterproof material and lines from his shop – and sold him their fish. He had something like seventy fishermen in his debt at any one time.

He stored fish in his warehouses in Boston and Salem, so the air in Elizabeth's new home must have needed her pomanders. Salem had begun to flourish as a port because it was so near the cod banks providing fish for much of Catholic Europe. Curwen's genius was to be like a friendly bank manager who never said no to extending the overdraft.

After their marriage, Elizabeth moved into his vast and imposing house in Salem, said to have had a front of 150 feet. The Curwen mansion also functioned as a shop and huge warehouse which received agricultural produce from all the local farmers within a radius of fifteen miles. Peas, pork and wheat were all brought to Curwen. He sold them on to fishermen or merchants or town-dwellers like himself. The new Mrs Curwen differed from her equivalents in London in that she would have taken her turn in the shop. A lady of Elizabeth's status in England would not have served in a shop, but in Boston and Salem hard work could not be avoided. Consisting of dry goods and hardware, the shop was a sort of Aladdin's Cave, while the warehouse was full of foodstuffs and the goods George Curwen imported from England: a 'silver case and doctor's instruments, costing five pounds', watches, barber's scissors, spring locks, 3,000 needles, beads, salt cellars, bridles, striped linen, silks, broadcloth, 'flowered ribbon', sheets, Scotch cloth (presumably tartan), silver-topped canes, silver hat bands, silver cases – and cash, some of it Elizabeth's. Her husband allowed her money to make her own ventures in his ships.

In a tough world where trickery was a constant anxiety Elizabeth had married the sharpest man in Salem. Her fortunes were transformed. There were 1,500 acres in farmland; in Salem harbour were not only the boats he financed but the ketches and ocean-going vessels he built for himself, including the *Swallow* and *George*, as well as warehouses and a wharf. Meanwhile, his wharf in Boston made sure he was at the heart of business there.

The gathered wealth in Elizabeth's new home was irresistible to some of the many Curwen servants. In March 1683 a combined gang of a servant named Elizabeth Godsoe, her husband, a baker called Collier and others climbed into the house with the aid of a dark lantern. Godsoe claimed to have a key to Curwen's counting house. Curwen was supposed to keep a parcel of Spanish silver pieces of eight 'hidden in a cask in the warehouse cellar' covered with carrots and sand. Elizabeth's daughter Pen had said that there was £3,000 in gold buried underground. The thieves were caught and the Godsoes sentenced to be branded in the face, whipped and fined. Their accomplices had lesser punishments. Collier was soon released from prison on the grounds that 'his wits were distracted', i.e. he was mad.

By 1650 the Bay area was home to over 15,000 people. Jutting out into the ocean, Boston was a place where all deep-water ships could swing easily at anchor. Compared to London, the population of which was 350,000, Boston with its 4,000 people was tiny, but it was full of luxuries demanded by newly wealthy inhabitants. New Englanders disapproved of Charles II for many different reasons, but they were not immune to the subtle vagaries of fashion. The climate of social extravagance generated by the Restoration drifted over to New England. A well-to-do woman's dressing table became crowded with expensive objects – bud vases, portraits in silver frames, silver-backed hairbrushes.

There is a famous portrait of George Curwen in which he is dressed as extravagantly as a royal courtier. His brocaded coat with silver gilt lace and satin waistcoat embroidered with gold proclaim he was much more than a mere shopkeeper, which was not only correct, but also of course the impression he wanted to convey. Curwen was probably painted by the accomplished artist Thomas Smith, who began a Boston school modelled on English painters such as Sir Peter Lely and Sir Godfrey Kneller. Previously portraits tended to be made by sign painters or local craftsmen who painted their friends and relations who were often important officials.

Josiah also had an appetite for grand clothing that would not have been out of place at court. He owned several showy buckles for his shoes, and spurs – a calculated indication of gentlemanly rank.

There is an eighteenth-century portrait of Josiah's much younger cousin, the silversmith Edward Winslow junior, made by the visiting fashionable British painter John Smibert. Nothing about his calm expression and his exquisite linen suggests an ancestry of spiritual agony – his grandmother was Anne Hutchinson. His forebears would have frowned at the silver chalices he produced for New England churches.

In Boston, there was a 'small but pleasant common where the gallants a little before sunset walk with their madams as we do in Moorfields'. At nine o'clock in the evening a bell rang to send them home and 'constables walk their rounds to see good order kept and to take up loose people'. New England was beginning to have the security to be a more easeful, cultured and literate society. The air was breezy and invigorating but always with a slightly astringent tang to it, like its inhabitants' speech today. Tradesmen and gentry, the movers and shakers of Boston, lived near one another with their similar shops, and the wharves and docks facing onto the Atlantic.

In 1663 the English visitor to New England John Josselyn wrote one of the last seventeenth-century paeans to the Indians. He described 'bold Barbarians' whizzing down waterfalls 'with desperate speed but with excellent dexterity, guiding his Canoe that seldom or never it shoots under water, or overturns, if it do they can swim naturally, striking their paws under their throat like a dog, and not spreading their Arms as we do; they turn their Canoe again and go into it in the water'. Their boats and bravery reminded Josselyn of 'vessels the Ancient Britons used'. Josselyn furnishes one of the last descriptions of Philip walking confidently through the streets of Boston. He was adorned with so much *wampum* Josselyn calculated the beads on his coat and buskins were worth £20, the year's salary of a workman.

By the end of the decade the colonists were no longer interested in the Indian monarchical system, or the way the *wampum* was so cunningly made that no one other than an Indian could fashion it. Dishes made of bark and coats of woven turkey feathers no longer had the power to charm. The next time Philip was written about, he was dead, described as 'a doleful, great, naked, dirty beast'.

The Marshfield house built in 1636 by Susanna and Edward eventually disintegrated. All that remains now is a commemorative stone. Archaeologists have found signs that in the 1650s and 1660s Penelope and Josiah built a brand-new house beside the old one. It possessed two stone cellars full of glassware and earthenware of a kind that suggests Penelope made her own medicines. There was an extra room of ten feet by fourteen feet which may have been a separate kitchen.

Josiah had been looking after his mother since 1646, and possibly decided it was time to build a separate dwelling now he was married. In general Plymouth houses had an idiosyncratic style because local carpenters had their own building methods, and things were not as sophisticated as they were in Boston and the north shore. Nevertheless Penelope had been brought up in the imposing Bellingham house on Tremont Street in Boston. The combination of Elizabeth Curwen's new establishment and Penelope's memories of her own childhood may have meant Penelope demanded a dwelling more in keeping with her position. It is believed Josiah built his new house abutting his mother's in a more gracious fashion, with many gables and chimneys like houses in Boston. It probably had an overhanging porch jetty two storeys high, which was very unusual at the time for Plymouth.

Many Plymouth houses continued to have halls which were both meeting places and sleeping areas. But life at Careswell was more formal. The upper floors were for private life and the ground floor for public functions. There was a parlour not just a hall, a parlour chamber, a porch chamber, middle chamber, closet, middle kitchen, garret and cellar.

Josiah was a more stately being than his father, and his governor-ship was marked by lordly ceremonial. Four halberdiers had to attend the governor and magistrates at the annual elections, and two during the session of a court. Such pomp was unlike the usually simple ways of the old colony.

Despite their elegant way of life Penelope and Josiah lived with a certain level of determination and willed bravery. Their failure to start a family cast a shadow at a time when most New England families had upwards of eight children. An infant daughter died at two days about seven years into their marriage. Not for another six years did Penelope fall pregnant again. A daughter, Elizabeth, was born on 8 April 1664. A son, Edward, was born on 14 May 1667 but did not survive. Isaac arrived in 1671. 'Isaac' was a Winslow family name but its choice here probably reflects the story in Genesis of Isaac, son of the patriarch Abraham, whose wife Sarah was past childbearing age. The birth of Isaac Winslow was viewed as a semi-miraculous – and much prayed for – event by parents who were already middle-aged.

With such delicate children Penelope and Josiah may have been relieved that their pastor, Reverend William Witherell, had a common-sensical approach to baptism. He just wet the head. Pastor Chauncy, whom Edward had supported, believed in total immersion. New England writers nearer Josiah and Penelope's era, remembering their own experience of the New England winters, were horrified to think total immersion could be practised on small babies in freezing churches. Each winter brought a ton of snow to wooden roofs which never dried out. Ice frequently had to be broken in the christening bowl. Babies had deeply hooded cradles carved for them, much like curtains round four-poster beds, to keep out the freezing draughts.

In October 1664 baby Elizabeth, who had been born that April, was christened alongside Mercy Baker at the Second Church of Scitu-ate, the church established by Edward's enemy William Vassall, where Josiah and Penelope worshipped regularly, though it was ten miles from their home.

Having children of a similar age is a good way of bonding. Penel-ope's son Isaac was born around the same time her sister-in-law Elizabeth Curwen produced two girls to make more of a family for her son, John Brooks, now in his teens. Elizabeth named her daughters after her sister-in-law and her mother: Penelope was born in 1670 and Susanna in 1672. But Elizabeth did not forget her first husband, Robert Brooks. Amongst her prized possessions was a chest of linen which had belonged to him. It was 'always reserved to myself and kept in my possession'.

Josiah became reliant on George Curwen as a friend and mentor, perhaps for his commercial wisdom. The sober, practical Curwen was in awe of what he perceived as Josiah's noble, lordly character. Amongst the Curwen papers is an October 1672 IOU from Josiah asking his executors to pay Curwen the large sum of 'fifty pounds stout in the current silver money of New England' before the following October. Josiah most likely had ventured some money on one of Curwen's ships.

As transatlantic trade took off and business boomed, the opinionated, proud nature of the Boston merchants grew more pronounced. The gold- and silversmith John Hull was typical of the new Boston establishment, of which Josiah was now part. Hull was sent to England by the Massachusetts government to negotiate with Charles II's ministers to make sure that England did not interfere with the charter. Unsurprisingly, Charles II viewed New England as the home of regicides. Indeed two very well-known regicides – Edward Whalley, a cousin of Cromwell, and his son-in-law, the millenarian-minded General William Goffe – had fled there in July 1660, and had been openly welcomed.

Samuel Maverick, one of the earliest settlers in New England and a dedicated Anglican, hated the Congregrational churches. He had signed Child's Remonstrance, for which he had been imprisoned by the Massachusetts government. At the Restoration he had his revenge. He told Charles II he should send over commissioners to pull the colonies into line, and was himself appointed as one of them. The New England colonies were not only independent-minded and largely Parliamentarian in sympathy, they were also literally a law unto themselves.*

The Massachusetts government refused to accept the Royal Commissioners' jurisdiction, calling out trained bands onto the streets. They also hid the regicides. Edward Whalley lived in a cave outside New Haven, Goffe under a pseudonym in Hadley, Massachusetts.

Eventually the commissioners returned home, furious at the insulting way in which they had been received at Boston. Their only success was

---

* Since 1652, John Hull had been making shillings stamped with a pine tree. After 1660, in order to outwit the English government for whom the shillings were illegal, they were always dated 1652.

to seize New Netherland in what is known as the Second Dutch War, renaming the island of Manhattan New York, after the Duke of York, Charles II's brother James. Penelope's uncle, Governor Bellingham, was loudest in his defiance to Charles II. He had always been an outrageous character and had lost none of his fire in his old age. He refused to go to England to discuss New England's behaviour. Instead he sent over a ship laden with pine trees for masts for the Royal Navy. The king, preoccupied by other matters, thereafter left New England alone.

Where the English commissioners were effective was with the Atherton Company. Helped by Samuel Gorton, who had hung on to the 1644 petition in which they submitted themselves to Charles I, the Narragansetts once more petitioned the Royal Commissioners for justice. They got it: the Atherton Purchase was declared illegal. The commissioners named the Narragansett country 'the King's Province' and the tribe were considered to be taken under Charles II's protection but this was one victory for the Indians in a series of defeats.

In acknowledgement of Charles II's overlordship, the Narragansetts were to pay him two wolfskins a year on 29 May, his birthday. As a sign of their pleasure the chiefs sent extra gifts which included 'a feather mantle and a porcupine bag for a present to the Queen'. (These curios never reached Whitehall. The ship in which they were travelling was seized by the Dutch.)

The English began to foreclose on loans that the Plymouth Indians did not have the cash to pay for. Josiah saw nothing wrong with such practices. He kept adding to his own acres. In what was called the Major's Purchase, in 1662 he and forty-four others bought a considerable area of Indian land. In 1671, in what looks like a cynical manoeuvre to benefit a syndicate of Boston businessmen, he sued one of Massasoit's great-nephews – William, the son of Tispaquin the sachem of Namassaket – for £20 because he had not paid for a horse and other goods worth £10. To pay the fine, William's father Tispaquin agreed to hand to Josiah over a hundred acres of land.* In August 1672, to settle an £83 debt Philip mortgaged four square miles of land near Taunton River.

---

* Jeremy Bangs notes that Josiah's draft revision of Plymouth's laws soon afterwards made it 'legal to attach real estate for the recovery of debts even if the real estate had not been previously identified as mortgaged to guarantee the repayment'. Bangs says that because of the inequality of the Indians' financial position it was tantamount to confiscating land. As with the Atherton Purchase, by the 1670s the diminished fur trade and the demonetisation of *wampum* meant the Indians could never repay a debt made in European money. But the debts and resulting sales continued.

Such questionable practices became the norm. The settlers' desire for land, and the Indians' desire for goods, meant that by 1675 the Wampanoag chief was completely surrounded by English settlers to whom he had sold thousands of acres. Hemmed in by the English colonists' houses which obstructed his view, Philip no longer even had the right to fish off his ancestral peninsula of Mount Hope.

King Philip was proud and ambitious, temperamentally more fiery than Massasoit, and far less able to compromise. He felt betrayed by Josiah, who seemed to have completely forgotten the history of the two families. The clergyman William Hubbard, who interviewed many leaders of the colony to write his book, reported that Philip's malice against the English 'was mixed with a particular prejudice against Governor Winslow'.

Philip felt humiliated by his treatment and kept expecting things to improve. But they did not. As a result, over the next decade Indian dances (at which they plotted war) became increasingly frequent. Held at Mount Hope on a regular basis, they added to the threatening atmosphere.

And the festering issues continued. The Indians were not used to fencing their fields, so English livestock trampled their corn; and 'the English made them drunk and then cheated them in bargains'. Philip was bitterly aware of growing powerlessness. By the 1670s as many as one-fifth of Indians of Massachusetts and Connecticut lived in Praying Towns such as Lowell, Grafton and Marlborough where their wigwams had once stood. They had English houses, meeting houses, clothing and schools where they read the Bible. The Indians wore English clothes, and had short hair. The Christian religion undermined the Indian leaders' powwows and their own power. Philip's great fear was that his Wampanoags would be forced to be Christians. The Indian culture, where rule and tribute were enforced by powwow magicians, was under threat.*

In a conversation with John Eliot, who became known as the Apostle to the Indians, Philip revealed his horror at praying Indians rejecting their sachems: 'if I should pray to [the English] God, and all my people with me, I must become as a common man among them and so lose all my power and authority over them'. Despite his amiability Massasoit

---

* In 1663 John Eliot published a translation of the Bible in Algonquian, a copy of which remains at Jesus College, Cambridge. He preached every two weeks at Natick, close to where Waban of Nonantum became his first Indian convert in the 1640s.

himself had been resistant to Christian instruction. Non-praying Indians were shocked by the way their kin had abandoned the hunting which had been the sign of a man's status.

Tragically Philip was also interested in progress. He was one of the most anxious of all the sachems to learn from the Europeans. He experimented with keeping a herd of hogs and asked John Eliot to teach his people to read, not for religious reasons, but so they could get on in the modern world. John Eliot sent one of his best students, a high-achieving Indian named John Sassamon, to live with Philip and teach the Wampanoags to read. Sassamon was one of the few Indians who had studied at Harvard. He asked the Plymouth government to give him encouragement, by which he probably meant money.

Unfortunately Philip's contemptuous behaviour towards John Eliot – during a meeting Philip plucked at a button on Eliot's coat and said he cared as much for his Gospel as that button – did nothing to shore up his credentials.

In July 1669, just when the Winslows were bound up with the organisation of Elizabeth's wedding to George Curwen, news came that some of Philip's senior men had been meeting with the chief of the Niantics, Ninigret. Although Philip said it was to teach his men a new dance the English became increasingly suspicious. The thought of the two most powerful tribes in New England plotting together ramped up tension.

Philip's younger brother Takamunna had just reached adulthood and he seems to have been stirring up other braves for the war which was the traditional way of young men proving themselves. Contemporary commentators, including Philip's chief commander Annawon, excused Philip, blaming the pressure of 'others of the youngest sort of his followers, who coming with their several tales (which he likened to sticks laid on a heap) till by a multitude of them a great fire came to be kindled'.

By 1671 the die seems to have been cast. Philip, probably forced by the younger braves urging war on him, had secretly made up his mind. Hundreds of Indians were making their way to Mount Hope. Philip's men were seen preparing for war, sharpening their tomahawks and cleaning their guns. Settlers were fleeing their territories in Rhode Island because they heard the Narragansetts were also in the plot and intended to 'slay them like cattle'.

To add to the strain for Josiah, there was a new baby in their house. Penelope had just given birth to their son Isaac. Susanna herself was really quite old. In the event of an Indian attack she would not be able to run.

Some authorities think Philip was playing for time as his preparations were not yet ready. He agreed to attend a peace conference at Taunton on 12 April 1671, where he was ordered to surrender his guns. He gave up some, though not all, and was released. But as the braves continued to assemble on Mount Hope, all the signs were he was still preparing to attack. Philip's friend James Brown – the son of Massasoit's confidant – went to Mount Hope to seek an audience but Philip was in the middle of a war dance with his braves, and knocked off Brown's hat when he tried to speak to him, saying it was disrespectful not to take off one's hat in the presence of a king.

Philip refused to go back to Plymouth and negotiate but he yielded to John Eliot's entreaties to go to Boston. The Massachusetts government agreed to mediate between the Plymouth government and Philip. Horrified by the thought of war, which would destroy the hopes he still retained of converting the Wampanoags, Eliot hoped to calm the situation.

At the meeting in Boston things appeared to go Philip's way. Echoing the Narragansetts, Philip said the governor of Plymouth 'was but a subject and he . . . would not treat except his brother King Charles of England were there'. In response Massachusetts wrote to Plymouth querying their authority over Philip.

By energetic lobbying Plymouth, however, managed to convert Boston to its view that Philip was indeed Plymouth's subject. Philip was charged with violating the Treaty of Taunton as well as having malicious and dangerous designs on Plymouth. A new treaty produced on 29 September achieved all Plymouth wanted: Philip was subject to Plymouth's government and its laws. He could not make war or peace without the permission of the governor. Philip was to deliver up all his arms, and pay £100 for the trouble he had caused. He had no more free agency. Philip's humiliation was complete – and so was his determination to wage war.

All the evidence suggests that over the next four years Philip was making secret preparations. The question was not whether war would come, but when.

Josiah and Penelope were also preoccupied with the woes of Penelope's aunt, whose husband, Richard Bellingham, died on 7 December 1672 when he was still governor of Massachusetts. Bellingham's capacity to enrage his acquaintances reached epic heights with his will. He left the bulk of his estate to his beloved wife, Penelope, a tiny legacy to his son and the rest to godly preachers. This was an offence against male primogeniture – while the godly preachers were the wrong kind of godly. The will was the subject of lawsuits for over a hundred years.

Aggressive questions about the governor's state of mind in his last days were put to the widow Penelope Bellingham and her sister Elizabeth, in a manner they were quite unused to. Josiah came to the rescue. Lawyers for Bellingham's son Samuel, who eventually overturned the will, suggested that the governor must have been mentally ill to leave next to nothing to his male heir. Court documents mention George Curwen as one of Penelope Bellingham's friends present after the funeral to support her. Elizabeth Winslow had only been married to George Curwen for three years, but Curwen could be relied on in a tight corner. There was some bargaining with the trustees to make sure she got something out of her husband's property. Josiah managed to swap the less profitable farm she was left for the more lucrative one he claimed had always been known as hers in the governor's lifetime.

Meanwhile, affairs were moving to a climax out at Mount Hope. The Indians were both cowed and furious. In May 1675 it was reported that Philip's former sister-in-law, Weetamoo, sachem of the Pocassets opposite Rhode Island, was fearful of her land boundaries being eroded. She wanted her bounds to have a river at each end – north and south because of her tribe's dependence on fish.

In January John Eliot's missionary John Sassamon had made a perilous journey through ice and snow to Marshfield. Sassamon had been a teacher in the school at the Praying Town of Natick. Probably orphaned during the 1633 smallpox epidemic and brought up by an English family named Callicut, he had been an interpreter for the English since the Pequot War. Although he had worked as King Philip's teacher, secretary and translator, he had fallen out with him. Nevertheless the activities he had noticed in his travels round the countryside – the hostile faces, the secret gatherings – had convinced him something was up, and he had investigated. Philip seems to have guessed he was a spy and was watching his movements. Sassamon took his life in his hands to visit Josiah. He told Josiah he believed Philip was planning an uprising, but Josiah did not believe him.

Perhaps he did not want to think that he would have to act against Philip. Perhaps he did not want to face the future.

When Sassamon left Marshfield, assassins were waiting for him and in the dark on his way home he was murdered. His body was found under the ice of Assawompset Pond with his gun and hat nearby. Philip appeared at Plymouth of his own free will to deny the murder, but Patuckson, another Indian, courageously came forward to say he had seen three of Philip's men drown Sassamon. In June they were tried for murder with a jury consisting of twelve English jurors and six Christian Indians who were meant to assist. On 11 June – three days after they were hanged – news came from Rehoboth that the Wampanoags were preparing for war.

One of the signs of an Indian war was that women and children were sent away to be looked after by tribes who were out of danger. Philip's squaws with their papooses on their backs were seen leaving Mount Hope for the Narragansett country.

Most historians today believe that the execution of Sassamon's killers triggered a war that Philip had actually wanted – though not at a date of his planning. Once the murderers had been hanged, Philip believed that he would be hauled into Plymouth, accused of ordering the killing, and executed.

The war was Philip's pre-emptive strike. A week before it began the deputy governor of Rhode Island, John Easton, called an emergency meeting on the Mount Hope peninsula with Philip and his councillors. He was a Quaker so he had a good sense of what it meant to be the underdog. Several Rhode Island magistrates came with Easton across the narrow channel to meet Philip at the ferry. Philip arrived unarmed himself, but with forty of his men who were bristling with weaponry. Easton made one final attempt to stop the war, suggesting that a mediation system could be put in place. But Philip in his last recorded words burst forth that he did not believe in English justice: the Indians had done nothing wrong, the English had wronged them. There could be no hope of justice when 'if 20 of their honest Indians testified that an Englishman had done them wrong, it was as nothing; and if but one of their worst Indians testified against any Indian or their king when it pleased the English, that was sufficient'.

Arbitration would not work because by arbitration the Indians had already had 'many miles square of land so taken from them'. They thought the English would insist on English arbitrators, that they would confiscate their arms as had happened at Taunton, and then make them pay £100 to retrieve them: 'And now they had not so much land or money, that they were as good to be killed as to leave all their livelihood.' Philip said the English always cheated: 'Whomever the English had once owned for king or queen, they would later disinherit, and make another king that would give or sell them their land.' As a result 'now they had no hopes left to keep any land'. Most poignantly of all, Philip revealed his sense of personal betrayal. When the Pilgrims had first arrived his father had been 'a great man' and the English like little children whom Massasoit had protected from other Indians. His father had let the English have 'a hundred times more land now than the king had for his own people'.

John Easton believed that if independent arbitrators could have been arranged – such as the governor of New York and an Indian king – the war would not have taken place. But Plymouth never suggested this.

After the meeting Easton asked the Wampanoags to disarm. He said the English would be too strong for them. The Wampanoags responded they would be too strong for the English. They marched away.

Four days before war broke out Colonel Benjamin Church had an encounter demonstrating there was still room for manoeuvre. He had just started settling in at his new farm at Little Compton opposite Mount Hope and had become very friendly with his neighbour, Awashonks, the Squaw Sachem of the Sakonnets. Out of the blue she was visited by six braves of Philip's to persuade her to join his side. Instead of agreeing, Awashonks sent a messenger to Church summoning him to the conference as well. Philip's Wampanoag braves were in the state which Church knew 'among that nation is the posture and figure of preparedness for war'. Their faces were painted, their hair 'trimmed up in comb-fashion', with powder horns and shot bags on their backs. As Church remembered, 'Awashonks herself, in a foaming sweat was leading the dance' of hundreds of Indians from her territories.

But despite the war dance Awashonks was not immediately persuaded by Philip's braves. She asked Church if it was true that Plymouth was building an army to attack Philip. Church responded, probably truthfully, that he would not have settled so near Mount Hope if the government was planning a war. She told him she had been threatened by Philip that if she did not become part of his confederacy he would kill English cattle and burn houses on her side of the river. The English would think she was responsible and attack her. Church called Philip's men bloody ungrateful wretches, for the English had been nothing but good to them. He advised Awashonks to seek sanctuary with the English. She promised to remain neutral in the event of a war. Church was escorted home by two of her men. He decided not to move his goods in case that looked provocative. He asked the Sakonnets to bury them in the woods if war really did break out.

Church's confidence that the war could be contained was dealt a blow at nearby Pocasset, where he met Weetamoo. Her new husband, Peter Nunuit, was just arriving by canoe from Mount Hope. He told Church there would certainly be a war as Philip had just held a dance for several weeks, attended by young men from all over the area. Weetamoo's men had gone to Philip's dance though she had tried to stop them. Church advised her to seek shelter with the English at Aquidneck.

Peter Nunuit had been with Philip on Mount Hope when a peacemaking letter arrived from Josiah saying the English had nothing against him and had no intention of attacking him. The braves had wanted to kill the English messengers, but Philip stopped them, saying his friend James Brown must not be harmed, 'telling them his father had charged him to show kindness to Mr Brown'. Local histories note there were a number of English people Philip gave special instructions not to kill. But Josiah was not among them.

No warnings were sent round the Plymouth townships to prepare for war. Perhaps Josiah still thought it could all be settled, or perhaps he simply dreaded the onset of the fighting. He wrote to Weetamoo repeating Church's suggestion she hide herself at Aquidneck with the Rhode Islanders away from Philip's wrath. Perhaps Weetamoo had beauty and charisma that temporarily broke through Josiah's hostility. Perhaps chivalry had something to do with it. Benjamin Church described the two as friendly. Easton believed that Weetamoo had done much by back channels to try to avoid war. He may have been naïve. Locals had suspicions of the Indian queen. They would not take her in and burned her canoes. In fact, Weetamoo was probably always bent on joining Philip to make war. Not only did she desire vengeance for the death of Wamsutta, she was also a great princess who did not want her powers circumscribed by the English.

As midsummer approached, Josiah in Marshfield continued to hope for peace. But the settlers nearest Mount Hope in south Swansea started leaving their homes. On 20 June Philip's warriors began laying siege to Swansea. The inhabitants cooped themselves up in garrison houses. The long-predicted war had begun.

At break of day the next morning Josiah and Penelope were woken at Careswell by a messenger from Swansea. He had galloped all the way to let them know Philip was in action. Josiah sent messengers to call up seventy-five men from Taunton and Bridgewater to go to Swansea's assistance. He hoped to have another 150 in the field by the next day. Meanwhile he sent a note to the Massachusetts governor, John Leverett. In his usual courtly language Josiah entreated him to 'excuse the rudeness of my lines and to grant a word of answer by the post'. The situation was desperate. He feared that Swansea 'may be sorely distressed before they can have relief', though the messenger said the men were very cheerful. 'Our great request to your honour', he said, was that they used their influence 'to secure us from trouble' from the Narragansetts and Nipmucks, who were under Massachusetts protection. Josiah was confident that this would be a fight that could be contained: 'If we can have fair play with our own we hope with the help of God we shall give a good account of it in a few days.' And he continued to believe as he wrote that 'There hath been no occasion given by us, no threat, nor unkindness, but their own pride and insolency alone hath moved them to give us this trouble'. Boston replied they would send a mission with great speed to the Nipmucks and Narragansetts and to Philip. They said: 'pray let us have advice from time to time of what happens. We shall not fail to give you all needful assistance'.

The storm clouds that had been threatening for almost forty years had finally broken. The population of the English settlements trembled at what appeared to be the withdrawal of God's favour, on which they had presumed for so long.

CHAPTER XVII

King Philip's War

The revolt of the Indians was so dramatic that they drove the English towards the sea. Over half of the ninety New England towns were attacked. Seventeen were razed to the ground, their fine frame buildings, barns and fences reduced to heaps of ashes. Another twenty-five towns were badly wrecked.

By April 1676, ten months after the war began, it was not safe for the English to live beyond a certain point in the American wilderness. A third of all frontier towns in Massachusetts were abandoned. The colony begun by the *Mayflower* settlers was in danger of vanishing, as if the previous fifty years had never been.

When the Indian attacks had begun in late June 1675, no one could have predicted they would develop into what one historian has called 'the bloodiest war in American history in terms of its proportionate effect on a region'. It was assumed that the fighting would soon be over, and limited to Plymouth Colony, never that it could lead to the tribes of southern New England rising together against the English, the stuff of colonists' nightmares. The New England clergyman Increase Mather has left us a contemporary account of the war. He described how 'this fire which in June was but a little spark, in three months time is become a great flame, that from East to West the whole Country is involved in great trouble'.

On 22 June 1675, hoping to keep the mass of Indians away from the lure of Philip's warlike preparations, the governments of Rhode Island and Massachusetts went into action. But when the three captains entrusted with negotiating with Philip found mutilated English corpses on the way to Swansea, the peace mission was aborted. On 26 June Massachusetts soldiers were sent to Mount Hope.

The expedition started inauspiciously with an eclipse of the moon. The troops halted in total darkness, until the moon began to shine again and lit up the trail. To some, a black spot in the middle of the moon resembled an Indian scalp. To others, it looked like an Indian bow drawn against the English.

After a brisk rendezvous with the Plymouth troops at the minister's house at Swansea, which was within a quarter of a mile of Mount Hope, some Massachusetts troopers were so keen to get to the Indians that they impetuously ran over the bridge. It was a foolish action. Indians lurking in undergrowth attacked and Philip and his men seized the opportunity, leapt into canoes and escaped from Mount Hope across Narragansett Bay to the country of the Pocassets.

Once the massed ranks of English soldiers were ready to march across the Mount Hope bridge in formation, they found no Indians left. There was just a torn-up Bible, a very frequent occurrence in the war showing how much the Indians hated this symbol of English power.

A couple of miles on they came upon the hideous sight of heads, scalps and hands cut off the corpses of English people. These body parts had been stuck on poles. The commander insisted on cutting them down.*

Eventually the search was called off. The peninsula was empty. The soldiers came upon Philip's large wigwam which was deserted. Retreating back over the bridge to Swansea they were encircled by thirty or forty Indian dogs. So swift had Philip's flight been, the dogs had lost their masters.

Philip's dramatic escape had been masterminded by Weetamoo, who had finally shown her hand. Abandoning all pretence of supporting the English, she now threw her weight behind Philip. It was she who sent the canoes in which Philip fled, and it was she who enabled him to go to ground in her territories opposite Mount Hope. She sheltered him for a month. A crucial number of the warriors defending Philip in his hideaway turned out to be from Weetamoo's own tribe, the Pocassets. At last, Weetamoo was taking revenge against the settlers for what she regarded as the murder of her husband.

The colonists were hampered by lack of ammunition and food. They knew that Philip was holed up in the Pocasset Swamp on Weetamoo's land and they tried to make a firm treaty with the Narragansetts, to prevent him escaping to Narragansett territories nearby. Soldiers who

---

* Burying the dead became an unusual luxury. In the future the sheer numbers of English bodies, and fear of hidden Indians waiting to pick off survivors, meant soldiers had to leave them where they lay.

were all novices in war imagined that the unknown woods were full of hundreds of Indian warriors.

If failing to contain Philip on Mount Hope had been a great mistake, the Plymouth troops' inability to capture him in the Pocasset Swamp was catastrophic. The colonists should have had men at the swamp's northern end to catch him as he came out. But the Plymouth men were not professional soldiers. Ever since the New England Confederation was formed in the 1640s, militias had become more systematised, and each town had a trained band with two or three officers who drilled them in the use of weapons, but this took place just four or five times a year. Most of these officers did not have a grasp of military strategy.

Philip's warriors made deliberate diversionary attacks on the towns of Middleborough and Dartmouth, and on the night of 29 July, a hundred English troops were forced to go to the assistance of Dartmouth. Only twenty-five men were left guarding the swamp. Philip seized the opportunity to escape. He and his braves made their way north-west over the Taunton River on rafts and were now free in the Nipmuck country. The Nipmucks had given assurances of neutrality, but the promises were meaningless. They joined Philip, launching small-scale but alarming attacks on the Massachusetts towns of Mendon, Brookfield and Lancaster. And from then on the war spread across the whole of New England. Philip's breakout from the swamp was the beginning of a tremendous journey through New England rallying the tribes, largely on foot or by canoe. Philip was not to be seen in his home territories again for another year.

In the past the pragmatic Canonicus and Passaconaway had urged peace and accommodation; they recognised that in the long term the Indians could not defeat the English. But Miantonomo had warned it must be war if the Indians wanted to preserve their autonomous civilisation. The charismatic Philip had been preparing the ground with the war dances and conferences he had at Mount Hope over the past few years. Now his message of insurrection was out in the open. It spread amongst mutinous tribes like a hissing charge of dynamite. The nightmare had come to pass. Philip had united the tribes against the English.

Two weeks after the war began Josiah made his will. He had serious fears Careswell would be Philip's next port of call. He wrote to Governor Leverett at the end of July that he had heard 'my person . . . has been much threatened'. The Winslows had to decide what to do with Penelope and their two children. Elizabeth was eleven but Isaac was only four. The murder of Rachel Mann, 'a serious, modest, well-disposed woman', and the baby she was breastfeeding when Rehoboth was attacked was particularly horrifying. It seemed sensible to send the whole household north to Salem, outside the war zone, to the Curwens, who could look after them in their large house. Nowhere in Plymouth Colony felt safe.

At least Josiah did not have to worry about his mother. At some point before that summer, Susanna had died. In the autumn of 1673 her old friend Mistress Elizabeth Warren also passed away. They had known each other since Leiden, over half a century before. The Plymouth Colony records relate that Mistress Warren was 'honourably buried'. Having lived a godly life, she 'came to her grave as a shock of corn fully ripe'.

Meanwhile Susanna's grandchildren and daughter-in-law were clambering into canoes to go across the Marshfield creek to reach the sea. From the coast they could get a ketch to the safety of Boston. The household included a young female cousin, Elizabeth Gray. The Winslows seem to have brought her up perhaps as a companion for their daughter. Josiah's nephew William White was also living at Careswell to get an agricultural education, as was the custom, helping Josiah farm his considerable acreage. He was probably asked to protect the family on their journey north; he could return later to fight.

It was a frantic departure, but their journey was relatively well managed in comparison to the chaos as the war continued, when carts of desperate people evacuated burning towns all over New England. The practical Penelope managed to hand over a copy of Josiah's will to her brother-in-law.

Josiah would now be 'less encumbered'. He had twenty men with him at Careswell. He had resolved to stand and fight for as long as he could – 'as long as a man will stand by me', in a garrison where all were taking watches night and day. Josiah had built protective extensions onto the house. At an angle to the fence round the property there was a well and beyond it a pond and a cedar tree. Legend has it that from a window of the house one of the garrison spotted an Indian sniper hiding in the tree and shot him. The pond became known as Long Tom Pond. Some say there was a tunnel from the house which came up outside the stockade onto the marsh.

The countryside was so dangerous that Josiah could not return to

Plymouth town. As governor he had to conduct the war temporarily from Careswell. Fortunately he had been Plymouth's military leader for almost twenty years. He was increasingly gloomy. It had become clear that the war was going to need to be a joint enterprise involving the United Colonies. Josiah asked that Boston organise support for a defensive war, because it was not safe to send a messenger cross-country to Connecticut. He told Captain Cudworth, commander of Plymouth Colony's small army, that the ablest men, with the Massachusetts soldiers 'and our Indian allies', should be made into 'as many small parties as you shall judge convenient and so to range down this way or where your best intelligence may guide you to speak with the enemy'. The rest should go home to protect their towns and families.

Though Josiah spoke of 'Indian allies', he believed most of the Indians in the Plymouth Colony would eventually join Philip. Even Indians who were their friends would be too frightened of Philip to oppose him. The arrival of an Indian named Vickus and his son and a party of men offering to help put him into a dilemma: 'I am not well assured of their fidelity, yet in as much as they are come down to tender their service, we are not willing to put such a discouragement upon them to refuse them least it should cause them to take part with the Enemy.'

The Narragansetts swore they would not join Philip. Yet while Philip was still on Mount Hope locals had seen their canoes passing across Narragansett Bay with emissaries to Philip. A hundred Narragansett warriors had marched to Warwick, but they retreated. As usual Uncas stirred the pot in Boston: he lost no opportunity to tell the government that the Narragansetts were treacherous. But in this case he had some reason. After Philip escaped from the Pocasset Swamp, English colonists saw Weetamoo and her Pocassets heading down to the Narragansett main camp thirty miles to the south-west.

By August the impenetrable Narragansett country was hiding Weetamoo and several hundred Pocasset warriors. As always in such moments of crisis Massachusetts called in Roger Williams as interpreter and ambassador. But his influence was no longer what it had been. Miantonomo's son Canonchet had grown up in the shadow of his father's death. Canonchet was as stoical and fierce as Philip. The history of being menaced by the English meant he had abjured the desire for peace the Narragansetts had once been known for.

Ninigret held himself aloof. He had intimidated the English colonies for twenty years with his war threats. But his actions at this time reveal that he had been a clever diplomat, exploiting whatever powers he could against the English to attempt to keep hold of Narragansett territory. Ninigret had no intention of going to war. He began to distance himself from the Narragansett leadership, and offered to broker a peace, suggesting he went with an English envoy to the Mohawks to stop them joining in on Philip's side. When this offer was not taken up, Ninigret removed his people from their home territories. For the rest of the war they largely secluded themselves in unknown country. The Pennacook tribe similarly believed that no good could come from joining either side. They too vanished.

The war coincided with a widespread belief that God was not pleased with New Englanders, who would have to pay for deserting their promises by becoming so worldly. For some time there had been great anxiety amongst New England clergy about their covenant with God. Increase Mather's sermon of February 1674 had warned 'The Day of Trouble is near' when a sinning people would be punished. He had not known when. It was clearly now. The warnings about what would happen to a backsliding people were about to be verified. In his account of the war he observed that 'great and public Calamities seldom come upon any place without Prodigious Warnings to forerun and signify what is to be expected'. There had been various portents: the noise of a 'great piece of Ordnance' at Hadley and other towns; in Malden people talked of the sound of drums passing.

From August 1675 onwards, when it became clear how many Indians were responding to Philip's call, the mood of the English colonists became more desperate. God's will was urgently sought. What did it mean? Reverend Thomas Walley on Cape Cod struggled to interpret the divine significance of the war. A Quaker had told him it was punishment for persecuting them. But some thought it was because the colony allowed them 'public exercise of their false worship'. Like so many, Josiah interpreted it as God using the Indians to punish the colonists, to 'scourge and chasten us', as he told John Winthrop junior soon after the war began. The terrible destruction was for the population's own good. Throughout New England the churches advised people to beg God for forgiveness, through days of humiliation and fasting.

The thought that the Indians were a merciful God's way of restoring his chosen people to righteousness was – ironically – a comforting one. Issues to do with the treatment of the Indians were conveniently ignored. To more thoughtful settlers another truth was that the catastrophe was caused not by sinfulness but by neglect of the Indian point of view, by the loss of Indian lands, livelihoods and autonomy. But these were not thoughts Josiah entertained. All he would admit in the future was that when it came to Indians there had been a need to 'improve that great blessing of peace better than we have done'.

By no means all the Indians in Plymouth joined Philip. They began to give themselves up in quite large numbers, particularly the squaws whose husbands had vanished to fight. Slavery without trial was Josiah's preferred way of dealing with them. Around 200 Indians who surrendered were taken straight to Plymouth harbour, and sold in the West Indies.

It was an uncontroversial fact of English seventeenth-century life that rebels could be treated harshly. In 1685, 800 soldiers from Monmouth's rebellion in England were sentenced to be slaves in the West Indies. It was expensive to support captured Indians and dangerous to allow them to remain in New England, since men could not be taken away from the fighting to guard them. Nevertheless a good number of Plymouth colonists objected. Captain Eels of the Dartmouth garrison and Benjamin Church had got local Indians to surrender on friendly terms after the attack on Dartmouth. They pleaded for the Indians to be treated fairly. But the Indians were sold nonetheless. This was 'an action so hateful to Mr Church, that he opposed it, to the loss of the good will and respects of some that before were his good friends'. To agree to peace terms and then ignore them was dishonest and treacherous and not gentlemanly.

There was unease too about the slavery of innocent Indians without any attempt at a trial. The Old Testament might support slavery, but Reverend Thomas Walley complained about the 'rash cruelty of our English towards Innocent Indians'. In Massachusetts John Eliot petitioned the government, to remind them that the proclaimed purpose of their charter was to convert the Indians to the Gospel, not to 'extirpate them'. Not only would selling the Indians into slavery prolong the war, it also consigned their souls to eternal perdition. He begged for an orderly discussion to 'weigh the reason and religion that laboureth in this great case of Conscience'. He told the government that the English were behaving like the Spanish, the greatest insult in an English colonist's vocabulary. They were destroying men and depopulating the land. He reminded them the country was large enough for all to have land, Indians and English.

Daniel Gookin was one of the officials in charge of administrating the Praying Towns. He believed the Praying Towns, which were spaced at intervals along the western frontier, could have been a 'living wall' to guard the greater part of Massachusetts. With their superior ranging skills the friendly Praying Indians could have roamed the woods and protected the English to whom they had benevolent feelings. Instead, wrote Gookin in his eight-volume history of the New England tribes, 'those counsels were rejected, and on the contrary a spirit of enmity and hatred conceived by many against those poor Christian Indians'. And in return Praying Indians turned against their English friends and joined Philip.

For their own safety it was decided that the inhabitants of the Praying Towns should be interned on Deer Island in the middle of Boston harbour. In the spring of 1676 some Bostonians bayed for the Praying Indians to be killed or enslaved and sent out of the country. But more moderate voices, as Gookin reported, reminded them 'their ancestors had a covenant with the English about thirty years since, wherein mutual protection and subjection was agreed'. A search in the records ordered by the General Court produced the treaty. The furore temporarily died down as it was agreed – reluctantly by some – that Massachusetts was bound by its terms.

In fact nature did their dirty work for them. By the end of the war only 167 Praying Indians were still alive. There was nowhere for them to hunt and they slowly faded away, dying from malnutrition and exposure, living on what they could scavenge off the shore.

Benjamin Church believed that had the promises to the Indians been kept, and had they been treated fairly, it would have gone a good way to shortening the war. Most if not all the Indians in those parts would have surrendered.

As the war continued, such was Walley's concern he asked the prominent and influential Plymouth pastor John Cotton junior to have a word with Josiah. He too feared that the severity shown to numbers of 'poor squaws' sent to the West Indies was a massive provocation. 'What the effect will be God only knows. I could wish our honoured Governor would send for them back and return them to their friends.' There was 'much discontent about it; some fear we have paid dear for former acts of severity and how dear we may yet pay God knows'. If Cotton could do anything to change Josiah's mind he would be doing a good service: 'it will not be thought unreasonable that they should be returned again'.

But Josiah's never very warm feelings had hardened. In Josiah's extenuation, as governor from late June 1675 onwards he was not only having to direct a war, he was also having to deal with the effects of the Indian raids on the colony's towns. As the Indians became bolder and burned more houses all over Plymouth Colony he had the perpetual administrative headache of helping homeless widows and their children who came stumbling into Plymouth town from their ruined farms. The injured had to be looked after at public expense. Josiah was arranging to put up and feed hundreds of tired, terrified inhabitants. When it was a matter of practical survival there was little time to think about ethics. Running the war was a hideous and depressing strain. The ghastly tales of what was going on may have warped his judgement. Indians practised fiendish tortures: they dismembered the bodies of the English once they had stripped them naked and often flayed the skin off them, as well as scalping them.

The horrors of the war strengthened his view that there was no room for mercy to the Indians. They were the enemy, 'known many of them' to be of those that have burned this and that town, 'and killed many of the inhabitants'. He needed God's help 'to distinguish aright between the innocent and the guilty, if they are distinguishable'. This was total war where nothing was sacred for either side. His reactions, though not admirable, were executive. Josiah's swift actions and rapid orders saved lives, in the short term.

But he was also not in good health. Perhaps he should not have continued as governor. Throughout that autumn and winter his friends and those he governed worried about his 'frail body' and refer to weakness, though it is not clear what this consisted of.

Despite having smaller numbers than the English, the Indians had considerable advantages. Widely acknowledged to be more accurate shots than the English, they had good hearing and almost supernaturally good eyes due to their expertise at hunting. Indian forest craft was legendary. In a land where forest dominated the theatre of war the Indians knew the terrain better than any English. Increase Mather wrote: 'They have advantages that we have not, knowing where to find us, but we know not where to find them . . . every Swamp is a Castle to them, and they can live comfortably on that which would starve Englishmen.' As the English had learnt during the Pequot War, Indians were exponents of what was later called guerrilla warfare.

Guerrilla warfare was developed in America by what are now called Rangers following Indian example. John Eliot called it 'the skulking way of war'. It took some time for English settlers to abandon their prejudices against the despised – because uncivilised – Indian battle tactics, to realise that they had to adapt their manoeuvres to the forest warriors if they wanted to defeat them. King Philip's War was not a European war of soldiers in uniform tramping in tight formation across plains. War games and stalking the enemy were part of the Indians' culture and tradition. They were invisible, specialising in ambushes and deadly raids on towns by night. The Indians had largely discarded their bows and arrows in favour of flintlocks. These portable guns were much better for quick reloading than the heavy old muskets and matchlocks the Pilgrims had brought with them to America. By 1675 the tomahawk was only used at close quarters. Contemporary accounts show the Indians believed that English soldiers were slow and unfit. Plymouth's troops were farmers on horseback who knew how to shoot but had little interest in manoeuvres or supply chains. But the Indians had been thinking about tactics for centuries.

Even the commander of the colony's armed forces, James Cudworth, had little time for military action. In the past he had been unwilling to go on a mission against the Dutch because he was overwhelmed by domestic chores and his hay was still in the ground. His wife had always been unwell and was getting worse with age. He had very little help with his farm other than an Indian boy. He burst out to Josiah that he was as ready to serve his king and his country as any man 'in what I am capable and fitted for'. But he did not see why a man had to serve his country if it resulted in 'the inevitable ruin and destruction of his own family'. In 1675 ruin and destruction of farms and family were threatening to happen anyway.

When Penelope fled Marshfield, Salem was far from the fighting. But a couple of weeks after the Nipmucks started burning towns in Massachusetts the country between her and Josiah was no longer safe. A group of experienced Massachusetts military men – including Captain Edward Hutchinson, the son of Anne Hutchinson, and Ephraim Curtis, who was well known for his friendships with the Indians – attempted to broker a peace deal. As they travelled towards Brookfield north-west of Boston they noticed that all the Nipmuck villages were deserted. That should have warned them. They were ambushed in a narrow ravine and had to retreat to one of the garrison houses at Brookfield, by this time crowded with much of the town's population. Curtis and his friend Henry Young tried to escape to raise the alarm, but were forced back.

Captain Hutchinson died a lingering death of his wounds. One unwary colonist who ventured out of the garrison had his head cut off and used as a football. Eventually under cover of night Curtis somehow got to Marlborough – thirty miles away – to raise the alarm. He returned with forces to lift the siege of Brookfield. The trembling people in the garrison house had fought off an Indian attack of flaming arrows and barrels set on fire pressed up against the walls. They had been saved by a providential rainstorm. But Brookfield had to be evacuated and abandoned. This was only August. There was much worse to come.

On 1 September Deerfield in remote western Massachusetts was attacked unexpectedly. This was the furthest outpost of the English frontier. It was clear that the war could not be stopped, and the conflict spread north-east to Maine. The Abenakis, who had once been the trading partners of the Pilgrims, began to attack individual farms, perhaps in revenge for cruel behaviour by rough traders.

Along the Kennebec, over fifty settlers were killed and their houses burnt. In north-east Maine colonists led isolated lives. In search of land and prosperity, newcomers had fanned out. Their farms, whose green acres were so vast and exciting, proved dangerously vulnerable to attack by marauding Indians who felt they had suffered too long at the hands of foreign usurpers. Roger Williams had told Canonchet dismissively that Indian warfare was just 'commotion', and that they had not won any battles or seized any forts. But that was an Anglocentric notion of warfare. The Indians had indeed won no battles but their tactics were working. Settlers were deserting their land in droves. The geographical distances were so vast it was hard to get troops to the attacks in time. Atrocity followed atrocity. The Indians attacked the carts of settlers, with women and children fleeing their homes. The bands of roaming Indians bent on destruction were often 500 strong. The average New England town was no match for such swift raids.

Being a settler had always required courage in the great empty spaces. Now that courage was undermined. Men and women who had seen their friends scalped, and their brains spilling out, and no mercy shown even to babes in arms were terrified and lost their spirit. They began to fear they could never defeat the Indians and that the hand of God was truly against them.

In late September the towns of the upper Connecticut Valley gave a deadline to the river Indians to hand in their arms. A week later, on 4 October, Springfield, once the valley's most powerful and successful settlement, was wiped out. Springfield had been pioneered by the Pynchon family. They had built up a business empire which stretched to Antigua in the West Indies, where they had interests in sugar and rum. The Indians burnt their warehouses and 300 homes.

Since the summer the Narragansetts had been sheltering Philip's chief ally Weetamoo in the middle of a secret and impassable swamp. Most colonists believed that the Narragansetts were helping Philip to his dramatic and alarming successes in western Massachusetts. Without them his army could not have had such huge numbers. Dying or wounded Narragansetts were found amongst Philip's warriors.

According to the traders living on the edge of Narragansett country, the Pocassets were treated like kin. In point of fact they *were* now kin. Shortly after her arrival, having put aside her pro-English husband Peter Nunuit, Weetamoo quickly married Quinnapin, one of the Narragansett princes. Because the tie of family was sacred amongst the Indians, the Pocassets could not be yielded up, even if the Narragansetts were bound to do so by treaty. The English did not know this. But they were deeply suspicious.

Roger Williams retained his tight connection to the Indians. After suggesting in his usually eccentric way that an informal straw poll of all of New England was needed to see what God had in mind, he did good practical work with the Narragansetts. Using the moment when he was ferrying Canonchet in his large canoe, Williams delivered blunt advice to the new young chief. He told Canonchet that Philip was 'Cawkakinnamuk' – that is, his own looking glass: he was deaf to all advice. Moreover Philip was 'Cooshkouwawi' – that is, he caught 'at every part of the country to save himself' – but he was done for.

Williams reported Canonchet 'answered me in a consenting, considering way'. He warned the young chief that if the Narragansetts were false to their treaty, the English 'would pursue them with a Winter's War, when they should not as mosquitoes and rattle snakes in warm weather bite us'.

But even Roger Williams was losing his influence. He did not know that Canonchet had secretly decided to join Philip.

By 9 December the largest army New England had ever seen, over 1,000 troops from all the New England colonies except Rhode Island, was preparing to attack the Narragansetts on their own territory. It was a bold move.

The United Colonies leaders have been criticised by historians for attacking the neutral Narragansetts in a pre-emptive strike. But Narragansett neutrality was a ruse. They had failed to surrender Weetamoo and her warriors, and many of their young braves were helping Philip's troops. The United Colonies commissioners meeting at Boston that November had come to the grim conclusion that they must destroy the Narragansetts before the Narragansetts rose up and destroyed them.

Although it was a matter of some discussion who should take charge of the United Colonies forces, Josiah's long-standing military expertise, and his conduct of the war in Plymouth, meant that for many he was the natural choice. The clergyman William Hubbard, who was present at many episodes in the war, thought Josiah 'a pattern to the succeeding race, that may come after', full of courage, resolution and prudence. Josiah could have commanded 'a far greater army than ever is like to be gathered together in this part of the world', a wonderful example, as the first governor of a New England colony to be born there.

Even if there were reservations about Josiah's harshness, most of his contemporaries thought no man fitter 'for this great service' of saving New England, to execute 'the vengeance of the Lord upon the perfidious and bloody heathen', as Increase Mather called it. But those who knew Josiah worried whether he was physically strong enough. On 18 November, Reverend Walley hoped God would set aside his weaknesses and Plymouth's need of him and 'make him a saviour to this poor distressed land'. They must do what they could 'to keep him alive and in health by our prayers'.

On 10 December the army marched out of Boston in gusts of snow and ice. They were to rendezvous with the Connecticut men at Wickford on the edge of the Narragansetts' territory. There was a stone garrison house there under the command of Jerry Bull. Because of Connecticut's long history of good relations with Uncas, alongside the 300 Connecticut soldiers were fifty Mohegans and some Pequots. But after the army had crossed the Seekonk River on a pontoon raft made of canoes and treetrunks, they discovered the Wickford garrison had been massacred. The buildings where they would have had cover for the night had been burnt to the ground.

Despite the heavy snow the army started marching thirty miles south-west, to the Chipuxet River. The Indians had gone into the swamps where no Englishman wanted to go without a guide. Fortunately the soldiers found stores of food buried in the ground, and saw an Indian named Peter watching them. Threatened with hanging if he did not take them to the Narragansetts' hiding place, he led them to a swamp they did not even know existed. Because of the weather, the usually near-impassable swamp was frozen solid. Peter took them to a huge palisaded fort, concealed on an island where the Narragansetts and their allies the Wampanoags and Pocassets were hiding.

Seeing a way in, the English forces charged at the fort and fought bravely with the Indians. Six captains were killed and William Bradford's son got a bullet in him which was still there a year later. Hundreds of Indians escaped.

In an echo of the Mystic massacre in the Pequot War, the English set fire to wigwams with old women and children in them. According to Connecticut historian Benjamin Trumbull, a number of the English soldiers were unhappy at this unchristian behaviour. Drawing on accounts in contemporary manuscripts, Trumbull wrote that 'The burning of the wigwams, the shrieks and cries of the women and children, and the yelling of the warriors exhibited a most horrible and affecting scene, so that it greatly moved some of the soldiers. They were much in doubt then, and afterwards, often seriously inquired whether burning their enemies alive could be consistent with humanity and the benevolent principles of the Gospel.' But there were not enough of such dissenters to call a halt.

It was thought best to evacuate the swamp, in case the Indians were hidden in the trees and launched a second attack. Although some thought the wounded would be better off in sheltered surroundings, Josiah decided it was safer to march back through the deep snow to Wickford. But it was a ghastly journey. They lost their way and had to walk all night in the biting wind. Provisions arrived by boat from Boston for the weary troops but there were not enough. Josiah gave orders to local farmers to slaughter sheep.

Although the swamps were famously difficult to attack, under Josiah the English troops had managed to destroy the Narragansetts' lair. At last the Indians had been defeated in straightforward battle. To the victors it seemed an extraordinary and emblematic victory over an apparently unbeatable foe, a triumph for the English way of life. The engagement was ever after called the Great Swamp Fight. (John Winthrop's son Wait Still Winthrop's poem 'Some Meditations', written ten days after the battle, pronounced Indians 'a swarm of flies'. This line has been seen as the beginning of a dehumanisation of the Indians.)

The Great Swamp Fight became a touchstone of New Englanders' valour. It reversed the psychological trauma of the chosen people not having God on their side. It appeared that – after all – He was. But the Narragansetts were no longer neutral, or semi-neutral. Having now officially joined Philip they began to rain down terror on the rest of New England.

After the Great Swamp Fight the Narragansett leader Canonchet had asked for a truce, which Josiah impatiently refused. Had the truce been given and peace terms made, New England could have been spared the warfare that now ensued. Josiah's iron will at the beginning of the Indian insurrection had been viewed as a strength. Now flexibility was called for. Perhaps Josiah was no longer so in command of himself as he had been. His friend the secretary and historian of Plymouth Colony, Nathaniel Morton, thought he probably ruined his own health from exposure. The beginning of what appears to have been a clotting or thrombotic problem may have manifested itself and made him blinkered and short-tempered. Nevertheless he had the reputation of a 'stout commander'.

Since Josiah would not allow a peace parley, in the view of some critics he should have pursued the Narragansetts immediately, for Canonchet began a series of terrifying raids seizing cattle and horses. But it took two long weeks for fresh troops to come from Connecticut. Like so many farmer soldiers called up, colonists were unwilling to campaign for long periods of time. They wanted to be at home guarding their families, and sowing their crops to make sure they had a harvest and didn't starve the next winter.

At the end of January the army set off after Canonchet, always hoping for another pitched battle, but they never caught up with the main party of the fleet-footed Narragansetts. The English travelled north for seventy miles, always seeing the fires of the Indians in the distance. The skeletons of the animals the Narragansetts butchered lay all around, but for the colonists it was known as the Hungry March. Boats with food could not get to them because of the frozen water. The soldiers had to eat their own horses in the snow.

Josiah finally stopped at Marlborough because he was in Nipmuck country. Despite mutterings then and after, that in one more day they would have cornered the Narragansetts, Josiah opined it was not so. He made tracks for Boston, where the army was disbanded.

The official position was that New England still had not done enough to please the Lord. He had 'deferred our Salvation', wrote

273

Increase Mather. Josiah was furious with Rhode Island, which had not allowed the army to be sheltered in their houses during the Narragansett campaign. That had added to the exhaustion and poor health of his soldiers.

On 8 February Josiah had to stop serving through ill health. He was paid £32 for service in war. He may have gone to Salem to be nursed briefly by Penelope. But he was still governor of Plymouth so he had to return there. John Cotton junior's wife Joanna was well known for her medical skills and may have been called on to help Josiah recover.

Meanwhile in January the governor of the recently acquired colony of New York, Edmund Andros, had finally given the United Colonies news of Philip. The Indian king was sick but had 400–500 men within fifty miles of Albany.

Governor Andros had only arrived in North America the year before, but he had already done a deal with the Mohawks. When the English had seized New Netherland in 1664 this had had a knock-on effect on the local system of Indian alliances and the Mohawks became allies of the English at New York. In response to Andros, they now unleashed themselves against Philip in his winter hideout, driving him away from the Hudson River.

The English colonists continued desperately warding off the Narragansetts who were still attacking their settlements. All New England towns now enhanced their fortifications. Extra garrison houses were built with loopholes for guns to poke out of the backs of chimneys. Salem threw up a wall across the neck of the peninsula on which the town was built, an order signed by George Curwen. Refugees from Maine were driven west to Salem because it was the nearest safe town. Did Penelope learn to use a gun?

In February 1,000 screaming Indians attacked Medfield. A helpful Indian spy who had watched the town burn came through the night on snowshoes to tell Daniel Gookin that Lancaster would be next. From then on settlers became more receptive to using friendly Indians to scout; they could slip in and out of camps; they overheard plans and secrets. As they had always been, they were priceless guides through the wilderness.

As English soldiers began struggling to get through from Boston, several hundred Indians surrounded Lancaster. They used the town's winter log pile to burn the garrison house. Around two dozen people were taken prisoner, including Mrs Mary Rowlandson, the wife of Reverend Joseph Rowlandson.

She wrote a celebrated history of her captivity, which begins: 'On the tenth of February 1676, came the Indians with great numbers upon Lancaster: their first coming was about sunrising; hearing the noise of some guns, we looked out; several houses were burning, and the smoke ascending to heaven.' The Rowlandsons' own house was set on fire. As Mary opened the door to leave with her children,

> the Indians shot so thick that the bullets rattled against the house, as if one had taken an handful of stones and threw them, so that we were fain to go back. We had six stout dogs belonging to our garrison, but none of them would stir, though another time, if any Indian had come to the door, they were ready to fly upon him and tear him down ... But out we must go, the fire increasing, and coming along behind us, roaring, and the Indians gaping before us with their guns, spears, and hatchets to devour us. No sooner were we out of the house, but my brother-in-law (being before wounded, in defending the house, in or near the throat) fell down dead, whereat the Indians scornfully shouted, and hallooed, and were presently upon him, stripping off his clothes.

Mrs Rowlandson was dragged away, having been wounded by a bullet. In her arms she was clutching her six-year-old daughter Sarah, who was bleeding from the bowel and the hand. Mrs Rowlandson's mind was full of dreadful sights, her friends and relations 'bleeding out their heart-blood upon the ground. There was one who was chopped into the head with a hatchet, and stripped naked, and yet was crawling up and down.'

The Indians put Sarah on a horse because she was plainly dying, and after six days of travelling in the woods of northern Massachusetts they buried the little girl. Mrs Rowlandson was both grieving and ill herself. Every night she heard of new Indian triumphs and fresh assaults on New England towns: 'They began their din about a mile before they came to us. By their noise and whooping they signified how many they had destroyed.' And though God upheld her through her ordeal she felt she was being punished for being lazy about her observance of the Sabbath. She worried about the effect on her other daughter of living with the Indians. But as she would relate, the Indians were not unkind either to her or her children.

Mrs Rowlandson was sold to Weetamoo and her new husband the Narragansett chief Quinnapin. Mary did not like the arrogant Weetamoo, whose personal maid she became: 'a severe and proud Dame ...

bestowing every day in dressing herself neat as such time as any Gentry of the land: powdering her hair, and painting her face, going with Necklaces, with Jewels in her ears, and Bracelets upon her hands'. Weetamoo was spiteful to her and slapped her face. She was a fearsome warrior queen who fought with her men.

King Philip appeared, to coordinate campaign plans with Weetamoo. Mrs Rowlandson found herself sewing a shirt for Philip's son. Despite the war, English clothing remained prestigious amongst the Indian community. In return Philip gave her a small cake of corn and a pancake fried with bear grease. He treated her with gentleness, offering to smoke tobacco with her, and reassured her that her ordeal would soon be over. 'Philip came up and took my hand, and said, two weeks more and you shall be mistress again.' Her book is full of information about the Indians: Weetamoo made 'girdles of *wampum* and beads', and her braves left women alone and neither tortured nor raped them.

Mrs Rowlandson endured three months of captivity. A meeting was called to decide how much she could be ransomed for. Rather pathetically the Indians told her they were the 'General Court' and she was to stand up and say how much she was worth. Worried by the destruction of her home and all her family's possessions when Lancaster was stormed, she said £20. That was what she was ransomed for on 3 May.

At the end of March, in a terrible blow for Roger Williams, his own plantation, Providence, was burned by 1,500 Narragansett warriors. He had cultivated the tribe's friendship for over forty years.

In an extraordinary rendezvous with the warriors – a meeting which the town and his sons begged him not to undertake – Williams confronted them. Even as he did so, his own house was torched. Pointing at it, Williams said 'this house now burning before mine eyes hath lodged kindly some thousands of you these ten years'. Williams asked why they attacked a neighbour who had always been good to them. The Narragansetts responded that the people of Providence had helped their enemies in Plymouth and Massachusetts. They also told Williams the English God had deserted them. Williams replied that on the contrary, 'God had prospered us'. It was an exchange that left Williams shaking. The world he had built, the friendships he had cherished, were literally going up in flames in front of his eyes.

In the end he was numbered on the side of his own kind. But, as many of his statements show, he believed that the English greed for land bore a heavy responsibility. An articulate Indian named John

Wallmaker (or Stonewall John) said, 'You have driven us out of our own country and then pursued us to our great misery, and your own, and we are forced to live upon you.' That was an accurate if unwelcome summing-up.

At the end of March from Plymouth Josiah wrote to Boston begging to be sent troops. As governor he was in a mood of utter despair. He put it baldly: 'we are very weak and unable to defend ourselves'.

The Indian army had returned to Plymouth Colony with force. They massacred the Eel River garrison three miles from Plymouth town. The warriors knew most people would be at the meeting house on the Sabbath. This garrison was believed to be one of the safest places in the colony. Benjamin Church had been advised to send his heavily pregnant wife there; fortunately she preferred Rhode Island. Mrs Clark, the wife of the commander of the garrison, was killed along with eleven others.

This was followed by the grisly death of Captain Pierce of Scituate and eighty men, sixty English and twenty Wampanoag Christian Indians, who were lured into a trap on 26 March at Pawtucket Falls on Rhode Island. Surrounded by Canonchet and 500 screaming Narragansetts, they died valiantly in a circle defending one another. That same day the minister of Marlborough left church because he had a toothache. As he opened the door he saw the town was completely surrounded by Indians, who had approached silently. Marlborough was destroyed.

In Salem Penelope had no idea whether Josiah was dead or alive. For all she knew, Careswell might have been destroyed along with the rest of Marshfield. In fact Marshfield itself was never attacked, but a number of houses were burned in an attack on Scituate just nine miles away. The minister of Bridgewater wrote: 'We are in expectation every day of an assault here. The Lord prepare us for our trial.' By late April the protective circle of the outlying Massachusetts towns of Lancaster, Groton, Marlborough and Medfield was no more. All their inhabitants had fled. Farmhouses were burning in an arc across New England from eastern Maine to Connecticut. Hostile Indian forces were in striking distance of New England's main port. All the northern settlements on the Connecticut River, from Northfield to Deerfield, were ghost towns.

New England's international trade had come to a halt. With the whole country in a state of siege there were no men on the wharves to land goods, no merchants to commission ships, no farmers to cut down trees and make lathes to send abroad. As communications were reduced the English were largely reliant on friendly Indians for news of what was happening. And there was a constant anxiety about whether those Indians would stay friendly.

The very bitter feeling against the English was expressed not just by murderous attacks. The Indians struggled to deliver an explicit message that they felt oppressed by English culture. Mrs Rowlandson had noticed the hatred of the Bible – Weetamoo snatched Mary's copy out of her hand 'and threw it out of doors'. After Medfield was burned in February 1676 a Nipmuck pinned a tragic letter to a cart which said: 'We will fight you twenty years if you will. There are many Indians yet. You must consider the Indians lost nothing but their life; you must lose your fair houses and cattle.' Written by a literate Indian who probably once lived in a Praying Town, it was the end of a dream.

All over New England, in the isolated English outposts which had been havens of neat fields, the golden corn rotted. There was no one to gather in the harvest. Those who survived were too frightened to go into the fields because their Indian enemies could be waiting for them. Every tap on the window, every rustle in the bushes, could be the beginning of a shocking domestic massacre.

On 21 April 1676 Captain Wadsworth and his men were massacred trying to relieve the burning settlement of Sudbury. Indian braves had suddenly risen up from the long grass. It was Sudbury which at last convinced the Massachusetts Council that Indians must be used as scouts. This decision made an incalculable difference. Indian scouts were sent ahead 'to give speedy notice of the Indians' movements and disappoint their mischievous designs'.

The tide began to turn when Canonchet of the Narragansetts was captured. Like the citizen soldiers, the Narragansetts and the Wampanoags longed to return home. They were beginning to starve because they could not get at their food stores buried in the earth. 'General Hunger' was a potent weapon against them.

Canonchet had gone to Mount Hope to find seed corn when a hunting party of English soldiers came upon him. They did not realise it was him until, as he was running, in order to go as fast as possible he started throwing off his clothes, including the silver-laced coat the English had given him. In his haste his foot slipped on a stone crossing the Pawtucket River, he fell and was caught. When he was asked to reveal Philip's whereabouts and submit to the English, this proud son of the tragic Miantonomo said he would fight it out to the last man. Just before he was executed he said, 'I like it well. I shall die before my heart is soft, and before I have spoken a word unworthy of myself.'

Canonchet told the English that killing him would not end the war because all the Indians wanted to destroy them. In fact, however, most Indians had had enough of being fugitives. Philip's allies were exhausted and feared that the Mohawks would come for them. They were living on groundnuts and English cattle that they stole in the night. Once the planting season passed without them having put seed in the ground, they would starve. They could no longer peacefully smoke their fish on frames by rivers in preparation for the winter. They started to surrender in large numbers. An Indian known as James Printer, John Eliot's typesetter assistant, reappeared. He threw himself on the authorities' mercy, reporting that many Indians were dying of disease.

An atmosphere of acute anxiety and sadness prevailed also amongst the English. Weakened by the war, they fell prey to a flu epidemic. John Winthrop junior died, aged seventy. So many perished in Boston that the funeral processions bumped into one another.

Philip was being forced slowly back to his old territories. It was rumoured that he was calling Indians to him for a last stand at Mount Hope. He might regroup and then fall on Plymouth Colony again.

In spite of all that had happened Philip retained affection for those English who were his friends. In a tragic episode Hezekiah Willett, the son of Philip's former trading partner Thomas Willett, stepped out of his door in Swansea, when Narragansetts leapt up and beheaded him. His body was stripped and his black servant Jethro was carried off. Jethro later reported poignantly that 'the Mount Hope Indians that knew Mr Willett, were sorry for his death, mourned, combed his head, and hung peag in his hair'.

Benjamin Church, meanwhile, was coaxing Philip's neighbours, the Sakonnet Indians under their Squaw Sachem Awashonks, into coming over to the English side. Awashonks said she would abandon Philip on condition all her tribe's lives were spared. Church gave his word, and said how pleased he was at the thought of the return of their former friendship. Awashonks responded forthrightly they would get Philip's head before the Indian corn was ripe.

When he picked up his new brigade, Church was treated to an

extraordinary sight. At sundown the Sakonnet Indians came running from all directions, carrying the tops of dry pine trees to build a huge fire. The tribe surrounded it in three rings: Awashonks and the oldest of her people, 'men and women mixed', kneeling down formed the first ring next to the fire; all the 'lusty stout men' standing up formed the next; and then 'all the rabble in a confused crew surrounded on the outside'. The chief captain danced between the rings and the fire with a spear in one hand and a hatchet in another, listing all the nations of Indians who were enemies to the English and mock-fighting fire-brands in the fire. He was followed by another and another with increasing fury. Awashonks explained they were all now engaged to fight for Church. He might call upon them at any time and any place. She presented Church with what he called 'a very fine firelock'.

Church had been told a great Indian secret: that they always travelled 'thin and scattered' for safety. The English 'always kept in a heap together' so that it was as easy to hit them as a house. The English never scattered and the Indians always did.

As the summer sun blazed down on the bracken, the forces of colonists and Church's Indians scoured the thick woods. Four times they narrowly missed capturing Philip. The Indian king had cut his hair to disguise his appearance. Church was so near that his men found Philip's camp kettles still boiling over a fire, though the Indians were nowhere to be seen. Church's men frequently found flattened grass, showing they were being watched.

On 30 July Philip attempted to cross the Taunton River to attack Bridgewater again. His braves had pulled down a large pine tree and placed it across the river in preparation. Church and his men approached very early in the morning. On the stump of a tree an Indian warrior was sitting by himself. Church was about to fire when one of the Indians shouted he was friendly. As he was looking down the barrel Church realised he had had Philip himself in his sights. But Philip leapt down a bank on the side of the river and escaped.

That day not only did Church capture 133 Indians but he also retrieved Philip's wife Wootonekanuska, and their nine-year-old son. One of his prisoners told him, 'Sir, you have now made Philip ready to die, for you have made him as poor and miserable as he used to make the English; for you have now killed or taken all his relations.'

All English writers noted the warmth of the affection the Indians had for their children. And, as clan leader of the Wampanoag peoples,

Philip had plenty of reason for heartbreak now that the Sakonnet braves of his close cousin Awashonks were helping his enemies.

On 6 August a treacherous Indian offered to reveal the hiding place of the Squaw Sachem Weetamoo, Philip's one remaining ally. Her men were captured but Weetamoo herself managed to flee. She tried to get over the river on a makeshift raft, but it fell apart and she drowned. Perhaps she was too broken, cold and miserable to struggle. Her naked corpse was found not far from the waterside where she had helped Philip make his escape the year before. The soldiers who came across her body sliced off her head and put it on a pole in Taunton. Some Indians in the prison there recognised her. They started to howl with anguish, crying out that 'it was their queen's head'.

Six days later Philip himself and his closest comrades were cornered in his old home. Perhaps Philip had given up all hope. He no longer had much reason to live. In a state of extreme exhaustion, he had killed one of his followers who disagreed with his future plans. This man's brother had found his way to Benjamin Church. When Church learnt Philip was just across the water, he crossed onto the peninsula. Philip was on a little spot of upland on Mount Hope, below which was a swamp. Church knew it well. Telling his men to be silent and crawl on their bellies, under the cover of darkness he positioned them throughout the trees. As the sun rose they were to make a noise, in effect beat Philip out and then ambush him. They now knew Philip's techniques for escape. He was always first out of a trap so they were well prepared to fire at anyone who came silently out of the swamp.

The story goes that Philip woke to find the swamp surrounded. At an opening to the swamp, where he was sure Philip would exit, Church had positioned two men – an Englishman and a Sakonnet Indian named Alderman. Sure enough Philip's lithe figure raced out. They both took aim. The Englishman's gun did not fire because it was damp. But Alderman had an old musket, a more reliable weapon, and an extraordinary eye. Philip fell stone dead on his face in the mud and water, with his gun under him.

As they saw him fall, his men escaped. They did not see their leader dragged out of the mud by his stockings and breeches, or his head cut off and his body quartered by their Sakonnet cousins.

No one at that time would have found this very shocking, but the Wampanoag braves would have resented the impertinence of the unimportant Sakonnet chosen to dismember their leader. As he stood with his hatchet he made a disrespectful speech over their chief's body: Philip had been 'a very great man, and had made many a man afraid of him' but, however important he had been, the Sakonnet was now going to 'chop his arse for him'.

In the centre of another swamp in woods above Rehoboth, Church had another coup. He tracked down Annawon, one of Philip's most important commanders – 'a very subtle man of great resolution'. He had also been a valiant captain under Massasoit. An old squaw was making supper in the camp. Under the noise of her pounding corn, Church and his men lowered themselves down the cliff and seized Annawon. Church told Annawon's Indians he could guarantee their lives would be spared, and that although he would plead for Annawon's, he could not guarantee it. There followed an extraordinary scene.

All except Church and Annawon went to rest. For an hour in the bright moonlight the two stared at one another. Church could not speak Algonquian, and he thought Annawon could not speak English. Annawon suddenly produced a package. It was Philip's ceremonial dress, and included what Church called Philip's belt, a sort of stole that reached the ankles, 'curiously wrought with black and white *wampum*, in various figures and flowers, and pictures of many birds and beasts', as well as a headband with two flags at the back. Falling on his knees Annawon said in plain English, 'Great Captain, you have killed Philip and conquered his country, therefore these things belong to you.' Annawon told Church all the objects were Philip's 'royalties which he was wont to adorn himself with when he sat in state'. They were edged round with red hair which Annawon said was got from the Mohawk country. Annawon had saved them after Philip's desperate flight. The night passed in good conversation as Annawon related his war deeds and life with Massasoit.

As soon as it was light they marched out of the swamp. Annawon and his Indians were taken to Plymouth while Church had business in Boston. He was sure his men would soon capture the last of Philip's captains, his brother-in-law Tispaquin, another superb soldier. Church had given his word that if Tispaquin surrendered he would not be executed. He thought it was much more sensible to incorporate the captured chiefs along with other good fighters into the colonists' army against the Maine Indians.

But though Church had given his word to Tispaquin and intended to plead for Annawon, it was to no avail. When he returned to Plymouth their heads were stuck on poles there, along with Philip's.

Despite the amnesty, all male Indians over the age of fourteen who surrendered were sold into slavery in the West Indies. At least 1,000 were sent to work on the sugar plantations. It was their punishment as rebels, as one of Josiah's surviving certificates declared.

Most people felt harshly towards the Indians. They paid to see an exhibition of Philip's hands and the powder scar where he had burned himself, which were displayed in Boston and other towns. But finer feelings were not altogether dead. In his memoirs Benjamin Church wrote how in a cleaning-up operation in 1677 to make sure the woods were safe, he met an old Indian whose name was 'Conscience'. 'Then the war is over', said Church, 'for that was what they were searching for, it being much wanted.'

But it was to the slave markets of the Caribbean that Philip's young son was probably sent. The Elders of Plymouth and Boston made use of the Old Testament to debate what to do about what they described as 'a child of death'. This was the boy, whose name is not known, for whom Philip had asked Mrs Rowlandson to sew a shirt. Deuteronomy said a child should not be put to death for his father's sins, but there were precedents when children of notorious rebels and traitors who had been 'the principal leaders' against a whole country could be executed, even if they themselves were not culpable. But the kind-hearted Reverend James Keith of Bridgewater, who, tradition relates, hid Philip's wife Wootonekanuska and their son before they were captured, urged mercy. He wrote to John Cotton junior on 30 October 1676, 'I long to hear what becomes of Philip's wife and his son.' The last mention of him is in a letter John Cotton junior wrote from Plymouth to Increase Mather on 20 March 1677: 'Philip's boy goes now to be sold.' What became of Philip's wife and son is not known. There are many legends that his descendants – and thus of course the descendants of the great Massasoit – can be found in Bermuda or the West Indies.

Philip's death was a sign of God's blessing, that New England's providential destiny was still on course. Nevertheless colonists remained crushed by what seemed to many to be God's judgement that they were a sinful people who had lost sight of their covenant. Penelope herself had some kind of nervous crisis that was so severe she had to be counselled by Elders at Plymouth and Marshfield.

At the end of the war a fire broke out in Boston, which burnt forty-six houses before it was brought under control. It was another sign of God's power. He could turn their dwellings to ashes without the help of either foreign or domestic enemies.

Though Josiah was regarded as a hero in Plymouth, some contemporaries in Rhode Island and Massachusetts were angry about what many saw as an unnecessary war. Josiah himself was too well connected and well liked to come in for much personal recorded criticism. The war had killed perhaps ten per cent of the population of New England as a whole, with half the population of Indian tribes being wiped out. Those Indians who managed to escape the wrath of the Puritan colonies either hastened west to New York or north-east to Maine where the fighting was continuing. Governor Andros welcomed the pathetic refugees fleeing their homeland. Good relations with the Mohawks and their Iroquois relations were a keystone of his administration. Whether they wanted to be or not, numerous Indian refugees were adopted members of the Mohawk tribe.

The fourteen Praying Towns were reduced to four. The relationship between the Indians and English had been irremediably altered. It was not until the nineteenth century, when the new American Republic was in search of a national myth, and the Indians were no longer dangerous, that they were once again upheld as noble savages.

Such was the feeling in 1676 against Daniel Gookin, the superintendent of the Indians, he was not re-elected to the Massachusetts Court of Assistants. Gookin's account of what he called *The Sufferings of the Indians* was not published in America in his lifetime.

In 1690 John Eliot died. His Latin School at Roxbury continues to this day. Eliot's Algonquian Bible went out of print. After the war Harvard University's Indian College saw no more Indian students. The building fell into ruins by the end of the century. Despite the best intentions, its most successful students – John Sassamon and James Printer – had not done well straddling the English and Indian peoples.

With the death of Roger Williams in 1683 another great champion of the Indians passed away. He had denounced Philip as an 'ungrateful monster', but to his dying day Williams defended the point of view of the Narragansetts, nostalgically recalling the great friendship they had shown him for forty years. He did not abandon his controversial championing of their customs. English settlers' cheating over land grants 'stunk in their pagan nostrils' and was one of the reasons for 'their late great burning and slaughtering of us'. As was often the case with early settlers, Williams decided to be buried in his own garden. When an enthusiast tried to find the grave in the nineteenth century, all that he could retrieve was an apple-tree root. It was as if New England's vegetation had taken over his body just as the native inhabitants had taken over his heart.

CHAPTER XVIII

Penelope Alone: the widow's bed 'not priced'

The war had been ruinously expensive, and especially terrible for Plymouth. A contemporary report to the English government said 1,200 houses in New England had been burnt, 8,000 cattle had died and huge quantities of food had been destroyed. In August 1676, thanks to an initiative by Increase Mather's brother, a minister in Dublin, Irish Protestants sent a ship called the *Katharine* with cargo to be sold for the poor people of New England. Everywhere Josiah looked there was misery. Plymouth could not even pay its creditors. During the Narragansett campaign Josiah had persuaded the local grandee Peleg Sanford to advance money for bandages for his men after the Great Swamp Fight, but Sanford was still dunning for his money six years later.

Plymouth was particularly devastated because so much of the war took place on its land. In addition to blackened fields there was a shortage of labour because so many men were dead. The English had not gone in for scalping or skinning their enemies as the Indians did on a regular basis. (One Englishman had his stomach cut open and a Bible stuffed into it.) But the English had burned Indian villages. And there were other atrocities – particularly at the hands of the privateer turned Massachusetts soldier Samuel Moseley and his band of thugs. On 16 October 1675 Moseley ordered a captured Indian woman resisting questioning 'to be torn in pieces by dogs'. On two occasions he shot prisoners in his care. The rest were sold into slavery. His position as a relation of Governor Leverett seems to have protected him from criminal proceedings.

Unlike the Indians, most of the colonists eventually returned to their own homes, but getting back to normal was hampered by mental anguish as well as lack of manpower. Amidst the wreckage of clothing and linen were the broken remains of chairs and tables carved so painstakingly in happier times. Precious sentimental objects, often the last relics of ancestors and deceased relations, were blown away by the wind, and lost forever. The wilderness, which had been beaten back, returned.

286

Careswell was battered by its spell as a garrison house where twenty men had lived. Penelope had to face the fact that, like Careswell, her husband would never be the same again. Josiah was no longer the athletic young man of his portrait. Wearied by leadership, by dealing with the injured, maimed and homeless, his aims were now a return to order and restoring the public finances.

The tax rate for Plymouth needed to be set at ten times what it had been before the calamitous war, but people were nervous about returning to their homes to start the vast task of rebuilding on their own. Sporadic attacks were feared. The mood throughout New England was sombre. Men were dying of their wounds and disease. As Mary Rowlandson would recall: 'I can remember the time when I used to sleep quietly without workings in my thoughts, whole nights together, but now it is other ways with me.'

The solution preached by Elders in meeting houses all over New England was greater orthodoxy, greater repentance and a harsher attitude to heterodoxy. The war had happened because the colonists had retreated from the values which had brought them to America. Eastern Maine was still uninhabitable because of the continuing war with the Abenaki. The drying up of trade and the despair was inevitably seen as a sign of sinfulness exemplified for some by the Half-Way Covenant. The Old Testament showed how God had punished His people in the past if they had not pleased Him. Now He was doing it again.

In his poem 'New England's Crisis' the schoolmaster poet Benjamin Tompson pointed out that if New England had remained true to the simplicity of its early days – when settlers were happy to eat off wooden trays with clam shells – all might have been well. Tompson sighed for the Eden of their 'wiser fathers', when manners were plain, clothes not European but 'puritanick capes', and when graces were so long the food got cold. They had been 'golden times (too fortunate to hold)' sinned away 'for love of gold'.

The colonial administrator Edward Randolph was asked by the government in London to report on New England in the aftermath of the war. He related in amazement 'the government of the Massachusetts (to give it in their own words) do declare these are the great evils for which God hath given the heathen commission to rise against them', one of which was 'following strange fashions in their apparel'.

But the sin of pride was all part of the same problem, the new profaneness which made God angry. Now Plymouth Colony's inhabitants were graver, less accommodating and less open-minded than before.

There was a new brutality, as if they wanted to prove themselves by their harshness and intolerance. Plymouth had been much the most charitable to the Quakers of the New England colonies. There were several communities of them, especially on Cape Cod, but now feeling had grown that their strange religion bore a heavy responsibility for 'these dreadful frowns of providence'. The Quakers had earned additional obloquy because of their association with Rhode Island. Rhode Islanders had tried to claim some of Philip's empty land and had taken in many of the defeated Indians, although they felt that they had suffered badly from a war that was not of their making.

There was only one way of paying for the costs of the war: gain control of the rich agricultural Wampanoag lands at Mount Hope. It was Josiah's hope that these Indian territories be granted to Plymouth as opposed to their rivals, Rhode Island and Massachusetts. To this end, and to secure a proper charter, Josiah heavily cultivated the English government official Edward Randolph. Randolph was a frequent guest at Careswell. Josiah was becoming increasingly lame but Randolph was taken to shoot game in an elegant fashion. Over a glass of wine imported before the war, Randolph convivially discussed how to advantage Plymouth.

A man on the make, Edward Randolph had come to New England in 1676 on behalf of his wife's cousin, Robert Mason. Since the earliest days of the Pilgrims the Masons had links to land in New Hampshire. But once he arrived Randolph saw that his best chance for advancement was to work for the government in England. He turned himself into a spy on their behalf, writing a critical report of the highly irregular life across the Atlantic. By 1678 he was Collector of the Customs in New England, though this was a title honoured in the breach – Massachusetts ignored most of the English Navigation Acts. Exasperated by constantly coming up against Massachusetts' celebrated charter and insistence on self-government, Randolph was the key figure who in 1684 suggested the charter be removed and a royal governor be introduced.

Josiah's courting of Edward Randolph earned him a great deal of dislike in Massachusetts. Ultimately Josiah's loyalty was to Plymouth. Like many moderates – who were denounced as villains by fiery New England patriots – Josiah was a pragmatist. It was in his fellow colonists' interests at Plymouth to ingratiate themselves with the powerful English government, even if it broke the line with Massachusetts.

Charles II's government had been frequently insulted by Massachusetts but Plymouth's vulnerable position – it lacked a proper charter – meant that it had always been more accommodating. Josiah's father would have been astonished by Josiah's obsequious letters. He would never have called a king 'Dread sovereign' or compared him to the holy King of Kings. But like many a son with a powerful father, Josiah shrugged off his legacy of Puritanism, and told himself that these were different times.

In June 1677 Josiah sent Charles II the highly symbolic war trophies of King Philip's regalia which Annawon had handed over so solemnly to Benjamin Church. These extraordinary personal effects of the Indian chief who had terrorised New England might bring home to Charles the reality of what the settlers had experienced. The trophies were accompanied by a letter to remind the English king of the great losses Plymouth had endured defending the English Christian way of life they had planted in America. Josiah reiterated – as he was to do many times – that the war was not Plymouth's fault, that relations with the Indians had been peaceful and that Plymouth had borne by far the greatest cost of the war: '100,000*l*. besides inestimable damage sustained by particular persons and plantations, and the loss of the lives of many hundred of their brethren, children, and choice friends'.

Disingenuously, he claimed that Mount Hope was within the patent grant made to New Plymouth – a claim which would have astonished Massasoit. Josiah wrote 'earnestly to beg that they may not be deprived of it, not only because they have fought and paid and bled for it, but because this Colony for want of good harbours could never get considerable improvement of the sea, whereas these places are well accommodated for the settlement of a sea-port town or two'. Many have seen the war against Philip as an attempt to seize his land. But taking the whole of Philip's patrimony was something the colony was achieving by stealth in any case.

The regalia which had once adorned Philip's now decapitated and pathetic body were put on a ship to London for the attention of a merchant named Ashurst. It was to be despatched to Josiah's brother-in-law Waldegrave Pelham, at Ferriers in Suffolk, for him to present at court. Unaware of its importance, Waldegrave probably thought nothing of what to him were simply strips of material covered in shells. Entrusting this task to Waldegrave Pelham was a mistake. Josiah's ne'er-do-well brother-in-law never delivered the famous regalia of the Wampanoag chieftains. It vanished and has not been seen again.

But until February 1679 – when he received a letter from London about Mount Hope – Josiah was completely unaware of this. At a time when communications were sparse, Plymouth had assumed Charles II's silence meant acquiescence. Plymouth was already arranging the sale of the rest of the Mount Hope lands to Boston businessmen. No one in Plymouth could afford to be part of the consortium. Its economy did not recover for a hundred years.

It would be extremely embarrassing if Charles II were to decide this land was not Plymouth's to sell. As was explained to the English government: 'Having written about two years since and doubted not till now that the letters were received,' Plymouth 'did believe the King was satisfied and thereupon disposed of some of the conquered lands.'

Unfortunately Josiah's anxiety to become Edward Randolph's best friend made him overplay his hand. Boston politicians found out that Josiah had influenced Randolph's highly critical reports. It emerged that on Randolph's first visit to Careswell Josiah had suggested New England would do better and be more useful to the English government if 'the several Colonies and plantations were reduced under your Majesty's immediate government' – i.e. there should be a royal governor general. Josiah had 'expressed his great dislike of the carriage of the magistrates of Boston to your Majesty's royal person and your subjects under their government'. The daily breaches of the English navigation laws, and the exorbitant rates charged by Massachusetts for using their harbours, were destroying trade profits for other colonies as well as the English government.

Did Josiah really make these disloyal remarks? He denied them immediately. But he was a dying man, with little time perhaps for lofty thoughts of New England's historic self-government. Perhaps by now proud colonial independence had become simply 'the inconveniences of a divided government daily arising', as Randolph reported. What energy Josiah had left had become domestic and small-scale.

But Josiah and Randolph continued to be intimate. Randolph wrote regularly to Josiah. At the beginning of January 1680 from Maine he complained he had been received at Boston 'more like a spy than one of his majesty's servants'. He had been welcomed by a rude poem about himself – 'scandalous verses'. He added rather sinisterly that he took all the more notice because it reflected 'so much upon my master, who will not forget it'.

The word was out that Josiah simply would not live much longer. He had told Randolph he was too unwell to go to England. But in his clumsy way Randolph still urged Josiah to make the effort: 'Considering the necessity there is of renewing your charter, you can never do your colony greater service than to appear yourself at Whitehall.'

But Josiah never did. He was still managing to sit in court, but on bad days the session had to come to him in Marshfield. Thomas Hinckley became deputy governor, a position invented precisely because it was now often too arduous for Josiah to make the journey from Marshfield to Plymouth. The shades were lengthening for him, and Plymouth Colony itself.

But in January 1680 the cultivation of Randolph paid off. His Majesty's reception of Josiah's letters had been 'kind'. Because of Plymouth's 'Loyalty and good Conduct in that War' Charles II granted 7,000 acres of Mount Hope lands to Plymouth in exchange for a quit rent of seven beaver skins to be delivered to Windsor Castle every year on the feast of John the Baptist.

Though the governor was slowly dying, aged fifty-two, he had pressing personal legal concerns in England. Penelope's father, Herbert Pelham, had died, and in March 1676 his will was published. Ever since then a legal dispute had been raging between Waldegrave Pelham and Penelope's relations.

At first Penelope and Josiah were oblivious of this. New England was deep in a battle for its very survival. Travel was severely disrupted by the war. Even in May when Penelope's younger half-sister Anne and her husband Samuel Stannard began a suit against Waldegrave Pelham for another unpaid legacy – supposedly left them by Herbert in his dying days – Plymouth was still under threat. Most of its populations were gathered in stockades. But once Boston harbour reopened and it became safe to travel the countryside, communications resumed. Anne Stannard and her avid new husband had launched a suit very soon after their wedding, claiming £200 they said Anne had been left in a trust not mentioned in the will.

Much more importantly for Penelope and Josiah, Herbert's will did not mention the £450 left to Penelope by her grandfather Thomas Waldegrave, of which, since the mid-1650s, she had believed she was being deprived.

What her father left her was respectable but not on that scale. Like her aunts in New England, Penelope got a small income from the rents of a farm on his Lincolnshire estates, though her sister Katharine, and Anne were more generously provided for. The Winslows were in the queue (after other younger English Pelhams) for a year's rent here and there. Yet one of these sums was for money Josiah had been owed by Nathaniel Pelham, who had been dead for the past twenty years. Herbert had refused to pay up. Since Josiah was looking after Herbert's property and cattle for him, and doing Herbert the favour of being the guardian of Penelope's high-spirited brother Edward, it was rather grudging. Josiah was to administer Edward's rents for the property he was to inherit – or not inherit, if Edward failed to become (as the will put it) 'serious, sober and solid', and be 'reclaimed'. Penelope got half the goods, 'all other brass, bedding, linen, with all my books and other utensils and movables' which Herbert had in New England, but the family silver went to her younger brother.

Incomplete records mean it is hard to see what steps Penelope and Josiah had previously taken to obtain Penelope's grandfather's legacy in the twenty years since they had first learnt about it. But it seems that they let things slide and then hoped that they would retrieve the money from Waldegrave after Herbert's death. In the past, during the angry confrontations between Herbert and the Winslows, Waldegrave had been sympathetic to the need for his father to give his sister her grandfather's legacy.

Sending King Philip's trophies via Waldegrave may have been Josiah's attempt to please him by giving him the privilege of attending court. But it had no effect. Josiah now believed that Waldegrave by then owed them £1,000. The funds additional to the £450, Thomas Waldegrave's legacy, were most likely for business which Josiah had contracted on Herbert's behalf.

By the autumn of 1680 Herbert had been dead for six years, yet no money had appeared. Like everyone else in New England after the war the Winslows struggled financially. In September they sent a Letter of Attorney from Marshfield to Thomas Sergeant of the Middle Temple. It permitted Sergeant to receive 'all and every legacy and legacies as were given and bequeathed unto the said Penelope by her grandfather Thomas Waldegrave' and any rents from Waldegrave Pelham. It commissioned him to take any legal action necessary.

Josiah was fading fast. He was too ill to travel to England in person, and it was urgent they should sort out the matter while Penelope still had a powerful male at her side. Once she was on her own, as a woman, it would be far more difficult to be taken seriously, as she knew well from the experience of her aunt, Mistress Bellingham. Most lawsuits were much more effective if a man put his name to them, which was probably why Penelope got a dying Josiah to issue a writ.

Since the fifteenth century the Equity Courts of England had specialised in protecting the property of married women. Although upon marriage a woman legally became part of her husband's body, the Equity Courts, unlike the ordinary courts, recognised a married woman had separate rights. A married woman could initiate a suit there on her own, but it was looked on more favourably if a husband helped press his wife's claim.

It was the last action Josiah carried out for his wife, but nothing happened.

Penelope threw herself into the hopeless task of nursing a man dying before her eyes. She boiled sheets, kept broth going on the stove, and gathered herbs for purifying the blood, including elder roots, sage, comfrey and rosemary. The Charles River was frozen over, and we can imagine the sick Josiah trying to get warm at Careswell. Penelope would have liked him to be in bed but he insisted on trying to sort out the various claims to Mount Hope almost to the day he died. Penelope spent £20 on a doctor, a huge sum. Trained doctors in New England were rare. Ministers frequently combined healing with preaching. The country had not been an attractive arena for medical men. Settlers preferred divinity to cure them.

Prayers were offered in all the colony churches for Josiah. Penelope was made of sterner stuff: she was determined to find someone with medical training. The doctor came from Boston and probably stayed in the house for several days.

The appearance of a great comet generated a febrile and apocalyptic atmosphere. Josiah's old friend Thomas Hinckley could not help thinking it signified the governor's 'dying state'.

Poor Penelope had been badly hit by spiritual anxiety brought on by the war. Letters to her from Nathaniel Morton show that in the late 1670s she had passed through a painful religious crisis when she was in 'great affliction of mind' and 'God's people sought to God for you and God brought you through those difficulties'. Many New Englanders, however devout, passed through times of anguish about their faith or their godliness, or whether they were saved. Perhaps Penelope was angry with God for what happened to Josiah, and perhaps that made her feel sinful.

On 18 December 1680, which was almost the anniversary of the triumph against the Narragansetts, the fight was too much for Josiah. To Penelope's scarcely controllable anguish, he died. He had been her intimate companion for thirty years.

The colony was devastated. Josiah's pastor, William Witherell, said 'deep engulfing sorrow' had struck men dumb at the news Josiah was gone. The colony insisted on paying his funeral expenses as a mark of respect for his unstinting service during the nightmarish war. Samuel Sewall recorded that Josiah had died after terrible pain with gout 'and griping'. He noted: 'His flesh was opened to the bone on's legs before he died.' The description indicates it was an ulcer which would have had a more sinister origin, namely a thrombosis caused by disease of the veins.

In a condolence letter, addressing Penelope as his 'much respected Christian friend', Nathaniel Morton attempted to stem the inconsolable grief which he heard 'hath prevailed much on you', and which her church and community regarded with some alarm. There would be a resurrection, Josiah's soul would be in 'a blessed state', the poor governor would be free at last. Morton tried to explain that Josiah's death taught, as 'Mr Robinson sometimes our pastor in Holland' had said, that they were 'not to be fixated on the world here'. This 'lower world' was full of pain, temptation and sorrow, the times were 'like to be very sad and dangerous to professors of the Gospel' so men might seek death. But it should be remembered with thankfulness that Josiah had not fallen into the hands of the Indians: 'The Lord brought him to you again and he died in his bed under your inspection, care, and diligence and the manifestation of your utmost and best endeavours you could do for his recovery.'

Morton's words showed Penelope how she should behave, but the reality that her beloved helpmeet was gone was unbearable. Even the taking of probate was agony. She refused to open the door of what had been their shared bedroom. The inventory dolefully remarks that the widow's bed was 'not priced'. The men tramping round the house opening drawers, making notes about every possession, could not help but be painfully intrusive despite their tactful demeanour.

Josiah had been a major public official for Plymouth for a very long time. His tall figure investigating sites for mills, making sure the court ran properly, that all was orderly, had been a comforting sight for years. His determination had pulled the colony through the war and its aftermath. In Plymouth he was universally perceived as the man who had saved them from the Indians. It is clear from the outpouring of grief that Josiah's confidence that God was ultimately on Plymouth's side helped the community to fight through its darkest days. He had possessed the standing and confidence to negotiate aggressively on the colony's behalf, and that would be missed in the days ahead.

Despite air so cold it was painful to breathe, Josiah's funeral was a ceremony of considerable grandeur, probably involving the English fashion of giving rings and gloves as a memorial, especially to the pall-bearers.

The Puritan hatred of ceremony was dissolving, and religious occasions had become less plain. New Englanders prided themselves on their verses for every event, especially funerals. They were frequently published with skulls and crossbones adorning them. It was all part of the erection of a self-consciously English culture, a sign of the country's gentility, elegance and sophistication. The hundreds of lines of verse that poured out to 'New England's Phoenix, Plymouth's glory' were testimony to the overwhelming sadness. Who now could the colony trust to steer it to 'blissful times, and peaceful days'? Who now would be a 'tall Cypress' who could shelter them? No fewer than four people wrote elegies. Two were clergymen, and one of these clergymen was his close friend William Witherell. The kindly commonsensical pastor, who for thirty-nine years had guided the Second Church of Scituate, was now a very old man. He was more than fond of Josiah.

Over ploughed fields covered with hoar frost, Josiah's coffin was borne. A sorrowful procession of those who lived nearby followed to the old Winslow burial ground which overlooks the Green Harbour River Valley.

Overcome with emotion at the sight of Josiah's nine-year-old son Isaac standing by the grave, Reverend Witherell prayed 'that the Governor's son might be made half equal to his father'. The site is now surrounded with huge trees, horse chestnuts and pines, and Josiah's body lies there still.

Josiah's reputation waned over the next hundred years. The nineteenth-century historian John Gorham Palfrey viewed his decision to act unilaterally for Plymouth as a betrayal, writing sniffily: 'he cannot be described as a New-England patriot of the highest type'. The point was that Josiah was a *Plymouth* patriot. The Old Colony had his loyalty first and foremost, before New England.

Twelve years later, in 1692, the English government forced a reorganisation on the New England colonies. Plymouth became part of Massachusetts.

Penelope did not marry again. In this she was uncharacteristic. For reasons of protection in a harsh physical environment, most colonists lived as married couples. If a spouse died the survivor tended to marry again fairly swiftly. Even in seventeenth-century Europe men and women might marry several times because of high mortality rates, and the need for women to run households.

Penelope had been, in the Puritan phrase, Josiah's 'faithful yoke-fellow'. Like a swan she could only have one mate. She was to live almost another quarter of a century alone. She wore a mourning ring she had commissioned from the Boston silversmith John Coney, in which she kept a lock of Josiah's long dark hair.

Josiah had asked Kenelm's son, his first cousin Nathaniel, to be one of the overseers to help Penelope administer the estate. Penelope stayed in Marshfield to bring up Isaac and his sixteen-year-old sister, Elizabeth. Marshfield was a quiet New England town, a place cattle were driven to graze on the salt marsh where hundreds of wildfowl made their home within the sound of the sea. People were no longer afraid to go out of doors, but it could be a cold and solitary spot. Isaac was a scholarly boy. He seems to have avoided comparisons with his heroic father. Perhaps because of a rather lonely existence he did well at his studies. Josiah is said to have impatiently left Harvard after his first year, but Isaac grew up to be a distinguished lawyer who became judge of the Probate Court at Plymouth, and Chief Justice of the Court of Common Pleas. After Plymouth was absorbed into the new political entity demanded by the English government, he was briefly president of the Council of the Province of Massachusetts Bay.

Josiah had been especially close to his nephew, Elizabeth Curwen's son, the fatherless John Brooks. He left him a great deal of land at Middleborough which Brooks seems to have been farming for Josiah, and another hundred acres on the north side of the River Taunton.

Penelope was fortunate that, unlike most widowed women in Marshfield, she could escape from time to time to the busier world of Salem, where she was welcomed within the assured social circle of George and Elizabeth Curwen. Nevertheless anxiety about money afflicted Penelope as the very alarming picture of her father's affairs emerged. Voluminous records show that witnesses gave statements before commissioners of the High Court at inns in Sudbury and Bures

St Mary about Hebert Pelham's last days. He had not been in his right mind, and he was also burdened with debts and mortgages to neighbours; £600 was owed on Ferriers itself. It was a grim picture. Waldegrave claimed that his father's debts of £1,120 were so excessive that he could not pay out any of the legacies owed until those debts were settled, and he himself pleaded poverty.

Although some of the Pelham siblings saw Waldegrave as the villain of the piece, Penelope thought it was her father. To her, he had been a high-living crook.

The New England Penelope had grown up in was antagonistic to female assertiveness, but she had her brother-in-law and overseer, the litigious George Curwen, to support her. He was used to business deals. He may have told her she had every right to claim her own money. In February 1683 Penelope suddenly made an extraordinary public denunciation. She sued her brother and her father's estate in the Royal Courts of Justice in London for her legacy. In a vitriolic statement she accused them of fraud and criminal conspiracy to deprive her of her grandfather's money.

Being fended off by Herbert had been an embittering and alienating experience. Now Josiah was dead and she was facing life alone, her anger came tumbling out of her as she related how her grandfather had created a generous trust for all his grandchildren and she had never received her share. She said Waldegrave was now in possession of the said lands but now also refused to pay.

Penelope accused Herbert of denying that Thomas Waldegrave had the sort of estate that could stand such a legacy, 'that there were no such deeds made by the said Thomas Waldgrave though the will of the said Thomas doth mention the same'. Sometimes Herbert had claimed that the land had already been sold by the trustees and the money paid. Penelope believed Waldegrave knew the truth, and knew the whereabouts of the deeds. She demanded that he and his confederates, 'when discovered', produce them and also tell the truth about what had happened to the land. She believed it was being used and profited from – though it was meant to be sold 'for the benefit of your said orator and the other younger children'.

Penelope was used to being treated as an equal partner by Josiah. Out at Marshfield if a cow was calving and Josiah or his men were absent, there was no time for feminine sensibilities in an emergency. She just had to find a solution. Josiah had had a great deal of faith in

Penelope's character and judgement. His will stated that she could choose her own overseers to run his estate if any of the friends he named were not available. He insisted his family and community treat her with deference. Were his two precious children to die, Penelope could distribute £50 'to some other of my near relations who by their love and respect to her and hers she shall see best deserving'. When Isaac came of age the house and estate were to be divided between Isaac and Penelope once Elizabeth had her portion, but it was not up to Isaac to decide anything: 'In all divisions' it was 'my wife to have her choice'.

Penelope's devastating portrait of Herbert suggests a burning sense of personal indignation, but trashing her father seems to have come at considerable emotional cost. The court case coincided with Penelope's second spiritual crisis. She was overwhelmed by a sense of her own sinfulness, terrified she was not one of the elect. She was being assaulted by Satan and believed she was to be separated from Josiah for all eternity. What we might today call her nervous breakdown was so serious it necessitated another intervention by the community. An eight-page letter from Nathaniel Morton exhorted her to bear up during her current affliction.

Was that sense of sin related to her attack on her father? She lived at a time when all formal authorities, whether legal principles or etiquette books, reinforced patriarchal precepts, where a father and husband wielded what one historian has called 'absolute authority'. To charge her father with conspiracy had been an act of extraordinary daring which was almost sacrilegious, and perhaps created subconscious feelings of overwhelming wickedness.

Yet, for all her neuroses, Penelope did not withdraw from the litigation. Whatever her sense of sinfulness and unworthiness or the trauma of rebellion, her strong sense of what was owed to her in pecuniary terms was not invalidated. Penelope believed in her legal rights and was not afraid to enforce them.*

The lack of indexing of many seventeenth-century Chancery cases at the National Archives, and the fact that outcomes were not filed with

---

* Her aunt Mistress Bellingham had not received her own legacy of £30 a year from Waldegrave and could have sued at the same time, but she seems to have been a less forceful character. It was not until over ten years later, when her nephew Edward Pelham became interested in suing Waldegrave for further misdemeanours, that Mistress Bellingham was spurred to action.

cases, mean it has been impossible to find out how Penelope's case was resolved. All that survives of Penelope's is the writ to the sergeant and her 1683 deposition. It seems likely that Waldegrave either convinced his sisters that he had no money or that he gave them something out of court, though not the whole sum Penelope was owed. It was probably part of the proof for both sisters that on 2 July 1683, five months after Penelope's suit began, Waldegrave exhibited the probate inventory of Herbert Pelham and his executor's account in the Prerogative Court.

Waldegrave's mortgages increased dramatically from the late 1680s, so perhaps he borrowed more money in order to pay his sisters. In fact he was in far deeper financial water than anyone realised, but it would take another decade before that became clear.

CHAPTER XIX

Penelope's Final Actions

For half a century Massachusetts had fought against the threat to cancel its charter. External events had always intervened to save rebellious New England from interference when its bold characters – including Penelope's uncle, Governor Bellingham – became too provocative. The colonies had grown used to their independence. But with peace restored, England had the means to enforce a more streamlined imperial system.

Edward Randolph's information – which accused Massachusetts of being an illegal commonwealth, having an illegal mint, practising religious persecution, protecting regicides and avoiding the laws of England – made it easier to begin proceedings. In June 1684 not only was the Massachusetts Bay Charter revoked so were the charters of all the New England colonies, including Plymouth's. To uproar, it was announced they were to be directly ruled by a royal governor. Their proud representative assemblies were abolished.

Six months before the charter was declared void, in January 1684, Penelope's brother-in-law George Curwen dropped dead. A world only just restored to its old self started to totter again. George had been Penelope's protector and perhaps a bit of a father figure. He was only ten years younger than her own father, Herbert Pelham, with whom relations had become so troubled.

George Curwen had been a hectic leading citizen, but he never got round to making a will. Professional activities had used up all his attention. The ferocious scrutiny of detail which made him so successful in business stopped him tidying up his personal life. His wife Elizabeth had begged him for years to settle his affairs – 'which he always promised and really intended to do, for my Comfortable Subsistence and maintenance as his Widow'.

Elizabeth's domineering stepson Jonathan, George's executor, now claimed that much of his father's fortune had been made relying on his own mother's money and thus should not be shared with his step-mother. He attempted to stop Elizabeth having the sort of money she had been accustomed to spending.

Perhaps suffering from fear and depression as well as influenza, Elizabeth was in no condition to grapple with her stepchildren. Jonathan seized the moment to take over sole administration of the estate. 'What in Right belongs to me', Elizabeth said in her court deposition, 'but by reason of sickness I was unable then to manage so great a trust, and Mr. Curwen wholly refusing to join with me in it, but was very urgent that I should resign it solely to him.'

Living in Salem, Elizabeth was far from the people with whom she had grown up, at least a day's journey from her girlhood friends in Marshfield. But the years in London had toughened her up. She rallied to petition the county court to make sure she was not done out of what she continued to see as her fair share of a fortune valued at £6,000, the largest in the annals of New England at that date.

Elizabeth's magnificent affidavit won her case hands down. Savvy from living at the side of a master merchant, interested in money, she obtained almost half of her husband's estate. By a court decision of 1685 she got around £1,000 for herself and the same sum for each of her daughters. The intimidating Jonathan wanted to replace her as chief supervisor of the education of her younger daughter, Susanna. Elizabeth insisted she herself be appointed guardian. Court records show her battling furiously to get money to support herself in the luxurious style to which she had become accustomed, as well as portions for her girls.

Elizabeth's elder daughter Penelope married a well-connected young merchant named Josiah Wolcott. The date had been arranged long before. Without male support, suffering from distress in the middle of the rituals of the mourning period, Elizabeth still had to put on a wedding and make a fist at being joyful. But immediately after George's sudden death she had been very short of cash. Jonathan did not volunteer to pay for the wedding dress so she had to find the money out of her own funds. Penelope Curwen's wedding outfit was 'much short of what her father would have allowed'.

Elizabeth desperately needed the support of Penelope Winslow. Even for someone so masterful, a seventeenth-century widow's horizons shrank rapidly. It was an immediate loss of status, and in the Curwen family itself she was treated brusquely. Elizabeth seems to have been locked out of parts of what had been the marital home. She made a list of her personal possessions: 'that the several things given me some of them before and others after marriage (of which I have enclosed) may be restored to me'. Some were from her life with Robert Brooks. Others were probably imported by George Curwen from merchant connections round the world: the two calico quilts and her 'japanned box'; the two Turkish carpets which had been in the hall; and a fire screen. Elizabeth claimed a pair of tobacco tongs, used to pick up embers to light a pipe, suggesting she may have smoked. The flamboyant and independent Elizabeth also possessed an amazing set of 'chairs and screetoire [writing desk] of gilded leather' in what she called the Red Chamber, 'with the produce of some adventures the Captain had given me', i.e. the return of some ship in which he had given her shares.

At least Elizabeth now controlled her own funds absolutely. She made a handy income from interest on money lent to local merchants. She casually lists £8 worth of gold her husband got for selling an Indian boy. Since he was 'sent me from Plymouth per the Governor and council' the money belonged to her.

Penelope Winslow had been fortunate that her son Isaac was only nine when she was widowed so her house remained controlled by her. Elizabeth was entitled to use only one-third of the splendid mansion she had furnished. She could only walk in a third of the garden which she had planted. Though it had been her home for fifteen years, because George Curwen had failed to make a will, she received only the widow's thirds.

Even Elizabeth's spirited character could not help being ground down over the next decade. Her three children predeceased her. John Brooks died aged thirty-one in 1687. Three years later her daughter, Penelope, caught the highly contagious puerperal fever that was the premier hazard of childbirth. The girl whose wedding dress had not been good enough for her mother died aged twenty. Only a week earlier she had given birth to her second child, Elizabeth's first grandson, Josiah, named after Josiah Winslow. Seven days later on 4 January 1691 the baby was buried. Susanna, Elizabeth's younger daughter whom she had fought to bring up herself, died in October 1696 aged twenty-four, predeceasing her mother by two years.

Penelope Winslow's daughter Elizabeth married an apparently successful businessman, Stephen Burton. A widower, he was one of the four merchants appointed to purchase the 7,000 acres of Mount Hope lands. Having been exposed to her grand English relations, Penelope may have wanted to reproduce aspects of more elaborate English wedding traditions. But the bride and groom most likely wrote their own homespun vows which they said in the solemn heartfelt congregationalist fashion of Plymouth. Behind them stood Stephen's small children – aged seven, six and four – to whom Elizabeth was to be a young stepmother. Stephen's first wife had died earlier that year.

The Burtons built a house at Bristol, Rhode Island, which became Burton Street, named after Stephen. It was one of the 120 or so lots made out of King Philip's own land into small farms. The wild countryside was slowly transformed into fenced allotments. The Burtons lived there impervious to memories of Philip's death nearby. If they thought of him at all it was with a shudder.

To fulfil Josiah's wish that his land outside Marshfield should make up part of their daughter's portion, Penelope gave around a hundred acres on Mount Hope to Elizabeth in 1688, probably because Stephen Burton's business was not going well.

Sir Edmund Andros was a tough imperial administrator who had restructured the former Dutch colony New Netherland into the English colony New York, rebuilding the city and its trade. Appointed by the new Stuart king, James II, he looked forward to organising all the northern colonies – including Plymouth, Massachusetts Bay, New Hampshire, Maine, Connecticut, Rhode Island and New York – into one political entity called the Dominion of New England. Ruled by himself with the help of a council, it would be better defended against the French and Indian threats.

But the Dominion of New England rode roughshod over hallowed traditions, and trampled on colonists' rights. The town meetings which had been an integral part of New England life since its beginnings were suspended. New Englanders had hacked their towns out of the wilderness, yet they were no longer allowed to rule themselves. The congregational churches were forced to take second place to the (entirely absent) Church of England. All land grants were to be re-examined. It seemed to be the end of self-government and the beginning of direct rule from London.

Andros had been a successful governor of New York. His accomplished relations with the Iroquois Indians – especially the Mohawks – stood New England in good stead for decades. But his rule of Boston was blindly imperious and he imposed new taxes without consent. Imported English royal officials imprisoned those who protested. Careless of the sacred nature of the Old South Meeting House, Andros requisitioned it for Anglican services. Edward Randolph took a major role as inspector of customs to make sure the Navigation Acts were at last enforced.

John Winslow, Josiah's first cousin, arrived in Boston from Nevis with news of the Glorious Revolution in England which had thrown out James II, the author of the Dominion. John was a merchant and sailor, not the natural person to start a revolution. But all his life it had been dinned into him that New England had its own 'laws, liberties and customs'. When Andros imprisoned John for publishing William of Orange's *Declaration of Reasons for Appearing in Arms in England*, all hell broke loose.

With the approval of the most eminent Boston families, the militia seized Governor Andros and imprisoned him in Boston jail. He remained there for the next nine months until he was sent back to England. The venerable former governor Simon Bradstreet became president, and the Council of Safety administered the colony until a new charter was created. It was negotiated with the help of Increase Mather in London. The new king, William III, was in no position to resist the colonists' demands.

It was not until May 1692 that a new royal governor, Sir William Phips, arrived in Boston to rule what had become the Province of Massachusetts Bay. Massachusetts had become a Crown colony – but this time with its colonists' consent. Their representative assemblies were to continue. Phips had a massive task to restore order: the abolition of the Dominion had created an alarming vacuum of authority. Not only was there no legitimate government, the Indians in Maine were rumoured to be about to attack Boston.

In this febrile atmosphere, fears and emotions could easily get out of control. And in the town of Salem, they did.

Two hundred people were accused of witchcraft, over a hundred people were imprisoned and nineteen innocent people were executed. The youngest detainee was the four-year-old girl Dorcas Good, remanded to custody for witchcraft alongside her mother. Numbers grew rapidly as the apparently possessed young girls of Salem accused more and more decent people of being witches. Phips commissioned a new temporary oyer and terminer court to take over from the Salem County Court.

Salem had many refugees from the recent massacres in Maine carried out by Indians paid by the French, which were the opening shots
of a series of wars between the French and English. In the strange
unsettled mood, New England was regarded as being under attack –
from supernatural enemies who were getting the upper hand, and from
Indians who were perceived as agents of Satan. Cotton Mather, the
clergyman son of Increase Mather, and an equally influential personality of the day, gave chapter and verse to the fears that evil spirits were
present in large numbers. *Memorable Providences Relating to Witch-
crafts and Possessions* dealt with his attempt to exorcise a young girl
he believed to be possessed.

In the agitated climate the absurd accusations of overwrought teenage girls blew up into a major crisis. The new court to investigate what
was going on did nothing to calm the panicky atmosphere. In June
twelve ministers – including Increase Mather – protested at the court's
decision to allow what was called 'spectral evidence'. It eroded the rule
of law New England prided itself on. Spectral evidence – a witness said
he had seen the accused witch sitting on his stomach at midnight – got
Bridget Bishop hanged. Nathaniel Saltonstall resigned, disgusted by the
madness which had afflicted judges as much as plaintiffs. But Elizabeth's stepson Jonathan Curwen, one of the Salem County magistrates
in charge of committing the accused witches to prison before trial, had
no such qualms. He took Saltonstall's place.

Spectral evidence continued to be allowed because the judges genuinely believed there was a diabolic conspiracy against New England.
Behind the hysteria was social envy and long-standing feuds between
the poorer farming community and wealthy mercantile families.

Plymouth was unique amongst its fellow Puritan colonies in
having very little truck with witchcraft. Only one person was ever tried
in Plymouth. In 1677 Mary Ingham was accused of bewitching
Mehitabel Woodworth so that she fell into fits and was almost deprived
of her senses. Ingham was swiftly acquitted, perhaps because there
were so many reasons for people to be deprived of their senses after
the war.

It was hard not to be affected by the anxiety. If you believed in God,
the Devil was the other side of the coin. At a time when witchcraft was
dying out as a crime in Europe, there were ninety-three witch trials in
New England. At the end of the century when Isaac built his grand
modern house, with its wide windows and portico, he had anti-witches

marks carved into the beam over the fireplace in what is known as the winter kitchen.

Elizabeth Curwen's house overlooked the courtroom. Ashen-faced men and women were taken there by George Curwen's great-nephew, Sheriff George Curwen. They endured the ordeal of teenage girls falling down in self-induced fits because one of the accused had given them 'a look'. Most of them were highly respectable people of good character. Sheriff Curwen also confiscated the accused's goods on behalf of the government (in reality for himself).

On 30 April 1692 Elizabeth's pious neighbour Mary English was arrested in the middle of the night and dragged to Salem jail to join the rest of its terrified inhabitants. Married to Philip English, a merchant whose wealth rivalled George Curwen's, and a member herself of the distinguished local Hollingsworth family, Mary was sufficiently devout to have been admitted a full member of her church. A pillar of Salem society, as her granddaughter angrily recalled, she simply could not believe what was happening to her.

Mary's husband had been born Philip l'Anglais in Jersey. He was a French-speaker, an outsider, and a wealthy member of the mercantile elite. Powerful friends got Mary sent to the less dangerous jail in Boston. Philip English was persuaded he must join his wife there. In August Governor Phips seems to have helped spirit the Englishes away to New York to avoid the trial process, which he himself was beginning to deplore.

Meanwhile Sheriff Curwen took the opportunity to seize all Philip English's property. Twenty ships and 200 sheep were impounded. In appalling scenes the house so close to Elizabeth's was plundered. It shocked the town at a time when most people had become unshockable. Huge mirrors with elaborate frames, beautiful tables, ancient Dutch and French pictures, and lots of wine were ferried out of the front door.

The Mathers had a unique position in New England. One of the most influential and socially prominent families in the history of seventeenth-century Massachusetts, Increase Mather and his son Cotton were both ministers at the North Church, and both used their pulpits to extraordinary effect. Increase, who was president of Harvard, was in a difficult position because it would have been very peculiar if he had undermined Phips by criticising the trials. In the end, however, his uneasy conscience forced him to speak out. His pamphlet

Cases of Conscience of 3 October 1692 helped bring the trials to an end.

A few brave souls stood up to the process, including John Proctor, the rational wealthy farmer accused of being a witch, whom Arthur Miller made the central character of *The Crucible*. Proctor wrote a letter to five influential ministers of Boston's main churches pointing out that evidence was gathered through torture. In his view the 'magistrates, ministers, juries and all the people in general' were 'enraged and incensed against us by the delusion of the Devil'. He was nevertheless executed as a witch on Gallows Hill that August. His pregnant wife was reprieved, until she delivered her baby.

To prevent his property being confiscated the well-to-do farmer Giles Corey tried refusing to acknowledge the authority of the court by not entering a plea. For this he was pressed to death under stones, a punishment called *peine forte et dure*. Witnesses relate that because Sheriff Curwen was angry at being deprived of Corey's goods, he stuffed Corey's tongue back into his mouth with a stick as he died.

The witch-hunt menace spread to Plymouth with accusations against the son of John Alden. His trade with Indians was said to mean he was in league with the Devil. His father had been one of the most venerable of the *Mayflower* colonists. John Alden junior was a leading citizen and he treated the proceedings with robust disdain. Arriving in Salem to a court hearing, Alden was surrounded by what he contemptuously described as wenches with their 'juggling tricks'. They cried out that Alden was pinching them, though Alden was sitting far away from them on a chair in the courthouse. Alden described sorrowfully how even his old friend Judge Bartholomew Gedney, a Salem judge, believed their nonsense. 'I wonder at God in suffering these creatures to accuse innocent people.' To his complete astonishment he was detained for fifteen weeks to await trial.

Then 'observing the manner of Trials, and Evidence then taken', so little did Alden and his relations trust Salem's justice that he was sprung from jail. He was then hidden from vengeful witch-hunters in Duxbury, until, as he said, people regained their reason.

The frenzy at Salem became so uncontrolled even Jonathan Curwen's mother-in-law, Margaret Thacher of Boston, was named, though never arrested.

By the autumn Governor Phips was very uneasy. Respectable citizens had gone to their deaths screaming their innocence. Their corpses were still swinging on Gallows Hill. In November he heard there was a warrant out for his own wife's arrest. Saying Salem was a 'black cloud threatening this province with destruction', Phips took executive action to address a situation that was out of control. He dissolved the court and shut down the trials.

In the unfair way of events, affairs did not return to the status quo ante. Philip English's possessions could not be wrested from Sheriff Curwen. Estimating he had lost the enormous sum of close to £2,000, English was very angry indeed. Probably because of her ordeal his wife died young at the age of forty-four. Sheriff Curwen himself was carried off at the age of only thirty by what seems to have been a stroke – some said it was a curse by one of his victims. English is said to have seized Curwen's body during its funeral procession. He kept it in his cellar and refused to give it back until some of his property was returned.

Penelope Winslow had her own anxieties about her daughter in Rhode Island because of her son-in-law's condition. Stephen Burton was a cultivated and refined individual, supposed to possess a degree from Oxford. He became the first recording officer of his county, clerk of the peace, and was a conscientious deputy who five times represented Bristol to the General Court. He also suffered from depression. There were rumours he was neglecting his clerical duties 'in consequence of a disorder in the head'.

On 22 July 1693, he died. Whether the strain of business killed him is not clear. Perhaps it was a brain tumour. He may have wanted a mother for his children by his first marriage more than he wanted a second wife, though Elizabeth seems to have had at least two children of her own: Penelope and Thomas. (Thomas – a great-grandson of Edward Winslow – lived to see the American Revolutionary Wars begin, dying in 1779.)

Elizabeth had a house so immense that a cow was said to have got into one of the fourteen-foot fireplaces. But at some point she moved back to Marshfield, probably into her mother's home. She does not seem to have married again.

In 1700 Penelope's son Isaac married Sarah Wensley, a member of one of the most cultivated and well-to-do families in Boston. Six children were rapidly produced, all of whom were brought up at Careswell. The daughter of a Boston merchant, John Wensley, who had a large well-appointed house in the North End, Sarah may have found Marshfield isolated since Isaac's legal work took him to Plymouth and he also served on the Council for the Province of Massachusetts Bay in Boston.

Sarah brought substantial wealth into the family, but she may also have been a high spender. Her will shows she had a velvet cloak, along with a velvet handkerchief, a gold necklace, locket and earrings. She must have been a confident young woman who liked to make a striking impression. Isaac Winslow's will itemises several looking glasses. Sarah may have enjoyed catching a glimpse of herself as she bustled round their house, which was covered with printed wallpaper – a novelty for New England.

The witchcraft trials must have seemed a world away. Religion was losing its sway even in New England in the face of successful commercial society. The value placed on reason made way for the Enlightenment, driving out the hold superstition had had over the minds even of the educated.

By the late 1690s spectral evidence had been utterly discredited. There were church services in which the witchcraft accusers asked forgiveness. In the most thorough investigation of the Salem drama, historians Paul Boyer and Stephen Nissenbaum concluded the accusations were part of 'the Puritan temper during that final, often intense, and occasionally lurid efflorescence which signalled the end of its century-long history'.

Penelope's links with England had become attenuated. Josiah's Wake cousins were still alive but the relationship seems to have petered out; certainly there is no correspondence. Although Amie Wake had died young, William Wake lived to see their son, another William, rise high. Admired for his eloquence and emphasis on pastoral care, he became Archbishop of Canterbury in 1716, probably thanks to his close friendship with the intellectual, serious-minded Princess of Wales, the future Queen Caroline.

The passage of time had not been good to the Pelhams. In 1692 Penelope's nephew – son of her brother Waldegrave and named after him – was found guilty of homicide. He had hit a local man, Hugh Polley, with a wooden stick and Polley had died. Young Waldegrave opted to plead benefit of clergy and slunk home to his house at Chappell near Bures St Mary. He said he had been misled by a diabolic force: 'Not having God before his eyes' he had been 'moved and misled by the instigation of the devil'. It was another way of expressing the pressure he was living under. The finances of his father Waldegrave were in such poor shape that he needed dramatically to increase his existing mortgages. Then he ran out of land to raise money on. The last mortgage – which made his debts £4,800 in total – was secured on his younger brother Edward's property in Lincolnshire. By the end of his life Waldegrave's debts were treble those of his father Herbert.

In 1685 Dame Anne Robinson, who may have been a neighbour, swooped on the floundering Waldegrave. She took out a mortgage for £1,000 on the manor of Ferriers itself and bought his other large mortgage, for £2,000. Then in 1688 she sold on the Pelham mortgages to Richard Dickson, a wealthy haberdasher. In 1691 Waldegrave found himself short again. His new friend Dickson was happy to lend him an additional £1,000. Documents in the National Archives show that, like a Monopoly game, Dickson's collection of Pelham mortgages was now complete. Edward returned to England from Rhode Island, tried to enter his Lincolnshire property and was rebuffed. Everything was now controlled by Richard Dickson.

But because one of the terms of Herbert's will was that no monies had to be paid out until his debts were paid off, Waldegrave still held the trump card. He always denied Herbert's debts were entirely paid. In 1694 Edward set off for London. Perhaps he intended to sell his property as his life was so clearly fixed in New England. Since 1682 he had been married to Freelove Arnold, the daughter of the former governor of Rhode Island, and he was living in some splendour in her house in Newport. He may also have feared some of the possessions he was owed in Herbert's will might have been sold off – including 'one great silver tankard which was given him by his grandfather Godfrey Bossevile esquire with the inlaid cabinet and all in it that stands in the kitchen chamber at Ferriers'. Penelope and his aunts may have urged him to do something. Penelope was still hopeful of getting that legacy.

Despite Edward's wild ways he was a better businessman than his father and half-brother. Having also had the good fortune to marry a very rich wife, he hung on to his property in New England and probably increased it. He was enraged by Waldegrave. In his court deposition, Edward suggested that jewels and plate as well as papers detailing trusts and bonds had been secretly stolen from his father's study by Waldegrave, and the bonds not presented at the right time for payment because of incompetence. Whatever the truth, it was no good. The Pelham fortune was gone.

In 1697, either pushed by her nephew Edward or emboldened by his activities, Mistress Penelope Bellingham now entered the fray, and claimed arrears from her own annuity. She revealed that in the past

Waldegrave had said that there was a secret deed in existence that meant that nothing was owed. For many years she had felt too helpless to do anything, but now she asked for a subpoena to see the deed in court.

Because the judgements of the Pelham cases cannot be found it is not clear what happened next, but it seems likely Penelope Bellingham got her arrears. A year after his last appearance in court, in 1699 Waldegrave died, worn out from the strain. Edward was appointed estate administrator, by a grant from the Prerogative Court in February 1700. Waldegrave junior – the heir – was left out. This suggests Edward won.

Perhaps because he had got his own way in Old England, Edward decided the moment had come to claim Herbert's land in New England. In 1702 he asked the Massachusetts government not only for Herbert's 400 acres, but also Thomas Waldegrave's.

Penelope Winslow was fond enough of her larger-than-life half-brother. She probably attended his wedding to his heiress wife and was lavishly entertained in Newport. But when Edward asked the court for land owed to Thomas Waldegrave, he crossed a line. Penelope fired off a furious counter-petition to the General Court claiming all Thomas Waldegrave's stake, on the grounds that Edward was not even related to Thomas. Edward's grandfather, Penelope dictated, probably to her lawyer son Isaac, was not Thomas but Godfrey Bosseville. It was outrageous that he was laying claim to *her* land or her children's land when not a drop of Waldegrave blood flowed in his veins.

On 30 June 1703, less than six months before she died, in a vehement, bold and highly personal piece of writing, the seventy-year-old Penelope refused to accept her father's will, petitioning the General Court to stop Edward. He had 'no right at all to the said lands of the said Mr Waldgrave being no way related or of kin to him', she wrote furiously.

Perhaps Penelope was made more furious by the slow disappearance of all her old friends and a wish to put down a marker about the world she had known that was passing. Elizabeth Curwen had been laid to rest with a magnificent funeral, so that in death she retrieved some of her former state. Elizabeth had been more like a sister. Yet now she lay in the ground of the Broad Street Cemetery in Salem beside her husband.

Penelope went further than just claiming the 400 acres of her grandfather Waldegrave's land. She also wanted half of her father Herbert's own grant. It was she who should take the lion's share, 'to whom of right the greatest grant of said lands doth appertain. And not to the said Edward Pelham who though he be a son of the said Herbert Pelham yet not his sole heir, and not being the eldest son hath no more right to said land than your petitioner.'

On 21 July the House of Representatives accepted Penelope had some kind of interest – though not to her father's land. Edward's laying out of the disputed acreage was suspended. Ten years later the General Court finally found in favour of Penelope's claim that she was the only heir in New England to her grandfather's 400 acres, which were granted to her children. Her suit had been successfully pursued by her daughter Elizabeth Burton and her son Isaac. He may have lent his legal expertise to helping draft his mother's petition to the General Court, but the tone of angry outrage was all hers. It was the final act in her attempt to retrieve some portion of her Waldegrave legacy. This time she would not be deprived.

Roger Williams described land as one of 'the gods of New England'. In such an atmosphere it was natural for Penelope to take a keen interest in her father's and grandfather's property. In her own way she succumbed to the lure of the American land she had known since she was a little girl. She had seen it all planted, burnt and replanted. This was her land, which her husband had fought for. Penelope's actions also speak of a desire for recognition for herself and her children. Part of that was being her grandfather's heir in New England. It was a quest that was as much psychological as financial. Cut off from her birth family in England, she had become stronger and created her own small tribe.

Penelope Winslow died in December 1703. Her daughter Elizabeth moved to Pembroke, Massachusetts, where her son Thomas became the town clerk and schoolmaster. She supported herself by selling her land in Rhode Island.

Mistress Bellingham's good friend Samuel Sewall had marked her death in May 1702 in his diary, writing that she had been a 'vertuous gentlewoman *antiquis moribus, prisca fide* [of ancient customs, of ancient faith]'. Sewall had been the sole judge in the Salem witchcraft trials publicly to repent. In 1700 his conscience had again pricked him at the increasingly widespread practice of slavery. His pamphlet deploring this custom, *The Selling of Joseph*, may not have found many buyers amongst later Winslows. There were a series of black servants at Careswell. An eighteenth-century sampler shows a small black slave in attendance on a young lady. One of Isaac's sons, Edward Winslow (1713–84), was a Loyalist general in the Revolutionary Wars and had to flee to Nova Scotia in 1783, arriving with three black servants.

By the end of the eighteenth century historians note that references to slaves cease and there was sympathy for the anti-slavery movement. Careswell was inherited by another of Isaac's sons, John Winslow (1703–74), who was a general in the British army. Although he had to effect the removal of the French, now known as Cajuns, from Acadia, he personally settled two French families of refugees in Plymouth because he felt sorry for them. His son Dr Isaac Winslow inherited Careswell. He was a Loyalist but so popular for his selfless work as a medical man that his house was not seized, as most Loyalists' were. He was the last of the family to occupy the house. Although a kind physician, he was not especially good with money. He died in debt and the house passed out of the family. Many of the 1,000 acres were bought by neighbours, and for a brief time the gifted orator Senator Daniel Webster made Careswell his summer retreat.

Today the Winslows and all the other people in the *Mayflower* story are so long gone that it is almost as if they never lived. What they felt and thought frequently has to be imagined or put together from the tiniest pieces of evidence. Penelope and Josiah lie beneath a tomb devised by their son Isaac with a coat of arms. Where the mutilated body of the Indian King Philip lies, no one knows.

The spot where Philip died has never been built over, being too marshy. The hill of Mount Hope where Wampanoag chiefs used to look out is still there. What was once the swamp is covered with ornamental garden shrubs, part of the elegant grounds of Brown University.

Notoriously in history, success is about choosing the winning side. The Mohawks and Iroquois who chose to be on the English side flourished in the eighteenth century. Nevertheless the nineteenth century saw southern Indians forced off their hereditary territory by the 1830 Removal Act. Under President Andrew Jackson huge numbers were sent west of the Mississippi. Thousands died on the journey, today known as the Trail of Tears. But nowadays the concept of Indian sovereignty is recognised. Three hundred and more years after King Philip's War, coexistence is the predominant theme. There are still Wampanoags on Cape Cod. Many of the Mashpee Wampanoags were Christian and did not join Philip. In 1685 Plymouth Court confirmed the Mashpee title to their lands. In 2014 the Mashpee participated in the city of Taunton's 375th anniversary parade. Their tribal chairman, Cedric Cromwell, is at the time of writing a member of Harvard Provost's Advisory Council, designed to increase opportunities for Native Americans, as was intended at Harvard's founding. The Algonquian language had more or less died out by the mid-eighteenth century but recent years have seen a strong revival of interest in Indian languages and history. When asked if Thanksgiving is 'a time of celebration or mourning', Cedric says, 'It's both. Historically, Thanksgiving represents our first encounter with the eventual erosion of our sovereignty and there is nothing wrong with mourning that loss. In fact, as long as we don't wallow in regret and resentment, it's healthy to mourn. It is a necessary part of the healing process.'

The Mashpee Wampanoags live by Provincetown on their own land as they did in 1620. They are descendants of the people who saw a ship called the *Mayflower* appear over the horizon, and watched the Pilgrims, including Edward Winslow, alight.

On 20 July 1704, Josiah's half-brother Peregrine White died at the age of eighty-three. His iconic birth on the *Mayflower* meant that his death marked the end of a heroic generation. His land included the 200 acres granted to him as the first New Englander to be born in the New World. Peregrine's final thoughts make moving reading. 'Being aged,' he wrote, 'and under many weaknesses and bodily infirmities but of sound disposing mind and memory', yet in daily expectation of what he called 'my great change', he humbly committed 'my soul to Almighty God that gave it and my body to decent burial when it shall please him to take me hence'. It was the final journey for the youngest pilgrim.

The Pilgrims had their eyes fixed on their heavenly home, but they founded a new world. If you had asked Peregrine's stepfather Edward Winslow where home was, he might have had difficulty responding. In his case, it was wherever the godly cause was. For his stepson Peregrine, it was here in Marshfield amidst gentle green hills.

Acknowledgements, and a note about the book and its sources

Personal records are few and far between about the courageous people of modest origin who founded New England. So often these heroes and heroines are mere names in the Calendar of State Papers Colonial. Yet the Winslows and their friends were actors in momentous events. Settling in America and getting to know the Indians, they created a new society where they were not ruled by a monarch, and where they agreed the laws between themselves. But they also lived through the horror of Indian war, as greater numbers of Europeans eroded the trust of the early days.

When lives are poorly documented, lawsuits can be a means of getting information. Fortunately the Winslows married into the litigious Pelham family. Legal depositions at the National Archives in London, unseen for 300 years, shed rare light on the lives of the second generation of Winslows and their links to England.

William Bradford's history of Plymouth Plantation, Edward Winslow's own writing, the John Winthrop letters and his journal have been important authorities, as have the records of Plymouth Colony and the correspondence of Roger Williams. John Demos's *A Little Commonwealth* inspired this book. Jeremy Bangs's archival work on the Pilgrims in Leiden and New England, George D. Langdon Jr's *Pilgrim Colony* and the research of Cynthia Hagar Krusell on the Winslows have been essential.

I have modernised all spellings for the reader's convenience. Nowadays the terms Native American and American Indian are used interchangeably to describe the first inhabitants of North America. Native American has also come to mean Samoans and Micronesians, as well as Eskimos. I have elected to use the term 'American Indian' or the name of the tribe, as is preferred by the Bureau of Indian Affairs. For clarity I have used the name Massasoit throughout the text in preference to Osamequin. I have also used the English names Alexander and Philip, for Massasoit's sons Wamsutta and Metacom.

I am grateful to the following learned societies and institutions who permitted me to quote from the papers they hold: the Massachusetts Historical Society for Josiah Winslow's letters in the Davis Papers; the Boston Athenaeum Library for letters from Nathaniel Morton to Penelope Winslow; the New England Historic Genealogical Society for John Easton's letter describing the anxieties of Weetamoo, the Squaw Sachem of the Pocassets; the Phillips Library, Peabody Essex Museum, Salem, for items in the Curwen Family Papers; the National Archives in London for the Pelham family lawsuits; Christ Church, Oxford for permission to quote from 'The Original Autobiography and Journal of William Wake Archbishop of Canterbury', MS 541A (Parts 1 and 2).

I wish to thank the following individuals for their help: in America, especially Cynthia Hagar Krusell; the late Karin Goldstein; Craig Chartier; Aaron Dougherty of the Winslow House; Donna Curtin, Director of Pilgrim Hall Museum; Peggy M. Baker; Dr Walter V. Powell, Executive Director at the General Society of Mayflower Descendants; the late Alice Teal; Kathleen O'Connor; Betty Magoun Bates; Stephen C. O'Neill; Ann Young; Professor Francis J. Bremer; Cora Currier; Mrs Judy Smith. At the Massachusetts Historical Society: Anne E. Bentley, Curator of Art; Brenda Lawson; Elaine Grublin; Anna Clutterbuck-Cook; Sabina Beauchard; and Kim Nusco. At the Massachusetts State Archives: Jennifer Fauxsmith, Reference Archivist for tracking down the Winslow petitions. Elizabeth Bouvier, Head of Archives, Massachusetts Supreme Judicial Court. At the Boston Athenaeum Library: Mary Warnement, William D. Hacker Head of Reader Services; Stephen Z. Nonack; Stanley Cushing, Curator of Rare Books and Manuscripts. At the New England Historic Genealogical Society: Timothy Salls; Alicia Crane Williams; Mary Chen. Roberta Zonghi, Keeper of Rare Books and Manuscripts, Boston Public Library. Drew Bartley; Patti Auld Johnson and Patsy Hale, Archives & Special Collections, Harriet Irving Library, University of New Brunswick. Andrew Smith at the Judicial Archives of the Supreme Court of Rhode Island for assistance with Freelove Pelham's controversial will. Paul Royster at the University of Nebraska-Lincoln. David Taylor; Laure de Gramont; Edward Jay Epstein; Alden Brewster; Michelle Marchetti Coughlin; Angus Trumble; Penelope Rowlands.

In England, Christopher Vane, Portcullis Pursuivant, for his superb detective work about the Wake family; also to Thomas Woodcock,

Garter Principal King of Arms. Dr Nat Alcock, OBE gave vital help with the Pelham lawsuits; Hilary Marshall, Fellow of the Society of Genealogists, for her tireless transcriptions. Dr Stephen Roberts of the History of Parliament Trust for assistance with the MPs of the Interregnum; Dr Patrick Little; Professor Charles Mitchell. Sir Geoffrey Owen. The late Pamela Neville Sington for help with early American travel literature, and also Antony Payne.

Etain Kabraji Todds and Lord Phillips of Sudbury; the late Judge Francis Petre for showing me Ferriers, the former home of Herbert Pelham. Local historian Alan Beales of Bures Online. Jeremy Hill and Ida McMaster. The Reverend Canon Robin King, former vicar of Bures St Mary Church; Suffolk historian Clive Paine.

Dr Frances Willmoth, Archivist at Jesus College, Cambridge; Anna Reynolds of the Royal Collections; Karen Hearn, former Curator of sixteenth- and seventeenth-century painting at Tate Britain; Mrs Clare Brown, Archivist at Lambeth Palace Library; Professor Hugh Thomas; the late Professor Barry Coward. Laura Lindsay of Christie's London; Sir Stephen Sedley; Sir Ian Bosville Macdonald of Sleat and Christopher Simon Sykes for their assistance with the Bosville family. Mr Alan Palmer; Lord Mair, former Master of Jesus College, Cambridge; Charles Glass. The Duke Humphrey Library at the Bodleian Library, in particular Mike Webb, Curator of Early Modern Archives and Manuscripts; Rhodes House in Oxford; the Guildhall Archives; the British Library; the London Library; Mia Hakl-Law; Quincy Whitaker; the Leicestershire Record Office; Lord Hazlerigg; the Lincolnshire Archives; Liz Street, the Staffordshire Record Office; Essex County Record Office; the Suffolk County Record Office; Dr John Adamson; Dr David Scott; Timothy Otty QC; Dr Mike Macnair. Judith Curthoys of Christ Church, Oxford. Peter Hayward; Michael James; Dr Tom Charlton; Professor Munro Price; Laurence Kelly; Sir Geoffrey Owen; Celia Pilkington, Archivist of the Inner Temple; Geoffrey Robertson QC; Lord Waldegrave; Colin Cohen; Alison Samuel; Heather Holden Brown.

Clara Farmer at Penguin Random House and Charles Spicer at St Martin's Press for all their help; Charlotte Humphery for her great assistance in the final stages, and Penelope Hoare for editorial suggestions.

American relations helped to inspire this book – Mary Frediani and her family, and the memory of Cornelia Fitzgerald and Cornelia Ensign Claiborne. I thank the late Betty Pollock for her enthusiasm, and Claiborne Hancock. Also the late Coleman Saunders for continuous interest in this project.

Especial gratitude to Ed Victor, and my family: my mother Antonia Fraser and stepfather the late Harold Pinter, my daughters Blanche, Atalanta and Honor, and my husband Edward Fitzgerald – without whom this book would not have been written.

Notes

References to authors by surname alone indicate that the work is listed in the Bibliography, where full details can be found.

Prologue: 1676

Benjamin Church's eyewitness account of Philip's death is published in Benjamin and Thomas Church's *Entertaining Passages Relating to Philip's War* (1716), ed. Henry Martyn Dexter (B. Green, 1865).

Chapter I: Droitwich

Bangs, *Pilgrim Edward Winslow*, is the definitive biography. Brandon Fradd summarises genealogical information about the Winslows, including Edward Winslow senior's expectations, in *The Winslow Families of Worcestershire, 1400–1700* (New England Historic Genealogical Society, 2009). Thomas Habington describes the Winslow property in *A Survey of Worcestershire* and the eighteenth-century antiquarian Treadway Russell Nash mentions 'another considerable freehold estate' in Kempsey Parish. 'The middle sort of people': Keith Wrightson, *English Society 1580–1680* (Routledge, 2003). For apprenticeships, see Patrick Wallis and Cliff Webb, *The Education and Training of Gentry Sons in Early-modern England* (Economic History Working Papers, 128/09, LSE). For extensive information on Beale and Bellamy, see Bunker. For the separatist church in Sandwich, Kent, which included the Chiltons, see Paulick, 407.

Chapter II: Leiden

William Bradford's *Of Plymouth Plantation* is the most important source for the Pilgrims' lives, which he wrote around thirty years after they landed in America. Edward Winslow's *Hypocrisy Unmaskd* also contains important details. Bangs, *Strangers and Pilgrims*, provides much new information from the Walloon Church Archives. For the unusually democratic nature of the Scrooby church, see Langdon. The Dexters have a detailed description of the Green Gate house. Information about patents is from Peggy M. Baker, Director Emerita of the Pilgrim Hall Museum, Plymouth, Massachusetts. Thomas Coventry's name appears in the list of Adventurers who had to be paid back in 1626, noted in William Bradford's *Letter Book*.

Chapter III: Leaving Holland

Following Jeremy Bangs's research it is believed that about eighty people on the *Mayflower* were in some way connected to the church, even if they had not lived in Leiden and came from England. For whether Susanna White could have been the sister of the Fuller brothers, see Jeremy Dupertuis Bangs, *New England Historic Genealogical Society Register*, 154 (January 2000), 109–18. For Elizabeth Warren, see Peggy M. Baker, 'A Woman of Valour: Elizabeth Warren of Plymouth Colony'. Samuel E. Morison's edition of Bradford's *Of Plymouth Plantation* fn. 9, p. 121, and fn. 6, p. 363, drew attention to the fact that copies of the English translation of Jean Bodin's *Six Books of the Republic* were included in the estate inventories of both William Brewster and William Bradford. Morison believed Robert Cushman was also informed by Bodin. For attitudes towards the elect and non-elect, see Gerald F. Moran and Maris A. Vinovskis, *Religion, Family, and the Life Course: Explorations in the Social History of Early America* (Ann Arbor, 1992).

Chapter IV: The Voyage

For William Brewster's inventory, see John Davis Papers, Massachusetts Historical Society. The Brewster notebook belonged to both

William Brewster and his son Jonathan. It has recently been transcribed. For New England millenarianism, see Woodward. For the settlers' fears of European corruption, see Douglas Anderson. For women and midwifery, see Ulrich, 126–35. 'Beastliness': John Winthrop's *Journal*, 17 April 1630. On crossing the ocean in November 1619, see Ferdinando Yate, 'The Voyage to Virginia', *New York Public Library Bulletin*, Vol. I (1897), 68–72, Smyth of Nibley Papers.

Chapter V: Land

The original document known as the Mayflower Compact has vanished. It was written down in various places in the signatories' lifetime and included by Bradford in *Of Plymouth Plantation*. The form of government on the private or particular plantation was left up to the settlers. In Plymouth Colony there was no legal necessity for freemen, that is voters, to be members of the Plymouth Church. See George L. Haskins, 'The Legal Heritage of Plymouth Colony', *University of Pennsylvania Law Review*, Vol. 110, No. 6 (April 1962). The John White paintings remain in the British Library, too fragile to be on display. 'They marvel to see no monuments over our dead . . . the graves all alike': Thomas Morton's *New English Canaan* in Dempsey (ed.), 44. De Champlain's map in 1605 shows Patuxet (Plymouth) as a village. For the effects of European plague, see Richter, *Before the Revolution*, 153, and Jared Diamond, *Guns, Germs, and Steel: The Fates of Human Societies* (W. W. Norton, 2005), 78. For women in the early days of the colony, see Caleb Johnson, 'Women on the Mayflower' at Mayflowerhistory.com. 'Long in silence' from *The Courtship of Myles Standish*. God had 'brought his people hither': Edward Winslow, *New England's Salamander* (1647).

Chapter VI: Massasoit

Powhatan's cloak is now believed to be a wall hanging, though John Smith mentions a cloak being given by Powhatan to Captain Newport. Charles V commissioned a public debate about the treatment of the American Indians between the Dominican priest and Bishop of the Chiapas in Mexico, Bartolome de las Casas, and the academic Juan Gines Sepulveda. Sepulveda discussed the Indians along Aristotelian lines of classification. For the rediscovery of classical texts and their profound effects on English colonisers, see Andrew Fitzmaurice, *Humanism and America: An Intellectual History of English Colonization 1500–1625* (CUP, 2003). For Indians coming to represent degeneracy, see Richard Slotkin and James Folsom (eds.), *So Dreadfull a Judgement: Puritan Responses to King Philip's War 1676–1677* (Wesleyan University Press, 1999). Professor Neal Salisbury believes Edward was one of the few Pilgrims engaged in dialogue with the Indians about points of Christian doctrine: see Salisbury. For Massasoit's relations with other tribes, see Richter, *Before the Revolution*, 155–6.

Chapter VII: The Building of 'Our Town'

Scurrilous rumours about women and children: letter to the Adventurers in London, 8 September 1623, *American Historical Review*, VIII (1902–3), 299. One of the few pieces of personal information about Susanna Winslow is contained in a letter from Edward to her uncle Robert Jackson, *New England Historic Genealogical Society Register*, Vol. 109 (1955), 242–3. See the Lincolnshire Archives Report, 30 March 1954 – 25 March 1955, 'Robert Jackson gent. of Spalding . . . Clerk of Sewers for Holland, Kesteven and the City of Lincoln from about 1608 to his death early in 1625'. A 'pivot of almost all local business . . . He was perhaps the son of his predecessor John Jackson, the servant of the earl of Lincoln (506/65)'. Edward Jr and John were the Winslows' first children together. Both sons are named in the 1627 Division of Cattle. In 1651 William Bradford wrote that Edward Winslow married 'the widow of Mr White, and hath two children living by her marriageable, besides sundry that are dead'.

Chapter VIII: Good Farms

The Secretary of the New Netherlands colony Isaac de Rasieres described how 'the maize seed' was sent 'in sloops to the north for the trade in skins among the savages': James (ed.), 76–8. See Thwaites for a description of John Winslow in 1650 near Cushnoc by Father Gabriel Drouillettes. For Indians and the scenery of New England, see Cronon. 'Those poor savages, whose country we challenge, use and possess': John Smith, *The Description of New England 1616*.

Before he returned to England Gilbert Winslow may have gone with the Hilton family – successful English fishermen – to join their salt-works on the Pisquataqua River. All quotations from Thomas Morton refer to *New English Canaan* in Dempsey (ed.). For the Venetian ambassador, see Andrews, Vol. 1, 275.

Chapter IX: Massachusetts Begins

'Religion stands on tiptoe in our land', 'The Church Militant': George Herbert, *c*.1633. John Winthrop 'ruling with much mildness and justice': Captain Thomas Wiggin, *The Calendar of State Papers Colonial, America and West Indies, Volume 1* (November 1632). Edward was always 'employed for the Colony in occasions of great weight': Hubbard, *A General History of New England*. Letter from Emmanuel Downing to Sir John Coke: Historical Manuscripts Commission, *Manuscripts of Earl Cowper*, 19 December 1634. The only record of Roger Williams's lost treatise is in John Winthrop's *Journal*, 5–27 December 1633. For John Cotton and Thomas Weld quotations, see LaPlante. The stillborn baby appeared to have horns. For 'monstrous conception of his [Winthrop's] brain', see Kibbey.

Chapter X: The Pequot War

The 'mintmasters of New England': Kupperman, 213. Alfred A. Cave's *The Pequot War* is the most scholarly account. For Uncas, see Oberg. 'Very great captains and men skillful in war': Mason. 'Sometimes the Scripture declareth women and children must perish with their parents': Underhill. 'The Indians' persistent expectations of equality and reciprocity': Pulsipher, 25. For land transfer from Indians to the English see Bangs, *Indian Land Deeds*, 27.

Chapter XI: The Pan-Indian Conspiracy

For the account of Miantonomo's speech, see Gardiner. 'Testimonies of the Indians': Edward Winslow, *Hypocrisy Unmaskd*. The Pelhams were an early colonising family. John Humfrey's second wife was Herbert's aunt. Settler Edward Johnson describes the travails of founding Concord and other New England towns in *Wonder Working Providence 1628–1651*, Franklin (ed.). For Gorton's account see his *Simplicities Defence against Seven-Headed Policy*. For Miantonomo as a statesman see Salisbury, 232. Daniel R. Mandell described the situation as a 'Cold War' in *King Philip's War*, 19. There are many versions of Passaconaway's speech. See Alvin G. Weeks, *Massasoit of the Wampanoags* (originally published 1920; digital scanning 2001), 64.

Chapter XII: Leaving for London, 1646

For the Winslow family's church and Vassall's views see Deane, 389–90. For Mary Latham see John Winthrop's account in his *Journal*, 501. Adultery was briefly a capital crime in Plymouth, but it was never punished as such. In Massachusetts the death penalty did operate – though like all colonies, lack of population meant it tended to be observed in the breach. The death of Edward's old friend and patron Lord Keeper Coventry and resignation of Sir John Coke was 'very sad: for New England in those two is stripped at once of our best friends at the Board: so that now we must live by Faith without any dependance on means at all': Edward Winslow to John Winthrop, 27 April 1640, *Winthrop Papers*, Vol. IV, 258. For theories about the Indians and Jews, see Cogley, and Clark (ed.), 26.

Chapter XIII: Republican England

Details of the Wake family in Hutchins, 121, and Dr John Walker, *The Sufferings of the Clergy of the Church of England during the Great Rebellion*. Also MS 541A, 'The Original Autobiography and Journal' of William Wake, Archbishop of Canterbury, Christ Church, Oxford. Details of Colonel Godfrey Bossevile, Herbert Pelham and Sir Arthur Hesilrige from the forthcoming History of Parliament: *Commons 1640–1660*. Edward Winslow's millenarian views: 'The very years, in which many eminent and learned Divines, have from Scripture grounds, according to their apprehensions foretold the conversion of the Jews' in the Epistle Dedicatory, *The Glorious Progress of the Gospel Amongst the Indians in New England* (London, 1649). Josiah Winslow's Memorandum in the Massachusetts Historical Society, *Winslow Papers*, Vol. II, MSN 487, 16 December 1656, 'Copies of

Letters to London in ye year 1656', reveals Josiah was in business with his brother-in-law Robert Brooks. Elizabeth Winslow married Brooks, a London merchant, earlier that year – see Caleb H. Johnson, 'The Marriage and Children of Elizabeth Winslow, Wife of Robert Brooks', *Mayflower Descendant*, Vol. 60, Issue 1 (Spring 2011). For Edward's desire to return to New England, Shurtleff and Pulsifer (eds.), Vol. 9, *Acts of the Commissioners of the United Colonies of New England*.

Chapter XIV: Hercules

Character of Magdalen Winslow, and Amie Cutler wedding vow: Wake, *Autobiography*. Penelope Winslow never left New England with her father; see deposition in the National Archives, C8/338/282 'Plaintiff Penelope Wenslow [*sic*] widow 12th February 1682/3'. Anna Reynolds, curator of the Royal Collections, estimates the date of Penelope's portrait to be around 1651; information in email, 21 January 2014. For Hesilrige, John Lilburne and the Harraton Colliery controversy, see Aylmer. Rumours about Edward: Thomas Stanton to John Winthrop Jr, 'Mr Winslow out of prison and out of office only attends the Indian Corporation' [before 24 November 1653], *Winthrop Papers*, Vol. VI, 345–6. 'That the way of the kings of the east might be prepared (Rev.16:12)': see David Armitage, 'The Cromwellian Protectorate and the Languages of Empire', *Historical Journal*, Vol. 35, No. 3 (September 1992), 537–8. Roger Williams: 'his poor wife will miss him', 23 March 1655, Williams, *Complete Writings*, Vol. 6, 288. Edward's death: 'His grave being the whole ocean sea': Appendix E: Extracts from Henry Whistler's journal of the West India expedition, in *The Narrative of General Venables*, ed. C. H. Firth (Longmans, Green and Co., 1900); also *Memorials of the professional life and times of Sir William Penn, Volume II: From 1644 to 1670. By Granville Penn, esq.* (James Duncan, 1833).

Chapter XV: Generational Change

For the Winslows' international business with Brooks, Barbadian merchants, and references to 'Cuz Ed Wake' see 'Discussion of Previously Unpublished 1656 Memorandum of Josiah Winslow at the

Massachusetts Historical Society', *Mayflower Journal* (Fall 2016). For a list of Pelham lawsuits at the National Archives, see Bibliography. TNA C5/14/109 *Pelham, Herbert vs Wincoll, Isaac* was the attempt by Herbert Pelham to obtain possession of Ferriers, and other estates to which he believed he was entitled. For Penelope's accusations, see Fraser, 'Penelope Pelham and a Taste for Litigation', where TNA document C8/338/282 is printed in full. For the Misses Goodricke, see 'Letters to Governor Bellingham from the Massachusetts Archives', *New England Historic Genealogical Society Register*, Vol. 7, 186, April 1853. Information about Edward Pelham from Joseph Dudley's 1698 witness statement TNA C22/998/33. The exiled Dudley said he had known Edward 'ever since he was about the age of twelve years for the space of about thirty years now last past'. Edward had been 'bred at the Free School and College [i.e. Harvard] at Cambridge in New England within five miles of this deponent's own seat there'.

Chapter XVI: The Coming of War

For Ninigret, see Fisher and Silverman. For the Atherton Company, see Martin. For population figures in New England, see James D. Drake, 240, quoting Sherburne F. Cook, *The Indian Population of New England in the Seventeenth Century* (University of California Press, 1976). Philip's belief his brother was poisoned: Easton. For George Curwen's activities, see Vickers. Philip 'would not treat except his brother King Charles of England were there': Nathaniel Saltonstall's 'Continuation of the State of New England', Pulsipher. For Josiah and Governor Bellingham's will, see Chamberlain, Vol. 1, 405. Weetamoo's fears: letter from John Easton to Josiah Winslow, 26 May 1675, at the New England Historic Genealogical Society, MSS C 357, R. Stanton Avery Special Collections.

Chapter XVII: King Philip's War

The best histories of the war are Leach; Lepore; Mandell; George M. Bodge, *Soldiers in King Philip's War* (Boston, 1891); James D. Drake; Schultz and Tougias. See Bibliography for contemporary accounts by Benjamin Church, William Hubbard, Increase Mather and Mary

Rowlandson. 'The bloodiest war in American history in terms of its proportionate effect on a region': Mandell, op. cit., 134. For the Revd Walley's letters, see McIntyre and Travers (eds.). Josiah Winslow's unpublished letters are at the Massachusetts Historical Society. For Indian military techniques, see Patrick M. Malone, *The Skulking Way of War: Technology and Tactics Among the New England Indians* (John Hopkins University Press, 1993). For Roger Williams's confrontation with the Narragansetts in Providence, see LaFantasie (ed.), Vol. 2, 723. The death of Hezekiah Willett: Samuel Sewall diary, 1 July 1676. For tribal losses, see James D. Drake, 172. Of the rebel Indians, the Wampanoags, Narragansetts and Nipmucks, 'on average the region lost 60 to 80 per cent of the population'.

Chapter XVIII: Penelope Alone

'These dreadful frowns of providence': John Cotton Jr, 3 January 1676. Waldegrave Pelham 'detains from his sister above £1,000 due to them as legacies by her father and grandfather': *State Papers Colonial, America and West Indies*, 1 May 1680. For Pelham lawsuits, see Bibliography. Nathaniel Morton letters for Penelope's spiritual crises, 'you were in great affliction of mind some years since', 28 December 1680, and an undated letter in feeble writing probably 1685, shortly before Morton's death: Boston Athenaeum Library. For women keeping taverns, and property sales, see Krusell, *Plymouth Colony to Plymouth County*; also Mary Beth Norton, *Founding Mothers and Fathers: Gendered Power and the Forming of American Society* (Vintage, 1997); 'absolute authority', Salmon, 9. John Cotton Jr, 'I saw Madam Winslow & Mistress Pelham; Ned well in O:E [Old England] a 1000pd & more is due to them with Mistress Bellingham, which they have reason to think he will bring them this summer', 22 March 1695, in McIntyre and Travers (eds.), 468.

Chapter XIX: Penelope's Final Actions

The Curwen family papers, including Elizabeth Winslow Curwen's Inventory, are at the Phillips Library, Peabody Essex Museum, Salem, Massachusetts. For John Alden's trial, see Boyer and Nissenbaum, *Salem Possessed*. For Cotton Mather and the witchcraft crisis, see

Silverman. For Edward Pelham, see Sibley, Vol. 2. For the land petitions of Penelope Winslow and her children, see Massachusetts Archives Collection, 45:296, 30 June 1703, SC1/series 45X, and *Records of the Governor's Council: Acts and Resolves, Public and Private, Province of the Massachusetts Bay*. Governor Benedict Arnold's will refers to Freelove as 'my dearly beloved and youngest daughter'. Indian sovereignty 'however convoluted and contradictory, remains an important part of federal Indian law': see Peter P. d'Errico, 'Native Americans in American Politics', in *The Encyclopedia of Minorities in American Politics, Volume 2: Hispanic Americans and Native Americans*, ed. Jeffrey D. Schultz et al. (Oryx Press, 2000).

Bibliography

On account of the huge amount of secondary literature, this is emphatically a select bibliography.

Primary Sources

Legal papers of Sir Matthew Hale, MS 3476, 1577–1672. Case and opinion in *Isaac Wincoll vs Harbart* [*sic*] *Pelham*, Lambeth Palace Library. Pelham cases at the National Archives, London, include C5/14/109, 1649, *Pelham, Herbert vs Wincoll, Isaac*; Samuel and Anne Stannard cases against Waldegrave Pelham beginning 8 May 1676, C8/303/127, C22/825/11 1679, C22/707/30 1681. Herbert Pelham, PROB 32/24/98-100 1683 [1674] and C8/338/282, *Wenslow* [*sic*], *Penelope vs Pelham, Waldegrave*. Edward Pelham's suit against Waldegrave Pelham from 1696 to 1698: C9/152/15, C9/146/20, C5/118/39, C9/148/6, C9/322/24, C9/148/11, C5/131/22, C9/134/36, C22/998/33, C22/998/34. Penelope Bellingham vs Waldegrave Pelham is C9/151/43. *Acts and Resolves, Province of the Massachusetts Bay: Resolves 1702*, ch. 68; *Resolves 1703/4*, ch. 28; *Resolves 1713/14*, ch. 104; *Resolves 1718/19*; and 45:296, Petition from Penelope Winslow, 30 June 1703, Massachusetts Archives Collection. Josiah Winslow: 'Copies of Letters to London in ye year 1656 December 16 Memorandum That in October 56 I wrote to my brother Brook by Mr Garrett', and Josiah Winslow 'Letter of Attorney to Thomas Sergeant of London', September 1680, Massachusetts Historical Society. Estate Papers: 1684–5 Capt George Curwen, Phillips Library, Peabody Essex Museum, Salem, Massachusetts. Freelove Pelham's will, *Pelham vs Coggeshall*, September 1733, the Supreme Court of Judicature Archives, Rhode Island. Two letters from Nathaniel Morton to Penelope Winslow, Boston Athenaeum Library. MS 541A, 'The Original Autobiography and Journal of

William Wake Archbishop of Canterbury', Christ Church Library, Oxford. 'Sermon Preached at the Funeral of Mrs Smythee Harlakenden June 28 1651 by R.J.', the Earl's Colne Project Database. New England Historic Genealogical Society Register, The American Genealogist, Mayflower Descendant. Pilgrim Hall Museum. *Calendar of State Papers Colonial, America and West Indies. Acts and Ordinances of the Interregnum, 1642–1660. Calendar of the Proceedings of the Committee for Compounding, 1643–1660.*

Arber, Edward (ed.), *The story of the Pilgrim fathers, 1606–1623 AD: as told by themselves, their friends, and their enemies* edited from the original texts (Ward & Downey and Houghton Mifflin, 1897)

Bowden, Henry W. and Ronda, James P. (eds.), *John Eliot's Indian Dialogues: A Study in Cultural Interaction* (Greenwood Press, 1980)

Bradford, William, *Of Plymouth Plantation, 1620–1647*, ed. Samuel Eliot Morison (Rutgers University Press, 1952)

Church, Thomas and Church, Benjamin, *Entertaining Passages Relating to Philip's War* (1716), ed. Henry Martyn Dexter (B. Green, 1865)

Clark, Michael P. (ed.), *The Eliot Tracts: With Letters from John Eliot to Thomas Thorowgood and Richard Baxter* (Prager, 2003)

Cushman, Robert, *The Cry of a Stone*, eds. James W. Baker and Michael R. Paulick (General Society of Mayflower Descendants, 2016)

Dugdale, Sir William, 'Letter to John Langley Fol. 5 September 15 1655', Appendix to the Fifth Report of the Historical Manuscripts Commission, Manuscripts of His Grace the Duke of Sutherland at Trentham, Co. Stafford, Vol. 5.

Dunn, Richard S., Savage, James and Yeandle, Laetitia (eds.), *The Journal of John Winthrop, 1630–1649* (Belknap Press, 1996)

Easton, John, *A Relation of the Indian War, by Mr Easton, of Rhode Island, 1675*, ed. Paul Royster (University of Nebraska-Lincoln, online)

Franklin, Jameson J. (ed.), *Edward Johnson's Wonder Working Providence 1628–1651* (Charles Scribner's Sons, 1910)

Fuller, Thomas, *The History of the Worthies of England* (1662), ed. Austin P. Nuttall (T. Tegg, 1840)

Gardiner, Lion, *Relation of the Pequot Wars (1660)*, ed. W. N. Chattin Carlton (Electronic Texts in American Studies, Paper 38, University of Nebraska-Lincoln, online)

Gookin, Daniel, *An historical account of the doings and sufferings of the Christian Indians in New England, in the years 1675, 1676, 1677* (Arno Press, 1972)

Gorton, Samuel, *Simplicities Defence Against Seven-Headed Policy* (1646), ed. William R. Staples (Rhode Island Historical Society, 1835)

Hinckley, Thomas, *The Hinckley Papers* (Collections of the Massachusetts Historical Society, Vol. V, Fourth Series, 1861)

Hubbard, William, *A General History of New England* (Little, Brown, 1815); *A Narrative of the Indian Wars in New England from the First Planting thereof in the year 1607 to the year 1677* (William Fessenden, 1814)

Hutchins, John, *The history and antiquities of the county of Dorset,* eds. W. Shipp and J. W. Hodson (3rd edn, British Library, 1863–8)

James, Jr, Sidney V. (ed.), *Three Visitors to Early Plymouth* (Plimoth Plantation, 1963)

LaFantasie, Glenn (ed.), *The Correspondence of Roger Williams,* 2 vols. (Brown University Press, 1988)

Macfarlane, Alan (ed.), *The Diary of Ralph Josselin, 1616–1683* (OUP, 1991)

McIntyre, Sheila and Travers, Len (eds.), *The Correspondence of John Cotton Jr* (Publications of the Colonial Society of Massachusetts, 2009)

Mason, John, *A Brief History of the Pequot War* (1736), ed. Paul Royster (Electronic Texts in American Studies, Paper 42, University of Nebraska-Lincoln, online)

Mather, Cotton, *Magnalia Christi Americana or, The Ecclesiastical History of New England* (1702), 2 vols. (Silas Andrus and Son, 1855)

Mather, Increase, *A Brief History of the War With the Indians in New-England* (1676), ed. Paul Royster (Electronic Texts in American Studies, Paper 31, University of Nebraska-Lincoln, online)

Matthews, A. G., *Walker Revised: Being a Revision of John Walker's Sufferings of the Clergy During the Grand Rebellion 1642–60* (Clarendon Press, 1948)

Morton, Nathaniel, *New England's Memoriall* (1669) (republished by Boston Congregational Board of Publication, 1855)

Nash, Treadway Russell, *Collections for the History of Worcestershire* (printed for John White, 1799, republished by Gale Ecco, Eighteenth Century Collections Online Print Editions)

Poole, William F., *The Case of Ann Hibbins, Executed for Witchcraft at Boston in 1656,* ed. Justin Winsor, deposited by Paul Royster (Joshua Scottow Papers, University of Nebraska-Lincoln)

Roser, Susan E., *Mayflower Births & Deaths: from the files of George Ernest Bowman at the Massachusetts Society of Mayflower Descendants* (Genealogical Publishing, 1994); *Mayflower Deeds and Probates: from the files of George Ernest Bowman at the Massachusetts Society of Mayflower Descendants* (Genealogical Publishing, 1994)

Rowlandson, Mary, *The Sovereignty and Goodness of God Together with the Faithfulness of His Promises Displayed being a Narrative of the Captivity and Restauration of Mrs Mary Rowlandson* (Samuel Green, 1682)

Sewall, Samuel, *The Diary of Samuel Sewall, 1674–1729, Vol. II, Commonplace Book* (Collections of the Massachusetts Historical Society, vol. VI, 5th Series)

Shurtleff, Nathaniel and Pulsifer, Daniel (eds.), *Records of the Colony of New Plymouth*, 12 vols. (1856–61)

Smith, John, *Travels and Works of Captain John Smith*, ed. Edward Arber (John Grant, 1910)

Thwaites, Reuben Gold, *The Jesuit Relations and Allied Documents. Travels and Explorations of the Jesuit Missionaries in New France 1610–1791*, vols. 35 and 36 (The Burrows Brothers Company, 1898)

Toppan, Robert Noxon (ed.), *Edward Randolph: including his letters and official papers 1676–1703, 5 volumes with a Memoir* (Prince Society, 1899)

Townshend, L. P. (ed.), *Some account of General Robert Venables . . . with the autobiographical memoranda or diary of his widow, Elizabeth Venables*, Chetham Society, 83 (1872)

Underhill, John, *News from America; Or, A New and Experimental Discovery of New England; Containing A True Relation of Their War-like Proceedings These Two Years Last Past with a Figure of the Indian fort or Palizado*, ed. Paul Royster (Electronic Texts in American Studies, Paper 37, University of Nebraska-Lincoln, online)

Vaughan, Alden T. (ed.), William Wood, *New England's Prospect* (EDS Publications Ltd, 1994)

Williams, Roger, *The Complete Writings of Roger Williams*, 7 vols., Introductions by Edwin Gaustad (Wipf and Stock, 2007); *A Key into the Language of America* (originally published by Gregory Dexter, London, 1643; 5th edn reprint, Applewood Books, 1936)

Winthrop Papers, 6 vols. (Massachusetts Historical Society, 1929–44)

Young, Alexander, *Chronicles of the Pilgrim Fathers of the Colony of Plymouth from 1602 to 1625* (Charles C. Little & James Brown, 1851)

Secondary Sources

Anderson, Douglas, *William Bradford's Books: Of Plimmoth Plantation and the Written Word* (Johns Hopkins University Press, 2003)

Anderson, Robert Charles, *The Great Migration Begins: Immigrants to New England 1620–1633*, 3 vols. (New England Historic Genealogical Society, 1995); *The Pilgrim Migration: Immigrants to Plymouth Colony, 1620–1633* (New England Historic Genealogical Society, 2004)

Andrews, Charles M., *The Colonial Period of American History*, 4 vols. (Yale University Press, 1934–38)

Axtell, James, *The Invasion Within: The Contest of Cultures in Colonial North America* (OUP, 1985)

Aylmer, G. E., *The State's Servants: The Civil Service of the English Republic 1649–1660* (Routledge and Kegan Paul, 1973)

Bailyn, Bernard, *The New England Merchants in the Seventeenth Century* (Harvard University Press, 1955)

Baker, James W. (ed.), *History of the Town of Plymouth: From the Pilgrims to Beyond* (Old Colony Club, 1993)

Baker, Peggy M., '"A Touch of Purple": Penelope Pelham Winslow' (www.pilgrimhallmuseum.org); 'A Woman of Valour: Elizabeth Warren of Plymouth Colony' (www.pilgrimhallmuseum.org)

Bangs, Jeremy Dupertuis, *Indian Land Deeds: Land Transactions in Plymouth Colony, 1620–1691* (New England Historic Genealogical Society, 2008); *Pilgrim Edward Winslow: New England's First International Diplomat* (New England Historic Genealogical Society, 2004); *Strangers and Pilgrims, Travellers and Sojourners: Leiden and the Foundations of Plymouth Plantation* (General Society of Mayflower Descendants, 2009)

Baylies, Francis, *An historical memoir of the colony of New Plymouth* (Hilliard, Gray, Little and Wilkins, 1830)

Behrens, Pene, *Footnotes: A Biography of Penelope Pelham 1633–1703* (Spentpenny Press, 1998)

Bolton, Charles Knowles, *The Founders: Portraits of Persons Born Abroad Who Came to the Colonies in North America Before the Year 1701, With an Introduction, Biographical Outlines and Comments on the Portraits*, 3 vols. (Boston Athenaeum Library, 1919–26)

Bourne, Russell, *The Red King's Rebellion: Racial Politics in New England 1675–78* (Atheneum, 1990)

Bourque, Bruce J., *Twelve Thousand Years: American Indians in Maine* (Bison Books, 2004)

Boyer, Paul and Nissenbaum, Stephen (eds.), *Salem-Village Witchcraft: A Documentary Record of Local Conflict in Colonial New England* (Wordsworth Publishing Company, 1972)

Boyer, Paul and Nissenbaum, Stephen, *Salem Possessed: The Social Origins of Witchcraft* (Harvard University Press, 1974)

Bremer, Francis J., *John Winthrop: America's Forgotten Founding Father* (OUP, 2003)

Brenner, Robert, *Merchants and Revolution: Commercial Change, Political Conflict, and London's Overseas Traders, 1550–1653* (Verso, 2003)

Brotton, Jerry, *The Sale of the Late King's Goods: Charles I and his Art Collection* (Pan, 2007)

Bunker, Nick, *Making Haste From Babylon: The Mayflower Pilgrims and Their World: A New History* (Vintage, 2010)

Cannadine, David, *Ornamentalism: How the British Saw their Empire* (Allen Lane, 2001)

Cave, Alfred A., *The Pequot War* (University of Massachusetts Press, 1996)

Chamberlain, Mellen, *A Documentary History of Chelsea*, 2 vols. (Massachusetts Historical Society, 1908)

Cogley, Richard W., *John Eliot's Mission to the Indians before King Philip's War* (Harvard University Press, 1999)

Cook, David S., *Above the Gravel Bar: The Native Canoe Routes of Maine* (Polar Bear and Company, 2007)

Coons, Quentin and Krusell, Cynthia Hagar, *The Winslows of 'Careswell'* (Pilgrim Society, 1975)

Coughlin, Michelle Marchetti, *One Colonial Woman's World: The Life and Writings of Mehetabel Chandler Coit* (University of Massachusetts Press, 2012)

Coward, Barry, *The Cromwellian Protectorate* (Manchester University Press, 2002)

Cressy, David, *Coming Over: Migration and Communication Between England and New England in the Seventeenth Century* (CUP, 1987)

Cronon, William, *Changes in the Land: Indians, Colonists, and the Ecology of New England* (Hill & Wang, 1983, revised edn 2003)

Cutler, Charles, *O Brave New Words: Native American Loan Words in Current English* (University of Oklahoma Press, 2000)

Davis, William T., *History of the Town of Plymouth* (J. W. Lewis & Co., 1885)

Deane, Samuel, *History of Scituate, Massachusetts* (Boston, 1831)

Deetz, James and Deetz, Patricia Scott, *The Times of their Lives: Life, Love, and Death in Plymouth Colony* (Anchor Books, 2001)

Demos, John, *A Little Commonwealth: Family Life in Plymouth Colony* (OUP, 1970)

Dempsey, Jack (ed.), *New English Canaan by Thomas Morton of 'Merrymount'* (Digital Scanning, 2000)

Dexter, Henry Martyn and Dexter, Morton, *The England and Holland of the Pilgrims* (Houghton Mifflin and Co., 1905)

Drake, James D., *King Philip's War: Civil War in New England, 1675–1676* (University of Massachusetts Press, 1999)

Drake, Samuel G., *The Book of the Indians, or, Biography and History of the Indians of North America from its First Discovery* (Benjamin B. Mussey, 1848)

Elliott, J. H., *Empires of the Atlantic World: Britain and Spain in America 1492–1830* (Yale University Press, 2006)

Ellis, George W. and Morris, John W., *King Philip's War* (The Grafton Press, 1906)

Fisher, Julie A. and Silverman, David J., *Ninigret, Sachem of the Niantics and Narragansetts: Diplomacy, War, and the Balance of Power in Seventeenth-Century New England and Indian Country* (Cornell University Press, 2014)

Francis, Richard, *Judge Sewall's Apology: The Salem Witch Trials and the Forming of an American Conscience* (Harper, 2005)

Fraser, Rebecca, 'Penelope Pelham and a Taste for Litigation', *Mayflower Quarterly* (September 2015); 'Discussion of Previously Unpublished 1656 Memorandum of Josiah Winslow at the Massachusetts Historical Society', *Mayflower Journal* (Fall 2016)

Gaskill, Malcolm, *Between Two Worlds: How the English Became Americans* (OUP, 2014)

Gildrie, Richard P., *Salem, Massachusetts, 1626–1683: A Covenant Community* (University Press of Virginia, 1975)

Godbeer, Richard, *The Devil's Dominion: Magic and Religion in Early New England* (CUP, 1992)

Goldstein, Karin, 'The Creation of a New England Gentry: The Winslows of Plymouth Colony' (Masters thesis, University of Massachusetts, 2001)

Grumet, Robert S. (ed.), *Northeastern Indian Lives, 1632–1816* (University of Massachusetts Press, 1996)

Habington, Thomas, *A survey of Worcestershire*, 2 vols., ed. J. Amphlett (Worcestershire Historical Society, 1895–9)

Hagar, Joseph C., *Marshfield: The Autobiography of a Pilgrim Town* (Marshfield Tercentenary Committee, Rapid Service Press, 1956)

Hall, David D. (ed.), *The Antinomian Controversy, 1636–1638: A Documentary History* (Wesleyan University Press, 1968)

Hunter, Phyllis Whitman, *Purchasing Identity in the Atlantic World: Massachusetts Merchants, 1670–1780* (Cornell University Press, 2001)

Israel, Jonathan, *The Dutch Republic: Its Rise, Greatness, and Fall 1477–1806* (Clarendon Press, 1998)

Jameson, J. Franklin, *Johnson's Wonder-Working Providence 1628–1651: Original Narratives of Early American History* (Charles Scribner's Sons, 1910)

Jennings, Francis, *The Invasion of America: Indians, Colonialism, and the Cant of Conquest* (W. W. Norton, 1976)

Johnson, Paul, *A History of the American People* (Harper Perennial, 1999)

Karlsen, Carol, *The Devil in the Shape of a Woman: Witchcraft in Colonial New England* (W. W. Norton, 1998)

Kawashima, Yasuhide, *Igniting King Philip's War* (University Press of Kansas, 2001)

Kellaway, William, *The New England Company 1649–1776* (Barnes and Noble, 1961)

Kibbey, Ann, *The Interpretation of Material Shapes in Puritanism: A Study of Rhetoric, Prejudice, and Violence* (CUP, 1986)

Krusell, Cynthia Hagar, *Marshfield, A Town of Villages, 1640–1990* (Historical Research Associates, 1990); *Plymouth Colony to Plymouth County: The Land, the Church, the People 1680–1690* (Pondside Publishing, 2010)

Kupperman, Karen Ordahl, *Indians & English: Facing Off in Early America* (Cornell University Press, 2000)

Langdon Jr, George D., *Pilgrim Colony: A History of New Plymouth 1620–1691* (Yale University Press, 1966)

LaPlante, Eve, *American Jezebel: The Uncommon Life of Anne Hutchinson, the Woman Who Defied the Puritans* (Harper San Francisco, 2004)

Leach, Douglas Edward, *Flintlock and Tomahawk: New England in King Philip's War* (1958, reprinted W. W. Norton, 2009)

Lepore, Jill, *The Name of War: King Philip's War and the Origins of American Identity* (Vintage, 2009)

McCusker, John J. and Menard, Russell R., *The Economy of British America, 1607–1789* (University of North Carolina Press, 1985)

McIntyre, Ruth A., *Debts Hopeful and Desperate: Financing the Plymouth Colony* (Plimoth Plantation, 1963)

Mandell, Daniel R., *King Philip's War: Colonial Expansion, Native Resistance and the End of Indian Sovereignty* (Johns Hopkins University Press, 2010)

Martin, John Frederick, *Profits in the Wilderness: Entrepreneurship and the Founding of New England Towns in the Seventeenth Century* (University of North Carolina Press, 1991)

Moore, Susan Hardman, *Abandoning America: Life-stories from Early New England* (Boydell Press, 2013)

Morant, Philip, *The History and Antiquities of the County of Essex, Vols. 1 and 2* (reprint, EP Publishing, 1978)

Morison, Samuel Eliot, *Builders of the Bay Colony* (Houghton Mifflin, 1930)

Morison, Samuel Eliot and Chafee, Zechariah (eds.), *Records of the Suffolk County Courts 1671–1680* (Publications of the Colonial Society of Massachusetts, Vol. XXIX, 1933)

Newton, Arthur Percival, *The Colonizing Activities of the English Puritans* (OUP, 1914)

Norton, Mary Beth, *In the Devil's Snare: The Salem Witchcraft Crisis of 1692* (Alfred A. Knopf, 2002)

Oberg, Michael Leroy, *Uncas, First of the Mohegans* (Cornell University Press, 1999)

Paige, Lucius R., *History of Cambridge, Massachusetts 1630–1877* (H. O. Houghton and Co., 1877)

Palfrey, John Gorham, *History of New England* (Little, Brown, 1892)

Paulick, Michael R., 'The 1609–1610 Excommunications of Mayflower Pilgrims Mrs Chilton and Moses Fletcher', *New England Historic Genealogical Society Register*, Vol. 153 (1999)

Perley, Sidney, *A History of Salem Massachusetts* (1928) in *The Salem Witch Trials Documentary Archive and Transcription Project*, University of Virginia (salem.lib.virginia.edu)

Peterson, M. D., 'A Plymouth Pilgrim in Fleet Prison: Edward Winslow Confronts Archbishop Laud', Summary of Proceedings of the Annual Conference (American Theological Library Association, Vol. 49, 1995)

Philbrick, Nathaniel, *Mayflower: A Story of Courage, Community, and War* (Viking, 2006)

Powell, Chilton Sumner, *Puritan Village: The Formation of a New England Town* (Wesleyan University Press, 1970)

Pulsipher, Jenny Hale, *Subjects unto the Same King: Indians, English and the Contest for Authority in Colonial New England* (University of Pennsylvania Press, 2005)

Rabb, Theodore K., *Jacobean Gentleman: Sir Edwin Sandys 1561–1629* (Princeton University Press, 1998)

Ranlet, Philip, *Enemies of the Bay Colony: Puritan Massachusetts and its Foes* (University Press of America, 2006)

Ravenhill, W. W., *Records of the Rising in the West (1655)* (H. F. & E. Bull, 1875)

Richards, Lysander Salmon, *History of Marshfield* (Memorial Press, 1901)

Richter, Daniel K., *Facing East from Indian Country: A Native History of Early America* (Harvard University Press, 2003); *Before the Revolution: America's Ancient Pasts* (Belknap Press, 2013)

Russell, Howard S., *Indian New England before the Mayflower* (University Press of New England, 1980)

Rutman, Darrett B., *Husbandmen of Plymouth: Farms and Villages in the Old Colony, 1620–1692* (Beacon Press for Plimoth Plantation, 1967)

Salisbury, Neal, *Manitou and Providence: Indians, Europeans, and the Making of New England, 1500–1643* (OUP, 1982)

Salmon, Marylynn, *Women and the Law of Property in Early America* (University of North Carolina Press, 1989)

Schiff, Stacy, *The Witches: Salem, 1692* (Little, Brown, 2015)

Schultz, Eric B. and Tougias, Michael J., *King Philip's War* (The Countryman Press, 1999)

Sherwood, Mary B., *Pilgrim: A Biography of William Brewster* (Great Oak Press of Virginia, 1982)

Showalter, Elaine, *A Jury of Her Peers: American Women Writers from Anne Bradstreet to Annie Proulx* (Virago, 2009)

Sibley, John Langdon, *Biographical Sketches of Graduates of Harvard University, in Cambridge Massachusetts*, 3 vols. (Massachusetts Historical Society, 1873)

Silverman, Kenneth, *The Life and Times of Cotton Mather* (Harper & Row, 1984)

Sprunger, Keith L., *Trumpets from the Tower: English Puritan Printing in the Netherlands, 1600–1640* (E. J. Brill, 1994)

Starkey, Marion L., *The Devil in Massachusetts: A Modern Enquiry into the Salem Witch Trials* (Alfred A. Knopf, 1949)

Steele, Ian K., *Warpaths: Invasions of North America* (OUP, 1995)

Sterry-Cooper, William, *Edward Winslow* (Reliance Printing Works, 1953)

Stout, Harry S., *The New England Soul: Preaching and Religious Culture in Colonial New England* (OUP, 1986)

Stratton, Eugene Aubrey, *Plymouth Colony: Its History & People 1620–1691* (Ancestry Publishing, 1986)

Temin, Peter (ed.), *Engines of Enterprise: An Economic History of New England* (Harvard University Press, 2002)

Thacher, James, *History of the Town of Plymouth* (1835) (Higginson Book Co., 1991)

Thompson, Roger, *Mobility and Migration: East Anglian Founders of New England, 1629–1640* (University of Massachusetts Press, 2009)

Tinniswood, Adrian, *The Rainborowes* (Jonathan Cape, 2013)

Trigger, Brice G. (ed.), *Handbook of the North American Indians, Volume 15* ('Northeast') (Smithsonian Institution Press, 1978)

Trumbull, Benjamin, *A Complete History of Connecticut, Civil and Ecclesiastical, From the Emigration of its First Planters, From England, in the Year 1630, to the Year 1764; and to the Close of the Indian Wars* (H. D. Utley, 1898)

Ulrich, Laurel Thatcher, *Good Wives: Image and Reality in the Lives of Women in Northern New England, 1650–1750* (Knopf, 1982)

Vaughan, Alden T., *The New England Frontier* (Little, Brown, 1965)

Vickers, Daniel, *Farmers and Fishermen: Two Centuries of Work in Essex County, Massachusetts 1630–1850* (University of North Carolina Press, 1994)

Waselkov, Gregory A., Wood, Peter H. and Hatley, Tom, *Powhatan's Mantle: Indians in the Colonial Southeast* (University of Nebraska Press, 2006)

Woodward, Walter W., *Prospero's America: John Winthrop, Jr., Alchemy, and the Creation of New England Culture, 1606–1676* (University of North Carolina Press, 2010)

Wolkins, George C., 'Edward Winslow, Scholar and Printer', *Proceedings of the American Antiquarian Society*, 60 (1950)

Zelner, Kyle F., *A Rabble in Arms: Massachusetts Towns and Militiamen during King Philip's War* (New York University Press, 2010)

Index